GUIDE TO

Universities & Colleges

IN

CANADA

GUIDE TO

Universities & Colleges IN CANADA

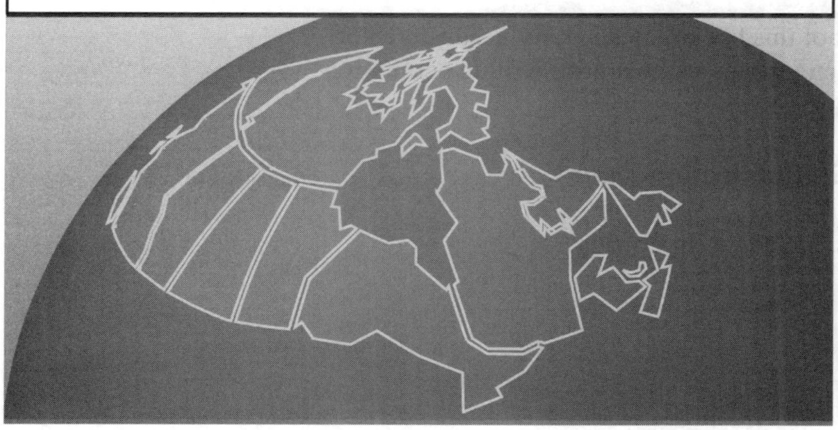

detailed institution profiles

student admissions, expenses and study options

informative articles
answer all your questions

education international

EI Education International Ltd.
205 - 5325 Cordova Bay Road
Victoria, BC V8Y 2L3 Canada
Internet: http://www.eiworldwide.com
email: educate@eiworldwide.com

Canadian Cataloguing in Publication Data

Guide to universities & colleges in Canada

1999 ed.-
Annual.
ISSN 1561-1965
ISBN 1-894122-24-0 (1999 ed.)

1. Universities and colleges--Canada--Directories. I. Education International (Organization) II. Title: Guide to universities and colleges in Canada.

L905.G84 378.71'025 C99-900222-8

Printed in Singapore by SNP Printing Pte Ltd.
Researched in Victoria, Canada by EI Education International Ltd.

The publisher has made every effort to ensure the accuracy and completeness of the information contained in this book; however, no responsibility can be taken for any errors or omissions.

Contents

Welcome

We know that choosing the right school is the key to your success, and if you wish to explore the postsecondary educational opportunities open to you in Canada EI's *Guide to Universities and Colleges in Canada* is the perfect resource for you. This guide provides an introduction to select postsecondary institutions, detailing both their educational philosophies and program highlights. By supplying concise and comparable information about tuition costs, student body statistics and admission requirements, it provides much of the preliminary information you will need to make an informed decision in the face of an almost overwhelming number of options. And the complete *Fields of Study Index* helps you immediately find the schools in this guide that offer majors in your area of interest. Do you want to know where you can study marketing management, chemical engineering, nursing? Are you interested in combining co-op work experience with your academic studies? Are you eager to learn which universities offer the widest range of services for international students? All of these questions, and many more, are answered in this guide.

The guide is intended to help students, their parents and educational counsellors explore the world of undergraduate education in Canada. You are advised to use this information to compile a short list of potential programs, and then seek further information directly from university staff or Canadian embassy representatives.

All of the schools whose programs appear in the EI guides are well respected. While we have included noteworthy reputational information, such as awards won, external rankings and prominent alumni, we have imposed no subjective judgements of our own. You are free to assess each school according to the criteria of most importance to you and to rank the schools based on your personal preferences and career goals.

Good luck in your studies!

David Boag
President, EI Education International Ltd.

Take the Next Step!
EI's Reader Response Card Service

Now that you've begun to explore the range of postsecondary programs available, your next step is to determine which university or college program is right for you.

AIR MAIL

You can also fax the other side of this card to us at 1-250-658-6285

ATTACH AIR MAIL POSTAGE

EI EDUCATION INTERNATIONAL LTD
#205 - 5325 Cordova Bay Road
Victoria, British Columbia Canada V8Y 2L3

education international

To receive information on all of the schools that are profiled in this guide from a specific region, check the appropriate box below, complete the form and send the card to the address on the back.
You can also fax this card to EI at 1-250-658-6285.

- ❐ **British Columbia**
- ❐ **The Prairie Provinces** (Alberta, Saskatchewan, Manitoba)
- ❐ **Ontario and Quebec**
- ❐ **The Atlantic Provinces** (New Brunswick, Nova Scotia, Prince Edward Island, Newfoundland)
- ❐ **The Northwest Territories**

Last Name ________ First Name ________ Age ____ Sex ____
Address ________
________ Postal/Zip Code ________ Country ________
Telephone (Area Code) ________ Fax (Area Code) ________ Email ________
Areas of Interest ________

CUC '99

education international

The Reader Response Cards in this guide provide a quick, convenient way for you to request program information from specific universities or colleges. You will find two kinds of Reader Response Cards: general Education International cards and institution-specific cards. The following guidelines will help you use EI's Reader Response Card Service to make an informed, educated decision!

1. As you read through this guide, keep a record of schools that interest you.
2. If the school has an institution-specific Reader Response Card, you should fill this out and return it directly to the university or college.
3. If the school does not have an institution-specific card, fill out a general EI card and return this to us. We will make your request and the school will return the information directly to you. By completing EI's Reader Response Cards, you will provide the institutions that interest you with clear contact information.
4. Be sure to print clearly and to affix the proper postage to the cards—you want your request to be addressed as quickly and as efficiently as possible. This will speed up your request for catalogues, brochures, application forms and financial aid.
5. Try to keep your options open! The purpose of this guide is to help you to choose the right program—the more program information you request, the more chances you will have of finding the perfect program for your needs.

How to Use the Guide

This guide has been set up to help you find the ideal program in Canada for you. By following the steps listed below, you will have the tools you need to determine which schools can meet your personal education goals.

✓ Read the introductory articles to gain an understanding of the educational system in Canada. Various articles provide information on enrolment patterns; different types of schools; new program options including co-op/internship possibilities, distance education and joint degrees; the application process; standardized tests; financial support possibilities; and tips for succeeding when you get there. International students can also benefit from a special feature section with articles designed to help them prepare for study in the Canada (page 19).

✓ Develop a list of criteria for schools to meet your goals and needs. As you do this, consider fields of study offered, program details (e.g., special options such as joint degrees and work experience opportunities), housing options and English language support, if you are a non-native speaker. Other items to consider are admission requirements, entry dates and tuition costs.

✓ If you already know what areas of study you are interested in, use the *Fields of Study Index* at the back of the guide to find specific programs that match your interests.

✓ Consult the listings of Universities and Colleges in Canada at the back of the guide to gain quick reference information on potential schools (including both those profiled in the guide and AUCC and ACCC member schools).

✓ Use the *University & College Quick Facts* chart (page 44) to quickly compare individual programs based on specific statistics.

✓ Read the profiles—particularly those that matched your list of criteria when using the *University & College Quick Facts* chart and/or the *Fields of Study Index*—and highlight the programs you find interesting so that you can easily refer back to them. Try to eliminate any program that does not match your search criteria.

✓ Re-read the programs you highlighted. Based on the criteria you selected earlier, prioritize them into a list of tier one schools (the ones you are most interested in) and a list of tier two choices (other schools that could meet your needs).

✓ Send or fax in your EI Reader Response Card (found at the back of this guide) requesting information on all of the schools in your tier one list. It could take anywhere from three to six weeks to receive the information from the schools. You can also contact the schools directly for information.

✓ Once the information arrives from your selected schools, review the calendars and brochures, as well as each school's specific admission requirements. You may want to consult an academic counsellor to ensure that you have the right qualifications. Narrow your choice down to a manageable list of schools (approximately three to five) whose admission criteria you meet.

✓ If you are an international student needing to upgrade your English skills, you may want to consider registering for some English language preparation classes and tests. If any of the schools you are applying to have set a minimum English proficiency test score for admission, you should register for the test as early as possible, as you may want to take it more than once in the hope of increasing your score.

✓ Good luck…you are now ready to complete your applications for admission.

Selecting the School That's Right for You

Whether and where to go to school are decisions that will have a large impact on the rest of your life. Your educational and social experiences, your network of friends and colleagues, your options for professional and graduate schools, and your ties to various parts of Canada and the world will all be affected by your decisions about school. Going to school is one of the important decisions that you will make in your life and you want the experience to be as rewarding and productive as possible.

There are often many influences at work on individuals who are researching their schooling options. Students sometimes select a school because their friends are going there or their parents went there, because the school is well regarded or the city well known, or for any number of other reasons that may or may not be related to their own educational, personal and career needs. In weighing the available options, all students should carefully consider how well a school will fit them.

Sometimes, a student who might flourish in a small friendly school, where most students know each other, can become discouraged and alienated by an urban commuter campus, where it is harder to make friends. Similarly, a student who might thrive at a large cosmopolitan university might feel stifled in a small school with more limited entertainment, athletic or cultural opportunities.

A great deal of time, effort and money can be wasted when a poor fit occurs, but this does not have to happen. Forethought and planning will increase the chances of finding a good fit and will help ensure that the school you select is the right one.

The First Step

The first step in selecting a school is to decide between the four types available in Canada—universities, colleges, university colleges and institutes.

In Canada, unlike some countries, universities and colleges are significantly different from each other. They both fall within the postsecondary category, but universities typically provide professional training leading to a degree, while colleges typically offer certificate and diploma programs in career and vocational training or university transfer courses.

Forethought and planning will increase the chances of a good fit.

University colleges are a blend of both college and university offerings; they offer some, usually undergraduate, degree programs in addition to college programs.

Institutes are generally specialized schools that offer selected degrees and some college-level programs.

There are about 90 degree-granting institutions in Canada and about 150 community colleges. Unlike institutions in some countries, Canadian postsecondary schools are not formally—and generally not informally—ranked. Educational quality is closely monitored by the Canadian government, however, and the standard of education is high.

Universities

Universities generally offer bachelor's degrees that require from four to five years to complete, as well as master's and doctoral degree programs.

Canadians' perceptions of their universities are changing. In the past, many people believed that the undergraduate experience at any one Canadian university was interchangeable with the experience at all or most other Canadian universities. It was common to hear, "It doesn't matter where you do your undergraduate work." As a result, most students attended the university closest to their home without investigating options at other schools.

In the last few years, however, federal and provincial budget cutbacks have started to change university offerings significantly. Today, most schools cannot afford to offer the wide range of programs, degree options and extracurricular activities that they once did. Whole programs have been eliminated or reduced; others have been amalgamated into joint offerings with nearby schools. The more than 50 undergraduate degree-granting universities in Canada are redefining their mission statements and objectives, carving out niches to differentiate themselves, doing fewer things in order to do those things well, and building highly specialized centres of excellence. All of these pressures are causing students and their parents to look more widely and more carefully at their options for a university education.

Colleges

Colleges offer technical training, vocational training, and in some cases, university transfer programs. They are authorized to grant certificates or diplomas for programs that range in length from one week to three years. Students sometimes benefit by using college as a less expensive introduction to postsecondary education; university transfer programs allow students to study for up to two years in a smaller setting and then transfer to a university for the completion of a bachelor's degree.

University Colleges

These schools are fewer in number than universities and colleges, and offer a mixture of university and college programs. University colleges offer some undergraduate degrees, including general degree programs, and shorter, more specialized, college certificate and diploma programs.

Institutes

Canadian institutes are degree-granting schools that may also offer selected diploma and certificate programs. The focus at most institutes in Canada is on technology programming and applied knowledge, with an emphasis on career development. As a result, many of the programs offered at institutes are highly specialized.

Finding a Good Fit

How do you select a school? You start by identifying as clearly as possible the features that you are looking for in a school. Once you know what you are looking for, you can compare schools against your list of features and make an informed choice. Whether you choose a university, college, university college or an institute, a school in the city or in the country, a large campus or a small one, you will need to choose the school most suited to your needs.

Each school has its own strengths and weaknesses. Each school has a slightly different educational philosophy or mission and each campus has its own feel. It takes some looking to find the school where you can meet your educational goals, enjoy being intellectually challenged by your professors and classmates, meet friends and future professional colleagues, and feel comfortable socially. Every school isn't right for every student; every student is different and every school is different.

Each school has its own strengths and weaknesses.

Campus Culture

The culture on a campus is hard to define in words, but it can make a big difference as to whether there is a good fit between a particular student and a school. Campus culture is an intangible combination of history, pride and school spirit; the attitude and friendliness of faculty and staff towards students; student attitudes towards learning and grades; the level of student participation in clubs, organizations and student government; how much time students spend on campus and what time of day most students leave the campus; and many other attitudes and behaviours that are hard to measure.

A campus culture is unique. What one student might see as a positive attribute, another might see as a drawback. The goal is for each student to find a school and campus culture that are a good fit.

A Final Word on Choosing the "Right" Program

Once the decision to enrol in a postsecondary program has been made, another staggering decision awaits. Which school would be the "best" school? The answer to this question is highly individual. Each applicant possesses a unique set of values, expectations and goals. As a result, self-knowledge is one of the most useful tools a student can possess. Applicants need to employ two critical skills: research and planning. Applicants should research carefully and apply only to those schools that are capable of meeting their needs.

An important point for applicants to keep in mind is not to limit their options too soon. Otherwise, students may eliminate schools that could best meet their needs, simply because the schools are too near or far, not large or small enough, too expensive, or unknown to friends and family. While family and friends may hold definite opinions about which school is "best," they are not the ones planning to invest a considerable amount of time and effort there. Students should always remember that the ability to succeed in a postsecondary program is closely related to how well suited they are to the program and the school.

Adapted from *Going to University*, by Beverly Cameron, PhD.

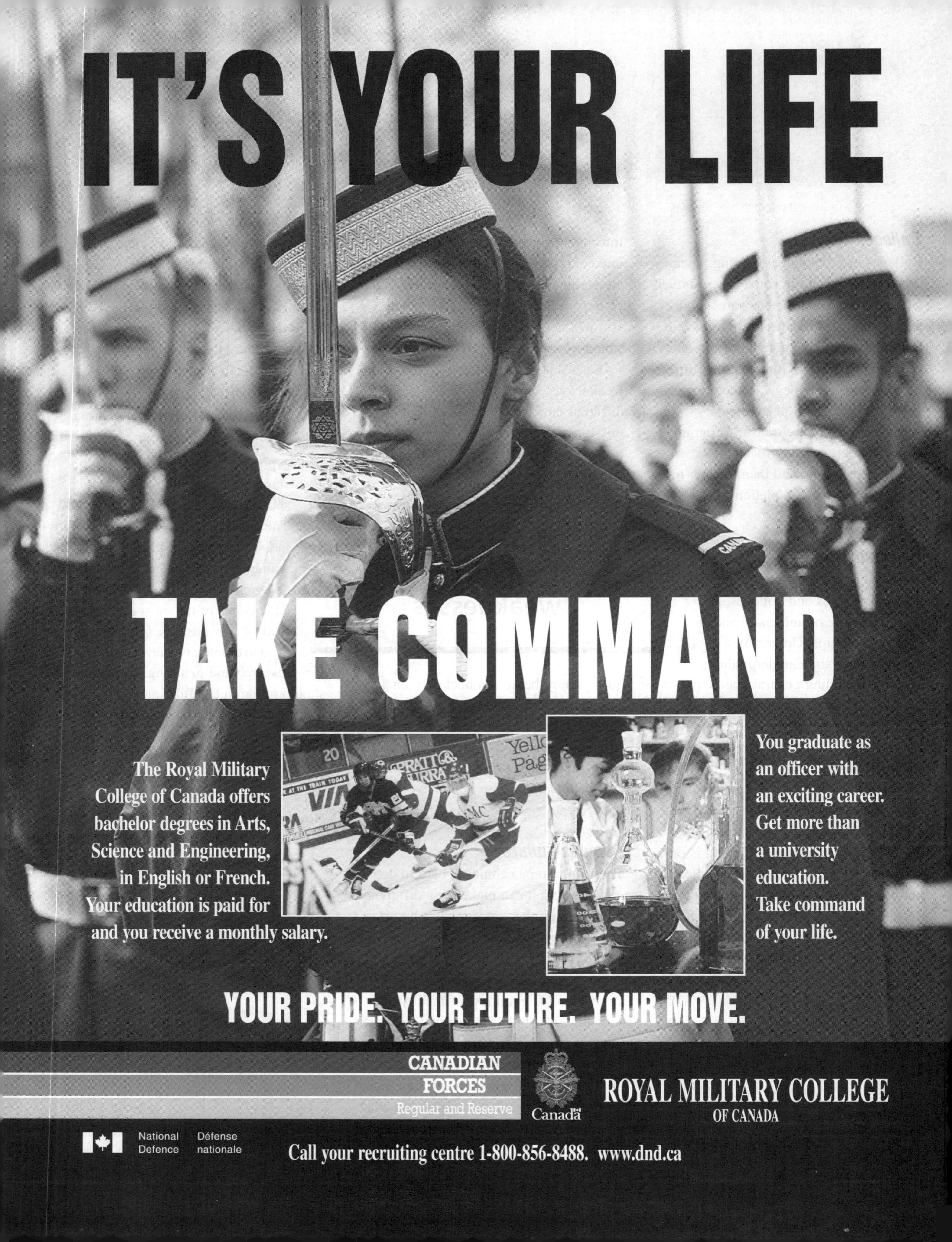
IT'S YOUR LIFE
TAKE COMMAND
The Royal Military College of Canada offers bachelor degrees in Arts, Science and Engineering, in English or French. Your education is paid for and you receive a monthly salary.
You graduate as an officer with an exciting career. Get more than a university education. Take command of your life.
YOUR PRIDE. YOUR FUTURE. YOUR MOVE.
CANADIAN FORCES
Regular and Reserve
Canada
ROYAL MILITARY COLLEGE OF CANADA
National Defence
Défense nationale
Call your recruiting centre 1-800-856-8488. www.dnd.ca

Tips for Researching Your Study Options

Students beginning to look into their study options should consider a number of approaches to their research and take into account the time available.

Planning Your Research

If you are in grades nine or 10:

- Think about why you might want to go to school.
- Assess your personal and academic strengths.
- Talk to parents and teachers about your interests and goals.
- Talk to current postsecondary students about their school and their experiences.
- Visit a postsecondary campus, just to look around.
- Obtain a school guide book or calendar to see what they contain.
- Attend an education fair in your area or at your school.
- Plan some extracurricular, volunteer, and work experiences for the next few years. These activities will help you think about what you want from your studies, and having them on your resume will give you an edge in gaining acceptance to highly selective schools. These experiences can also give you valuable insight into future career options.

If you're in grade 11:

- Ask a guidance counsellor if you can take an interest inventory to help you think about what you may want to pursue following secondary school.
- Ask a guidance counsellor, and do some research on your own, about scholarships you may be eligible for.
- Compare school handbooks, and meet with school representatives if they visit your secondary school.
- Look for information on course and program offerings, costs, enrolments, locations, admissions requirements, and application deadlines.
- Plan your courses to make sure that you meet the entrance requirements for your areas of interest.
- If possible, visit two or three schools—maybe on a summer or winter holiday trip—to help you narrow your choices.

Arrange campus visits to two or three schools you are seriously considering.

Graduating grade 12 students have several things to consider that are best broken down into manageable pieces and taken on throughout the year.

Between September and January you should try to:

- Talk to your parents and meet with your guidance counsellor if you're considering large changes in your school plans.
- Attend presentations by all schools that visit your secondary school even if you're only remotely considering the school. You could change your mind or get some other valuable information about the schools you are most interested in.
- Obtain application forms and scholarship applications forms for all the schools you are considering.
- Check on application and scholarship deadlines and prepare for them well in advance.
- Apply for any scholarships that you may be eligible to receive. Apply even if you think your chances are slim. If you don't apply, you definitely won't get a scholarship, and some have few applicants.
- Arrange campus visits, if possible, to schools under serious consideration.
- Try to talk to students originally from your secondary school who are attending the postsecondary schools to which you are applying. Remember that students in their second or third year may have a more informed view of university, university/college, college or institute life than those in their first year. You may learn more about which residence to ask for, how to get the classes you want, which professors are best, and so on.
- Encourage your parents to talk to the parents of students who are attending schools to which you're applying.
- Look into awards and financial aid packages.

Between December and February you should:

- Send in your applications to all the schools which interest you.
- Request that your secondary school send copies of your official transcript to schools you have applied to.
- Ask your secondary school teachers or any others if they would write you the reference letters you may require.

Between March and June you should:

- Notify your high school of acceptances, so they can send your final transcript after June graduation.
- Begin to consider which school or program you would choose if you are accepted into multiple schools or programs.

Visiting A Campus

A campus visit is probably the best way to get to know a school. Although a visit can be expensive, it is often worth the cost to gain a first-hand feel for the place where you may spend the next three or four years, as well as thousands of dollars. Many students know a school is right for them after a campus visit.

You can visit a school any time, but you'll get the best feel for campus life if you visit while regular classes are in session. This means going during the school year, but with some planning you can arrange a trip during a break or at another time when you'll miss as few days of school as possible.

The Tour

Most schools offer guided tours to potential students. Once you know when you will be able to go, call the university/secondary school liaison or admission office and sign up for a tour. A school representative or a student will generally lead these tours, which may be group or individual tours. Most tours provide you with an overview of the campus, a visit to a residence, the library, bookstore, computer and sports facilities, and may point out favourite campus hang-outs. A tour is also a good time to ask questions and to hear the answers to questions other students or parents on the tour may have.

If you are interested in becoming a member of a college that is part of the university you're visiting, be sure to make it a part of your visit. Even a quick visit can give you an idea of the opportunities and atmosphere at the college.

Following the formal tour, you can request that arrangements be made for you to sit in on classes and talk to students and professors in programs of particular interest to you. If you want to sit in on a class, the school will usually give you a list of several classes that are open to visitors. You may want to talk to an academic adviser or an athletic coach, or you may want to look through the library and check specific collections or see the athletic facilities available. You may prefer to wander around the campus, read bulletin boards, talk to students or have something to eat in the cafeteria. If you call several weeks ahead, arrangements can be made for you to talk to and see just about anybody and anything you want to.

A campus visit is probably the best way to get to know a school.

Interviewing a School

Ideally you want to interview a school during a campus visit by talking to an admissions counsellor, professors from specific departments and other students already enrolled at the school. This will let you form your own impression of the school and ensures that all your questions are answered. If a physical interview isn't possible, phone or email conversations with the appropriate people, followed by a careful rereading of the school's information, is the next best alternative.

Special Considerations for International Applicants

International applicants may have additional concerns or requirements they need to address when selecting a school. For example, international students need to determine whether or not they wish to attend a school with a large or small international student population; one with a high or low representation of students from their country of origin; or one where international students are completely integrated into the larger student population or enjoy a wide range of special services, activities and meeting places. International students must also consider the degree of orientation and English language support available or required at a potential school. International students can discuss these questions with the international office at the school you are considering attending, or by speaking with an international student adviser.

Special Considerations for Applicants with Physical or Learning Disabilities

Applicants with physical disabilities need to ensure that the schools they apply to have taken measures to accommodate their unique needs. These may include wheelchair-accessible classrooms, laboratories and dormitories, as well as the availability of speech pathologists and physical therapists on campus. A tour of the campus will quickly determine campus accessibility for differently abled students.

A Final Tip

Searching out the school that is right for you, is your first assignment as a postsecondary student. Have fun with it, involve your family and friends in your research, and ask questions. It's your right.

Adapted from *Going to University*, by Beverly Cameron, PhD.

Applications and Admissions Requirements

Admissions requirements vary greatly by school and by program. Some schools and programs pride themselves on being highly selective; others are equally proud that their open admissions policies make them accessible to most interested students. The majority of Canadian schools and programs have admissions standards that place them somewhere between these two extremes.

All admissions policies have strengths and weaknesses, so it is important to consider the implications of these policies when selecting a school. When a school has highly selective admissions criteria, its students tend to be self-sufficient, independent learners, and its professors will generally assume that they are teaching a well-prepared student body. The intellectual atmosphere may be exciting and stimulating, and the learning environment may be highly competitive and highly stressful. On the other hand, when a school has an open admissions policy that admits students with a range of secondary school grade averages, the student body will tend to be more diverse in its level of ability and professors will generally adapt their teaching styles and expectations to that diversity. Students often find the intellectual atmosphere and learning environment at an open school to be supportive and encouraging.

The Application Process

Canadian postsecondary schools place a great deal of emphasis on the grades earned in the last two years of secondary school (graduates of Ontario secondary schools applying to universities and some colleges are a notable exception to this rule, as many institutions will only consider applicants' grades earned in Ontario Academic Courses when determining eligibility). In addition, certain schools and programs may require the completion of, or weigh more heavily, certain secondary school mathematics, social science, English or science courses.

Some schools will accept secondary school students on the basis of their grade 12 midyear grades on the condition that their marks don't fall before graduation. Other schools require final grade 12 marks before accepting students. Some schools may also offer students credit for Advanced Placement (AP) courses taken in secondary school; however, Canadian schools are not required to accept AP courses. Although rarely a deciding consideration, certain schools may consider the academic performance of previous graduates from an applicant's secondary school.

All admissions policies have strengths and weaknesses...

Many schools ask that applicants provide information on secondary school awards and scholarships, leadership positions held, extracurricular activities, and special circumstances that may have influenced an applicant's secondary school performance. As the competition for places within Canadian schools and programs increases, admissions officers may start to ask for more information and take it into account in their admissions decisions.

Students who feel that completing a school's application form and package does not provide an accurate reflection of their activities, achievements and potential may want to include a resume or personal statement with their application. These are not required, but if an applicant's experiences and circumstances are out of the ordinary, a resume or personal statement provides the admissions office with more information on which to base its decision.

Letters of reference and admissions essays are generally not part of the application requirements for Canadian schools, but this may change in the future. Standardized test scores, such as the SAT and ACT, are also not required for Canadian school admissions; however, students who have written these tests may submit their scores to the schools they are applying to.

Application Deadlines and Offers of Admission

Application proceedures vary greatly and students should contact potential schools directly, or consult a guidance counsellor, for detailed information about the application process. Generally, application deadlines are in the spring or summer for students intending to enter in the fall; certain specialized or highly competitive programs may have earlier deadlines. Universities generally send acceptance notices from February to mid- or late summer. Colleges often accept applications and issue acceptance notices into the late summer.

Scholarship notification dates also vary widely. Some schools make scholarship offers in the spring and others wait until mid- or late summer before making offers. The deadline for scholarship applications often occurs several months prior to the deadline for application to the university

in general; it is not uncommon for students to be expected to have completed their scholarship applications to universities by early January for entry in the fall of the same year.

Additional information regarding application procedures and deadlines can often be found on the Internet at a school's website; increasingly, schools are allowing students to apply online and submit official transcripts and required materials later by traditional mail.

Admissions Standards

Canadian schools often use minimum entry requirements when describing their admissions standards and students should be aware that in some cases meeting this minimum requirement is not sufficient for entry. Certain schools and programs, which have limited enrolment available, may give priority consideration to students with the highest academic averages and qualifications. This may mean that no applicants near the minimum requirements are accepted. Information related to the actual cutoff point for entry is usually available from the school directly.

Considerations for International Students

International students interested in applying to Canadian schools will find well-developed support and information networks waiting for them that have been designed to help ease the transition to life and study in Canada.

For many students the Canadian Education Centre (CEC) in their area provides an initial point of contact and is an invaluable resource for researching education in Canada. CEC's are currently located in Thailand, Hong Kong, Indonesia, South Korea, Taiwan, Malaysia, Singapore, Chile, Argentina and Brazil. Students can contact the Canadian Embassy or Consulate in their area for the address of the nearest CEC office. Canadian Embassies and Consulates can also provide information about how to obtain an application for a student authorization, which is required by all international students studying in Canada.

Admissions requirements vary greatly by school.

Applying to schools in Canada

Schools in provinces other than Ontario require that students contact them directly, by mail, phone, fax or over the Internet, in order to obtain an academic calendar and an application package. Students considering applying to schools in Ontario should contact potential schools directly in order to obtain an academic calendar and additional information about the school; in order to apply to schools in Ontario students should contact the province's central application services: the Ontario Universities' Application Centre handles university applications, and the Ontario College Application Services handles college applications. These services provide and process standardized application forms for Ontario schools. In some cases, international students may apply directly to an Ontario school.

When contacting any Canadian school, international students should have a potential area of study, or studies, and an intended entry date in mind.

Academic Assessment

Official academic records, including all secondary and any postsecondary studies undertaken are required and assessed by each school or the appropriate central application service. Generally, transcripts not in English or French must be accompanied by certified translations. Each school or service applied to will assess any previous credit earned and determine whether or not that credit is acceptable.

Many schools can offer international students a list of admissions standards by region or educational system.

Language Proficiency

International students are required to provide proof of proficiency in the language of study, generally either English or French, at a potential school. The TOEFL is the most common measure of English language proficiency; however, both minimum TOEFL scores and alternative measures of proficiency vary greatly between schools. French language proficiency indexes also vary greatly and potential schools should be contacted directly for information related to accepted measures of proficiency.

Adapted from *Going to University*, by Beverly Cameron, PhD.

Financing an Education

Like many good things, an education isn't free. Going to school involves a sizeable financial commitment. At the very least, students need funds over and above their living expenses to cover tuition and books. Other expenses may be incurred depending on the choice of program, school and lifestyle.

Tuition

Canadian Students

Based on 1999 totals for tuition at Canadian universities, Canadian students can expect to spend between C$1,700 and $8,500 per year, and with ongoing government cutbacks these costs are continuing to increase. College tuition costs currently range from C$1,300 to $4,500 per year. Tuition fees vary significantly between schools and may vary between the programs offered at each school.

International Students

Tuition for international students at Canadian universities ranges from C$4,000 to $21,000 per year. International student tuition at Canadian colleges, for one year, ranges from C$1,500 to $10,000.

Other Costs

Room and Board

Apartment and food expenses can vary significantly, depending upon the town or city chosen, and whether the accommodation is private, in an on-campus residence or homestay (for international students). Students should expect to pay a minimum of C$3,000 for a two-semester academic year.

Health Insurance

The requirements for health insurance coverage vary by province and by school. Some schools include health insurance for international students, or additional coverage for Canadian students, in the registration fee. Students should contact the schools they are interested in for detailed information about health insurance policies.

...an education is probably the best investment possible for long-term stability.

Books and Materials

When calculating the approximate costs for books and materials, students should factor in fees for textbooks and supplies, including notebooks, paper, pens, photocopying and lab equipment; book and material costs for two full-time semesters average between C$500 and $3,000.

A good way to save some money is to look into purchasing used books from the campus bookstore; also, students often can resell their books to the bookstore for a reduced price at the end of the semester.

Calculating the Costs and Benefits

How does one weigh the costs of going to school against the costs of not going to school? In considering the expenses of an education students should take into account what they would do if they did not go to school, and how their choices would affect them in the long term, both socially and financially.

Going to school is costly; however, an education is probably the best investment possible for long-term stability. Labour force data shows that individuals with university degrees are much less likely to be unemployed than those who enter the workforce directly from high school.

Employers continue to look for individuals with well-developed analytical and problem-solving skills, and the rapidly changing economy requires educated, flexible individuals who can adapt to new situations. Rather than become discouraged at the cost of going to school, students should carefully consider their needs, expectations and career goals and determine the appropriate steps required; overall, students should ask as many questions as possible before committing time, money and energy to any school.

Forms of Financial Assistance

With a little searching a little searching and some initiative, students in Canada will discover a wide assortment of financial aid possibilities open to them. By taking the time to become informed about scholarships and aid, students can significantly reduce the expense of an education, leaving them with less debt upon graduation. Students should note that each year many scholarships are not awarded due to a lack of suitable applicants; even students who feel their chances are slim should apply to all scholarships for which they are eligible.

The following are the most common forms of financial aid:

- Scholarships, bursaries and grants are awards that do not need to be repaid. Scholarships are usually based on academic merit; some also take into account financial need and involvement in specific activities. Bursaries and grants are usually awarded on a combination of academic merit, financial need and involvement in specific activities.
- Loans offer money that has to be repaid, usually after graduation or a set period of time. The interest rate paid on student loans is usually lower than the standard consumer loan rate. International students are not eligible for some student loan programs.
- Work-study arrangements are arrangements in which the school provides students with jobs, usually on campus, helping to offset education costs. Because it is payment for work performed, the money earned does not have to be repaid. International students may be able to apply for work-study positions.
- Co-op programs allow students to alternate periods of study on campus with periods of paid work related to their area of study, usually off campus. Co-op job wages vary. Co-op programs usually require more time to complete than regular programs because of the time spent in job placements. International students should enquire about their eligibility for co-op placements prior to enrolling in a school

More on Scholarships

Most Canadian schools offer a variety of entrance and other scholarships as well as access to scholarships available from other sources, usually the government.

The amount of money offered by individual schools varies significantly and can change from year to year. The grades required by students to obtain these scholarships also vary by school; often schools with lower admissions averages are able to offer financial aid to students with a wider range of academic marks. In some cases students are automatically considered for scholarships when they are admitted; however, many scholarships require a separate application. Short essays are frequently required of scholarship applicants; as a result students are encouraged to start early when assembling their application packages.

It takes a little searching and some initiative to find financial aid.

There are also a number of general scholarships not tied to attendance at a specific school. The best way to find out about these general Canadian scholarships, as well as some university-specific ones, is by using *Canadian Scholarships on File*, a scholarship CD-ROM available through Canadian high school guidance counsellors.

Some provincial governments award scholarships to provincial residents who have secondary school grades in the top percentiles and who choose to attend a postsecondary school in that province.

Students are advised to contact potential schools directly to obtain information about scholarships and aid packages. The deadline for scholarship applications is often earlier than the deadline for general entrance applications; it is not uncommon for a school to have a December or January deadline for scholarship applications. Students are advised to investigate the dealines and apply early.

Government Loans for Canadian Students

Canada Student Loans come from the federal government and are interest free while students are studying full-time. Provincial loan programs are also available for residents who are studying full-time. Generally, Canada and provincial loan repayments start six months after full-time study ends.

Special financial awards or aid may be available from individual provinces for disabled, part-time or First Nations students. Since financial aid packages and eligibility vary by school and province, detailed information should be requested from the financial aid office of each school under consideration.

Athletic Scholarships

While athletic scholarships are more common at US schools, some Canadian schools have begun to offer financial aid to incoming students based on athletic excellence in a particular sport. These scholarships vary depending on the institution in question. Students should consult the athletic departments at potential schools for more information.

Adapted from *Going to University*, by Beverly Cameron, PhD.

Leaving Home to Study

As you prepare to enter your post-secondary studies, you are preparing for a time of significant change, whether you stay near home or go away. Probably the most noticible difference will be the increased independence you will have. You will have to organize your time and study plan on your own, you may be enrolled in some very large classes and some of the subjects may be new to you. In addition, you will have to get to know your way around campus and find the buildings where your classes are located; you will need to become familiar with the school's rules and regulations; and you will spend a great deal of time among people you have never met before.

Another key change may be the increased academic challenges you will face. If you are at a highly selective school, you may find that your initial marks are not as high as those you earned in secondary school. At first, you may wonder if you are up to the academic challenges and you may generally feel a bit overwhelmed.

Depending on your choice of institution, moving away from home, learning to live on your own, meeting hundreds of new people and making new friends may be added to the list of changes you will experience.

You will definitely be adding some stress to your life, but if you have done your best to ensure that there is a good fit between you and your school, the chances are very good that it will be one of the most exciting and intellectually stimulating experiences of your life. Having some days when you feel a bit homesick, when you wonder if you have made the right choices or when you miss your secondary school friends and family members, is to be expected. Most first-year students experience all of these feelings at one time or another.

Dealing With the Transition

How do you deal with all of this change? There are many things you can do:

- Make sure you attend all of the parts of any orientation program your institution offers to first-year students. These programs familiarize you with the layout of the campus, immerse you in the campus culture and the insitition's traditions, introduce you to advisers, administrators and older students who can answer your questions, give you valuable information about the insitition's rules and regulations, and allow you to meet other students who may be having the same thoughts and feelings you are experiencing. Make an effort to get out and become involved, rather than staying in your room for the first few weeks so that you do not miss the events designed to help acquaint you with your new school.

- Join any student organizations or clubs that interest you, become active in your residence organization, and/or join an intramural sports team. These activities will introduce you to new people, help you make friends and ensure that you are involved with life on campus. Becoming involved and active will help make the transition to life at school much easier.

- Seek out older students who have already been at your insitution for a year or two, and take advantage of the experiences and advice they have to offer.

- Call home and talk to your family. Some moral support or a care package from home can be very reassuring, even if the first few calls or packages leave you a bit homesick.

- Call your friends from secondary school. A friendly ear can help and many of your friends may be facing the same worries that you are in adjusting to a new school.

- Do not hesitate to ask for help or advice. Talk to your professor if you are having concerns about a particular course, assignment or test, or if you want a litle extra guidance. Professors have office hours during which they are available to talk to students.

- Talk to your residence floor adviser or a counsellor at your school's student services centre. They will listen and help you solve specific problems.

- Go to the academic-skills office if you have concerns about reading skills, essay writing, test anxiety,

Going to school can be a great deal of fun.

multiple-choice exams, time management or any other academic concerns. These offices usually have counsellors who can talk to you one-on-one and they may offer short workshops to improve your study skills.

- Remember that schools, especially highly selective schools, screen all their applicants to pick those that are most likely to succeed. They picked you because they thought that you had the academic talent, maturity and general ability to succeed at their school. The school that you will be attending wants you to succeed as much as you do, and they have many resources in place to help make your experience a good one.
- Do not study all the time. At least some of the time, relax and enjoy yourself. Going to school can be a great deal of fun.

Things to Take with You

You will obviously want to take your clothes, toiletry items, personal medications, a calculator, pens and pencils, but there are a few other things you may want to consider taking.

- a small table fan; the fall and spring can be warm if your room isn't air conditioned
- hangers; residence rooms rarely come with hangers
- extra long phone cord
- duplex plug for the telephone jack; if your computer modem doesn't support an auxiliary telephone
- telephone answering machine
- floor or table lamp
- small bulletin board and push pins
- alarm clock
- unbreakable plates, bowls, cups, glasses, knives, forks, spoons, a paring knife, microwave bowls, stirring spoons, a medium-size cooking pan, a frying pan, dishcloths and a dishtowel
- box of plastic bags
- can opener
- a few cans or boxes of easily made food

...relax and enjoy yourself.

- popcorn or other snacks
- stereo
- cold/hot gel pack
- a screwdriver, pliers and a small hammer
- bedding if the residence doesn't supply it (pillow, pillow case, sheets and a quilt or blankets)
- bath towels, hand towels and washcloths
- a bathroom caddy for taking your toiletries to the bathroom
- rolls of coins for washing or vending machines
- laundry bag, detergent and supplies
- posters and pictures for your room; many residences charge for damage to walls and paint, so ask what you can use to hang your decorations
- rain-gear
- hairdryer

Documents To Take With You

Before leaving home you should take the time to arrage all the papers you may require during your time at school.

- Social Insurance Number, passport, student visa or other personal identification
- provincial health insurance card; out-of-province health insurance coverage card if you are leaving your home province (many provinces will not cover you fully while you are out of province unless you let them know you are attending school and will return at the end of the academic year); or private health insurance
- credit card, with a separate record of the number, expiry date and the phone number to call if the card is lost or stolen
- bank account numbers, bank books and bank convenience cards
- immunization record
- driver's license automobile registration and insurance forms; if you are taking a car, copy all of these documents and leave the photocopies at home with a family member

A Final Word

The most important thing to remember as you begin your postsecondary career is that a new world of opportunities is opening up to you. Your time in school will be a period of incredible change and growth, and will shape many of the events to come in your life. Look forward to the opportunity and enjoy your days at school.

Adapted from *Going to University*, by Beverly Cameron, PhD.

ALGONQUIN COLLEGE

Come Join our International Family!

Algonquin College is one of Canada's largest community colleges offering career oriented programs to more than 11,000 full-time and 40,000 part-time students each year.

Located in Canada's National Capital - Ottawa is home to a population with the highest education and training in Canada.

ALGONQUIN COLLEGE OFFERS:

Diplomas/Certificates in:

- Business, Hospitality & Tourism
- Media Studies
- Health Studies
- Technology and Trades
- Teachers of English as a Foreign Language
- International Access Program

English as a Second Language:

- TOEIC/TOEFL Preparation classes
- Conversation and fluency classes
- Multimedia Language Labs

Airport pick-up
Homestay assistance
International Student Orientation

Our International Education Centre organizes events such as skiing, skating, tours, camping, and excursions to Montreal, Quebec City, Toronto, Niagara Falls, and New York.

Algonquin College of Applied Arts and Technology
International Education Centre
1385 Woodroffe Ave. Room C429
Ottawa, ON, CANADA K2G 1V8
TEL: (613) 727-4723 extension 7031/7038
FAX: (613) 727-7665
E-mail: intl1@algonquinc.on.ca
Web site: www.algonquinc.on.ca

"Give yourself the competitive advantage of a rich and diversified international education by joining us at Algonquin College in Canada's beautiful capital city."

Robert C. Gillett,
President

ALGONQUIN

ADDITIONAL INFORMATION FOR

International Students

Top 10 Reasons to Study in Canada

1	*The United Nations ranked Canada as* ***the best*** *among 173 countries to live in.*
2	*You can enjoy Canada's* ***breathtaking natural beauty*** *and four distinct seasons.*
3	*Canada's* ***education system is excellent;*** *it is subject to strict government standards.*
4	*It is a* ***multicultural society****, where customs and traditions are respected and valued.*
5	*Degrees earned at Canadian colleges and universities are* ***internationally recognized****.*
6	*Canada is* ***stable, safe and peaceful****.*
7	***Sport and cultural activities*** *are accessible and affordable everywhere, year-round.*
8	*The Canadian* ***health care system*** *is among the best in the world.*
9	*Canadian cities are remarkably* ***clean and environmentally friendly****.*
10	*As a bilingual and multicultural society, Canada is* ***a world leader in second language training*** *programs.*

Destination: Canada

Living in Canada

Former Canadian Prime Minister William Lyon Mackenzie King once remarked, "If some countries have too much history, we have too much geography."

Canada's vast size and variety of geography and people are its most striking features. For ordinary Canadians, as well as visitors, its abundant rivers, mountains, forests, lakes and beaches make for one colossal, bountiful playground! If you've chosen to study in Canada, we know that there is a world of things to discover awaiting you!

Country Facts

When it comes to geography, Canada has more variety than just about any other place: clear alpine lakes and glacier-fed rivers, forests, mountains, semi-arid grasslands, fertile farmland and coastal beaches. Canada has 24,400 kilometres of coast bordering on the Atlantic, Pacific and Arctic Oceans and about one-quarter of the world's freshwater lakes.

Geography has played a major role in Canada's historic and social development. While studying and living in Canada you will have a chance to learn about some of Canada's fascinating history—the establishment of fur trading posts, the building of its railroads, the gold-rush and later development of mining and forestry, and the way of life of its original inhabitants, or "First Nations" people.

Canada, though the second largest country in the world, has a population of a mere 27 million. Canadians are as diverse as the land on which they live. While most are of either British or French ancestry, Canadians of other ethnic backgrounds comprise more than one-quarter of its population, with the Asian Canadian population having one of the highest growth rates. Today, the First Nations people make up about 2 per cent of the country's population. In recognition of this immense diversity, Canada formally adopted a policy of multiculturalism in 1971. Canada is very proud of its "cultural mosaic."

Canada is divided into 10 provinces and two territories, each with a strong regional identity.

The Atlantic provinces on the east coast, frequently referred to as "the Maritimes," were among the first settled and retain much of the flavour of their historical and cultural past in their architecture, food and music. The province of Quebec, which has been referred to as "a nation within a nation," has a distinct social and cultural identity—unique in its language (French), culture, architecture and cuisine.

Of Canada's provinces, Ontario is the economic, political and cultural giant; nearly one-third of Canada's population lives in this province, which is renowned for its wine-producing areas and the Great Lakes, the world's largest bodies of fresh water.

A hearty, outgoing friendliness characterizes the western provinces, which include the three prairie provinces (Manitoba, Saskatchewan and Alberta) and British Columbia. This vast region, which stretches from the geographical centre of Canada to its west coast, encompasses farm and ranchland, foothills and mountains.

Canada's northern territories are roughly the size of Europe but have a very small population, mostly consisting of Inuit and Dene peoples. A visit to "the Great White North" can be a fascinating way to learn about the way of life of these native inhabitants.

Since the country is so vast, temperatures vary greatly. Generally, the west coast is temperate with moderate rainfall, the prairies and eastern provinces have extremes of temperature from very cold in winter to hot in summer. All regions of Canada experience, to some degree, four distinct seasons. Temperatures drop below freezing in the winter, and many places in the country receive snow, yet in some parts of Canada the summer can be as hot and humid as in the tropics! Winter is from December to February, and summer from June to August.

Canada is an independent, democratic nation with its federal government housed in the nation's capital, Ottawa. The government is headed by the prime minister and each of the 10 provinces is led by a premier. A constitutional monarchy, Canada recognizes Queen Elizabeth II as the formal head of state; she is represented by an appointed governor general.

The dollar is the basic unit of Canadian currency. Its $5, $10, $20, $50, $100 and larger denomination bills are colourful and easy to distinguish. Each dollar represents 100 cents, and $1 and $2 coins are now the standard. International banks operate in Canada and credit cards widely accepted include Visa, MasterCard and American Express. Canada's goods and services tax (GST) is 7 per cent and provincial sales taxes range from 0 to 13 per cent.

People and Culture

Canadians are polite and welcoming, if a little reserved. Because Canadians themselves represent almost every major racial and ethnic group in the world, you are unlikely to feel like a foreigner. Canadian cities have a rich ethnic diversity; most larger cities have well-established Asian and Latin American communities.

In Canada, women and men, regardless of their cultural background or economic status, are treated as equals.

Canadians are outdoor enthusiasts. Favourite pastimes include hiking, beachcombing, fishing and cycling. Canadians also enjoy winter sports, including downhill and cross-country skiing, ice-skating and, of course, their national pastime—hockey. Canada is

superb camping country, offering an almost unlimited choice of public and private camping sites. Having the world's greatest reservoir of freshwater lakes, Canadians love water sports. Favourites include kayaking (one of Canada's contributions to the boating world), scuba diving, sailing, rowing, whitewater rafting and canoeing. If they are not playing sports, they are frequently watching their favourite teams, often in a pub with friends.

The food in Canada reflects the diversity of its people. In almost every city, a wide range of different cuisines can be found, from Chinese to Indian and Italian to Ukrainian. Canadians generally eat three meals a day: breakfast, lunch and dinner. Meal times vary, though breakfast is usually between 7:00 and 9:00 in the morning, and dinner between 5:30 and 7:00 in the evening. The evening meal, usually called supper, is the biggest meal of the day. On weekends, many Canadians enjoy eating brunch: a late breakfast substantial enough to get you through until dinner time. Tipping in restaurants and for some other services (10 to 15 per cent) is customary.

Day-to-Day Living

Generally, Canadians dress more conservatively than in the US and less formally than in Europe. Students dress casually, usually in jeans and a T-shirt. Short sleeve dress is standard in the summer. You will need warmer clothes— wool sweaters or sweatshirts—in most places by late October or early November. You may need to buy winter wear once you arrive in Canada, depending on the part of the country in which you will be living.

Many universities have on-campus residences. Living on campus is a great way to meet Canadian students. You can apply for housing through the university according to the procedure specified in the main application form. Many students live separately or in groups in off-campus houses or apartments. Most universities operate a housing office that publishes lists of available rental units. A growing number of Canadian colleges and universities offer host family programs; in these, arrangements are made for you to live with a Canadian family for a period of time.

Most of the world's major airlines fly to Canada; the most common entry points are Vancouver, Toronto and Montreal. When travelling in Canada, keep in mind the size of the country! Flying is the main means of transportation to another province or far-away city, but it can be expensive. Buses cross the country, providing a comfortable and inexpensive way to travel shorter distances. Conducted bus tours or rail/bus excursions are offered, especially in the peak tourist months (July and August). Canada's cross-country train service provides travellers with a unique way to see a variety of breathtaking landscapes. The Canadian Hostelling Association, a member of the International Youth Hostel Federation, operates more than 120 hostels throughout the country, offering an economical alternative to hotels. For travel within the city, most students use city buses, their own cars or bicycles.

Studying In Canada

Internationalization of Education

Canadian postsecondary institutions have long recognized the benefits of having people from many different countries in their student bodies. In 1994-95, 60,000 international students were studying at the postsecondary level in Canada.

Many universities and colleges have an international office or liaison person dedicated to looking after the needs of international students and providing services designed to help them adjust to life in Canada.

Overview of Higher Education System

Among OECD (Organization for Economic Cooperation and Development) countries, Canada devotes the greatest proportion of its public expenditures to postsecondary education. All universities and colleges are government regulated and subject to very high standards, ensuring that degrees are nationally and internationally recognized.

In Canada, there are 89 degree-granting institutions, offering a range of undergraduate, graduate and English language programs. Most bachelor's degrees take three or four years of full-time study to complete.

The government supports technical, vocational and community colleges, of which there are about 150 across the country. These colleges offer certificates and diplomas in a variety of fields such as business, arts and technology, which can, in some cases, be used for transfer to a university degree program. A few community colleges in British Columbia offer full three- and four-year degree programs; these are known as university-colleges.

English language training in Canada is known as English as a Second Language (ESL) and is offered at almost every university, most colleges and many private institutions in the country. Most offer courses designed especially for students preparing for further study at a university or college, as well as a variety of other courses.

The academic year runs from early September to April, and is often divided into two semesters (September to December and January to April). Although September is the main entry date, some institutions also accept students into their programs in January

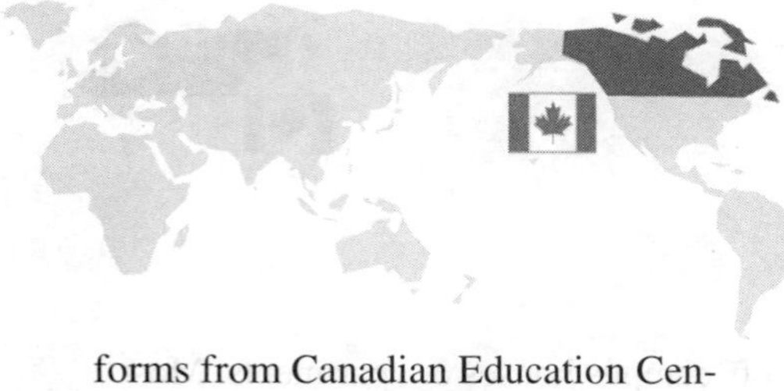

and/or May. Many offer a limited number of courses during the summer (May to August). ESL courses generally run year-round, offering students many possible entry points.

General Admission Requirements for Undergraduate Students

Each college and university in Canada has its own admission standards, which vary depending on the program to which you wish to apply. Undergraduate applicants must have the equivalent of a Canadian high school education. Universities recognize a wide range of secondary school certificates from other countries as being equivalent to the Canadian high school diploma. Generally, you will be required to submit official academic records and certified translations, where necessary, with your application.

You must also meet the institution's minimum English language requirement. The most common English proficiency test required by Canadian universities is the Test of English as a Foreign Language (TOEFL), though other tests such as the Michigan English Language Assessment Battery (MELAB) and the International English Language Testing System (IELTS) are becoming more widely accepted. Generally, students require a TOEFL score of 550 to 600.

All institutions in Canada have their own application forms, except those in the province of Ontario. Requests for applications to Ontario universities should be forwarded to the Ontario Universities' Application Centre, PO Box 1328, Guelph, ON, N1H 7PA. For all other provinces, write to the registrar's office at the university you wish to attend. You may also get forms from Canadian Education Centres, established in Thailand, Hong Kong, Indonesia, Malaysia, Korea, Singapore, Taiwan, Mexico, India, Australia and Beijing, China. Admission deadlines differ from one institution to another. These deadlines tend to be strict; if you do not anticipate receiving your marks before the deadline, send your application to the university, indicating when any outstanding documents can be expected.

Fees and Cost of Living

Costs can vary depending on the course you wish to study. Tuition costs for an undergraduate degree range from about C$2,500 up to about $15,000 per year (two semesters) and English language courses vary from C$230 to $5,000 depending on the type and length of course. You must have guaranteed funds to cover your study expenditures for one year.

You can expect to require between C$7,200 and $11,000 per year for living expenses, which will cover accommodation, food, transport, clothing, health and entertainment. Living costs in larger cities like Toronto may be higher.

Very little financial assistance is available to international undergraduate students. After you have completed one year of education in Canada, however, you are sometimes eligible to receive awards in your area of study.

Medical Insurance

Canada has an excellent public health system and medical insurance is inexpensive. At present, some provinces offer health care to international students, while in others students can purchase private insurance. When you register, the university will supply you with information about where to enrol in the provincial health plan.

Visa Requirements

To study in Canada, you will need to obtain a student visa, or student authorization, before you arrive. In order to be granted a student authorization, you must supply evidence that you have been accepted to an approved Canadian educational institution, have sufficient funds to cover your expenses, and have a valid passport.

Applications can be obtained through the Canadian High Commission in your home country. You will need to apply at least three months ahead of the school's registration date. The student authorization allows you to attend one institution for a specified period of time. You can apply to extend your visa while still in Canada, but you need to do this before your current authorization expires.

International students are permitted to work part-time on campus and to participate in cooperative work programs if they form a mandatory part of their degree programs. However, jobs can be difficult to find and you should not count on them to fund your studies.

The country's diverse geography and people, combined with its high quality of education, make Canada an ideal destination for study abroad.

For further information on accommodation, student visas and health insurance, please see page 25.

Visa, Health Insurance & Accommodation Information

CEC Network
Réseau des CÉC

Canada is a popular study destination for international students. Canadian educational institutions have international offices and/or staff committed to providing services that support international students throughout their stay. Such services include orientation, language assistance and counselling. Many of these institutions are also clients of the Canadian Education Centre (CEC) Network, which promotes and markets Canadian education internationally through a network of offices overseas.

Although it can be difficult to adapt to living and studying in a foreign country, international students can ease the transition by keeping themselves informed of their rights and responsibilities. Following is some critical information for international students who are thinking about applying to study in Canada.

Canadian universities are committed to providing services that support international students.

Student Authorizations

Student authorizations are required for international students taking academic, professional or vocational training courses at approved postsecondary institutions, secondary schools and private ESL/FSL schools in Canada. They are not required for English or French language courses that last a maximum of three months and that are not academic, professional or vocational in nature.

Students interested in studying in Quebec are required to obtain a Certificate of Acceptance (CAQ) from the Quebec government and a student authorization from the Government of Canada. Application forms for a CAQ are available at educational institutions in Quebec. A processing fee is incurred.

Student authorization forms can be obtained at Canadian embassies, high commissions or Canadian Education Centres (CECs) throughout the world. Applications and documentation must be submitted to the nearest visa office. Students must submit all requested documentation; missing documentation will delay the authorization process.

Only those who are national or permanent residents of the United States, residents of St. Pierre and Miquelon, or dependants of individuals who are in Canada on employment visas or student authorizations may apply for student authorizations at a Canadian port of entry.

Students under the age of majority (as defined by provincial law) must provide notarized declarations signed by their parents or legal guardians in their countries of origin and notarized declarations signed by their custodians in Canada. The declarations should state that adequate arrangements have been made for the custodian to act in place of a parent in times of emergency, such as when medical attention or intervention is required. For younger children, a broader declaration stating that the custodian is responsible for day-to-day care and supervision may be required.

When reviewing student authorization applications, visa officers must be satisfied that students meet the requirements of the Canadian Immigration Act and Regulations and that these students will only be in Canada temporarily. If they decide that an interview is necessary, they will contact individuals directly.

Students coming to study in Canada may be accompanied by their spouse and children provided that these individuals meet all the requirements for visitors to Canada. Family members may be required to provide evidence that they are law abiding and have no criminal record. They may also be required to have a medical examination and to obtain a visitor visa.

Spouses and children who will be accompanying students should be included in the appropriate space on the application for student authorization. Students will be required to provide a marriage certificate and birth certificates for any accompanying dependants. Spouses and children who will be following at a later date must make a separate application for admission.

Documentation to be Included in Student Authorization Applications

The following documentation must accompany all student authorization applications:

- a valid passport or travel or identity document that guarantees re-entry to the country that issued it and two recent passport-size photos of each accompanying family member, with the name and date of birth recorded on the back of each photo
- proof of financial resources to cover tuition fees, living expenses for students and their accompanying dependants and return transportation

for students and their accompanying dependants; documentation for this requirement may be proof of a Canadian bank account—if money has been transferred from another country—or bank statements for the past four months

- marriage certificate and birth certificates for any accompanying dependants
- proof of medical examination if staying in Canada longer than six months; students should note that medical processing will add several weeks to the time necessary to obtain a student authorization
- letter of acceptance from an approved educational institution
- appropriate notarized declarations from parents and custodians

After Arriving in Canada

Upon arrival in Canada, immigration officers determine whether students may enter Canada and how long they may stay. Students must leave Canada on or before the date set by the immigration officers unless their status has been extended by an immigration office in Canada.

Students wishing to extend their student authorizations are advised to ask the nearest Canada Immigration Centre to mail an application form to them at least two months before their authorizations expire. All applications from within Canada must be mailed to and processed by Citizenship and Immigration Canada's central processing centre in Vegreville, Alberta.

Students may transfer to comparable institutions and/or programs of study unless the terms and conditions on their student authorizations state that they are required to attend a specific school. In such circumstances, students must apply for new student authorizations through the nearest Canada Immigration Centre.

International students may work on the campus of any publicly funded, degree-granting institution. Full-time students at postsecondary institutions may obtain employment authorizations for employment essential to their degree program (unless they are accounting students, medical interns or medical residents); for employment related to approved research or training programs; or for employment on the campus of an institution where they are registered full-time. Additionally, those who have successfully completed a community college or university program in Canada may work for a maximum of one year in employment related to their field of study.

> *International students may work on the campus of any publicly funded, degree-granting institution.*

A spouse of a full-time student at a community college or university may apply for an employment authorization to work in the general labour market. The spouse should phone a Canada Immigration Centre in Canada to obtain more information about submission of an application for employment.

A spouse may work only during the validity of the student authorization. Any income earned while in Canada should not replace the need to meet the financial requirements for the student authorization. Also, a medical examination may be required.

Re-entering Canada

Legally, a person's status in Canada ceases when he or she leaves the country. The normal practice of Citizenship and Immigration Canada, however, is to allow re-entry on the basis of an existing student authorization. This means that every decision is made on a case-by-case basis. Individuals cannot be assured that they will be allowed to re-enter Canada.

Health Insurance

In the provinces of Alberta, British Columbia and Saskatchewan, international students are covered by provincial health care plans.

In Alberta, students and their dependants must register for the Alberta Health Care Insurance Plan within three months of their arrival. In most cases, dependants are defined as a husband or wife and children under 21 years of age who are single and wholly dependent on the parent(s). Coverage costs approximately C$34 per month for one individual and C$68 for a family, and is available for the term stated in the student authorization. To be eligible, students must be studying in Canada for more than 12 months. For more information, contact the Alberta Health Care Insurance Plan, PO Box 1360, Edmonton, Alberta, Canada, T5J 2N3. For telephone enquiries, dial 403-310-0000 and ask for either 403-427-1432 (Edmonton) or 403-297-6411 (Calgary).

Under the BC Medical Services Plan (MSP), students must hold a student authorization upon entering Canada to be eligible for medical coverage. As of January 1, 1998, new medical regulations state that international students with student authorizations for six months or longer must be covered under the province's medical service plan. There is a three-month waiting period and students should apply immediately upon commencement of studies. The cost is roughly C$36 per month. Students should take out private medical insurance for these first three months or if they will be studying for less than six months in total. Those studying for longer than six months should not acquire private insurance for any longer than this time period as it will still be mandatory for them to be covered by MSP. For more information, contact the BC Medical Services Plan, PO Box 1600, Victoria, BC, Canada, V8W 2X9. For telephone enquiries, call 1-800-663-7100.

Under the Saskatchewan Hospital Services and Medical Care Plan, students must register immediately upon arrival. Coverage, which is free, is available for students and their dependants for the duration of the student authorization or visa. For more information, contact Saskatchewan Health, Health Insurance Registration, T.C. Douglas Building, 3475 Albert Street, Regina, Saskatchewan, Canada, S4S 6X6. For telephone enquires, call 1-800-667-7551.

In the remaining seven provinces, international students must arrange for private medical coverage through private insurance companies.

Accommodation Options

Temporary Accommodation

Hotels

A wide range of hotels is available for temporary stays upon arrival in Canada. A Canadian hotel is defined as having inside access, private rooms, and daily maid service. Reservations should be made in advance, especially during peak tourist season such as the summertime (May-August). Most hotels accept major credit cards, and reservations can be made either directly or through a travel agent in a student's home country. Hotel services, price and quality will vary depending on the hotel; students should expect to pay anywhere from C$35 to $250 and upwards.

Although prices will vary, students should expect to pay anywhere from C$3,000 to $7,500 per school year for residence or dormitory accommodation.

Youth Hostels/YMCA

Hostelling is a temporary and inexpensive way to stay in major Canadian cities. Accommodation is basic but economical, and major facilities are shared. Rates are calculated daily, and costs are lower than major hotels. A Canadian hostel must be inspected and approved by the Canadian Hostelling Association. Students should contact the International Youth Hostelling Association in their countries to become members of this international network. Although prices will vary, students should expect to pay between C$10 to $20 per night.

School-Provided Accommodation

Residence/Dormitory

Many schools have accommodation conveniently located on or near their campuses. Students in need of accommodation are advised to contact the schools they are attending for more information. Dormitories are usually separated by gender. Rooms are usually furnished and can vary in size and in quality. Many dormitories have shared kitchens, toilets, baths and laundry facilities. In some cases, there are also cafeterias where daily meals can be arranged if the student wishes.

Although prices will vary, students should expect to pay anywhere from C$3,000 to $7,500 per school year for residence or dormitory accommodation.

Family Housing

Several universities offer residence accommodation specifically designed for family living. These facilities are frequently located on-campus and usually contain one to two bedrooms and a private kitchen, toilet and bath. Meal plans are generally not offered to family housing tenants; most individuals prefer to use the kitchen facilities provided to prepare their own food. The cost of family housing varies considerably from one region of the country to another, but students can expect to pay from C$3,200 to $8,000 per academic year for such accommodation. Waiting lists for family housing are common; students interested in this residence option are advised to contact the school they will be attending as early as possible for further information.

Homestay

Many Canadian families welcome international students. This may be an effective

Discover a World of Opportunity in Canada

At the University of Windsor, we offer more than 130 fully-accredited undergraduate, graduate, co-operative and professional degree programs recognized the world over for quality. We award degrees in fields such as computer science, engineering, mathematics, the sciences, the humanities, fine and performing arts, business, law, education and others.

The University of Windsor is located in Canada, on the border with the United States just across from Detroit in the manufacturing heartland of North America. Our university has world-leading research facilities, as well as a safe and supportive learning environment.

Our university has a tradition of celebrating cultural diversity. Each year, more and more students from around the world choose the University of Windsor for the quality of the education we provide and for the quality of life our students enjoy.

We cordially invite you to discover a world of opportunity in Canada at the University of Windsor. Please contact:

The Registrar
University of Windsor
Windsor, Ontario
CANADA
N9B 3P4

telephone: +1 (519) 253-3000
facsimile: +1 (519) 971-3653
or visit our **website** at:
www.uwindsor.ca

UNIVERSITY OF
WINDSOR

CEC Network
Réseau des CÉC

way for students to learn English and gain an understanding of daily life in Canada. Typically, a homestay consists of a Canadian family hosting a student in their home while the student attends classes in Canada. Meals and a room are provided in the home, and the host family encourages participation in family activities.

Homestays are arranged by the school, and students are matched with families who share similar interests. Amenities and location vary from home to home but preferences should be indicated to the school so that a suitable match may be found. Many schools can arrange for a school representative or homestay family to meet the homestay student at the airport upon arrival. Students should enquire about the availability of this service when applying to schools. Although prices will vary depending on location, they should expect to pay between C$400 and $800 per month.

> *While renting an entire house is usually too costly, renting a suite within a house is a popular option for students.*

Off-Campus Housing

Renting

Renting is another option for students, but they should be warned that price, quality and availability vary greatly; rental suites can cost anywhere from C$400 to $1,500 per month, depending on the location. Rents are particularly high in the major cities and apartments can be difficult to find in these areas, where vacancy rates are low.

While renting an entire house is usually too costly, renting a suite within a house is a popular option for students. Suites are self-contained units with a kitchen, toilet, bath and bedroom and are often found in homes near campuses.

Apartments are another option and typically contain a kitchen, toilet, bath and one or two bedrooms. Most rental apartments do not include furniture or meals.

Available apartments, houses and suites within houses are published weekly in local newspapers. Students may also contact their school's housing officers to obtain an up-to-date list of local rental accommodation. However, it is up to the student to determine whether accommodation is suitable as schools do not inspect these places.

Agreements with landlords should be made with care. Most landlords require a damage deposit and rent is usually paid on a monthly basis in cash or by cheque. Students are advised to carefully examine the terms and conditions of rental agreements before signing.

Contributed by the Canadian Education Centre Network.

The CEC Network

Founded in April, 1995, the CEC Network's mandate is to promote and market Canada as a destination for international students and as a source for international corporate and group training. It also provides high-quality service and support to subscribers and overseas clients, and supports Canada's foreign policy and development assistance objectives worldwide. The CEC Network is a wholly owned subsidiary of the Asia Pacific Foundation of Canada and is managed in partnership with the Government of Canada (specifically, the Department of Foreign Affairs and International Trade, the Canadian International Development Agency, and Citizenship and Immigration Canada). CEC offices are located in the following major cities:

- Bangkok, Thailand
- Beijing, PRC
- Buenos Aires, Argentina
- Canberra, Australia
- Hong Kong
- Jakarta, Indonesia
- Kuala Lumpur, Malaysia
- Mexico City, Mexico
- New Delhi, India
- São Paulo, Brazil
- Santiago, Chile
- Singapore
- Seoul, Korea
- Taiwan
- In Canada:
  Montreal, Quebec
  Toronto, Ontario
  Vancouver, BC (Head Office)

For information on how to contact these centres, please contact the Vancouver office by telephone at 604-684-5986 or by fax at 604-681-1370, or visit the CEC Network website at http://www.studyincanada.com.

English Language Tests: Steps to Success

International study is rapidly gaining in popularity as students worldwide recognize the cultural and educational advantages of overseas experiences. An increasing number of international students are pursuing studies in a language other than their own. Not surprisingly, international students who wish to pursue postsecondary studies in an English-speaking country sometimes view the language skills requirement as a barrier. Non-native speakers of English will almost always be required to prove their English language proficiency for admission into a postsecondary institution whose primary language of instruction is English. Conversational English abilities alone are not enough; when admitted to an institution in an English-speaking country, international students are competing at the same academic levels as native English speakers, and must have corresponding language skills. Required language skills are determined by each institution individually, and may vary from program to program within an institution.

Choosing a Proficiency Test

Although certain colleges and universities do administer their own institution-specific English language tests, there are several standardized international proficiency tests. For students who wish to improve their English language skills in an English-speaking environment, there are also several recognized institutes, such as the ELS Language Centers, designed to provide international students with the language skills necessary for university or college study. An individual university or college may request scores from one or several of the following tests:

TOEFL

The Test Of English as a Foreign Language (TOEFL) is the most widely accepted test of English proficiency in North America, and is offered 12 times per year at more than 1,200 test centres in 170 countries and regions. More than 2,400 universities in the US, Canada, and other English-speaking countries require prospective international students to submit TOEFL scores. Many countries now offer the TOEFL in a computer-based format, allowing students to schedule their own exam appointments year-round in comfortable, computer-equipped cubicles. By the year 2000, the computer-based TOEFL will have replaced the paper-based exam internationally.

> ...international students are competing at the same academic levels as native English speakers

IELTS

The International English Language Testing System (IELTS) is accepted by most Commonwealth academic institutions and is becoming increasingly recognized for admission by colleges and universities in Canada. The IELTS is available in over 250 centres across 100 countries, including more than 174 testing centres in the UK, 61 in Australia, 19 in New Zealand and 39 in Canada. Testing dates are flexible and each IELTS centre offers a testing date at least once per month.

MELAB

The Michigan English Language Assessment Battery (MELAB) is recognized by many educational institutions in Canada and the US as an alternative to the TOEFL. Although after June 30, 1998, the MELAB will be available only at testing sites in Canada and the US , and at limited international locations where the TOEFL is not administered, international group MELABs may be arranged for institutions or organizations.

Cambridge Exams

There are three levels of Cambridge Exams: the First Certificate Examination (FCE), the Certificate in Advanced English (CAE), and the Certificate of Proficiency in English (CPE). It is this final certificate that fulfils English language entry requirements at many universities in the UK, as well as universities in other English-speaking countries. Each Cambridge Certificate Exam is offered twice a year, in June and December.

What to Expect

Most English language proficiency tests generally take between two and three hours to complete. Depending on the number of candidates present for a given testing date, students should normally expect to spend at least three and a half hours writing the test.

The majority of the English language tests are presented in multiple-choice formats and are divided into three general sections: listening comprehension, structure & written expression and reading comprehension. Students registered for certain TOEFL testing dates must also complete the Test of Written English

(TWE), a short essay demonstrating their ability to write in English. International students planning to pursue graduate studies in English-speaking countries are also often required to submit scores for the Test of Spoken English (TSE), a third optional element to the TOEFL. The MELAB, although similar in structure to the TOEFL, requires all students to complete a written examination. Similarly, all IELTS candidates complete a test module on spoken English.

English language test scores are normally valid for a maximum of two years after the testing date. There are generally no pass or fail marks: scores are given and evaluated according to each institution's English proficiency standards. The average paper-based TOEFL requirement for undergraduate students is a score of 550, while the average IELTS requirement is a score of 6.5 and the average MELAB requirement is 85.

How to Prepare

Students with advanced English language abilities may only need to prepare for two to four months before writing a proficiency test. Students with elementary to intermediate abilities will need anywhere from six to 10 months of intensive language courses to achieve the skills they will need to succeed on a standardized English language proficiency test.

Students planning to write an English proficiency test should prepare to do so by writing the sample tests provided by most testing centres. Studying using a centre's practice exams enables students to review their English language skills while becoming familiar with the format of the exam. By writing practice tests under the same circumstances they will experience on the actual testing day (completing a sample test within the set time limit, for example), students should gain useful insight into the nature of the exam, and be able to approach the actual testing day feeling confident, well prepared and relaxed.

Students should remember that they are not allowed to use dictionaries, watches with alarms, scratch paper, highlighters or notes during most English language tests, and should therefore avoid using these tools during their practice sessions.

Students should be able to approach the actual testing day feeling confident, well prepared and relaxed

What to Bring

Most testing centres will send admission tickets to all candidates. These tickets function both as receipt of payment and for examination entry. Students who do not bring their admission ticket with them to the testing centre may be unable to write their test. In addition to admission tickets, all test-takers should bring the following:

- Photo File Record—candidates will normally receive these in the mail along with their admission tickets and must attach current photos of themselves to each signed, completed form.
- Official Identification—as specified on their admission tickets, students are required to bring two pieces of official photo identification, such as a passport and driver's license, with them to the testing centre.
- Pencils—most tests must be completed with soft-lead (#2 or HB) pencils. Students are advised to bring at least two, a pencil sharpener and an eraser.
- Watch—although official time will be kept by the proctor, candidates may want to monitor their own progress. Students should remember to avoid bringing watches with alarms.
- Lunch—since cafeteria facilities are not available at all testing centres, students should bring snacks to eat after the test or during break periods.

Test Administration

Students registering for English language tests should remember to use the same form of their names on all testing and identification documents. Students using variant spellings or name orders may not be permitted to take the proficiency test.

Students are encouraged to register early for their chosen testing dates, as some centres fill up quickly.

English language test administrators inform students of their test scores within a varying amount of time. Students receive results from the paper-based TOEFL approximately one month after the testing date, and IELTS candidates receive their scores within a two-week period. The new computer-based TOEFL offers students the opportunity to view unofficial exam results immediately upon completing the exam.

Students should remember that in most cases they may rewrite the examination if necessary.

Before You Go

Once you have received an acceptance letter from your school, there are many things that you need to think about and do to prepare yourself for a rewarding international experience. The following is a short list of some of these things:

- ✓ ***Learn more about where you are going.*** It is very important to invest time into researching and reading about your destination country. Learn about its culture, geography, economy, and political and legal systems. The more you learn about where you will be living, the more you will appreciate the experience and the faster you will adjust to your surroundings. Everyone experiences a different degree of culture shock, but certainly the more you learn about the culture, the better prepared you will be for your new way of life. Talking to other people who have visited, lived and studied there is one of the greatest sources of information, but remember, everyone has different experiences.

- ✓ ***Make sure your passport is in order.*** You will need your passport to enter most countries, as well as for other things like banking. It sometimes takes quite some time to obtain a passport, so be sure to apply early. If you already have a passport, you may want to make sure that it does not expire while you are overseas. Have a plan to keep your passport in a safe place. We recommend that you make several photocopies, and you may want to consider keeping your passport in a safety deposit box at a bank.

- ✓ ***Obtain a student visa.*** You will need a visa to live and study in most countries for any extended period of time. Visit an education centre or an embassy to obtain an application and to learn exactly what is needed to apply. This process can be very lengthy, so apply as early as you can.

- ✓ ***Book your flight.*** Investing time into booking a flight is worthwhile. Often, as a student, you can find low-cost flights, but they sell out early. If you begin your search early enough, you may learn of a special seat sale that could save you hundreds of dollars.

- ✓ ***Buy additional health insurance.*** Many institutions offer health insurance to students at a very reasonable price. There may be a waiting period before you are eligible to apply for a health plan, during which you will want to carry extra health insurance. You can organize this from your home or you may be able to purchase a health plan when you arrive. Keep a copy of your insurance plan in a safe place.

- ✓ ***Make money arrangements.*** Once you are overseas, you will want to open a bank account. Before you go, however, you should arrange to obtain some local currency and traveller's cheques to use during the first few days after your arrival.

- ✓ ***Prepare an arrival plan.*** Before you leave, you will want to know that all arrangements for your first few days or weeks in your new home have been made. Some schools offer airport pickup or provide very detailed directions on how to get from the airport to your destination. If you know that you will not be able to move into the residence hall upon arrival, or if you do not yet have permanent accommodation organized, you may want to reserve a few nights at a local hotel or International Youth Hostel.

While You Are There

Once you arrive at your school, there are a number of steps that you should take to ensure a safe and rewarding international experience. The following list includes some of the most important:

✓ ***Register at your country's mission or embassy if there is one.*** They may be able to help you in an emergency and can provide you with information on the local customs, laws, health insurance, etc.

✓ ***Check in with a contact person at the institution you will be attending.*** They can help orient you to the city and your new lifestyle and provide details about the school year.

✓ ***Be careful! Take extra precautions—foreigners are sometimes at greater risk than locals of theft.*** Do not carry or show large amounts of money. Never carry all of your information (passport, ID, cash, credit cards, etc.) together.

✓ ***If you promised your family you would phone home, do it!***

✓ ***While you are in a foreign country, you are subject to its laws.*** Make sure you know them and abide by them. If you do find yourself in an illegal situation, contact the nearest embassy of your country.

✓ ***Familiarize yourself with the country's culture, laws, regulations and structure.*** Always ask before you take a picture of someone and be respectful of religious sites.

✓ ***Don't forget to reconfirm any onward flights you are on.*** Usually, you should do this 72 hours before the flight's departure.

✓ ***You may want to arrange to have your mail forwarded to a post office box.***

Dealing With Culture Shock

Almost everyone who studies, lives or works abroad experiences some degree of culture shock. This period of cultural adjustment involves everything from getting used to the food and language to learning how to use the telephone. No matter how patient and flexible you are, adjusting to a new culture can, at times, be difficult and frustrating. It is easy to get lost, depressed and homesick. You may even want to go back home!

Don't panic...these are all normal reactions and you are not alone. You are on an adventure—a wonderful opportunity to grow and learn—even though it does not always seem that way. Although you cannot avoid culture shock entirely, the following tips may help you:

- ✓ ***Start a journal*** of the new things you come across every day and your reactions to your new home. Writing things down will help you keep them in perspective, and journal entries are funny to look back on!
- ✓ ***Never confuse your ability to speak the new language with your intelligence***; it is easy to get frustrated, but there is no reason to. It takes everyone some time to adjust and become comfortable with a new language.
- ✓ ***Be physically active!*** Walk, swim, run, play tennis or do some other physical activity you enjoy often. You will feel better, meet new people and keep in shape.
- ✓ ***Keep your sense of humour.*** Try, no matter how hard it is, to see something of value in every new experience and challenge you come across. Laugh now, not just later!
- ✓ ***Take advantage of services that your school, church or community offer.*** Contact a counsellor at the International Students Office, a resident adviser if you live in residence halls, someone at your church, etc. If you are having a problem with something, tell someone! They will want to help you, and you will feel a lot better having people to support you. Don't be afraid to speak up.

Adjusting to a new culture can be difficult and frustrating, but it can also be a wonderful, thought-provoking time of your life during which you will grow as a person. Living in a foreign country will open new doors, introduce you to new ways of thinking, and give you the opportunity to make lifelong friends.

REMEMBER: All international students share in what you are going through; you are not alone. Even more importantly, it is only a matter of time before you are well-adjusted and comfortable in your new home.

PROFILES OF Universities & Colleges IN CANADA

List of Profiled Universities & Colleges in Canada

List of Profiled Institutions by Province or Territory

Canada

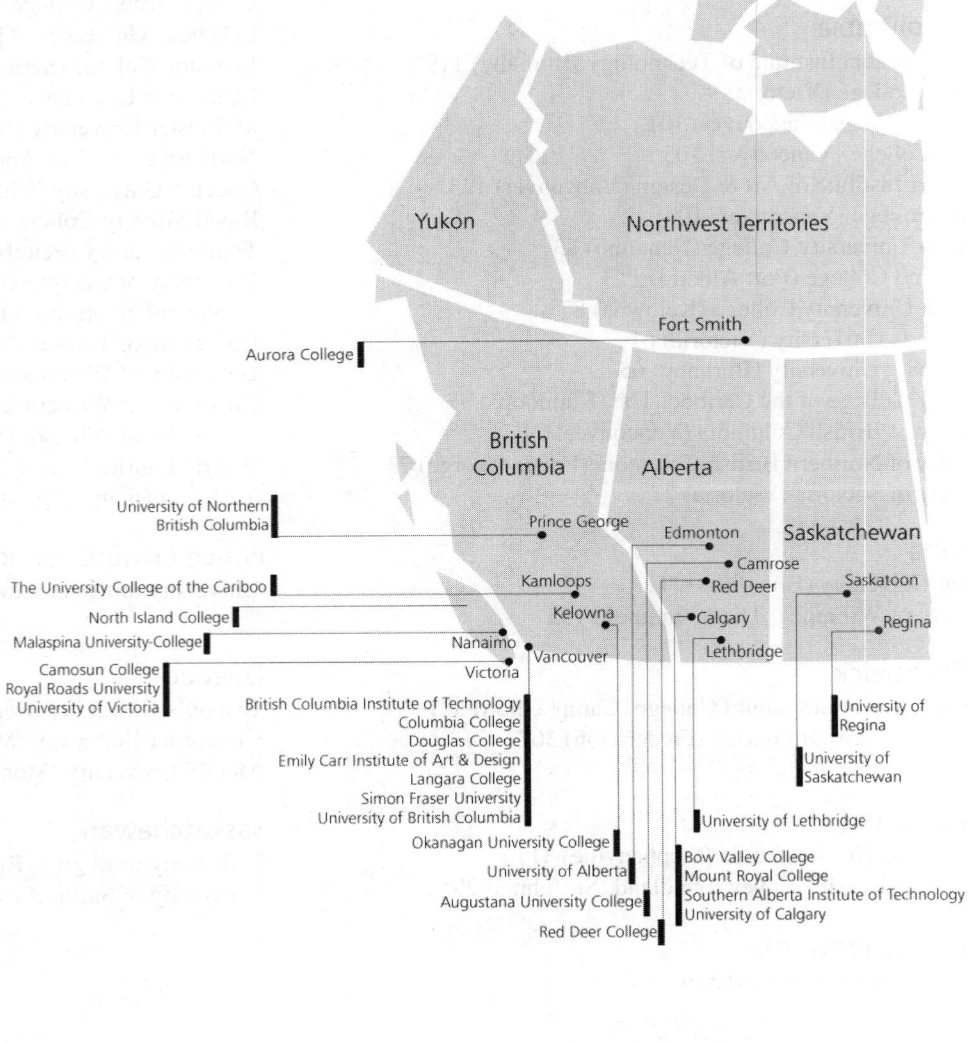
Yukon
Northwest Territories
Fort Smith
Aurora College
British Columbia
Alberta
Saskatchewan
University of Northern British Columbia
Prince George
Edmonton
Camrose
The University College of the Cariboo
Kamloops
Red Deer
Saskatoon
North Island College
Kelowna
Calgary
Regina
Malaspina University-College
Nanaimo
Vancouver
Lethbridge
Camosun College
Royal Roads University
University of Victoria
Victoria
British Columbia Institute of Technology
Columbia College
Douglas College
Emily Carr Institute of Art & Design
Langara College
Simon Fraser University
University of British Columbia
University of Regina
University of Saskatchewan
University of Lethbridge
Okanagan University College
University of Alberta
Augustana University College
Red Deer College
Bow Valley College
Mount Royal College
Southern Alberta Institute of Technology
University of Calgary

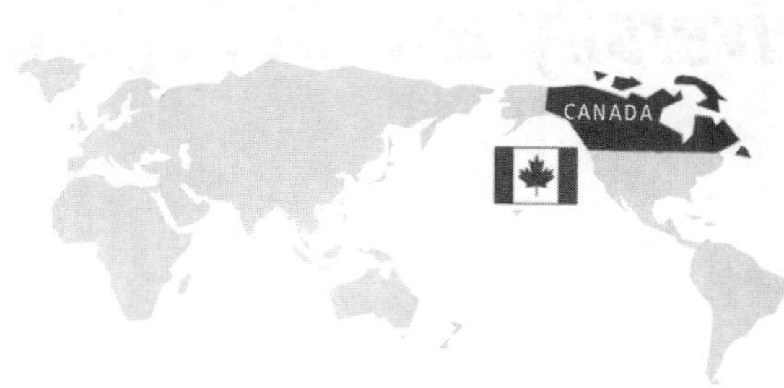
CANADA

Newfoundland
St. John's
Memorial University of Newfoundland
Stephenville
College of the North Atlantic
Prince Edward Island
University of Prince Edward Island
Quebec
New Brunswick Community College Network
Manitoba
Charlottetown
Campbellton
Nova Scotia
Antigonish
St. Francis Xavier University
New Brunswick
Halifax
Ontario
Fredericton
Dalhousie University
Saint Mary's University
Timmins
Montreal
University of New Brunswick
Brandon
Winnipeg
Thunder Bay
Sudbury
Lennoxville
Bishop's University
Concordia University
McGill University
Northern College of Applied Arts & Technology
Peterborough
Ottawa
Kingston
Carleton University
University of Ottawa
Algonquin College of Applied Arts & Technology
Lakehead University
Guelph
Toronto
The University of Winnipeg
Waterloo
Hamilton
Queen's University
Royal Military College of Canada
Sarnia
London
Brandon University
Windsor
George Brown College of Applied Arts & Technology
University of Toronto
York University
Laurentian University
Trent University
McMaster University
University of Waterloo
Wilfrid Laurier University
University of Guelph
Lambton College of Applied Art & Technology
The University of Western Ontario
University of Windsor

University and College Quick Facts

List of Profiles by Region & Type

	Page	Location: City	Location: City Population	Location: Cost of Living	Enrolment: Total Enrolment	Enrolment: Undergraduate Enrolment	Enrolment: International Enrolment	Enrolment: Student/Faculty Ratio
British Columbia								
Universities								
Royal Roads University	61	Victoria	325,000	high	750	400	10	10:1
Simon Fraser University	65	Burnaby	1,800,000	high	23,220	20,966	861	25:1
University of British Columbia	69	Vancouver	1,800,000	high	33,474	27,293	2,324	18:1
University of Northern British Columbia	73	Prince George	75,000	med	3,200	2,850	70	10:1
University of Victoria	77	Victoria	325,000	high	17,222	15,098	834	17.4:1
University Colleges								
Malaspina University-College	83	Nanaimo	75,000	low	7,000	7,000	575	–
Okanagan University College	87	Kelowna	100,000	–	7,500	–	225	12:1
University College of the Cariboo, The	91	Kamloops	80,000	low	7,500	3,600	365	21:1
Colleges								
Camosun College	97	Victoria	350,000	high	23,960	7,772	400	15:1
Columbia College	101	Vancouver	1,800,000	high	650	600	560	12:1
Douglas College	105	Greater Vancouver	1,826,000	high	22,700	9,254	373	11:1 (f/t)
Langara College	109	Vancouver	2,000,000	high	15,000+	6,350	435	35:1
North Island College	113	various	160,000 (combined)	med	10,600	2,000	10	21:1

KEY

[–] - not available
assoc - associate degree
avg - average
bac - baccalauréat
c/b - computer-based
cert - certificate
dgr - degree
dip - diploma
sup - supérieures
f/t - full-time

Expenses				Academics		
Application Fee	*In-Province Tuition*	*Out-of-Province Tuition*	*International Tuition*	*Academic Options*	*Minimum GPA*	*Minimum English Requirement (TOEFL, MELAB & IELTS)*
$50 (Cdn and int'l)	$2,500-8,500/yr	$2,500-8,500/yr	$5,000-17,000/yr	undergrad/grad	B-	TOEFL 570 (p/b), 233 (c/b)
$65 (Cdn and int'l)	$2,310/yr	$2,310/yr	$6,994/yr	undergrad/grad	67% (Cdn), 85% (int'l)	TOEFL 230 (c/b) with TWE 4.5; TOEFL 250 (c/b); IELTS 7.5
$22 (i/p), $54 (o/p), $100 (int'l)	$2,295/yr	$2,295/yr	$13,830/yr	undergrad/grad	varies by faculty	TOEFL 570-580, MELAB 90, IELTS 6.5
$10 (i/p), $35 (o/p, int'l)	$2,500/yr	$2,500/yr	$5,400/yr	undergrad/grad	65% (BC high school)	TOEFL 570
$25 (i/p), $65 (o/p), $70 (int'l)	$2,265-2,896/yr	$2,265-2,896/yr	$6,795-8,688/yr	undergrad/grad	70-74% (1998-99)	TOEFL 575, MELAB 90, IELTS 7.0
$30 (Cdn), $100 (int'l)	$756/sem	$756/sem	$6,800/yr	cert/dip/undergrad	n/a	TOEFL 213 (c/b) or 550 (p/b); IELTS 6.5
$20 (Cdn), $100 (int'l)	$1,410/yr	$1,410/yr	$3,350/yr	cert/dip/undergrad	varies	TOEFL 550
$15 (Cdn), $75 (int'l)	$1,230/yr	$1,230/yr	$3,350-3,965/sem	dip/undergrad	no set minimum	TOEFL 550, IELTS 6.0
$25 (Cdn), $100 (int'l)	$450-901/sem	$450-901/sem	$3,400/sem	dip/cert/assoc	varies	no set minimum
$100 (Cdn and int'l)	$3,900/yr	$3,900/yr	$8,000/yr	cert	n/a	TOEFL 520-530, IELTS 5-6.5, MELAB 77-79
$25 (Cdn), $100 (int'l)	$1,400/yr	$1,400/yr	$7,050/yr	assoc/dip/cert/citation	n/a	TOEFL 550 (academic programs)
$40 (Cdn), $100 (int'l)	$1,578/yr	$1,578/yr	$7,500/yr	cert/dip/assoc	grade 12 or equivalent	TOEFL 550, IELTS 6.5
$25 (Cdn), $100 (int'l)	$1,186/yr	$1,186/yr	$1,800/yr	dip/certs/assoc	no set minimums	TOEFL score not required

grad - graduate
hs - high school
i/p - in province
med - medium
n/a - not applicable
p/b - paper-based
o/p - out of province
undergrad or ugrad - undergraduate
sem - semester
yr(s) - year(s)

University and College Quick Facts

List of Profiles by Region & Type

	Page	Location: City	Location: City Population	Location: Cost of Living	Enrolment: Total Enrolment	Enrolment: Undergraduate Enrolment	Enrolment: International Enrolment	Enrolment: Student/Faculty Ratio
Institutes								
British Columbia Institute of Technology	119	Burnaby	3,000,000	high	44,277	15,134	611	20:1
Emily Carr Institute of Art & Design	123	Vancouver	2,000,000	high	1,600	945	45	15:1
The Prairie Provinces								
Universities								
Brandon University	131	Brandon	40,000	low	2,605	2,555	70	10:1
University of Alberta	135	Edmonton	850,000	med	30,000	25,000	–	15:1
University of Calgary	139	Calgary	828,500	med	23,638	20,472	900	~15:1
University of Lethbridge	143	Lethbridge	66,000	low	5,503	5,289	214	19:1
University of Regina	147	Regina	200,000	low	11,625	10,716	347	16:1
University of Saskatchewan	151	Saskatoon	210,000	low	17,078	15,290	698	29:1
University of Winnipeg, The	155	Winnipeg	700,000	low	6,500	7,000	250	15:1
University Colleges								
Augustana University College	161	Camrose	14,000	low	848	742	38	15:1 (f/t)
Colleges								
Bow Valley College	167	Calgary	830,000	med	10,520	3,258	120	15:1

KEY

[–] - not available
assoc - associate degree
avg - average
bac - baccalauréat
c/b - computer-based
cert - certificate
dgr - degree
dip - diploma
sup - supérieures
f/t - full-time

Expenses				Academics		
Application Fee	*In-Province Tuition*	*Out-of-Province Tuition*	*International Tuition*	*Academic Options*	*Minimum GPA*	*Minimum English Requirement (TOEFL, MELAB & IELTS)*
$30 (Cdn); $200 (int'l)	$2,338/yr*	$2,338/yr*	$4,350/ term	cert/dip/ ugrad/grad	varies	varies, TOEFL 500-580 or equivalent
$30 (Cdn and int'l)	$2,520/yr	$2,520/yr	$9,222/yr	dip/ undergrad	2.5 (for yr 2000)	TOEFL 570 (p/b); TOEFL 230 (c/b)
$35 (Cdn and int'l)	$2,808- 3,050/yr	$2,808- 3,050/yr	$4,914/yr	undergrad/ grad	Man: hs dip; others: 60-65%	TOEFL 550, MELAB 80, IELTS 6.5
$60 (Cdn and int'l)	$3,700/yr	$3,700/yr	$7,400/yr	undergrad/ grad	varies (65-70%)	TOEFL 580 (p/b), 237 (c/b)
$65 (Cdn and int'l)	$3,841/yr*	$3,841/yr*	$7,682/yr*	undergrad/ grad	65-80%	TOEFL 560, IELTS 7.0
$50 (Cdn and int'l)	$1,680/ sem	$1,680/ sem	$3,360/ sem	undergrad/ grad	2.0-2.75 (4.0 scale)	TOEFL 550, IELTS 6.0
$50 (Cdn and int'l)	$2,812/yr	$2,812/yr	$5,625/yr	undergrad/ grad	65%	TOEFL 550
$50 (Cdn and int'l)	$3,000- 3,780/yr*	$3,000- 3,780/yr*	$6,450- 8,901/yr*	undergrad/ grad	65% or C average	TOEFL 550 (p/b), 213 (c/b); MELAB 85; IELTS 6.0
$35 (Cdn), $60 (int'l)	$3,300/yr	$3,300/yr	$5,778/yr	undergrad/ grad	60% or special approval	TOEFL 570, IELTS 6.5
$30 (Cdn); $50 (int'l)	$4,695/yr	$4,695/yr	$6,260/yr	cert/dip/ undergrad	2.5/4.0; 5.0/9.0; 60% or C (avg)	TOEFL 550
n/a (Cdn); $100 (int'l)	varies	varies	$1,500 (f/t ESL)	hs dip/ GED/cert	n/a	n/a

grad - graduate
hs - high school
i/p - in province
med - medium
n/a - not applicable
p/b - paper-based
o/p - out of province
undergrad or ugrad - undergraduate
sem - semester
yr(s) - year(s)

University and College Quick Facts

List of Profiles by Region & Type

	Page	Location: City	Location: City Population	Location: Cost of Living	Enrolment: Total Enrolment	Enrolment: Undergraduate Enrolment	Enrolment: International Enrolment	Enrolment: Student/Faculty Ratio
Mount Royal College	171	Calgary	828,500	med	21,453	5,443	567	17:1
Red Deer College	175	Red Deer	60,000	low	10,309	5,800	23	18:1 (f/t)
Institutes								
Southern Alberta Institute of Technology	181	Calgary	828,500	med	8,800	8,800	250	13:1
Ontario								
Universities								
Carleton University	189	Ottawa	1,026,900	high	17,445	15,084	893	28:1
College Militaire Royal du Canada	193	Kingston	140,000	moyen	1,100	900	n/a	6:1
Lakehead University	197	Thunder Bay	125,000	med	6,600	6,267	115	20:1
Laurentian University	201	Sudbury	92,059	med	6,384	6,026	137	17:1
McMaster University	205	Hamilton	350,000	med	17,019	11,861	240	23:1
Queen's University	209	Kingston	120,000	med	12,982	10,998	763	11:1
Royal Military College of Canada	213	Kingston	140,000	med	1,100	900	n/a	6:1
Trent University	217	Peterborough	68,000	med	5,160	3,800	135	19:1
University of Guelph	221	Guelph	95,000	med	13,746	12,192	224	21:1
University of Ottawa	225	Ottawa	1,000,000	med	22,695	19,345	800	20:1

KEY

[–] - not available
assoc - associate degree
avg - average
bac - baccalauréat
c/b - computer-based
cert - certificate
dgr - degree
dip - diploma
sup - supérieures
f/t - full-time

Expenses				Academics		
Application Fee	***In-Province Tuition***	***Out-of-Province Tuition***	***International Tuition***	***Academic Options***	***Minimum GPA***	***Minimum English Requirement (TOEFL, MELAB & IELTS)***
$30 (Cdn and int'l)	$2,800-3,000/yr	$2,800-3,000/yr	$6,168/yr	cert/dip/ applied dgr	equivalent to Alberta hs dip	TOEFL 560
$40 (Cdn), $50 (int'l)	$2,564-3,495/yr	$2,564-3,495/yr	$7,511-8,422/yr	dip/cert/ undergrad	n/a	TOEFL 550
$25 (Cdn), $500 (int'l)	$1,780-3,033/yr	$1,780-3,033/yr	$8,500-9,500/yr	cert/dip/ undergrad	no set minimum	TOEFL 560
$80-95 (OUAC), $75 (Carleton)	$3,822-4,432/yr	$3,822-4,432/yr	$10,202-11,242/yr	undergrad/ grad	2.8-3.2 (4.0 scale)	TOEFL 580
n/a	$1,524/ année	$1,524/ année	n/a	bac/ études sup	75-80%	n/a (aisance dans une des langues officielles)
$80 (Cdn), $90 (int'l)	$2,345-$3,550/yr	$2,345-$3,550/yr	$4,850-$7,000/yr	dip/under-grad/grad	65%	TOEFL 550
$85 (Cdn), $95 (int'l)	$3,486/yr	$3,486/yr	$7,560/yr	undergrad/ grad	varies	TOEFL 550, MELAB 90
$80 (Cdn), $95 (int'l)	$3,900/yr	$3,900/yr	$12,000/yr	undergrad/ grad	varies	TOEFL 560
$85 (Cdn), $95 (int'l)	$3,551-3,915/yr*	$3,551-3,915/yr*	$10,000-16,300/yr*	undergrad/ grad	70% (may vary)	TOEFL 580, MELAB 90, IELTS 7.0
n/a	$1,524/yr	$1,524/yr	n/a	undergrad/ grad	75-80%	n/a; fluency in at least one official language
no application fee for students	$4,231/yr*	$4,231/yr*	$10,796/yr (includes	undergrad/ grad	2.5	TOEFL 550 (p/b), 213 (c/b)
$60 (Cdn and int'l)	$3,223-3,500*	$3,223-3,500*	$5,140-8,380*	undergrad/ grad	60-79%	TOEFL 600, IELTS 6.5, MELAB 85
$85 (Cdn), $95 (int'l)	$3,653-5,003/yr	$3,653-5,003yr	$8,005-8,778/yr	undergrad/ grad	B- (70%)	TOEFL 550-580 (p/b), 213-237 (c/b), MELAB 85-90, IELTS 7.0

grad - graduate
hs - high school
i/p - in province
med - medium
n/a - not applicable
p/b - paper-based
o/p - out of province
undergrad or ugrad - undergraduate
sem - semester
yr(s) - year(s)

University and College Quick Facts

List of Profiles by Region & Type

	Page	Location			Enrolment			
		City	City Population	Cost of Living	Total Enrolment	Undergraduate Enrolment	International Enrolment	Student/Faculty Ratio
University of Toronto	229	Toronto	4,338,400	high	54,000	30,484	3,168	9:1
University of Waterloo	233	Waterloo	275,000	med	18,125	16,300	428	20:1
University of Western Ontario, The	237	London	412,600	med	26,538	23,572	–	18:1
University of Windsor	241	Windsor	290,000	med	12,500	11,900	400	25:1
Wilfrid Laurier University	245	Waterloo	275000	med	6,000	5,200	200	20:1
York University	249	Toronto	3,000,000	high	38,500	34,400	1,700	16:1
Colleges								
Algonquin College of Applied Arts & Technology	255	Ottawa	1,027,000	high	11,000	11,000	350	18:1
George Brown College	259	Toronto	3,000,000	med-high	52,000	10,000	200	15:1
Lambton College	263	Sarnia	75,000	med	12,600	2,675	9	50:1
Northern College of Applied Arts & Technology	267	Timmins	45000	med	1,400	1,400	10	20:1
Quebec								
Universities								
Bishop's University	275	Lennoxville	5,000	med	2,361	2,333	141	16:1
Concordia University	279	Montreal	3,328,300	high	25,984	24,353	1,104	16:1
McGill University	283	Montreal	3,000,000	low	29,729	23,802	3,953	12:1 (avg)

KEY

[–] - not available
assoc - associate degree
avg - average
bac - baccalauréat
c/b - computer-based
cert - certificate
dgr - degree
dip - diploma
sup - supérieures
f/t - full-time

Expenses				Academics		
Application Fee	*In-Province Tuition*	*Out-of-Province Tuition*	*International Tuition*	*Academic Options*	*Minimum GPA*	*Minimum English Requirement (TOEFL, MELAB & IELTS)*
$95 (OUAC), $60 (U of T)	$3,516-5,808/yr	$3,516-5,808/yr	$8,320-11,345/yr	undergrad/grad	no set minimum	TOEFL 600, IELTS 6.5, MELAB 90
$80 (Cdn), $90 (int'l)	$3,454-4,858/yr*	$3,454-4,858/yr*	$12,174-20,848/yr*	undergrad/grad	70%	TOEFL 600 (p/b), 250 (c/b); IELTS 7.5; MELAB 90
$80 (i/p); $85 (o/p); $90 (int'l)	$4,200/yr	$4,200/yr	$10,000/yr (approx)	undergrad/grad	B or 75% average	evaluated on a case-by-case basis
$95 (Cdn and int'l)	$1,725-1,874/sem	$1,725-1,874/sem	$4,572-5,947/sem	undergrad/grad	2.75 (B-)	TOEFL 550 (p/b), 213 (c/b)
$90 (Cdn and int'l)	$3,300/yr	$3,300/yr	$7,000/yr	undergrad/grad	70%	TOEFL 560 (p/b), 220 (c/b), IELTS 7.0, MELAB 90
$60 (int'l)	$3,550/yr	$3,550/yr	$10,200-12,654/yr	undergrad/grad	varies by program	TOEFL 560 (p/b), 220 (c/b); MELAB 85; IELTS 7.0

$65 (Cdn), $250 (int'l)	$1,947/yr	$1,947/yr	$9,895/yr	dip/cert	no set minimum	TOEFL 550
$65 (OCAS); n/a (George Brown)	$1,473-$1,836/yr	$1,473-$1,836/yr	$9,375/yr	cert/dip/postdip	n/a	TOEFL 550
$65 (Cdn and int'l)	$1,702/yr	$1,702/yr	$9,215/yr	dip/cert	no set minimum	evaluated on case-by-case basis for ESL students
$40 (Cdn and int'l)	$1,801/yr	$1,801/yr	$9,740/yr	dip/cert	no set minimum	TOEFL 500

$55 (Cdn and int'l)	$1,700/yr	$3,200/yr	$8,200-9,200/yr	undergrad/grad	73%	TOEFL 550, MELAB 85, IELTS 6.5
$40 (Cdn and int'l)	$1,668/yr	$3,170/yr	$9,170-10,000/yr	undergrad/grad	n/a	TOEFL 550, MELAB 85, IELTS 6.5
$60 (Cdn and int'l)	$1,670/yr	$3,170/yr	$8,300-12,000/yr	undergrad/grad	varies	TOEFL 550, IELTS 6.5, MELAB 85

grad - graduate
hs - high school
i/p - in province
med - medium
n/a - not applicable
p/b - paper-based
o/p - out of province
undergrad or ugrad - undergraduate
sem - semester
yr(s) - year(s)

University and College Quick Facts

List of Profiles by Region & Type

	Page	Location: City	Location: City Population	Location: Cost of Living	Enrolment: Total Enrolment	Enrolment: Undergraduate Enrolment	Enrolment: International Enrolment	Enrolment: Student/Faculty Ratio
The Atlantic Provinces								
Universities								
Dalhousie University	291	Halifax	350,000	med	13,423	9,891	940	13:1
Memorial University of Newfoundland	295	St. John's	175,000	med	15,852	14,366	359	10:1
Saint Mary's University	299	Halifax	342000	med	7,200	6,800	800	17:1
St. Francis Xavier University	303	Antigonish	6,000	low	3,554	3,210	110	17:1
University of New Brunswick	307	Fredericton	65000	med	9180	8,100	400	15:1
University of Prince Edward Island	311	Charlottetown	31,400	med	2,439 (f/t)	2,400	81 (f/t)	12:1
Colleges								
College of the North Atlantic	317	Stephenville	172,000 (St. John's)	low	12,000	6,500	–	10:1
New Brunswick Community College	321	various	various	med	21,458	6,958	–	8:1 (f/t)
The Northwest Territories								
Colleges								
Aurora College	329	Fort Smith	varies by campus	med to high	1,900	850	n/a	8:1

KEY

[–] - not available
assoc - associate degree
avg - average
bac - baccalauréat
c/b - computer-based
cert - certificate
dgr - degree
dip - diploma
sup - supérieures
f/t - full-time

Expenses				Academics		
Application Fee	*In-Province Tuition*	*Out-of-Province Tuition*	*International Tuition*	*Academic Options*	*Minimum GPA*	*Minimum English Requirement (TOEFL, MELAB & IELTS)*
$35-50 (Cdn and int'l)	$3,850/yr*	$3,850/yr*	$6,550/yr*	undergrad/ grad	70%	TOEFL 580, MELAB 90, IELTS 7.0
$40 (1st-yr), $80 (int'l, transfer)	$3,300/yr	$3,300/yr	$6,600/yr	undergrad/ grad	70%	TOEFL 550, IELTS 6.0
$35 (Cdn and int'l)	$3,820/yr	$3,820/yr	$7,130/yr	undergrad/ grad	65%	TOEFL 550 or equivalent
$30 (Cdn and int'l)	$3,956/yr	$3,956/yr	$6,956/yr	undergrad/ grad	65%	TOEFL 550
$25 (Cdn and int'l)	$3,290/yr*	$3,290/yr*	$5,590/yr*	undergrad/ grad	varies	TOEFL 550 (p/b), 213 (c/b); MELAB 85; IELTS 6.5
$35 (Cdn and int'l)	$3,310/yr	$3,310/yr	$6,710/yr	cert/dip/ ugrad/grad	65%; 75% (Que Secondary V)	TOEFL 550 or equivalent
$30 (Cdn and int'l)	$726/sem	$726/sem	$3,300/ sem	cert/dip	2.0	TOEFL 550 (direct admission)
$15 (Cdn), $100 (int'l)	$2,000/yr*	$2,000/yr*	$5,000/yr*	dip/cert	n/a	TOEFL 550, MELAB 85
$15 (Cdn)	$1,300/yr	$1,300/yr	$1,300/yr	cert/dip	varies by program	varies by program

grad - graduate
hs - high school
i/p - in province
med - medium
n/a - not applicable
p/b - paper-based
o/p - out of province
undergrad or ugrad - undergraduate
sem - semester
yr(s) - year(s)

PROFILES OF Universities & Colleges IN British Columbia

British Columbia, World Class Education in

BCCIE

British Columbia's (BC) public universities, university colleges, colleges and institutes have been at the forefront of welcoming international student bodies, internationalizing curricula, pursuing international contracts and establishing faculty and student exchange programs worldwide. The majority of the public postsecondary institutions in the province include internationalization goals within their strategic plans, have a central office for coordinating international student services and international activities, and plan to increase their international involvement in the next five years.

Top 10 Reasons to Study in BC

Canada has been selected as the number one country in the world in which to live by the United Nations for most of this decade, and British Columbia has seen a continuing increase in the numbers of international students wanting to study here. There are several reasons for BC's prominence:

1. World-class education system
   BC has an excellent public education system that is recognized as being among the best in the world.
2. Wide range of choices
   An education in BC offers many options from certificates to graduate degrees with a choice of hundreds of programs.

> BC has an excellent public education system that is recognized as being among the best in the world.

3. Qualified and experienced instructors
   In the BC public postsecondary system, courses and programs are delivered by a dedicated group of highly qualified and experienced instructors in top-quality facilities.
4. Excellent support services for international students
   BC's public institutions offer a variety of excellent support services for international students including homestay, on-campus accommodation and orientation services.
5. Affordable costs of study
   Reasonable tuition fees combined with the fact that the Canadian dollar is 40 to 45 per cent lower than the US dollar makes education in BC affordable.
6. Spectacular natural environment
   Beautiful BC offers spectacular scenery with the lush rainforests and islands of the coastal areas; the open spaces, lakes and rivers of the interior and northern regions; and the snow-capped Rocky Mountains of eastern BC.
7. Welcoming multicultural society
   With a culturally diverse population, BC welcomes individuals from around the world and provides a tremendous range of cultural opportunities.
8. Safe, clean towns and cities
   BC is home to over 3.7 million people who live in major cities, small towns and rural communities that are among the safest and cleanest in North America.
9. A variety of recreational activities
   BC has an accessible outdoors and a climate to suit all kinds of sporting and recreational activities from mountain climbing to sailing.
10. Moderate climate
    BC is blessed with a moderate climate with four distinct seasons.

Increased Student Enrolment

The presence of international students is a way to encourage a broadening of the international perspectives of institutions, students and faculty, and communities.

Contact Information

To receive more information about studying in BC, write, phone, fax or email the BCCIE at the address below or visit the BCCIE website:

British Columbia Centre for International Education
6th Floor A, 1483 Douglas Street
Victoria, British Columbia
Canada V8W 3K4
phone: 1-250-978-4242
fax: 1-250-978-4249
email: bccie@bccie.bc.ca
internet: http://www.bccie.bc.ca

Canada: a Spectacular Setting

BCCIE

British Columbia has experienced a consistent and significant increase in the numbers of international students coming to the province. In 1996–97 the number of international students in BC at the postsecondary level was close to 18,000—representing nearly a 130 per cent increase in enrolment from the beginning of the decade. During the same time period, BC's share of Canada's total international student population at the postsecondary level grew from 12 per cent in 1990 to 26 per cent in 1996.[1]

These increases came about for the most part because institutions in BC became a strong presence in the Asia-Pacific region, expanded their interests in South America and began to see increased awareness of their excellence in Europe and the United States. As a result of these international activities and the increased awareness of the global marketplace, international students and faculty are increasingly taking advantage of the opportunity to see the high quality of programming that BC public institutions offer.

Extensive Program Choices

The British Columbia public postsecondary system offers international students a wide variety of programs. Short-term programs range from ESL programs to study tours to international executive training. Graduate programs in a wide range of fields are available at BC's six universities, while long-term undergraduate programs in the humanities, sciences and professions are available at BC's four universities and two specialized universities as well as the five university colleges. BC's university colleges, colleges and provincial institutes offer excellent university transfer, career, technical and vocational training.

Diverse Student Body

British Columbia's public postsecondary campuses have students from around the world representing over 115 countries. Many of the students who come to BC are from the Asia-Pacific region, though a growing number are from the United States, Mexico, South America and Europe. This kind of diversity helps to bring an international dimension to BC's campuses.

BC Institutions Working Together

In British Columbia a great deal of effort has been made to ensure that transfer from institution to institution within the province is as convenient and understandable as possible. The 26 integrated public universities, university colleges, colleges and institutes in BC have agreements in place that allow students to track how their education can progress from institution to institution until their educational needs have been met. So, for example, a student may choose to start their biology degree at a college and after successful completion of their first two years of prerequisites, decide to transfer into the third year of a biology degree program at one of BC's universities or university colleges. The system is flexible enough to accommodate the special needs of most students.

BC's Higher Education Institutions

UNIVERSITIES

Royal Roads University
Simon Fraser University
Technical University of British Columbia
University of British Columbia
University of Northern British Columbia
University of Victoria

UNIVERSITY COLLEGES

Kwantlen University College
Malaspina University College
Okanagan University College
University College of the Cariboo
University College of the Fraser Valley

COLLEGES

Camosun College
Capilano College
College of New Caledonia
College of the Rockies
Douglas College
Langara College
Northern Lights College
North Island College
Northwest Community College
Selkirk College
Vancouver Community College

INSTITUTES

British Columbia Institute of Technology
Emily Carr Institute of Art & Design
Justice Institute of British Columbia
Open Learning Agency

1. Source: "The National Report on International Students in Canada" 1996–97.

Universities

IN

British Columbia

ROYAL ROADS UNIVERSITY VICTORIA, BRITISH COLUMBIA

University Mission

...to provide innovative, market-driven education to equip our graduates with the life-long learning skills they need to meet the challenges and opportunities of a rapidly changing world

Student Voice:

They encouraged me to run with new ideas, to take the reins and get involved. The accelerated program was great, too, because I can get into my career sooner.

Chantal Cadieux
Bachelor of Commerce
1997 Graduate

CONTACT INFORMATION
Office of Learner Services & Registrar
Royal Roads University
2005 Sooke Road
Victoria, British Columbia
Canada V9B 5Y2
PH 1-800-788-8028
FAX 1-250-391-2522
EMAIL rruregistrar@royalroads.ca
INTERNET http://www.royalroads.ca

UNIVERSITY OVERVIEW

Formerly known as the Royal Roads Military College, a degree-granting naval and army cadet college, Royal Roads University (RRU) was established in 1995 by the provincial government of British Columbia and the first civilian students registered in September 1995. RRU is the province's newest public university, offering smaller class sizes and teacher to student ratios. In addition to several highly specialized programs at the master's level, RRU confers Bachelor of Commerce (BCom) and Bachelor of Science (BSc) degrees.

Bachelor of Commerce

The BCom in Entrepreneurial Management program is both integrative and interdisciplinary, and incorporates the study of marketing, organizational behaviour & human resources, and communications. The curriculum focuses on the changes in the global economy that both challenge and support entrepreneurial ventures. Information about Asia Pacific cultures and economies is integrated into the curriculum to enhance students' awareness of global issues as well as their understanding of international business. One of the program's central beliefs is that studies in entrepreneurship and international business should not be separated.

Bachelor of Science

The BSc in Environmental Science program at RRU is grounded in the study of sustainability and its interrelationships. The approach to the subject is interdisciplinary and includes the study of the social, economic and environmental implications of the decision making process. The program is designed to provide a well-rounded education that combines business, communications and technical skills. The curriculum is designed to prepare graduates for responsible roles as leaders in a changing world.

Calendar Year

The calendar year at RRU is organized on a quarter system, with each quarter consisting of 10 weeks of instruction, followed by a two-week period for the completion of projects and examinations. There are two advantages to this format: there are a greater number of entry dates (although at present students can only enter in September); and, the longer breaks associated with traditional programs have been eliminated, granting students greater flexibility and enabling them to maximize their savings. Students generally enter the program after completing two years of training at a university or equivalent institution. RRU's undergraduate programs condense the third and fourth-year curricula into one calendar year, which enables students to earn a degree in three years instead of four.

Highlights

- Accelerated learning schedule combines traditional third and fourth years into one combined year
- Distance learning opportunities in selected programs allow students to study while continuing their employment with no loss of income

University Statistics

Year Founded: 1995
Academic Options: undergraduate/graduate
Calendar Year: first quarter (Sept-Dec); second quarter (Jan-Mar); third quarter (Mar-Jun); fourth quarter (Jun-Sept)

DISCIPLINES/MAJORS OFFERED

Entrepreneurial Management

Environmental Science

ADMISSIONS CRITERIA & PROCEDURES

Candidates for admission must complete an application form obtained from RRU's Office of the Registrar or the RRU website. In addition, the application package should include the nonrefundable C$50 application fee, two letters of reference (one academic and one work-related), official postsecondary transcripts, a resume and a personal statement detailing the reasons why the candidate wishes to enter the program. All candidates must prove their proficiency in written and spoken English, and will be tested on their language skills during the Prior Learning Assessment (PLA) normally required of candidates. All official documents should include certified English translations, where applicable. International students are responsible for any costs incurred during the evaluation of their international credentials by the International Credential Evaluation Service.

Prior to a program's commencement, students take the PLA to assist the university in identifying any potential academic areas students may need to improve before entering their first quarter. The PLA process examines each student's potential using methods including the preparation of the student's academic portfolio, demonstrations of competency, examinations, questionnaires, interviews and references.

All undergraduate students are required to take a three week Foundation Program that is designed to reacquaint students with some of the necessary skills needed at RRU.

Admissions at a Glance

Minimum GPA: B-

Minimum English Requirements:
TOEFL 570 (paper-based), 233 (computer-based): with TWE and TSE

Application Fee: C$50 (Canadian and international)

Application Deadlines: May 15 (undergraduate)

ACADEMIC FACILITIES

RRU's Learning Resource Centre (LRC) is a facility that combines an extensive library with several alternative information centres and data resources. The LRC houses a collection of 120,000 monographs and journals, 5,000 government documents, 30 CD-ROM databases and provides access to several on-line periodical databases. The campus bookstore, which provides university textbooks, RRU clothing and accessories, transit passes and photocopy cards, is also located in the LRC.

RRU has almost 100 computer terminals located in the Grant Block, the LCR, the Millward Residence Annex and the Millward Residence. All the terminals in the residence buildings are connected to the campus-wide RRU LAN system and many are available 24 hours a day.

Student & Faculty Profile

Total Enrolment: 750

Undergraduate Enrolment: 400

# of Faculty: 75

Student/Faculty Ratio: 10:1

Male/Female Students: 53%/47%

First-Year Class Sizes: 50

Undergraduate Acceptance Rate: 54%

Undergraduate Enrolment by Discipline:

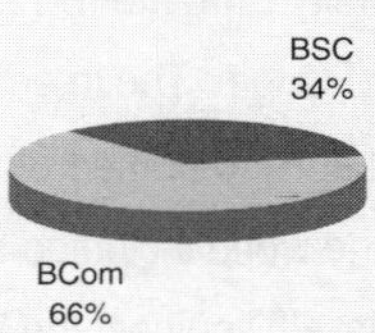

SCHOLARSHIPS & FINANCIAL ASSISTANCE

RRU grants C$20,000 in entrance scholarships every year. Application forms and information regarding scholarship eligibility are available at the Office of the Registrar. Scholarships are awarded based on academic achievement or proven ability in subject areas including sustainable development, entrepreneurship, leadership, conflict analysis and management. Scholarships available to undergraduate students include BCom in Entrepreneurial Management and BSc in Environmental Science awards.

Expenses at a Glance

Tuition (undergraduate, full-time):
In-Province: C$2,500-8,500/year
Out-of-Province: C$2,500-8,500/year
International: C$5,000-17,000/year

Fees, Books, Materials: C$800-1,600/year

Accommodation:
Private: C$400-875/month
Residence: C$665/month (approx)
Homestay: n/a

Health Insurance: not available

CAMPUS & LOCATION

City Population:	325,000
Cost of Living:	high
Climate Range:	0° to 30°C
Campus Setting:	suburban
# of Students in Residence:	200

Royal Roads University's campus is situated on over 250 hectares of historic grounds and gardens owned by the government of British Columbia. The campus is located on Hatley Park, an estate formerly owned by James Dunsmuir, premier of British Columbia in the early 1900s. Hatley Castle was built on the property for Dunsmuir in 1909 and was maintained by the family until its sale to the government in 1940.

RRU offers its undergraduate students 106 residence rooms on campus, overlooking the Strait of Juan de Fuca and the snow-capped Olympic mountains in nearby Washington state. All floors of the undergraduate residence are coeducational and contain many modern conveniences, including TVs, VCRs, refrigerators, microwaves and coffee makers. There are over 100 spaces available in the graduate residences, which offer views of Hatley Castle and the campus gardens; all floors of the graduate residence are also coeducational.

The RRU campus is 25 minutes from downtown Victoria, the capital city of British Columbia. Victoria is renowned for the wide variety of outdoor activities possible in and around the city, including hiking through some of Vancouver Island's mature rainforest, mountain biking through the local mountains or whale-watching off the west coast of the island. In addition, Victoria offers numerous cultural activities and a clean, safe living environment.

ATHLETICS & EXTRACURRICULAR ACTIVITIES

Victoria's temperate climate provides many opportunities for outdoor recreation at RRU, both on and off campus. RRU offers a wide range of recreation facilities including an indoor pool, squash courts, tennis courts, playing fields and a weight room; the nearby lagoon is perfect for such water activities as sailing, kayaking, windsurfing and canoeing. RRU's Rowing Centre provides students with the opportunity to train under national-level coaches and former Olympic Rowers.

Students are encouraged to join, and have the opportunity to develop, the academic, recreational and social student associations and clubs on campus. There are also several student-organized committees and councils on campus including the Environmental Stewardship Committee, Activities Committee, Board of Governors, and the Residence and Academic Councils.

University Recognition

- RRU's research division has undertaken 14 major consulting and research projects
- Member of the Association of Commonwealth Universities
- Agreement with Capital University of Economics and Business of Beijing

STUDENT SUPPORT SERVICES

Counselling services are available to all RRU students in need of professional personal counselling with any kind of problem. The university also offers career counselling for students seeking advice on career path choices. Aid is available for students as they search for job opportunities by providing information resources, contacts in the industry, coaching on interview and resume skills.

The Foundation Programs is designed to support students in need of academic aid. The program's professional staff will assess the student's exact learning needs and cater the program to suit the student. Students may be referred outside institutions for any specific academic needs that RRU cannot supply.

International Students

University Enrolment: 10

% of University Enrolment: 1%

Countries of Origin: The international students at RRU come from countries around the world including Hong Kong, Indonesia, Philippines, the West Indies and the US.

SIMON FRASER UNIVERSITY
BURNABY, BRITISH COLUMBIA

...to be Canada's number one

comprehensive university

Student Voice:

SFU is rated one of the best universities in Canada, and I can see why—top professors, lots of academic options and a flexible trimester system. Best of all, and thanks to the co-op education program, I'm learning and using leading edge technologies both in the classroom and on the job.

Marko Vasiljevic
Third-Year, Engineering Science

CONTACT INFORMATION
Simon Fraser University
8888 University Drive
Burnaby, British Columbia
Canada V5A 1S6
PH 1-604-291-3224
FAX 1-604-291-4969
EMAIL
undergraduate-admissions@sfu.ca
INTERNET http://www.reg.sfu.ca

UNIVERSITY OVERVIEW

Founded in 1965, Simon Fraser University (SFU) is a comprehensive, public, mid-sized university. The university offers undergraduate and graduate programs in a wide variety of disciplines as well as distance, co-op and continuing education programs. SFU was ranked as the nation's best comprehensive university in Maclean's 1998 national reputational survey.

Academic Programs

SFU offers undergraduate and graduate programs through its Faculties of Applied Sciences, Arts, Business Administration, Education and Science. The university is proud of its tradition of offering innovative programs that facilitate study across disciplines. Students may choose to engage in interdisciplinary studies within their major or pursue double major, joint major, joint minor or minor options. SFU encourages its students to explore all the possibilities of a postsecondary education.

The university's trimester system allows students to enter into any of the three terms and continue their studies year-round. Each semester has its own registration and exam period. SFU understands that not every student can participate in a traditional study period; therefore, the university offers many classes at night or on weekends to accommodate its students.

SFU is focused on providing students with the analytical and practical foundation required for success in today's global environment.

Practical Experiences

Many of the programs in a wide variety of fields include co-op or internship programs, which provide students with real-world experience and the opportunity to make important career contacts. These paid, study-related positions are arranged through the university and include both public and private sector placements.

A Global Perspective

There is a strong international presence on the SFU campus, an attribute the university strongly promotes. The International & Exchange Student Services Office is responsible for coordinating the university's international exchange program and other international activities.

SFU is committed to developing a global perspective in its programming and among its students. The university has exchange agreements with 130 universities in 24 countries including Argentina, Australia, China, England, Fiji, Korea, Norway, Philippines, Switzerland and the USA.

Highlights

- Trimester system allows students to study year round
- Co-op and internship opportunities in a wide variety of disciplines
- International exchange opportunities with 130 universities in 24 countries
- Beautiful campus with award-winning architecture

University Statistics

Year Founded: 1965
Academic Options: undergraduate/graduate
Calendar Year: fall semester (Sep-Dec); spring semester (Jan-Apr); summer semester (May-Aug)

DISCIPLINES/MAJORS OFFERED

Faculty of Applied Sciences: Communication, Computing Science, Communication, Engineering Science, Kinesiology

Faculty of Arts: Archeology, Asia-Canada, Canadian Studies, Cognitive Science, Contemporary Arts, Criminology, Critical Studies, Dance, Economics, English, Film, First Nations Studies, French, Geography, Gerontology, History, Latin American Studies, Linguistics, Humanities, Interdisciplinary Studies, Mathematics, Music, Philosophy, Political Science, Psychology, Sociology & Anthropology, Spanish, Statistics, Theatre, Visual Arts, Women's Studies

Faculty of Business Administration: Accounting, Business Administration, Finance, Human Resource Management, International Business, Management Information Systems, Management Science, Marketing, Policy Analysis

Faculty of Education: Mathematical Sciences Specialization, Professional Development Program

Faculty of Science: Applied Mathematics, Biochemistry, Biological Sciences, Chemical Physics, Chemistry, Earth Sciences, Environmental Science, General Science, Geography, Management & Systems Science, Mathematics & Computing Science, Mathematics & Statistics, Mathematical Physics, Physics, Quaternary Studies, Statistics

ADMISSIONS CRITERIA & PROCEDURES

Generally, students who have completed the highest level of secondary education in their region, or its equivalent, are eligible for admission; however, admission to SFU is competitive. Domestic students typically require a minimum of 67 per cent for consideration, or higher, on four senior subjects, including English for admission. International students typically require a secondary school average of 85 per cent or higher to be considered. The minimum grade average may be higher for certain programs and individual programs may have specific subject prerequisites. Prospective students should contact the Office of the Registrar for further information on specific programs. Additional admission requirements may include auditions, portfolios and standardized test scores.

A completed application form must be accompanied by official academic transcripts, any additional information requested by the program applied to and a C$65 application fee. Students applying for on-campus housing should complete the appropriate section at the back of the admissions application and include an additional C$20 fee. Application can be made for entry into any of SFU's three terms. Many programs allow only limited enrolment; students are encouraged to apply early.

Those students who are not native speakers of English must submit a TOEFL score of 230 (computer-based) including a minimum essay score of 4.5, a TOEFL score of 250 (computer-based), an International English Language Testing System (IELTS) score of 7.5, or a TOEFL score of 207 (computer-based) and completion of SFU's English Bridge Program, which is an intensive ESL program designed to improve academic English-language skills.

Admissions at a Glance

Minimum GPA: 67% (Cdn), 85% (int'l)

Minimum English Requirements:
- TOEFL 230 (computer-based) with TWE 4.5; TOEFL 250 (computer-based); IELTS 7.5; TOEFL 207 (computer-based) and completion of SFU's English Bridge Program

Application Fee: C$65 (Cdn & int'l)

Application Deadlines: Apr 30 (fall semester); Sept 30 (spring semester); Feb 1 (summer semester)

ACADEMIC FACILITIES

SFU offers technologically advanced learning facilities. The research and experimental laboratories on campus are continually updated to ensure that students have access to modern equipment. There are 34 centres and institutes located on campus that conduct research in a wide variety of disciplines. Students work closely with faculty members through these centres.

The W.A.C. Bennett Library on the Burnaby campus is fully automated and features online computer services. The library has over 2.4 million items, including books, periodicals and microform materials. All SFU students have Internet and email access. The university-wide Unix system at SFU gives students access to the library database, the World Wide Web and department servers through a high-speed fibre-optic network. There are more than 400 microcomputers available to students throughout the campus.

Student & Faculty Profile

Total Enrolment: 23,220

Undergraduate Enrolment: 20,966

# of Faculty: 615

Student/Faculty Ratio: 25:1

Male/Female Students: 43%/57%

First-Year Class Sizes: 80 (average)

Undergraduate Acceptance Rate: 58%

Undergraduate Enrolment by Discipline:

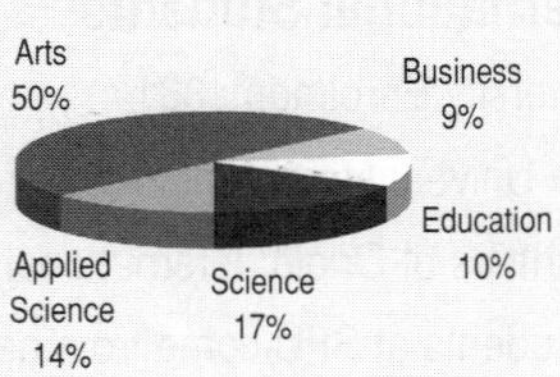

SCHOLARSHIPS & FINANCIAL ASSISTANCE

Students are eligible for a variety of financial assistance programs including entrance or continuing scholarships, bursaries, awards and loans. Entrance and continuing scholarships are awarded to students with a high level of academic achievement. Awards at SFU are merit-based and bursaries are need-based. Domestic students may be eligible for both federal and provincial need-based loan programs. Students should contact the Office of the Registrar for further information.

International students who have studied for at least two semesters at SFU may compete for scholarships and awards. Students apply for bursaries in their first semester.

Expenses at a Glance

Tuition (undergraduate, full-time):
- In-Province: C$2,310/year
- Out-of-Province: C$2,310/year
- International: C$6,994/year

Fees, Books, Materials: C$1,560/year

Accommodation:
- Private: C$450-750/month
- Residence: C$400-475/month
- Homestay: n/a

Health Insurance: C$500/year

CAMPUS & LOCATION

City Population:	1,800,000
Cost of Living:	high
Climate Range:	0° to 25°C
Campus Setting:	suburban
# of Students in Residence:	1,200

The Burnaby campus, with its distinctive, award-winning architecture, serves as SFU's main campus. Designed by Arthur Erickson, the Burnaby campus buildings are terraced and unobtrusively follow the contours of the landscape; many of the buildings are connected by covered walkways giving the campus a unified feel. The campus extends along the ridge of Burnaby Mountain and students enjoy spectacular views of Vancouver, the Coast Mountains and Georgia Straight.

The Harbour Centre campus, located in downtown Vancouver, opened in 1989. The campus is housed in a modern facility comprising over 123,000 square feet, which contains a wide variety of specialized instructional resources.

SFU's main campus is in Burnaby, British Columbia, just 16 kilometres from the major urban centre of Vancouver. Vancouver is Canada's gateway to the Pacific Rim and is one of the most ethnically diverse cities in the world. Vancouver is the largest commercial, industrial and financial centre on Canada's west coast. SFU students can take advantage of the many cultural opportunities the city offers including its theatre and ballet companies, symphony, numerous galleries and museums. Vancouver is a clean, safe city with a cosmopolitan atmosphere and numerous parks. The region enjoys the mildest climate in the country and the local mountains, ocean and forests offer many outdoor recreational activities.

ATHLETICS & EXTRACURRICULAR ACTIVITIES

SFU students enjoy a comprehensive athletic and extracurricular system. The university strives to provide students with a rewarding and diverse experience while studying at SFU.

SFU has a proud tradition in athletics. The university competes against North American opponents in many men's and women's varsity sports in the National Association of Intercollegiate Athletics (NAIA). An intramural system offering a wide range of sporting activities is also an important part of university life. Students can participate in activities such as basketball, badminton, ice hockey and volleyball. The university also offers a number of recreational and instructional programs in areas that range from belly dancing to fencing. Athletic facilities housed in the Chancellors Gymnasium Complex include two multi-purpose gymnasia, an Aquatic Centre, weight training facilities, squash and racquetball courts and a cardio-vascular gym.

There are nearly 100 student organizations meeting on the SFU campus, which allow students to encounter peers with similar interests. A student-run radio station and newspaper keep the student body informed and entertained. The Simon Fraser Art Gallery and School for the Contemporary Arts offer a program of cultural events each year.

University Recognition

- SFU was ranked as the best comprehensive university in Canada in Maclean's 1996, 1997 and 1998 national reputational survey
- SFU's University/Industry Liaison Office has successfully launched over 34 active spin-off companies
- SFU accounting students again earned a gold medal and the highest pass percentage rate (92%) in Canada in the 1998 Chartered Accountancy Uniform Final Examination (UFEs)

STUDENT SUPPORT SERVICES

Campus Community Services supports and enriches campus life by providing programs and services to students and the university community. Students will find a wide variety of services available. Health and Counselling Services is committed to helping students, staff and faculty maintain physical, social and emotional wellness. Both peer and professional counselling are available on campus. Other services include a Chaplain's Service, Student Employment Centre, Residence & Housing, Centre for Students with Disabilities, First Nations Student Centre, Recreational Services & Athletics, and the Volunteer Resource Centre.

The Centre for International & Exchange Student Services helps ease foreign students' transition to university life and Canadian culture. The centre can assist students with concerns about immigration, housing, university life, cultural issues and finances.

International Students

University Enrolment: 861

% of University Enrolment: 5%

Countries of Origin: International students at SFU come from nearly 100 countries around the globe.

University of British Columbia
Vancouver, British Columbia

University Mission

...to be a world renowned institution of

higher education and research

Contact Information

Undergraduate Admissions
University of British Columbia
2016-1874 East Mall
Vancouver, British Columbia
Canada V6T 1Z1
PH 1-604-822-3014 (Cdn);
1-604-822-8999 (int'l)
FAX 1-604-822-3599 (Cdn);
1-604-822-9888 (int'l)
EMAIL
registrar.admission@ubc.ca (Cdn);
international.reception@ubc.ca (int'l)
INTERNET
http://www.admissions.ubc.ca (Cdn);
http://www.international.ubc.ca (int'l)

Student Voice:

Having a UBC degree will open up many doors to new and exciting opportunities in the field of science. It is broad enough in scope to allow me to find a job in industry, yet focused enough to allow me to pursue further studies.

Carol
Biology & Chemistry major
Faculty of Science

UNIVERSITY OVERVIEW

The University of British Columbia (UBC) was incorporated in 1908 and admitted its first 379 students in 1915. Now Canada's third largest university, UBC has become a premiere teaching and research institution.

Academic Programs

UBC offers undergraduate and graduate instruction in 12 faculties and 11 schools, and provides instruction in all the major disciplines and professions. The majority of undergraduate programs require four years of study and culminate in a bachelor's degree.

The Faculty of Graduate Studies offers master's and doctoral degrees and administers a number of interdisciplinary research centres and institutes.

UBC's preprofessional programs include medicine, law and dentistry and typically require a minimum of three years of preparatory study. Other programs, including commerce and pharmaceutical sciences, are normally entered after completion of a preparatory year of study in another faculty. Diploma programs are also offered in specialized areas of study.

The university's Student Exchange Programs offer opportunities for third-year students to study at one of UBC's 83 partner institutions in Europe, Asia, Africa, Australia or the US.

Undergraduate Academic Options

Arts One and Science One provide an alternative to the traditional first-year undergraduate programs at UBC.

Arts One is an optional first-year program for students enrolled in the Faculty of Arts. In cooperation with the faculty, students in the program are able to focus on a single theme and study from a select group of fiction and nonfiction books and films, and pieces of music. In small work groups, students are able to discuss the course materials and its thematic elements, allowing for a more intimate and personalized program of study.

Science One is an innovative first-year program in which traditional biology, chemistry, mathematics and physics courses are presented in a unified, integrated format. The program emphasizes interdisciplinary studies and offers a rigorous academic focus that incorporates lectures, tutorials and laboratory work.

Cooperative Education

UBC's co-op coordinators work with employers across Canada to create career-related positions for co-op students. UBC offers co-op programs in selected academic areas in the Faculties of Arts, Applied Science, Forestry, Commerce & Business Administration, and Science. Enrolment in the co-op program is limited and dependent on the number of qualified students and available placements.

Highlights

- Special first-year undergraduate programs in the Faculty of Arts and the Faculty of Science
- Cooperative education programs available in five faculties
- Student exchange and study abroad opportunities

University Statistics

Year Founded: 1908

Academic Options: undergraduate/graduate

Calendar Year: fall semester (Sept-Dec); spring semester (Jan-Apr)

DISCIPLINES/MAJORS OFFERED

UBC offers more than 300 degree programs, including programs in the following areas.

Faculty of Agricultural Sciences: Agricultural Econ, Agriculture, Agroecology, Animal, Food, Int'l Resource Systems, Plant, Soil

Faculty of Applied Science (Engineering): Bioresource, Chemical, Civil, Electrical, Eng Physics, Geological, Mechanical, Metals & Materials, Mining & Mineral

Faculty of Arts: Anthropology, Archeology, Classics, Creative Writing, Econ, English, Env Studies, Ethnic Studies, Film, Fine Arts, Geography, History, Int'l Relations, Language & Literature, Linguistics, Math, Music, Philosophy, Political Science, Psychology, Religious Studies, Sociology, Theatre

Faculty of Commerce & Business Administration: Accounting, Commerce & Econ, Finance, Bus Mgmt, Industrial Relations Mgmt, Int'l Bus, Mgmt Info Systems, Mktg, Transportation & Logistics, Urban Land Econ

Faculty of Dentistry

Faculty of Education

Faculty of Forestry

Faculty of Law

Faculty of Medicine

Faculty of Pharmaceutical Sciences

Faculty of Science: Aquaculture, Astronomy, Atmospheric, Biochem, Bio, Chem, Comp, Env, Geography, Geological, Geophysics, Math, Microbio, Nutritional, Oceanography, Pharmacology, Physics, Physiology, Psychology, Statistics

ADMISSIONS CRITERIA & PROCEDURES

Admission to UBC is competitive and is based on a strong academic background. Broader based admissions criteria may be used in some programs in the selection of a limited number of qualified students.

All applicants must complete an application for admission, accompanied by the appropriate nonrefundable application fee. Applicants should arrange to have official secondary school transcripts (and postsecondary transcripts, where applicable) sent directly to the Office of Undergraduate Admissions.

All undergraduate applicants, regardless of country of origin or citizenship status, will be required to demonstrate competence in the English language prior to admission. Students from within British Columbia may submit a grade of 80% or higher on the BC English 12 or English Literature 12 part of the provincial exam. Applicants may also submit one of the following: a grade of 6 or 7 on the IB Higher Level English course, a grade of 5 on the AP English, 570 (580 for the Faculty of Arts) on the TOEFL, 90 on the MELAB, or a 6.5 on the IELTS with no band lower than 6.

The minimum academic qualifications for undergraduate admission include graduation from a secondary school with an acceptable university preparatory curriculum and the applicable program prerequisites.

In addition to regular admission requirements, international students should include certified English translations of all documentation in their application package, as well as documentation in the original language of instruction.

Admissions at a Glance

Minimum GPA: varies by faculty

Minimum English Requirements: TOEFL 570 (580 for the Faculty of Arts), MELAB 90, 6 or 7 IB Higher Level English course, 5 on the AP English, or 6.5 on IELTS with no band lower than 6

Application Fee: C$22 (in-province), $54 (out-of-province), $100 (American and international)

Application Deadlines: Feb 28 (fall, early admission; summer, regular admission); Apr 30 (fall, regular admission, but varies by program)

ACADEMIC FACILITIES

The university heads four federally funded Centres of Excellence that provide national networks for advanced research, including the Tri-University Meson Facility (TRIUMP), one of the world's largest nuclear accelerator facilities for research in subatomic physics. With 19 branches, the UBC library system is the second largest university library in the country and holds approximately three million volumes. The central libraries at UBC include the new Walter C. Koerner Library (social sciences and humanities) and the Main Library (physical sciences and engineering). UBC also boasts a fine arts gallery, an Asian centre, numerous museums, an herbarium, specialty gardens and a research forest.

UBC's many computer labs provide access to PC and Macintosh computers, and specialized workstations for advanced applications; Internet access is provided in all labs and email accounts are available to all students.

Student & Faculty Profile

Total Enrolment: 33,474

Undergraduate Enrolment: 27,293

# of Faculty: 4,000 (part- & full-time)

Student/Faculty Ratio: 18:1

Male/Female Students: 52%/48%

First-Year Class Sizes: 60 (average)

Undergraduate Acceptance Rate: not available

Undergraduate Enrolment by Discipline:

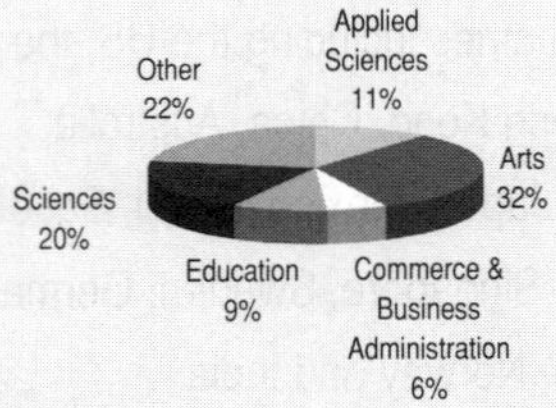

SCHOLARSHIPS & FINANCIAL ASSISTANCE

The university offers a number of merit-based awards for undergraduates, including major entrance scholarships for students of high academic calibre who enter UBC from secondary school. UBC's University Scholars' Program recognizes students who have achieved academic excellence in secondary school.

Students should contact UBC's Office of Awards & Financial Assistance for more information about application deadlines and qualifications.

Expenses at a Glance

Tuition (undergraduate, full-time):
- In-Province: C$2,295/year
- Out-of-Province: C$2,295/year
- International: C$13,830/year

Fees, Books, Materials: C$800/year

Accommodation:
- Private: C$600-800/month
- Residence: C$6,400/year
- Homestay: C$168/week (minimum stay 2 weeks)

Health Insurance: C$49/month

CAMPUS & LOCATION

City Population:	1,800,000
Cost of Living:	high
Climate Range:	0° to 28°C
Campus Setting:	urban
# of Students in Residence:	8,370

The University of British Columbia, the province's oldest university, is located on the west coast in the city of Vancouver, Canada's gateway to the Pacific, and the third largest city in the country. UBC's sweeping 403-hectare campus with its many buildings, walkways and gardens is surrounded by forests, mountains and beaches.

Vancouver is renowned around the world for its beauty. Clean and safe, this modern, multicultural city of 1.8 million offers an abundance of natural and cultural attractions. Vancouver's parks, public beaches and the nearby snow-capped Coast Mountains offer a wide variety of outdoor activities that can be enjoyed year-round as a result of the temperate climate.

Several different types of on-campus housing are available. UBC's Totem Park and Place Vanier are generally used by first- and second-year students and the Walter Gage, Fairview Crescent and Thunderbird residences are usually occupied by upper-level students. Residences accommodate more than 6,000 students and their families. Off-campus housing and a homestay program are also readily available.

ATHLETICS & EXTRACURRICULAR ACTIVITIES

UBC's extensive sports facilities include swimming pools, tennis courts, gymnasia, playing fields, skating rinks and a golf course. UBC's recreation program, known as the Birdcoop, provides students with access to some of the best fitness equipment available.

The UBC Thunderbird Athletic Program is one of the most prestigious and successful interuniversity athletic programs in Canada. UBC's Thunderbirds compete on both men's and women's teams in 20 different varsity sports, including soccer, basketball, volleyball, hockey, and football.

UBC supports over 200 student clubs and organizations that cater to a wide variety of academic and social interests. Students can participate in the activities of one of the 32 ethnic and cultural societies on campus, including AIESEC, the Pacific Rim Club, the Muslim Students' Association, the Japanese Network and the Indo-Canadian Cultural Association.

University Recognition

- UBC is consistently ranked among Canada's top four medical/doctoral universities by Maclean's magazine
- Approximately 80% of all university research in British Columbia is done at UBC
- UBC ranks third in North America behind MIT and Stanford for the number of spin-off companies formed through its research programs

STUDENT SUPPORT SERVICES

UBC's Counselling Centre offers personal and academic counselling for all students; group workshops and one-on-one counselling sessions are available. Career advising is also available to all students.

UBC's International Student Services provides a wide range of support and social services to the over 2,000 international students at UBC, including orientation and peer partner programs, personal advising services, and social/cultural and recreational programs that bring international and Canadian students together.

UBC's English Language Institute (ELI), located in a new building with modern multi-media labs, offers a variety of short-term intensive language programs from the elementary to the advanced level, as well as university-readiness programs to strengthen students' academic and communication skills.

International Students

University Enrolment: 2,324

% of University Enrolment: 7%

Countries of Origin: UBC's international student population comes from over 114 countries including the US, the UK, Hong Kong, China, Australia, Korea, Japan, Mexico, Brazil, Saudi Arabia, Singapore, Sweden, Germany, Taiwan, Norway and India.

UNIVERSITY OF NORTHERN BRITISH COLUMBIA PRINCE GEORGE, BRITISH COLUMBIA

UNBC The University of Northern British Columbia

University Mission

...to improve the quality of life in its region, the province and beyond, by attaining the highest standards of undergraduate and graduate teaching, learning and research

CONTACT INFORMATION
International Centre
University of Northern British Columbia
3333 University Way
Prince George, British Columbia
Canada V2N 4Z9
PH 1-250-960-5702
FAX 1-250-960-5546
EMAIL lward@unbc.ca
INTERNET http://www.unbc.ca

Student Voice:

I was attracted to UNBC for the opportunity to see something new and experience something different from that which I was used to.

Robert Karanja

UNIVERSITY OVERVIEW

The University of Northern British Columbia (UNBC) is a new, small university, created to meet the needs of northern and central British Columbia. Founded in 1990, the university now has over 3,000 students working towards undergraduate and graduate degrees. Although most of the courses are offered at the main Prince George campus, the university also has regional campuses throughout central and northern British Columbia. The university offers full-time and part-time options, and particularly welcomes mature and First Nations students. The small size of the university ensures that students receive a personalized education that is unavailable at other, larger universities.

Programs Offered

UNBC has 27 undergraduate programs and 18 graduate programs. The university also offers a number of certificate programs. Collaborative arrangements with community colleges in northern British Columbia and elsewhere enable students to transfer blocks of credit in programs such as business administration, forestry, social work and nursing. Natural resources management and business administration are the most popular degree programs at UNBC.

Interdisciplinary Studies

UNBC programs are interdisciplinary in approach, removing the forced boundaries between areas of study. Areas such as environmental studies, First Nations studies, international studies, northern studies, women's studies and gender studies exemplify the university's commitment to interdisciplinary programs. UNBC students have extensive options for combining fields of study across traditional divisions.

Co-op Education

UNBC offers a cooperative education program in nearly all undergraduate programs. The co-op program combines traditional learning with four semesters of paid, on-the-job training. Employers are increasingly employing graduates with co-op experience, recognizing the potential brought by new employees with both theoretical and practical knowledge. Interested students should contact the Office of Cooperative Education.

Exchange Programs

UNBC offers international exchange programs with 12 universities in eight countries around the world. Exchange programs are available regardless of students' degree programs. Students can participate in exchange programs lasting anywhere from six weeks to one full academic year.

Highlights

- Education opportunities ranging from certificate to graduate programs
- Co-op education available
- Exchange programs with 12 universities from eight countries around the world

University Statistics

Year Founded: 1990
Academic Options: undergraduate/graduate
Calendar Year: fall semester (Sept-Dec); winter semester (Jan-Apr)

DISCIPLINES/MAJORS OFFERED

Undergraduate Programs: Anthropology, Arts, Biology, Business Administration, Chemistry, Computer Science, Economics, English, Environmental Planning, Environmental Science, Environmental Studies, First Nations Studies, Geography, History, International Studies, Mathematics, Natural Resources Management, Northern Studies, Nursing, Physics, Political Science, Psychology, Resource-Based Tourism, Science (General), Social Work, Women's Studies

Certificate Programs: First Nations General Studies, First Nations Public Administration, First Nations Nisga'a Studies, Political Science, Public Administration

Graduate Programs

ADMISSIONS CRITERIA & PROCEDURES

Admission to UNBC is granted on a general, not program-specific, basis. The minimum requirement for admission from a British Columbia secondary school is successful graduation with an average of 65 per cent based on English 12 and three academic grade 12 courses (including Advanced Placement, International Baccalaureate and immersion courses). All students meeting these requirements are guaranteed admission to UNBC. Secondary students from outside of British Columbia should contact the Admissions Office for detailed admission requirements.

Students who have completed a minimum of 24 credit hours of university transferable coursework with a 2.0 GPA (C average) are guaranteed entry to UNBC.

Applicants who do not meet the published requirements may be eligible for admission as mature students or under the special entry category that takes extenuating circumstances into account.

Students whose first language is not English are required to provide evidence of English language proficiency. Submission of a TOEFL score of 570 or higher is required prior to being admissible to UNBC.

International students are advised to submit all relevant documentation well in advance of their intended date of entry. Each international application is reviewed on its own merits and is subject to the availability of space.

Admissions at a Glance

Minimum GPA: 65% (BC high school)

Minimum English Requirements:
- TOEFL 570

Application Fee: C$10 (in-province), $35 (out-of-province, international)

Application Deadlines: March 2 (priority admission); April 1 (fall semester); August 1 (winter semester)

ACADEMIC FACILITIES

The University Library occupies two floors of the Library Building. The library is open seven days a week during the fall and winter semesters, providing books, journals, audiovisual resources and other materials to support the university's academic programs. The collection consists of over one million items, including 170,000 books, 1,200 current journal subscriptions, 1,750 audiovisual items and 800,000 microform titles. The library also has an extensive collection of Web-based and CD-ROM indexes, which support the research needs of faculty and students. It also houses several specialized collections.

An online computerized catalogue system enables students to access other libraries and information sources.

Student & Faculty Profile

Total Enrolment: 3,200

Undergraduate Enrolment: 2,850

# of Faculty: 150

Student/Faculty Ratio: 10:1

Male/Female Students: 50%/50%

First-Year Class Sizes: 35 (average)

Undergraduate Acceptance Rate: not available

Undergraduate Enrolment by Discipline:

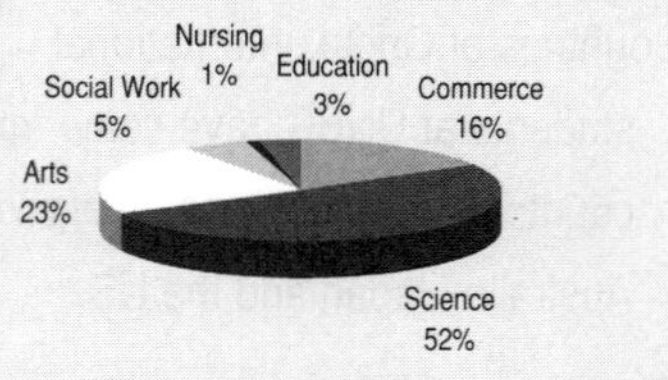

SCHOLARSHIPS & FINANCIAL ASSISTANCE

Scholarships, bursaries and awards are available to both new and continuing students. The Awards & Financial Aid Office administers a growing number of scholarships and bursaries to assist students financially. Last year over C$230,000 in scholarships and bursaries was awarded to 223 students. Students requiring financial aid should contact the office to enquire about government and bank loans; private, corporate and public scholarships and bursaries; the work study program at UNBC; and employment opportunities.

Expenses at a Glance

Tuition (undergraduate, full-time):
- In-Province: C$2,500/year
- Out-of-Province: C$2,500/year
- International: C$5,400/year

Fees, Books, Materials: C$1,000/year

Accommodation:
- Private: C$500-700/month
- Residence: C$3,000/year
- Homestay: n/a

Health Insurance: C$36/month

CAMPUS & LOCATION

City Population:	75,000
Cost of Living:	medium
Climate Range:	-30° to 30°C
Campus Setting:	suburban
# of Students in Residence:	550

The University of Northern British Columbia's Prince George campus is located on Cranbrook Hill overlooking the city of Prince George and the foothills of the Rocky Mountains. The award-winning Prince George campus is a showcase for the use of modern materials: there are granite columns, slate floors and soaring atriums with wood beams. The campus is just a few minutes' drive from Prince George, a growing community of 75,000, which serves as the educational, economic and cultural centre for northern British Columbia. Other regional centres serve as affiliated campuses throughout central and northern British Columbia.

Outdoor opportunities abound in the area: there are five ski hills within a two-hour drive of the city; numerous hiking opportunities; canoeing on the lakes and rivers; and biking on the 40 kilometres of bike trails adjacent to the campus. The campus is next to the Forests for the World park, a protected area of land made up of two lakes and dozens of trails.

The city of Prince George is located in the centre of British Columbia, approximately an eight-hour drive from Vancouver, Calgary or Edmonton. Located at the fork of the Fraser and Nechako Rivers, Prince George offers the amenities of a city of its size. Prince George boasts numerous fine restaurants and shops, a symphony orchestra, an art gallery, golf courses, theatres and dance clubs.

ATHLETICS & EXTRACURRICULAR ACTIVITIES

The Northern Timberwolves men's and women's basketball teams entered their first exhibition season in the British Columbia College Athletic Association (BCCAA) in 1998.

In addition to the varsity teams, the university offers an ever-expanding selection of intramural sports and recreational pastimes. Students can take part in tournaments in sports such as sand volleyball, basketball, rugby, soccer and squash. Noncredit courses such as guitar, jujitsu, line dancing, jive dancing, yoga, French, Spanish and sign language are also offered. Intramural sports included three-on-three basketball, volleyball, floor hockey and indoor soccer.

The UNBC Fitness Centre is available to all students at UNBC. Students have access to its squash courts, gym, weight room and intramural facilities.

UNBC offers an extensive list off student clubs, ranging from the Environmental Club to the Society of Creative Anachronism.

University Recognition

- Member of the Association of Universities & Colleges of Canada (AUCC)
- Association of Commonwealth Universities
- Association of Circumpolar Universities

STUDENT SUPPORT SERVICES

UNBC offers a wide variety of services to its students including the Awards, Financial Aid & Student Employment Centre, the Counselling Centre and the Learning Skills Centre. The university offers a Health & Wellness Centre to keep students healthy during their time of postsecondary study. UNBC also offers an interfaith chaplaincy and services for students with disabilities.

The International Centre has a special mandate to provide services and programs for international students.

International Students

University Enrolment: 70

% of University Enrolment: 2%

Countries of Origin: International students at UNBC have come from 36 countries around the world including Australia, Japan and the US.

UNIVERSITY OF VICTORIA
VICTORIA, BRITISH COLUMBIA

University Mission

...to offer a community of learning, knowledge and accomplishment that serves the people of British Columbia, Canada and the global community; to be judged excellent when measured against the highest international standards

Student Voice:

I came to UVic to earn my degree at a University that is respected and which has a tradition of excellence. I also came here because I felt my degree would be pertinent and timely.

Sarah-Beth Hogg
Third-Year Education

CONTACT INFORMATION
Admissions Services
University of Victoria
PO Box 3025, STN CSC
Victoria, British Columbia
Canada V8W 3P2
PH 1-250-721-8121
FAX 1-250-721-6225
EMAIL
srsad13@uvvm.uvic.ca (undergraduate)
INTERNET http://www.uvic.ca

UNIVERSITY OVERVIEW

Founded in 1963, the University of Victoria (UVic) is consistently ranked among the top comprehensive universities in Canada, with an active presence on the international stage. A medium-sized institution, UVic offers the advantages of both large and small universities: a broad selection of courses with relatively small class sizes. UVic has a reputation for innovation through its enterprising programs and interdisciplinary research.

Academic Programs

At the undergraduate level, students may undertake a program to earn a Bachelor of Arts, Commerce, Education, Fine Arts, Law, Music, Science, Science in Nursing or Social Work. Most undergraduate degrees require a minimum of four years of study, though education students require five years or more. Students enrolled in the co-op program (mandatory for some majors) may require additional time.

Students pursuing graduate-level studies may earn a Master of Arts, Applied Science, Business Administration, Education, Engineering, Fine Arts, Music, Nursing, Public Administration, Science or Social Work, and/or a PhD.

UVic also offers preprofessional programs in a number of areas, including applied science, chartered accountancy, dentistry, medicine and optometry, as well as distance education programs.

Co-op Program

UVic is renowned for its extensive co-op program. Students enhance their learning by undertaking paid relevant work experience. More than 3,000 students participated in the program in 1997-98, representing over 40 academic areas and working with more than 1008 employers. UVic has the third largest co-op program in Canada and the largest business co-op in western Canada. Co-op Japan, offered by a consortium of 22 Canadian universities and headquartered at UVic, enables UVic science and engineering students to work in Japanese industry.

Internationalism

Over the past several years, UVic has expanded its international dimension considerably. More than 111 exchange and cooperation agreements exist for students and faculty. International students have a considerable presence at UVic, with 100 attending through exchange agreements, another 738 as regular students and more than 1,400 as English language students each year. In 1997-98, 218 UVic co-op students worked in 41 countries. UVic holds courses for students in Hong Kong through a unique twinning arrangement, offers an MBA program in Thailand and operates an English Language Centre in South Korea.

Highlights

- Has Canada's only law and health information science co-ops
- Has established 111 exchange and cooperation agreements with institutions in 25 countries
- Is home to 11 interdisciplinary research centres and receives C$23.5 million in external research funding each year

University Statistics

Year Founded: 1963

Academic Options: undergraduate/graduate

Calendar Year: first term (Sept-Dec); second term (Jan-Apr); summer term (May-Aug)

DISCIPLINES/MAJORS OFFERED

Faculty of Business: Entrepreneurship, Hotel & Restaurant Administration, International Business, Tourism Management

Faculty of Education: Elementary, Secondary; School of Physical Education; Leisure Service Administration, Kinesiology

Faculty of Engineering: Computer, Electrical, Mechanical, Computer Science, Software

Faculty of Fine Arts: History in Art, Music, Theatre, Theatre History, Visual Arts, Writing

Faculty of Graduate Studies

Faculty of Human & Social Development: Child & Youth Care, Health Information Science, Nursing, Public Administration, Social Work

Faculty of Humanities: English, French Language & Literature, Germanic Studies, Greek & Roman Studies, Hispanic & Italian Studies, History, Linguistics, Medieval Studies, Pacific & Asian Studies, Philosophy, Slavonic Studies, Women's Studies

Faculty of Law

Faculty of Science: Biochemistry & Microbiology, Biology, Chemistry, Computer Science, Earth & Ocean Sciences, Mathematics & Statistics, Physics & Astronomy

Faculty of Social Sciences: Anthropology, Economics, Environmental Studies, Geography, Political Science, Psychology, Sociology

ADMISSIONS CRITERIA & PROCEDURES

Students who wish to apply to the University of Victoria should contact Admission Services. Alternatively, applicants with access to a computer may submit their application via the Internet through the Post-Secondary Application Service website (http://www.pas.bc.ca/). Students must submit two official copies of transcripts (with notarized translations if not in English), except BC students having transcripts sent directly from the Ministry of Education.

In addition to course prerequisites, applicants to the 1998-99 school year needed a minimum average of 74 per cent if they were entering from a grade 12 or OAC program or 70 per cent if they were transferring from a college or university (higher than stated minimum because number of applications exceeded space available).

Students who plan to complete preliminary studies at another institution should confirm with UVic that the courses are transferable. Transfer possibilities exist for students who are entering from colleges and universities, institutes of technology or Colleges of Applied Arts & Technology (CAAP), as well as those who have completed a cégep in Quebec, the International Baccalaureate or Advanced Placement courses.

Students whose first language is not English must have a TOEFL 575 (233 on computerized test), MELAB 90, IELTS 7.0, four years' secondary/postsecondary education taught in English in an English-speaking country, a postsecondary degree earned in English in an English-speaking country, transfer credit for English 115 or 215 or 3.0 units of other English credit, or completion of the University Admission Preparation Course offered by UVic's Language Centre.

Admissions at a Glance

Minimum GPA: 70-74% (1998-99)

Minimum English Requirements:
TOEFL 575, MELAB 90 or IELTS 7.0

Application Fee: C$25 (within BC), $65 (outside BC), $70 (international)

Application Deadlines: Feb 28 (early admission, Canadian), Feb 28-May 15 (regular admission, Canadian, depending on faculty), April 30 (international)

ACADEMIC FACILITIES

UVic's McPherson Library houses more than 1.6 million volumes, more than 1.7 million microforms and an extensive supply of videos, films and sound recordings. UVic is also home to a law library, a map library, an electronic library for business students and a curriculum library for education students. An advanced Language Centre offers instruction in 18 languages. UVic's main computer facility includes an IBM 9672 and an IBM SP system. Students have 24-hour access to these systems using facilities located throughout the campus. In addition, many laboratories and classrooms are equipped with IBM and Apple computers. The campus features several new academic buildings, including a technologically advanced Engineering Lab Wing and a new Centre for Innovative Teaching.

There are 12 interdisciplinary teaching and research centres on campus, including the Centres on Earth and Ocean Research, Global Studies, Environmental Health and Asia-Pacific Initiatives. UVic also shares research facilities with other universities, including the Bamfield Marine Station, and officially participates in nine federal Networks of Centres of Excellence.

Student & Faculty Profile

Total Enrolment: 17,222

Undergraduate Enrolment: 15,098

# of Faculty: 1,219

Student/Faculty Ratio: 17.4:1

Male/Female Students: 42%/58%

First-Year Class Sizes: 53 (average)

Undergraduate Acceptance Rate: 58%

Undergraduate Enrolment by Discipline:

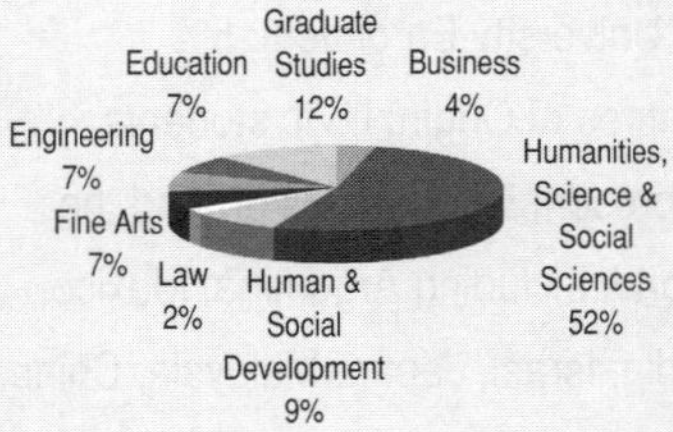

SCHOLARSHIPS & FINANCIAL ASSISTANCE

UVic grants C$630,000 in scholarships to entering students each year. Scholarship information may be obtained through the Administrative Registrar Secretary for the Senate Committee on Awards at UVic. Canadian students may apply for financial assistance through UVic's Student Financial Aid Services. Aid is available in three forms: provincial and federal government loans; short-term, interest-free emergency assistance; and bursaries awarded based on financial need.

Expenses at a Glance

Tuition (undergraduate, full-time):
In-Province: C$2,265-2,896/year
Out-of-Province: C$2,265-2,896/year
International: C$6,795-8,688/year

Fees, Books, Materials: C$1,025/year

Accommodation:
Private: C$550-685/month
Residence: C$4,536-5,160/year
Homestay: n/a

Health Insurance: C$102/year (Cdn)

CAMPUS & LOCATION

City Population:	325,000
Cost of Living:	high
Climate Range:	0° to 30°C
Campus Setting:	suburban
# of Students in Residence:	2,100

The University of Victoria is located on the west coast of Canada in British Columbia's capital city, Victoria. Mystic Vale, a 4.4-hectare section of old growth forest located at the southeast end of the campus, forms an ecological protection area with the university's Hobbs Creek ravine. UVic's Finnerty Gardens are internationally known for their rhododendron collection.

On-campus housing is available for 1,200 students in four coed residence halls with single and double accommodation in furnished rooms; residence hall costs include a meal plan. On-campus cluster housing, introduced for the 1994 Commonwealth Games, accommodates 376 students in 94 separate furnished units with cooking facilities. There are also 181 unfurnished family housing units. Students are advised to submit housing applications with their admission applications to improve their chances of being offered a position. Students opting to live off campus may make use of the university's listings of affordable, local apartments, suites and houses.

The 160-hectare campus is just a 15-minute drive from downtown. The rugged, forested, coastal geography of Canada's west coast, with the mildest climate in the nation, allows for a wide variety of recreational activities, including hiking, biking, skiing, sailing and kayaking. Although a small city, Victoria offers plenty of opportunities for economic and cultural activities, and is safe and clean.

ATHLETICS & EXTRACURRICULAR ACTIVITIES

UVic has a strong reputation for its athletics. Since it was founded 35 years ago, it has earned 69 Canada West University Athletic Association titles and 36 Canadian Interuniversity Athletic Union national championships. In 1998, the women's cross-country and basketball teams were the CIAU champions in their sports. UVic's men's and women's rowing and men's rugby teams were also Canadian university champions.

All students, faculty and staff at UVic benefit from comprehensive sports and recreational programs including aquatics, racket sports, intramural sports and fitness classes. An Athletics Program is offered to full-time students who wish to participate in competitive sports at the university varsity level.

UVic students organize and participate in a wide variety of clubs ranging from sailing to politics to international friendships, as well as an active student. A recently renovated Student Union Building is home to a pub, movie theatre, nightclub, photocopy centre and travel office. The Phoenix Theatre, one of the best educational theatre facilities in Canada, features frequent productions; a number of other events are hosted by the fine arts departments on campus.

University Recognition

- UVic's Health Information Science and Child and Youth Care programs are unique in western Canada
- Four faculty members have received national 3M Teaching Fellowships
- UVic's Faculty of Law has ranked number one in Canada three years straight in a survey of recent graduates conducted by Canadian Lawyer magazine

STUDENT SUPPORT SERVICES

Each of UVic's faculties offers academic advising to registered students. In addition, Counselling Services offers educational and career counselling; study and learning counselling through courses, study groups and workshops; and personal counselling. The Student Employment Centre helps students with job search strategies and posts part-time, summer and career job listings.

The International Student office helps international students during their time at UVic. An international student handbook, sent to all overseas students, includes information on immigration regulations and health insurance procedures.

An Interfaith Chapel is available to all students.

International Students

University Enrolment: 834

% of University Enrolment: 5%

Countries of Origin: UVic students represent 63 countries around the world, including Argentina, Mexico, India, Israel, Japan, Malaysia, China, the UK and Venezuela.

University Colleges

IN

British Columbia

Malaspina University-College
Nanaimo, British Columbia

University College Mission

...to develop the full potential of students in every program

Student Voice:

Malaspina is a really good environment in which to study: it's not too big, it's friendly and it really takes care of its students.

Yasuko (Japan)

CONTACT INFORMATION
Registration Centre (Cdn);
Int'l Education (int'l)
Malaspina University-College
900 Fifth Street
Nanaimo, British Columbia
Canada V9R 5S5
PH 1-250-755-8752 (Cdn);
1-250-755-8721 (int'l)
FAX 1-250-741-2494 (Cdn);
1-250-741-2745 (int'l)
EMAIL advise@mala.bc.ca (Cdn);
study@mala.bc.ca (int'l)
INTERNET http://www.mala.bc.ca

UNIVERSITY COLLEGE OVERVIEW

Malaspina University-College (Malaspina) has played an active role in the cultural and economic life of the central Vancouver Island region for 30 years. It was the first regional community college on Vancouver Island and today has a student body of approximately 7,000, including more than 500 international students. In addition, almost 20,000 students are enrolled in Community Education courses offered through Malaspina.

Founded in 1969, Malaspina was designated a university-college in 1989 and began offering selected university degree programs in conjunction with the University of Victoria. In January 1995, Malaspina began granting independent degrees.

Programs Offered

Malaspina strives to offer all its students a wide variety of educational experiences to choose from. A public degree-granting institution, Malaspina offers Bachelor's degrees, college certificates, college diplomas and English Language Certificate programs.

Malaspina offers programs in more than 70 fields of study. Its academic programs include undergraduate studies leading to bachelor's degrees in arts, education, science and tourism management. Malaspina also offers a wide variety of highly specialized, career oriented programs, including programs in business, health, technology and the trades. Malaspina has also become a leader in the areas of international education and contract training for business and industry.

Cooperative Education

Cooperative education is offered in several programs and allows students to combine classroom studies with paid work experience in their field. The programs currently offering a co-op component include the fisheries & aquaculture, hospitality management, recreation administration and tourism studies programs.

In order to successfully complete their work term, students must have received a satisfactory performance evaluation by the employer. Following their first co-op term, students can apply for advanced credit based upon their work experience.

This option is also available to international students.

Community Education

Malaspina offers a wide range of Community Education courses to serve the needs of part-time, life-long learners. These courses involve lectures, seminars, workshops, certificate programs and special events. Vocational and job training, business education and professional development, as well as courses in the arts, health, home improvement, languages, writing and other special interest areas are offered.

Highlights

- Small classes taught by experienced staff
- Wide range of certificate, diploma and degree programs
- Affordable tuition and living expenses

University College Statistics

Year Founded: 1969
Academic Options: certificate/diploma/undergraduate
Calendar Year: August-December (fall term); January-April (spring); April-August (intersession)

DISCIPLINES/MAJORS OFFERED

Degree Programs: Arts, Biology, Child & Youth Care, Computer Science, Education, First Nations Studies, Fisheries & Aquaculture, Nursing, Recreation, Tourism Mgmt

Business Programs: Accounting, Business Mgmt, Commercial Accounting, Continuing Health Care Admin, Hospitality Mgmt, Mgmt Skills, Microcomputer Applications, Microcomputer System Support, New Enterprise Mgmt, Office Admin

Fine & Performing Arts Programs: Art, Graphic Design, Interior Design, Music (classical), Music (jazz), Theatre

Health Programs: Dental Assistant, Dental Prosthodontic Module, Home Support/Resident Care, Nursing

Health Services Programs: Child & Youth Care, Early Childhood Education & Care, Human Services Certificate/Diploma, Recreation Administrator, Tourism Studies

Preparatory Programs: Access programs, Adult Basic Education, ESL

Technology/Technician Programs: Fisheries/Aquaculture Tech, Forestry Resources Tech, Horticultural Tech'n, Resource Management Officer, Science Foundation Courses

Trades & Technology: Automotive Service Tech'n, Baking, Carpentry & Residential Carpentry, Commercial Transport Vehicle Mechanic, Construction, Cook Training, Heavy Duty Mechanical Repair, Heavy Equipment Operator, Marine & Small Engine Tech'n, Welding

University Transfer Programs: Applied Science, Business Admin, Commerce-Hotel & Restaurant Mgmt, First Nations Studies, Theatre & Visual Art, Music, Physical Education, Science, Social Work

ADMISSIONS CRITERIA & PROCEDURES

Malaspina encourages students from all academic backgrounds to apply for programs. With course offerings that range from fundamental literacy skills to four-year university degree programs there is an entry level for all applicants.

Admission requirements at Malaspina are designed to allow access to higher education, while verifying that applicants have a background that provides a reasonable chance of success. The general admission requirement for Canadians is one of the following: a previous degree from a recognized university, graduation from a BC Secondary School or equivalent, deficiency in not more than two courses for BC Secondary School graduation or equivalent, mature student status or a special admission category. Applicants should be aware that there are specific admission requirements and prerequisites for some programs.

To apply for admission, Canadian students must complete the appropriate application form and submit it along with any required documents specified in the program outline. For degree programs, students should arrange for official secondary, or postsecondary, transcripts to be forwarded directly to the Admissions Office. The application must include the C$30 application fee. A C$200 commitment fee will be required to confirm acceptance.

Admission requirements for international students are as follows: graduation from a high school or equivalent (students lacking prerequisites for programs and courses can upgrade their schooling at Malaspina); minimum TOEFL score of 213 (computer-based) or 550 (paper-based), a minimum IELTS score of 6.5, successful completion of the university preparation level of Malaspina's English Language Certificate programs or completion of the Malaspina English language assessment test at the necessary level; and eligibility for a Canadian student authorization.

To apply for admission, international students must complete the international student application form (available on the website) and submit it along with any required documents. For degree programs, students should arrange for official secondary, or postsecondary, transcripts to be forwarded directly to the Director of International Student Services. The application must include the C$100 application processing fee.

Admissions at a Glance

Minimum GPA: n/a

Minimum English Requirements:
- Grade 12 English or equivalent, or TOEFL 213 (computer) or 550 (paper); IELTS 6.5; university preparation level of Malaspina's English Language Certificate Program; or Malaspina English language assessment test at the necessary level

Application Fee: C$30 (Canadian), $100 (international)

Application Deadlines: Canadian: March; international: Aug 1, Nov 15, Apr 1

Student & Faculty Profile

Total Enrolment: 7,000

Undergraduate Enrolment: 7,000

# of Faculty: 593

Student/Faculty Ratio: not available

Male/Female Students: 34%/66%

First Year Class Sizes: 28-34

Undergraduate Acceptance Rate: not available

Undergraduate Enrolment by Discipline:

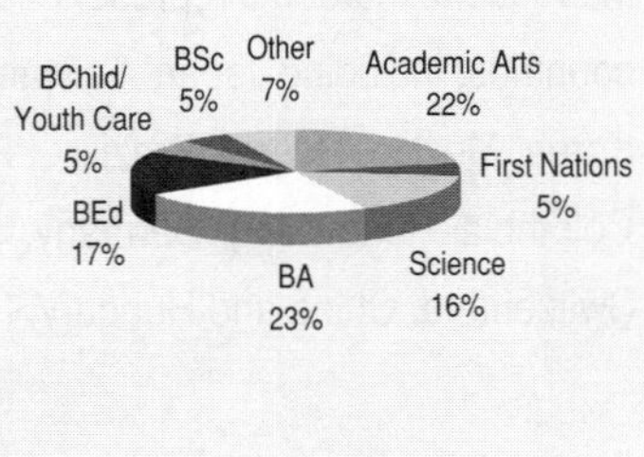

ACADEMIC FACILITIES

Malaspina's library facilities consist of the main library, centrally located on the Nanaimo campus, and branch libraries at the Cowichan and Powell River campuses. The university-college's collection contains over 100,000 books, journals, audio-visual and microform items. Access to the collection is provided at every campus through an on-line library catalogue. Faxable requests and courier services facilitate intercampus lending.

There are a number of computer labs on campus for student use.

SCHOLARSHIPS & FINANCIAL ASSISTANCE

Applications and information regarding scholarships and awards are available through the Student Support Services Office at the Nanaimo campus.

Malaspina's Financial Aid Office offers a wide variety of financial assistance, as well as information on provincial funds.

Expenses at a Glance

Tuition (undergraduate, full-time):
- In-Province: C$756/semester
- Out-of-Province: C$756/semester
- International: C$6,800/year

Fees, Books, Materials: C$1,200/year

Accommodation:
- Private: C$500-$800/month
- Residence: C$1,160-$1,320/semester
- Homestay: C$4,400/year

Health Insurance: C$439/year

CAMPUS & LOCATION

City Population:	75,000
Cost of Living:	low
Climate Range:	0° to 22°C
Campus Setting:	urban
# of Students in Residence:	189

To serve the needs of the 172,000 people in its region, Malaspina University-College has a main campus in Nanaimo and regional campuses in Duncan, Powell River and the Parksville/Qualicum area. The Nanaimo campus is located on a spectacular 50-hectare site on the lower slopes of Mount Benson, overlooking the city of Nanaimo, the Georgia Strait and the Coast Mountains across the straight. The campus has recently undergone a C$20-million facilities expansion to meet the requirements of new university degree programs. Noteworthy features on the campus include a 297-seat theatre, a well-equipped gymnasium, art studios and labs, two picturesque Japanese gardens donated by Tamagawa University and Okayama Women's College in Japan, a museum of natural history, an arboretum and the Nanaimo Art Gallery.

Nanaimo has approximately 75,000 residents and has recently experienced a tremendous population growth that has shifted the economy from mining, fishing and forestry to service-, information- and technology-based industries. The city is linked to the lower mainland through regular 90-minute ferry services and frequent 15-minute flights to Vancouver International Airport. The city is surrounded by the natural beauty of the mountains, forests and ocean, which provide many opportunities for outdoor recreation.

ATHLETICS & EXTRACURRICULAR ACTIVITIES

Malaspina offers a full athletic program to meet the needs of students involved at a varsity level of competition. The university-college is a charter member of the British Columbia College Athletic Association with 12 other BC colleges. The athletic department at Malaspina is traditionally one of the best in BC. Typically athletic sports teams include mixed badminton, men's and women's baseball, mixed golf, men's and women's soccer, men's and women's volleyball. The university-college also coordinates and supervises an intramural program which includes volleyball, indoor soccer, racquetball, squash, touch football, softball, basketball, road hockey, drop-in ice hockey and tennis. There is also a student subsidy for ski and driving range passes.

The Exercise Science, Fitness & Lifestyle Assessment Centre offers a variety of fitness-related activities, as well as a number of exercise and fitness assessment programs for faculty, staff and students. In addition to the fitness tests, nutritional assessments and personalized training the centre also provides Tai Chi, Tae Kwon Do, aerobic classes, dance and women's self-defense classes.

STUDENT SUPPORT SERVICES

Malaspina offers a wide selection of student services. The Career Resource Centre is available to provide assistance and resources for career-planning. Counselling Services aids students experiencing personal, career or academic difficulties. A First Nations Student Services Manager is available to assist First Nations students. Individual counselling, peer support, vocational assessments and group workshops are also available. In addition, the Students' Union administers and supports numerous student clubs, including the ESL Club, Nursing Club, History Club, Kayaking Club and Theatre Club.

Malaspina has a day care centre on its Nanaimo campus that serves students, Malaspina employees and the community.

An International Student Services office, with a director, student adviser and homestay coordinator, assists international students with cultural adjustment, career or academic planning, or housing options.

University College Recognition

- Recognized by the Government of BC
- Member of the Association of Canadian Community Colleges (ACCC)

International Students

University College Enrolment: 575

% of University College Enrolment: 8%

Countries of Origin: Malaspina's international students represent 25 countries, including Japan, Taiwan, Korea, Mexico, Russia, Brazil, Colombia, Hong Kong, Germany, Switzerland, China and Hungary.

OKANAGAN UNIVERSITY COLLEGE
KELOWNA, BRITISH COLUMBIA

University College Mission

...to provide programs, courses, and services of the highest quality....to reflect the diverse learning needs of the people we serve

Student Voice:

There are several reasons why I am staying at OUC to get a degree. First the professors have good qualifications and teaching experience. Secondly, the relationship between the professors and students is close because of the perfect class size. The most important point is that Kelowna is a very pleasant place for living and studying.

Iris Bar, Hong Kong
Second Year, Bachelor of Business Administration

CONTACT INFORMATION
Admissions, Office of the Registrar
Okanagan University College
1000 KLO Road
Kelowna, British Columbia
Canada V1Y 4X8
PH 1-250-762-5445 (Cdn);
1-250-862-5443 (int'l)
FAX 1-250-862-5470 (int'l)
EMAIL inted@okanagan.bc.ca (int'l)
INTERNET http://www.ouc.bc.ca

UNIVERSITY COLLEGE OVERVIEW

Okanagan University College (OUC) is a public, comprehensive postsecondary educational institution offering a wide variety of academic, continuing education and vocational programs. Established in 1965, the institution changed its name from Okanagan College to Okanagan University College in 1992 to reflect its new status as a degree granting institution.

OUC Programs

The programs offered at OUC are divided into five areas that comprise Career & Technology Programs, Degree Programs, Health & Social Development Programs, Adult Education Programs and Vocational Programs.

Career & Technology Programs are offered as two year diploma programs, which may include a cooperative education option. The areas of study available in these programs include business administration, civil engineering, commercial aviation, computer information systems, electronic engineering technology, fine arts, mechanical engineering technology and water quality technology.

Degree programs at OUC are academic in focus and lead to undergraduate degrees that include BA, BEd, BBA, BFA, BSc, BSW and BScN degrees. Part-time study is possible and many courses are offered at multiple OUC campuses, allowing students to design a highly flexible schedule.

In addition to the BScN and BSW programs, Health & Social Development Programs include certificate programs of less than two years duration that include certified dental assistant, early childhood education, home support/resident care attendant, human service worker, nursing, practical nursing and rehabilitation assistant programs.

Vocational Programs are offered in the areas of automotive mechanics, heavy duty/commercial transport mechanics, automotive collision repair/painting & refinishing, carpentry/joinery, recreation vehicle technician, automotive service technician, collision repair technician, culinary arts, welding, welder/fitter, office administration, litigation legal secretary program and corporate conveyancing legal secretary.

Cooperative Education

Students in the cooperative education programs at OUC are able to combine academic terms with paid work terms, offering students the opportunity to gain practical work experience while studying. The Cooperative Education Department posts part-time summer and graduate employment opportunities.

Highlights

- Academic, continuing education and vocational courses and programs offered
- Cooperative education option available
- Campuses throughout the Okanagan region of British Columbia

University College Statistics

Year Founded: 1965
Academic Options: certificate/diploma/undergraduate
Calendar Year: fall semester (Sept-Dec); winter semester (Jan-Apr)

ACADEMIC PROGRAMS

Division of Arts & Education: Anthropology, Economics, Education (Five-Year Program, Two-Year Postdegree Professional Program), English, General Arts, History, International Relations, Fine Arts, Latin American Studies, Mathematics, Philosophy, Politics, Psychology, Sociology, Women's Studies

Division of Adult & Continuing Education: Adult Basic Education, Adult Special Education, Business Administration (diploma, degree), ESL, Extension Services, International Education, Office Administration, Legal Secretary

Division of Trades & Technology: Apprenticeship/Certificate Programs (Culinary Arts, Heavy Duty Mechanic Commercial Transport, Carpentry/Joinery, Automotive Mechanic, Automotive Collision Repair, R.V. Technician, Welding)

Division of Science: Biology, Chemistry/Environmental Science, Freshwater Science, General Science, Mathematical Science, Physics

Division of Health & Social Development: Nursing (certificate, diploma, degree), Social Work, Several Certificate Programs Available (Dental Assistant, Early Childhood Education, Human Service Worker, Rehabilitation Assistant)

ADMISSIONS CRITERIA & PROCEDURES

New students, or those returning to school or changing programs, are required to fill out and submit an application form. Application forms are available at all OUC centres and are accepted on a rolling basis up to one year in advance of a students intended starting date. Applicants must submit their application together with the application fee, official transcripts from all secondary and postsecondary schools attended (where applicable) and proof of prerequisite requirements or test results as appropriate. Applications can be submitted by mail, in person, or online through the Post-Secondary Application Service of BC (PASBC). Students may access PASBC through the OUC homepage. Students are admitted on a first-come, first-served basis, with some exceptions. Admission requirements, application deadlines and starting dates at OUC may vary by program.

International applicants must submit their application for admission at least 10 weeks prior to the beginning of their intended first semester. In addition to the general requirements for admission, OUC requires international students to submit proof of English language proficiency; a TOEFL score of 550, or equivalent, is required for admission to most programs. International students who have received an OUC acceptance notice must submit a copy of their valid Student Authorization, issued by Canada Immigration Centre, prior to course registration.

Admissions at a Glance

Minimum GPA: varies

Minimum English Requirements:

TOEFL 550 or equivalent

Application Fee: C$20 (Canadian), $100 (international)

Application Deadlines: varies; March 31 (BA/BSc program)

ACADEMIC FACILITIES

In addition to the main library at North Kelowna Campus, OUC operates libraries at Salmon Arm, Vernon, Penticton at KLO campuses. Students have access to more than 192, 000 volumes, 6,862 videos, 1,602 journals and newspapers, along with maps and government documents. An inter-campus loan system exists, and materials can also be obtained from academic libraries throughout British Columbia and North America.

The campuses are equipped with relevant lab and trade facilities which allow students technical and research-based training on-campus.

The Research Services/Technology Access Centre, located at the North Kelowna Campus, provides research and industry information and liaison, along with a space suitable for testing shops, labs, prototype fabrication and other services.

Student & Faculty Profile

Total Enrolment: 7,500

Undergraduate Enrolment: not available

# of Faculty: 846

Student/Faculty Ratio: 12:1

Male/Female Students: not available

First Year Class Sizes: not available

Undergraduate Acceptance Rate: not available

Undergraduate Enrolment by Discipline:

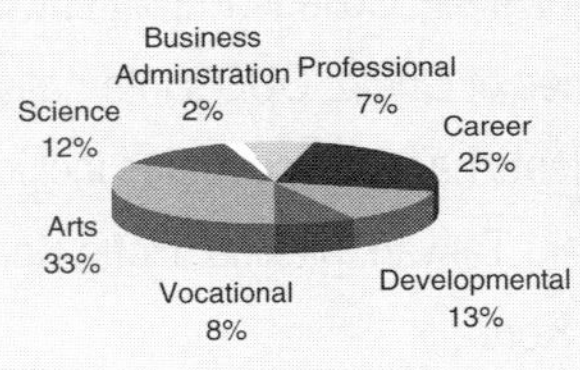

SCHOLARSHIPS & FINANCIAL ASSISTANCE

OUC gives financial aid to students in the form of government-approved loans, scholarships and bursaries. Students requiring financial assistance should contact the Financial Awards Office for more information. This program is only available to Canadian students.

Expenses at a Glance

Tuition (undergraduate, full-time):

In-Province: C$1,410/year

Out-of-Province: C$1,410/year

International: C$3,350/year

Fees, Books, Materials: C$100-400/year

Accommodation:

Private: C$600-800/month

Residence: C$600/month

Homestay: C$500/month

Health Insurance: C$115 (first 3 months); $216 (following 6 months)

CAMPUS & LOCATION

City Population:	100,000
Cost of Living:	not available
Climate Range:	-2° to 28°C
Campus Setting:	suburban
# of Students in Residence:	310

The region served by OUC consists of 37,750 square kilometres in the Okanagan region of the interior of British Columbia, extending from Osoyoos and Princeton, in the south and west, to Mica Creek and Revelstoke, in the north and east. OUC maintains the KLO and North Kelowna Campuses in the city of Kelowna, as well as campuses in the cities of Penticton, Vernon and Salmon Arm. The main campus is the North Kelowna Campus, which began operating in 1993 and saw the completion of its main facilities and new gymnasium in 1996.

The Okanagan Valley is famous for its beautiful and varied geography and its wide variety of recreational opportunities. Lakes, forests, mountains and desert terrain are nearby, and the climate allows for a wide variety of outdoor recreation during the year including boating, skiing, skating, swimming, hiking and hunting. Kelowna is the largest city in the Okanagan Valley and offers all the amenities of a young, mid-sized city. Kelowna is four hours by car and 40 minutes by air from the metropolitan centre of Vancouver, and eight hours from Calgary, Alberta.

ATHLETICS & EXTRACURRICULAR ACTIVITIES

OUC offers a variety of competitive and recreational athletic programs. OUC offers several men's and women's varsity teams, including basketball, volleyball and soccer teams, competing at the intercollegiate level. Team tryouts take place in late August through early September, and all students are encouraged to try out. In addition, each year hundreds of students take advantage of a variety of intramural sports and social activities including aerobics, volleyball, basketball, hockey, skiing and several fitness programs.

The C$6-million recreational facility at the North Kelowna Campus includes international standard volleyball and basketball courts, a soccer field and a fully equipped free weight and circuit training room. The recreation facilities are available to all OUC students.

Subsidized trips to sporting events, recreation activities and theatre productions are arranged throughout the year for OUC students.

STUDENT SUPPORT SERVICES

OUC offers a variety of student support services to help students overcome any hindrances to their educational and personal success while at OUC. Personal, academic and career counselling services are available to all OUC students. The Student and Graduate Employment Service is available year-round and posts job bulletins, liaises with employers, arranges both on- and off-campus recruiting tours, and provides career advising and labour market information to students. The KLO and North Kelowna Campuses operate daycare facilities for children between the ages of 12 months to five years.

International students can also take advantage of several specialized support services offered through the International Education Department. A full-time ESL program, specific ESL courses, summer immersion programs, short term ESL and cultural education study tours are offered through the department; housing services, personal advising and general assistance are also available.

University College Recognition

- Recognized by the Government of BC
- Member of the Association of Canadian Community Colleges (ACCC)

International Students

University College Enrolment: 225

% of University College Enrolment: 3%

Countries of Origin: OUC's international students hail from countries including Japan, Taiwan, Mexico, Hong Kong and Korea.

The University College of the Cariboo Kamloops, British Columbia

University College Mission

...to serve people and their communities through high-quality education, training and scholarship

Student Voice:

Many students agree that one of the benefits of study at UCC is to build close relationships with professors. The professors are friendly and always willing to give students a hand.

Kenji Takasaki
Business student
Toyohashi, Aichi, Japan

CONTACT INFORMATION
The University College of the Cariboo
Box 3010
900 McGill Road
Kamloops, British Columbia
Canada V2C 5N3
PH 1-250-828-5252
FAX 1-250-371-5513
EMAIL ckerr@cariboo.bc.ca
INTERNET
http://www.cariboo.bc.ca/intered

UNIVERSITY COLLEGE OVERVIEW

The University College of the Cariboo (UCC), located in Kamloops, British Columbia (BC), is both a fully independent university offering undergraduate degrees, and a college with many unique one- and two-year programs to prepare students for future careers. Founded in 1970 as Cariboo College, UCC is today a comprehensive institution that aims to provide accessible, high-quality academic instruction and practical skills training to the residents of the interior of British Columbia and surrounding area.

The college offers students the benefits of comparatively small classes, direct contact with faculty and opportunities to gain real work experience. It is now proud to offer nearly 100 degree and diploma programs. UCC also offers co-op education in a selection of two-year career and degree programs.

Highlights

- Offers nearly 100 programs in academic and vocational fields
- Located in the scenic interior of British Columbia
- Cooperative education offered for several programs

University College Statistics

Year Founded: 1970

Academic Options: diploma/undergraduate

Calendar Year: fall semester (Sept-Dec); winter semester (Jan-Apr)

Degree Programs

Students at UCC may choose from more than 30 four- to five-year degree options in 10 program areas. The college was given independent degree-granting authority in 1995, and developed its core degree programs directly in cooperation with three major westcoast universities (University of British Columbia, Simon Fraser University, University of Victoria) to ensure the credibility of the program curricula. UCC degrees are recognized by employers and by other postsecondary institutions.

UCC has made it possible for graduates of six of its diploma programs to progress directly into UCC degree programs. Students can also opt to undertake transfer programs, such as prelaw, that allow them to enrol at other BC universities upon completion.

Career & Vocational Programs

UCC's career & vocational programs are up to three years in length. A certificate is granted for completion of one-year programs; a diploma is granted to students who complete programs of two years or longer. UCC provides an extensive course pool for students preparing for direct entry into the workplace. The variety and scope of the career programs offered presents students with a wide selection of career options.

Trades & Technology Programs

UCC offers many trades & technology programs, categorized as either apprenticeship or pre-employment programs. The college also offers short vocational courses throughout the year.

ACADEMIC PROGRAMS

Bachelor's Degree Programs: Accounting, Animal Biology, Chemistry, Chemistry Environmental, Ecology & Environmental Biology, Elementary Education, English, Finance, General Arts-Canadian Studies, General Business, History, Human Resource Management, Journalism, Marketing, Mathematics, Mathematical Sciences, Natural Resource Science, Nursing, Physics, Psychology, Sociology, Social Work, Tourism Management

Associate Degree Programs: Arts, Science

Transfer Programs: Commerce, Engineering, Forestry, Predentistry, Prelaw, Premedicine, Prepharmacy, Pre-Rehabilitation Medicine, Pre-Veterinary Medicine

Career Programs: Accounting & Business, Agricultural Sciences, Childcare, Computers, Electronics, Fine & Performing Arts, Health Sciences, Human Services Worker, Office Administration, Tourism & Hospitality

Applied Industrial Technologies: Apprenticeship Programs, Construction Trades, Digital Art & Design, Electrical/Electronics, Engineering Design & Drafting Technologies, Food Trades, Mechanical Trades, Wood Process Technology

College Access: Adult Special Education, College Access, College Preparation, English as a Second Language, Health Sciences, Native Access Program

ADMISSIONS CRITERIA & PROCEDURES

Candidates may obtain applications for admission by contacting the admissions office or by visiting the UCC website. The basic educational requirement for academic & degree programs, and for the majority of career & technology programs, is completion of British Columbia grade 12, or the equivalent. In addition, each area has specific prerequisites and recommendations. Requirements for vocational programs vary from completion of grades 10 to 12; graduation from high school is recommended in all cases. Admissions decisions for first-year academic programs and for several career & vocational programs are determined on a first-come, first-admitted basis; qualified applicants are evaluated from the date by which all application requirements are met. Candidates are thus encouraged to apply as early as possible; UCC accepts applications beginning in October of the year preceding the student's intended start date.

Upper-level degree entry and many career program admissions are based on an established selective process, using grade point standing and other criteria.

Applicants who are at least 19 years old, who have been out of school for at least two years and who have a high school diploma can apply as mature students.

International students from around the world are eligible to attend UCC providing they meet the academic requirements and possess a valid student permit.

Admissions at a Glance

Minimum GPA: no set minimum

Minimum English Requirements:

English testing at college or TOEFL 550, IELTS 6.0

Application Fee: C$15 (Canadian), $75 (international)

Application Deadlines: rolling admissions; April 15 for priority applications

ACADEMIC FACILITIES

The UCC library collection, consisting of 100,000 volumes, 1,000 periodical subscriptions and extensive collections of government documents, pamphlets, microforms and audiovisual materials, is an important educational resource to the UCC community.

The Williams Lake UCC library collection consists of over 5,000 volumes and 300 periodical subscriptions. The library also serves as a testing and assessment centre.

Computer services are available for general student use. Media facilities include audiovisual resources, graphics, television, audio recording, media duplication, and design & media consultation.

Student & Faculty Profile

Total Enrolment: 7,500

Undergraduate Enrolment: 3,600

# of Faculty: 346

Student/Faculty Ratio: 21:1

Male/Female Students: 45%/55%

First Year Class Sizes: 25-35

Undergraduate Acceptance Rate: not available

Undergraduate Enrolment by Discipline:

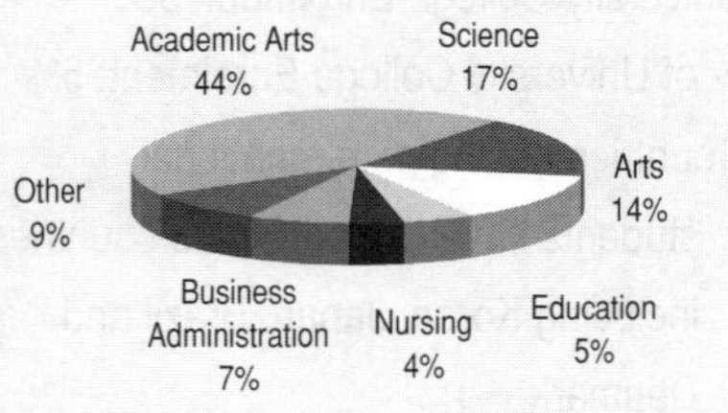

SCHOLARSHIPS & FINANCIAL ASSISTANCE

The rapid growth of the college is reflected in its increasing number of student awards & financial services. Application forms and pamphlets may be obtained from the financial aid & awards office. UCC offers a series of workshops on completing BC student assistance applications and provides general information on many aspects of student financial aid & awards. Among the programs that UCC offers is the work study program, which allows students to gain valuable paid work experience.

Expenses at a Glance

Tuition (undergraduate, full-time):

In-Province: C$1,230/year

Out-of-Province: C$1,230/year

International: C$3,350-3,965/semester

Fees, Books, Materials: varies

Accommodation:

Private: C$400/month

Residence: C$2,400/year

Homestay: C$525/month

Health Insurance: C$36/month

CAMPUS & LOCATION

City Population:	80,000
Cost of Living:	low
Climate Range:	-5° to 30°C
Campus Setting:	suburban
# of Students in Residence:	300+

The main campus of The University College of the Cariboo is located in Kamloops, a city of 80,000 in the centre of the southern interior of British Columbia. The main campus is spread over 100 hectares on a scenic and landscaped area just outside of Kamloops. UCC opened a new trades & technology centre in September 1997. UCC is also proud of its recently completed library and its science, arts & education, and campus activity centre buildings. The campus activity centre is the focal point for student activities and services.

UCC offers campus housing in 300 single units in the McGill student housing complex and the Upper College Heights student housing complex. Both the Upper College Heights and the McGill complexes are privately owned; students should initiate housing applications as early as possible.

UCC also serves Merritt and the Nicola Valley, Clearwater and North Thompson, Lillooet and the upper Fraser Canyon, as well as the historic region known as the Cariboo, from where the school drew its name. All are located within the spectacular scenery of BC's high country. This area is a popular destination, renowned for its natural beauty, pristine lakes and mountains. Skiing and hiking enthusiasts will be particularly impressed with the high country region.

Kamloops is a mid-sized city that boasts superb summers, sports and outdoor recreation opportunities, and a diversity of cultural activities. Nestled within the interior of BC, Kamloops is conveniently located within a day's drive from world-class destinations. Vancouver and Calgary are the most accessible large cities; and each provides the amenities of metropolitan centres, with exceptional cultural and recreational facilities.

ATHLETICS & EXTRACURRICULAR ACTIVITIES

The Department of Athletics & Recreation at UCC offers an intercollegiate program with other colleges and universities. Sports for men and women normally include soccer, baseball, volleyball, badminton and golf. A variety of recreational activities open to all students are conducted throughout the academic year in conjunction with the activities council.

Scholarships for varsity athletics are available to incoming high school graduates and returning students. The sports task force serves as a voluntary, community-based organization that raises approximately C$25,000 annually to support student athletes at UCC.

University College Recognition

- Member of the AUCC
- Member of the ACCC
- Accredited by the Government of British Columbia

STUDENT SUPPORT SERVICES

UCC offers advising services for students planning their future courses, seeking career changes, or making general enquiries about any aspect of student life at UCC. Specific services available include career planning workshops, study & stress workshops, services for students with disabilities, an employment centre, a health clinic and a campus activity centre. Services for First Nations students include liaison and communication with bands, as well as agencies, assistance and support to enhance student successes. The school supports a First Nations student association and a First Nations student centre. UCC also offers extensive awards & financial aid services, which provide information on scholarships, bursaries, student loans, application workshops and work study programs offered at UCC.

International Students

University College Enrolment: 365

% of University College Enrolment: 5%

Countries of Origin: International students have come from 23 countries including Korea, Japan, Brazil and Denmark.

Colleges

IN

British Columbia

CAMOSUN COLLEGE VICTORIA, BRITISH COLUMBIA

College Mission

...to serve the education and training needs of southern Vancouver Island and beyond...and to remain committed to work in international education that benefits students and strengthens the college, the community and international partnerships

Student Voice:

Camosun was a great experience for me. I started with English courses, and went on to complete a two-year diploma in business administration. Then I was able to transfer to year three at a local university where I completed my degree.

Jirar, International Student, Jordan
Business Administration

CONTACT INFORMATION
Camosun College
3100 Foul Bay Road
Victoria, British Columbia
Canada V8P 5J2
PH 1-250-592-1556 (Cdn);
1-250-370-3681 (int'l)
FAX 1-250-370-3551 (Cdn);
1-250-370-3689 (int'l)
EMAIL inted@camosun.bc.ca (int'l students only)
INTERNET http://www.camosun.bc.ca

COLLEGE OVERVIEW

Camosun College (Camosun) was established in 1971 as a two-year community college offering university transfer, vocational and upgrading courses. Camosun delivers programs in over 60 areas of study through the Schools of Access Programs & First Nations Education, Arts & Science, Business, Health & Human Services and Trades & Technology.

Schools

The School of Arts & Science includes the Departments of English, Humanities, Psychology, Social Sciences, Biology, Chemistry, Mathematics and Physics. It offers college preparatory courses, university transfer courses and career programs.

The School of Business offers university transfer courses as well as certificate and diploma career programs. Career programs such as hotel/restaurant administration offer hands-on training for students in real-world environments: students run a restaurant that is open to the public.

The School of Health & Human Services provides certificate and diploma programs in dental assisting, dental hygiene, early childhood education, nursing and recreational leadership. The school also offers continuing education opportunities for people wanting to update their skills within a field.

The School of Trades & Technology provides training in areas such as construction; mechanics; horticulture; civil, electronic and mechanical engineering technology; computer science; and nautical upgrading.

English as a Second Language (ESL) is offered through the School of Access Programs & First Nations Education. Instead of a minimum English language requirement, Camosun tests each incoming student whose primary language is not English and then individually places students at the appropriate level.

Cooperative Education

Many of Camosun's business and technology programs are taught in a cooperative education format, which is the integration of academic studies with paid periods of relevant work experience in their chosen field. The co-op staff is responsible for developing and monitoring co-op student work terms and in assisting students in the development of their own job search strategy.

International Education

Camosun College has been involved in international education since 1983 and is committed to contributing to the process of global education by reaching out to create relationships worldwide. International students on campus are served by the knowledgeable and experienced staff in the International Education Office.

Highlights

- Wide variety of program options
- Offers a cooperative education program in selected program areas
- 10,000 students currently participate in part-time studies at Camosun

College Statistics

Year Founded: 1971
Academic Options:
diploma/certificate/associate degrees
Calendar Year: fall semester (Sept-Dec); winter semester (Jan-Apr); spring term (May-Jun); summer term (Jul-Aug)

ACADEMIC PROGRAMS

School of Access Programs: Adult Basic Education; English as a Second Language

School of Arts & Science: Applied Communication; Biology; Chemistry & Geoscience; Criminal Justice; English; Environmental Technology; Humanities; Mathematics; Music; Physics; Psychology; Social Sciences; Visual Arts

School of Business: Accounting; Finance & Economics; Computing/Business Math & Quantitative Methods; Hospitality & Tourism; Marketing, Management and Public Administration; Office Careers

School of Health & Human Services: Continuing Care; Dental Programs; Human Services; Nursing; Recreation Leadership

School of Trades & Technology: Architectural Trades; Civil Engineering; Computer Science; Cook Training; Electrical; Electronics Engineering; Mechanical Engineering; Mechanical Trades/Metal Trades; Nautical

ADMISSIONS CRITERIA & PROCEDURES

Canadian applicants to Camosun must have completed grade 12 in a Canadian secondary school or its equivalent, or be 18 years of age or older.

International applicants must be at least 18 years of age and have completed the equivalent of 10 grades in a 12-grade system. They should fill out an International Application Form and submit the nonrefundable C$100 application fee with the form. International students should send official secondary, and any postsecondary, school transcripts with their application form accompanied by certified translations, where applicable. All international students are assessed at Camosun before registering for classes; international students should arrive at the college two weeks before the commencement of classes to complete their assessment, review the results, choose a course plan and register for classes.

All Canadian candidates should fill out an application for admission and send it along with the nonrefundable C$25 application fee to the Admissions/Registration Office. Candidates should include official copies of their secondary and postsecondary transcripts. Course and program requirements and prerequisites vary from program to program.

Admissions at a Glance

Minimum GPA: varies

Minimum English Requirements: no set minimum, all students assessed at Camosun

Application Fee: C$25 (Canadian), $100 (international)

Application Deadlines: Canadian: rolling admissions; international: May 31 (fall semester), September 30 (winter semester), January 31 (spring term), April 30 (ESL only, summer term)

ACADEMIC FACILITIES

The Lansdowne Campus's Young Building was originally built on three hectares of Hudson Bay Company property and, since its construction, has been used as Victoria's first Normal school in 1913, a military hospital during World War II and an institute for adult learning in 1967. The Young Building, with its Renaissance architecture and clock tower, provides a historic centre for learning that is equipped with modern technologies including the Applied Communication program's radio station (CKMO) and a television studio. The Fisher Building houses student services including the campus bookstore, cafeteria, classrooms, laboratories, and the nursing, biology, physics and chemistry offices. The Dental and Library Sciences Buildings opened in 1990 and 1991 respectively. The newest building is the Wilna Thomas Building.

The modern Interurban Campus features a two-storey atrium in the Centre for Business & Access. The Campus Centre opened in 1994 and houses the career resources centre, the admissions/registration office, the bookstore, meeting rooms, administrative offices, the Student Society Office and many classrooms.

Student & Faculty Profile

Total Enrolment: 23,960

Full-Time Enrolment: 7,772

# of Faculty: 399

Student/Faculty Ratio: 15:1

Male/Female Students: 47%/53%

Academic Class Sizes: 20-42

Enrolment by Program Type:

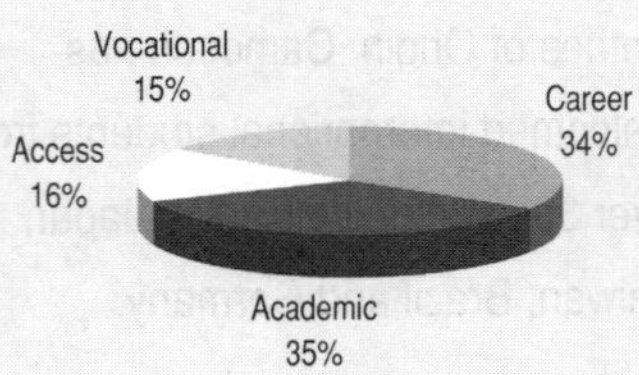

SCHOLARSHIPS & FINANCIAL ASSISTANCE

Canadian students requiring financial assistance may be eligible for scholarships, assistance programs, grants and bursaries. The Camosun College Foundation awards many bursaries and internal awards to those students who have applied for student loans. Students may also participate in the campus work study program, which offers part-time employment opportunities on campus for student loan recipients. The Government of British Columbia also provides international grants and offers the Asia Pacific Award for students who study abroad.

There is no financial assistance available for international students.

Expenses at a Glance

Tuition (full-time):

- In-Province: C$450-901/semester
- Out-of-Province: C$450-901/semester
- International: C$3,400/semester

Fees, Books, Materials: C$200-1,000/year

Accommodation:

- Private: C$650+/month
- Residence: n/a
- Homestay: C$600/month (int'l students)

Health Insurance: C$36/month

CAMPUS & LOCATION

City Population:	350,000
Cost of Living:	high
Climate Range:	0° to 30°C
Campus Setting:	suburban/rural
# of Students in Residence:	n/a

Camosun College has two campuses, the Interurban and Lansdowne Campuses. Camosun's Interurban campus is situated in rural Saanich, about 20 minutes from downtown Victoria. The Lansdowne campus is located 10 minutes from downtown and provides a combination of old and new buildings and facilities for over 4,500 students. Although Camosun does not offer on-campus residence, it does offer a homestay program for international students; the cost is C$600 per month and placements are arranged and reviewed by Camosun's Homestay Facilitator. Students seeking private accommodation are encouraged to consult the off-campus housing registry.

Victoria, the capital of British Columbia, is located on southern Vancouver Island and enjoys a temperate climate all year round. Victoria's relatively small population of 350,000 people lends it a comfortable, safe atmosphere that feels more like a small town community than the city that it is. Famous for its flower gardens and beautiful scenery, Victoria is a relaxing and enjoyable place to live and study. Many opportunities for outdoor activities such as sailing, hiking, biking and whale watching are available.

ATHLETICS & EXTRACURRICULAR ACTIVITIES

Camosun participates at the intercollegiate level in volleyball, basketball and golf in the British Columbia College Athletic Association (BCCAA). The college also offers a variety of personal fitness and drop-in recreational activities for students on both campuses.

There are various clubs, organizations and committees in which students can become involved including the International Club, the First Nations Students Association, the Women's Centre, student council, several outdoors clubs and many different course-related organizations. Club funding is provided by the student society and students interested in starting their own club are encouraged to contact the society.

College Recognition

- Accredited by the provincial government
- One of the largest publicly-funded colleges in British Columbia

STUDENT SUPPORT SERVICES

Camosun is committed to providing an extensive network of support services to ensure that all its students succeed. Comprehensive counselling services, Camosun's writing clinic, and academic and career advising are available to all students at either Camosun campus.

In addition, international students at Camosun are supported through the International Education office.

International student advisers, a homestay facilitator and an international counsellor are available at both Lansdowne and Interurban campuses.

International Students

College Enrolment: 400

% of College Enrolment: 5%

Countries of Origin: Camosun has welcomed international students from over 30 countries including Japan, Taiwan, Brazil and Germany.

COLUMBIA COLLEGE VANCOUVER, BRITISH COLUMBIA

College Mission

...to provide quality university transfer, senior secondary and English as a second language programs

Student Voice:

I like the environment of Columbia College and enjoy the facilities provided to us....Columbia College has given me the opportunity and confidence to reach further academic achievement.

Jing Sun
University Transfer
Business

CONTACT INFORMATION
Columbia College
500-555 Seymour Street
Vancouver, British Columbia
Canada V6B 6J9
PH 1-604-683-8360
FAX 1-604-682-7191
EMAIL admin@columbiacollege.bc.ca
INTERNET
http://www.columbiacollege.bc.ca

COLLEGE OVERVIEW

Columbia College (CC), formerly a private college, was founded in 1936 and offered high school completion programs to hundreds of students, including war veterans. As CC expanded, ESL and university transfer programs were added to accommodate the growing numbers of international students coming to the west coast of Canada; CC's current student body is drawn from over 40 countries around the world.

CC now offers eight certificate and diploma programs and over 125 courses in its University Transfer, Intensive ESL and Senior Secondary Programs.

University Transfer Program

The University Transfer Program is usually one semester in length and comprises four academic preparatory courses, including at least one Senior Secondary course. Students who have successfully completed a secondary school program, or equivalent, may enter the University Transfer Program.

First- and second-year university levels can be taken at CC and are fully transferable to universities; a student who completes 30 credits of university studies is eligible to apply for admission to second-year at Simon Fraser University, the University of British Columbia or any other approved postsecondary institution. Students in the program normally take 12 to 15 credits (three to four courses) per semester.

Intensive ESL Program

The Intensive ESL Program provides full-time English instruction to students who have been accepted into an academic program, but still require additional help with their English skills. The program offers intensive instruction in English language skills including speaking, listening, reading and writing. The program may also be taken by students who wish to learn English for business or social, rather than academic purposes.

Senior Secondary Program

The Senior Secondary Program is designed to allow students to complete the British Columbia Ministry of Education's requirements, including the Provincial Examinations in Academic Grade 12 subjects, for secondary school graduation.

In the last semester of the program, students are permitted to register concurrently in one or two university-level courses.

Highlights

- Almost 90% of student body is international
- Offers a full selection of courses in the summer
- Part-time options are available

College Statistics

Year Founded: 1936

Academic Options: certificate

Calendar Year: fall semester (Sept-Dec); spring semester (Jan-Apr); summer semester (May-Aug)

ACADEMIC PROGRAMS

University Transfer Program: Accounting, Anthropology, Applied Science (Engineering, Computer-Aided Engineering Graphics), Asian Studies (China, Japan), Biology, Chemistry (Organic), Composition, Computer Science, Economics, English (Academic, Business & Technical), Language & Composition, Literature, French, Geography (Landforms, Weather), Japanese, Mathematics (Analysis; Calculus I, II, III; Calculus for Business & Social Sciences; Linear Algebra & Differential Equations; Precalculus), Philosophy, Physics, Psychology, Sociology

Intensive ESL Program: Upper Beginner, Intermediate (Level I, II), Advanced (Level I, II), Academic Advanced (Level I, II), Cambridge Test Preparatory Program, Certificate in English Language Teaching for Adults (CELTA)

Senior Secondary Program

ADMISSIONS CRITERIA & PROCEDURES

Applicants to CC must submit a completed application form accompanied by secondary school transcripts from the most recent academic institute attended and a nonrefundable C$100 application fee. Potential students must be 16 years of age or older. International applicants should include the results of any external examinations taken (GCSE or HKCE for example) and a passport-sized photograph in the application package.

New students may be required to take CC's Language & Writing Assessment (LWA), which will be used to determine students' placement in the college's English program. Students with insufficient LWA scores will be required to enter the Intensive ESL Program in order to develop the necessary language preparation needed for CC's academic courses. International students should submit a minimum TOEFL score of 520, IELTS score of 5.0 or a MELAB score between 77 and 79 to be accepted directly into a regular academic program.

Admission to all programs is selective and based on the college's evaluation of the applicant's probable success in undertaking studies at CC. Acceptance into a specific program does not guarantee subsequent advancement into higher level programs at CC.

Admissions at a Glance

Minimum GPA: n/a

Minimum English Requirements: TOEFL 520-530, IELTS 5-6.5, MELAB 77-79

Application Fee: C$100 (Canadian and international)

Application Deadlines: September 14 (fall semester); January 15 (spring semester); May 14 (summer semester)

ACADEMIC FACILITIES

The Learning Resource Centre offers several services designed to assist students with their academic work. Individual English and math tutorials, interactive audiovisual and multimedia resources, and TOEFL preparation materials and advice are available through the centre. The campus library maintains an extensive collection of books, journals, periodicals, CD-ROM databases, government documents, maps, ESL materials and career-related resources. Professional librarians are on hand to provide reference and research services to CC students.

The Computer Centre is open to all CC students and provides services at four facilities including the 36-station Computer Laboratory, the Learning Resources Centre (with 15 stations), the library and Student Services. All workstations are connected through the NOVELL network and the Computer Laboratory is equipped with a Roland DPX-2000 Drafting Plotter capable of outputting advanced graphics.

CC has modern biology, chemistry and physics laboratories, equipped for experimental work at the university level.

Student & Faculty Profile

Total Enrolment: 650

Full-Time Enrolment: 600

# of Faculty: 55

Student/Faculty Ratio: 12:1

Male/Female Students: 50%/50%

Academic Class Sizes: 15-30

Enrolment by Program Type:

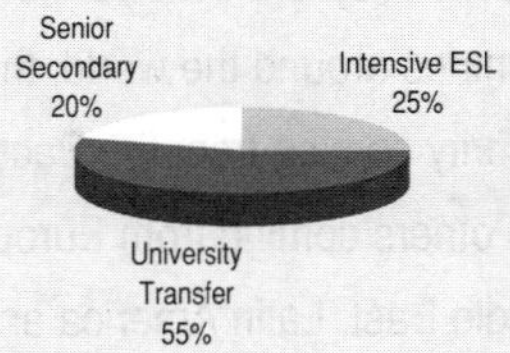

SCHOLARSHIPS & FINANCIAL ASSISTANCE

Each semester CC awards a number of scholarships including the Columbia College Academic Scholarship, the Jason Graham Memorial Scholarship and scholarships for students continuing on to university. These scholarships range from C$750 to $1,000 and are presented to students who display outstanding talent and academic standing in their area of study. Entry scholarships are available for well-qualified local students. For more information regarding applications and qualifications students should contact the Admissions Office.

Expenses at a Glance

Tuition (full-time):

- In-Province: C$3,900/year
- Out-of-Province: C$3,900/year
- International: C$8,000/year

Fees, Books, Materials: C$720/year

Accommodation:

- Private: not available
- Residence: not available
- Homestay: C$700/month

Health Insurance: not available

CAMPUS & LOCATION

City Population:	1,800,000
Cost of Living:	high
Climate Range:	0° to 25°C
Campus Setting:	urban
# of Students in Residence:	n/a

Vancouver is the largest city in western Canada, located on the southwestern coast of British Columbia. Vancouver enjoys a temperate climate year-round that rarely drops below zero degrees Celsius. Vancouver is a safe and clean cosmopolitan city of nearly two million people featuring shopping, fine dining, cultural facilities and an extensive public transportation system. Many opportunities for outdoor activities including golf, tennis, hiking and sailing are available throughout the year and the city is conveniently located near the Whistler/Blackcomb ski resort.

Columbia College recently moved to a new building situated in the heart of downtown Vancouver; CC shares this large building with the British Columbia Institute of Technology (BCIT). Simon Fraser University's downtown campus and Vancouver Community College are nearby. The campus is within walking distance of the Vancouver Library, the Queen Elizabeth Theatre, the Vancouver Art Gallery and the Ford Centre for the Performing Arts. CC offers an extensive homestay program for international students or the option of living in private accommodations in Vancouver.

ATHLETICS & EXTRACURRICULAR ACTIVITIES

The Student Coordinator organizes a wide variety of student activities outside of the centre including soccer, softball and basketball matches, and hiking and skiing excursions. In addition, CC's fitness centre is open to all college students.

CC provides three student lounges, one designated for quiet study, one for study and socialization, and a large social lounge equipped with vending machines, microwave ovens, as well as table tennis and pool tables.

Several student-organized activities occur each year and all students are invited to participate. Previous activities have included skiing, hiking and sailing trips.

STUDENT SUPPORT SERVICES

CC's support services are extensive and highly personalized. International students can arrange for airport pick-up services when they arrive in the country. A campus orientation is provided before each semester and is designed to introduce new students to the academic and social aspects of life at CC.

College Recognition

- Canada's oldest independent international college
- Senior Secondary Program certified by the province of British Columbia
- Incorporated as a Non-Profit Society under the Societies Act of British Columbia

The Student Resource Centre is located at Student Services. The centre provides university and college calendars and information on university transfer, career planning and TOEFL and SAT tests. Experienced counsellors are available to help students with course selection, career planning, university selection and personal and academic concerns. Counsellors are able to provide visa extension letters and other documents that may be needed by international students when dealing with Immigration Canada.

CC's homestay program is designed to allow international students to become familiar with Canadian culture and improve their English language skills by living as part of a Canadian family. Families are evaluated by CC and are selected from areas that provide easy access to the college.

International Students

College Enrolment: 560

% of College Enrolment: 86%

Countries of Origin: CC's international student body is drawn from over 40 countries around the world, the majority coming from the Pacific Rim, and others coming from Europe, the Middle East, Latin America and Africa.

Douglas College Greater Vancouver, British Columbia

College Mission

...to enhance the skills, knowledge and values of lifelong learners in meeting their goals and to respond to diverse community needs in a rapidly changing society

Student Voice:

Douglas College provided me with the formal knowledge and skill base to allow me to carry out my nursing duties more effectively. My program allowed for learning in a critical but constructive way that prepared me to confidently take on the role of a graduate nurse.

Mike Krabbendam
Graduate, Psychiatric Nursing Program
Director of Care, Scholem Home Ltd. Hope, British Columbia

CONTACT INFORMATION
Douglas College
PO Box 2503
Greater Vancouver, British Columbia
Canada V3L 5B2
PH 1-604-527-5400
FAX 1-504-527-5095
EMAIL registrar_office@douglas.bc.ca
INTERNET http://www.douglas.bc.ca

COLLEGE OVERVIEW

Founded in 1970, Douglas College is dedicated to excellence in instruction and offering accessible, flexible and affordable programs. Students benefit from personalized attention in small classes. By striving to make its programs accessible to all, Douglas College fosters a diverse, multicultural educational environment.

The Instructional Division of the college is responsible for all academic programs. Students may earn associate degrees, diplomas, certificates or citations.

University Transfer Programs

Douglas College has developed seven two-year university transfer programs in consultation with local universities: Diploma in Arts, Diploma in Commerce & Business Administration, Diploma in Criminology, Diploma in Performing Arts, Diploma in Science, Diploma in General Studies and Diploma in Physical Education. Transfer agreements have been established with most of the universities and university colleges in British Columbia, though transfer possibilities also exist outside of the province. Students in these programs complete 60 credits, equal to the first two years of a degree program.

Career Programs

Douglas College offers a wide variety of programs that train students for direct entry into the workforce. Programs last from one to six semesters and offer both theoretical and practical knowledge. Courses are taught by industry professionals and many offer students the opportunity to gain on-site, workplace experience.

Developmental Education

The Department of Student Development offers courses to help students prepare for future studies or personal achievement, including courses in literacy, numeracy, mathematics and study skills improvement, ESL and special needs programs.

Additional Programs

A wide selection of continuing education courses for professional development and general interest are offered through on-campus and community programs, workshops and conferences. Also, customized training programs are offered for employers, the self-employed, government agencies, labour organizations and community groups. In addition, Douglas College has established agreements with local school districts, enabling secondary school students to take college courses before graduation through Concurrent Studies.

Cooperative Education

To ensure that students gain practical, relevant experience to complement their education, co-op options are available in the following programs: Associate in Arts, Associate in Science, Business Management, Hotel & Restaurant Management, Office Administration and Print Futures: Professional Writing.

Highlights

- Wide range of university transfer, career developmental and continuing education programs
- Full- and part-time study options
- Campuses located in New Westminster, Maple Ridge and Coquitlam

College Statistics

Year Founded: 1970

Academic Options: associate degree/diploma/certificate/citation

Calendar Year: fall semester (Sept-Dec); winter semester (Jan-Apr); summer semester (May-Aug)

ACADEMIC PROGRAMS

Faculty of Child, Family & Community Studies: Child & Youth Care Counsellor, Community Social Service Worker, Community Support Worker, Early Childhood Education, Psychiatric Nursing, Sign Language Interpretation, Therapeutic Recreation

Faculty of Commerce & Business Administration: Accounting Mgmt, Accounting, Business Mgmt, Commerce & Business Admin, Computer Information Systems, Economics, Financial Services Studies, General Business, Hotel & Restaurant Mgmt, Marketing Mgmt, New Venture Mgmt, Office Admin, Office Assistant, Legal Stenography, Administrative Assistant, Financial, Legal Office Assistant, Medical Office Assistant, Office Admin

Faculty of Health Sciences: Dental Auxiliary, Dispensing Optician, General Nursing, Access to General Nursing, Health Information Services, Resident Care Attendent

Faculty of Humanities & Social Services: Anthropology, Criminology, Geography, History, Humanities, Philosophy, Political Science, Psychology, Sociology

Faculty of Language, Literature & Performing Arts: Communications, Creative Writing, English, Modern Languages, Music, Basic Musicianship, Print Futures: Professional Writing, Stagecraft, Theatre, Women's Studies

Faculty of Pure & Applied Science & Technology: Biology, Chemistry, Coaching, Computing Science, Environmental Sciences, Geology, Mathematics, Physical Education & Recreation, Physics

Interdisciplinary Studies: Habitat Restoration Program

ADMISSIONS CRITERIA & PROCEDURES

Students interested in enrolling in Douglas College courses should attend a free information session on campus before applying. Applicants should submit a completed application form along with official secondary and postsecondary transcripts and the application fee as early as possible, as admission and registration are determined on a first-come, first-served basis. Individuals are eligible for general admission if they meet one of the following criteria:

- they have graduated or are within one course of graduating from a British Columbia secondary school or the equivalent
- they will be at least 19 years old at the start of the semester
- they are at least 17 years old and have not attended school for one year
- they are special needs students, have completed a certificate or equivalent from a special program and have been in school for at least 12 years

Depending on their background, students may be required to complete preparatory courses before enrolling in certain programs. Programs offered on a limited enrolment basis only have their own application deadlines and additional admission requirements.

International students are permitted to enrol in most Douglas College programs. In addition to meeting the general admission requirements, international students must also submit a TOEFL score. Although a score of 450 is required for admission, students with scores between 450 and 549 must apply to the ESL program first. Students with scores of 550 or higher may take academic and ESL courses concurrently. Students with scores of 600 or 550 with a TWE of 5.0 are not required to take ESL courses

Admissions at a Glance

Minimum GPA: n/a

Minimum English Requirements: TOEFL 550 (academic programs)

Application Fee: C$25 (Canadian), C$100 (international)

Application Deadlines: August 1 (fall semester); June 1 recommended

ACADEMIC FACILITIES

The Learning Resources Department of Douglas College's Educational Services Division is responsible for library and audiovisual services. Also part of the division, the Centre for Educational Technology ensures that technology and media resources are available to support the educational process.

The New Westminster Campus houses classrooms, multimedia lecture theatres, laboratories and a major library. The Douglas College library has 2,500 videotapes, 3,000 sound recordings, government documents, computer programs, maps and pamphlets in addition to books and periodicals. The library is open to students from all British Columbia community colleges as well members of the community holding public library cards. Students may use study rooms in the library for private and group study.

SCHOLARSHIPS & FINANCIAL ASSISTANCE

Students requiring financial assistance may be eligible for funding from a number of sources, including government loans and awards as well as grants, awards, bursaries and scholarships from Douglas College. In addition, a number of entrance scholarships and graduation awards are granted each year. Students may undertake paid work-study programs. Students interested in applying for funding from the college should contact the Student Finance Office. Workshops are held year-round to help students with their loan applications.

Student & Faculty Profile

Total Enrolment: 22,700

Full-Time Enrolment: 9,254

# of Faculty: 520 (total)

Student/Faculty Ratio: 11:1 (full-time students)

Male/Female Students: 39%/61%

Academic Class Sizes: 18-35 (average)

Enrolment by Program Type:

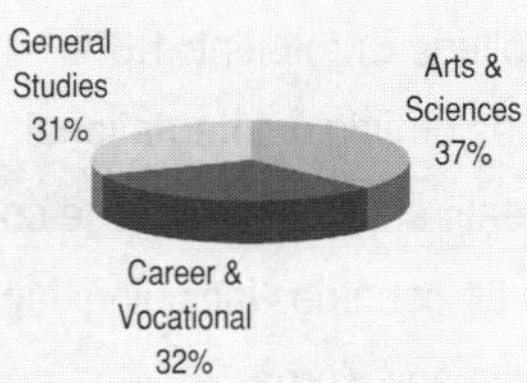

Expenses at a Glance

Tuition (full-time):

In-Province: C$1,400/year

Out-of-Province: C$1,400/year

International: C$7,050/year

Fees, Books, Materials: C$250/year (approx)

Accommodation:

Private: C$400-700/month

Residence: n/a

Homestay: C$640/month

Health Insurance: C$36/month (int'l)

City Population:	1,826,000
Cost of Living:	high
Climate Range:	0° to 27°C
Campus Setting:	suburban
# of Students in Residence:	n/a

CAMPUS & LOCATION

Douglas College's three campuses are located in Greater Vancouver on British Columbia's west coast. The main college campus, a large and modern site located in New Westminster, is just one block from a SkyTrain station, ensuring that students have easy access to all parts of the region. The Thomas Haney Campus, located in Maple Ridge, was the first facility in Canada designed to house both a secondary school and a community college. The new David Lam Campus, located in Coquitlam Town Centre, is next door to a major community centre, secondary school, cultural centre, aquatic centre and playing fields.

Although Douglas College does not have on-campus residences, the Student Society maintains an up-to-date listing of local off-campus accommodation. International students who wish to live with a local family may live with a host family; the Centre for International Education can arrange a homestay placement prior to the student's arrival in Canada.

Greater Vancouver offers extensive cultural and recreational activities. Downtown Vancouver is cosmopolitan and ethnically diverse, and the surrounding terrain is ideal for numerous outdoor activities including cycling and hiking.

ATHLETICS & EXTRACURRICULAR ACTIVITIES

Douglas College offers athletic opportunities for men and women in basketball, volleyball, badminton, golf, rugby, wrestling and soccer. Students may compete at the varsity level through membership in the British Columbia Colleges Athletic Association or at the national level through the Canadian Colleges Athletic Association.

Students may participate in non-competitive individual and coed team sports during the semester on Thursdays; sports activities include indoor soccer, floor hockey and volleyball. In addition, all students may use the college's athletic facilities, including the gymnasium and weight room. Various club sports, such as skiing and karate, are offered for a fee.

Students are encouraged to participate in college activities beyond their academic program. As members of the Douglas College Student Society, all students may become involved in student government. In addition, all students are encouraged to contribute to The Other Press, the college's independent student newspaper.

College Recognition

- Douglas College psychiatric nursing, dispensing optician, professional writing and financial services programs are unique in British Columbia
- The criminology course offerings at Douglas College are among the largest in British Columbia
- More students advance to Simon Fraser University from Douglas College than from any other institution

STUDENT SUPPORT SERVICES

Douglas College offers a variety of support services to ensure students' success. Information Sessions are held on a regular basis for prospective students interested in career and university transfer programs. Once students have enrolled, they may take advantage of academic advising services to obtain general program information and career guidance.

Career information is available through a number of courses, workshops and reference collections, as well as the Career Resource Centre, where services offered range from job search strategy instruction to provision of information on employment trends and volunteer activities. A Student Placement Office provides listings of part-time and summer job opportunities.

Career, personal and educational counselling are available at all campuses. Specialized assistance is also available through the First Nations Services Coordinator, the Women's Centre and Disabled Student Services.

International Students

College Enrolment: 373

% of College Enrolment: 1.6%

Countries of Origin: International students at Douglas College come from 31 countries including Japan, Taiwan and Korea.

Langara College
Vancouver, British Columbia

College Mission

...to be committed to excellence in teaching and the pursuit of life-long education by providing flexible, innovative and student-centred education

Student Voice:

Langara College has been the most helpful and supportive school that I have ever attended. I have received enormous support from the instructors for my academic life and from the International Education Department.

Hasan Chandra
Arts & Science/University Transfer Program

CONTACT INFORMATION
Langara College
100 West 49th Avenue
Vancouver, British Columbia
Canada V5Y 2Z6
PH 1-604-323-5511
FAX 1-604-323-5555
EMAIL gmcneil@langara.bc.ca
INTERNET http://www.langara.bc.ca

COLLEGE OVERVIEW

Langara College (Langara) offers a broad selection of courses and programs to serve the needs of individuals committed to pursuing postsecondary study. During its fall, spring and summer semesters the college enrols approximately 15,000 students in its first- and second-year arts and science courses and its 31 career programs. The college also serves about 8,400 continuing education students.

Programs Offered

Langara offers university transfer programs in the arts and sciences, and career programs.

The arts and sciences programs at Langara are designed to allow students to earn transferable credit towards a university degree. The areas of study offering transferable credit include English, the humanities, human performance, physical & life sciences and modern languages. A one-year engineering transfer program is offered that allows students to continue their studies in UBC's Faculty of Engineering.

The career programs are designed in conjunction with community advisory committees to ensure students are prepared for careers in the arts, business, industry and community services. Career programs are typically either two or four terms in duration, requiring one or two years to complete. Career programs are offered in business administration, community programs, creative arts, health applied science & human services and computer science, and a high degree of specialization is available in each of these fields.

Cooperative Education

Langara offers cooperative education programs that allow students to combine their academic knowledge with practical work experience. Co-op students are able to alternate terms of classroom studies with paid full-time employment. Through a competitive application, interview and selection process, students are matched with employers who have agreed to participate in the co-op program. There are normally two work terms in each program, with the work terms occurring in the spring and summer semesters; however, some programs may vary. The following programs offer co-op at Langara: Accounting; Business, Finance & Investment Management; Computer Information Systems; International Business; Applied Computer Science & Technology; Marketing & Sales and Real Estate Studies.

Credit is earned for each work term completed, with normal tuition fees applying to co-op terms.

Highlights

- Large cooperative education program
- Credit is transferable to any university in British Columbia
- Low tuition fees
- Small class sizes ensure personalized attention

College Statistics

Year Founded: 1965
Academic Options: certificate/diploma/associate degrees
Calendar Year: fall term (Sept-Dec); spring term (Jan-Apr); summer term (May-Aug)

ACADEMIC PROGRAMS

University Transfer: Arts, Commerce, Engineering, Sciences

Associate Degrees: Arts, Sciences

Two-year Diplomas: Accounting, Arts & Sciences (including Canadian Studies, Classical Studies, Commerce, Applied Computer Science & Technology, Environmental Studies, Family Studies, Latin American Studies, Pacific Rim Studies, Peace & Conflict Studies, Women's Studies), Business, Finance & Investment Management, Coaching & Instruction, Collaborative Nursing, Computer Information Systems, Coordinated Studies, Court Reporting, Criminal Justice, Display & Design, Early Childhood Education, Exercise Science, Fine Arts, General Education, International Business, Journalism, Leisure Studies, Library Technician, Marketing & Sales, Nutrition & Food Services Management, Professional Photo Imaging, Publishing Techniques & Technologies, Real Estate Studies, Recreation Facilities Management, Recreation Leadership, Theatre Arts

One-year Certificates: Accounting Postdiploma, Arts & Science Engineering, Computer Information Systems Postdiploma, Early Childhood Education, International Resource Systems, Journalism, Professional Computer Science & Technology, Real Estate Studies, Property Management, Realtime Reporting Postdiploma, Recreation Facilities Management Postdiploma, Recreation Leadership Postdiploma, Small Business Development, Social Service Worker, Special Education Assistant, Stenoscription

ADMISSIONS CRITERIA & PROCEDURES

New applicants to Langara must submit an application form along with official supporting documents to the Admission Office by June 30 for fall term, October 31 for spring term or February 28 for summer term. Applications received after this deadline will be considered if space is available.

Regular applicants must have successfully completed a BC secondary school program or the equivalent. Current BC grade 12 students are not required to submit an official transcript, provided they have directed the Ministry of Education to forward their final transcript to Langara and have included their BC Personal Education Number on their application. Canadian applicants who are not eligible for regular admission may be granted admission as mature students. All Canadian applications for admission must include a C$40 application processing fee.

International students must have academic qualifications equivalent to Canadian students, and must demonstrate proficiency in English prior to admission. Overseas applicants must submit a TOEFL score of 550 or an IELTS score of 6.5; international students in Canada may submit a minimum score of 2 from the Langara English Test (LET) or a score of 145 or better on the English Language Assessment (ELA) offered by Vancouver Community College.

Career program applicants must meet the program's prerequisite requirements. Applications for admission to career programs are evaluated on a first-come, first-served basis.

Admissions at a Glance

Minimum GPA: grade 12 or equivalent

Minimum English Requirements: TOEFL 550, IELTS 6.5, LET 2, ELA 145, LPI 4

Application Fee: C$40 (Canadian), $100 (international)

Application Deadlines: varies

ACADEMIC FACILITIES

The Langara library offers many services and several collections to assist students in their research and study. The resources available at Langara include books, magazines, newspapers, online databases and a variety of microfilm materials. In addition, the library's collection of audio-video materials is extensive, including videos, films, audio cassettes, CD's and interactive CD-ROM's. Langara, in partnership with the National Film Board, holds more than 2,500 films. A reference librarian is available to help students.

A networked microcomputer laboratory is also available to students during library hours.

Instructional Media Services (IMS) assists students with the production of materials for class presentations and assignments.

Student & Faculty Profile

Total Enrolment: 15,000+

Full-Time Enrolment: 6,350

# of Faculty: 410

Student/Faculty Ratio: 35:1

Male/Female Students: 50%/50%

Academic Class Sizes: 30-40

Enrolment by Program Type:

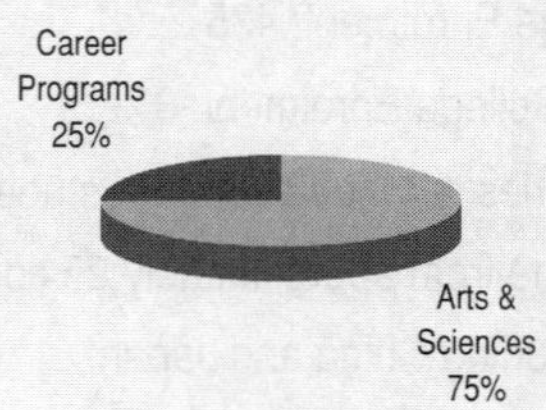

SCHOLARSHIPS & FINANCIAL ASSISTANCE

The Langara Financial Aid Department responds to the needs of currently enrolled and prospective students by administering a variety of assistance programs.

The federal government and the province of BC can provide some assistance to students through loans and grants. Langara also offers a work-study program which offers on-campus employment on a part-time basis. The Financial Aid Department provides information regarding scholarships, government assistance programs and the work-study program.

International students are not eligible for government assistance; however, scholarships are awarded each term to the two international students with the highest grades who continue to study at Langara.

Expenses at a Glance

Tuition (full-time):

- In-Province: C$1,578/year
- Out-of-Province: C$1,578/year
- International: C$7,500/year

Fees, Books, Materials: varies by program

Accommodation:

- Private: C$1,000/month
- Residence: n/a
- Homestay: C$650/month

Health Insurance: C$36/month

City Population:	2,000,000
Cost of Living:	high
Climate Range:	0° to 22°C
Campus Setting:	urban
# of Students in Residence:	n/a

CAMPUS & LOCATION

Langara College offers two modern instructional buildings housing lecture theatres, multi-use classrooms, study and seminar rooms, science laboratories, technical-vocational workrooms, studios for the cultural and performing arts, and athletics facilities.

Langara is located close to downtown Vancouver, in a residential area well-served by public transportation. The school also offers easy access to both the University of British Columbia and Simon Fraser University.

Vancouver was declared by the United Nations to be one of the 10 best places to live in the world. The city is located between the Pacific Ocean and the Coast Mountains, and offers outstanding multi-seasonal recreation activities. Offering a cosmopolitan setting, with excellent shopping and cultural opportunities, Vancouver is also a paradise for skiers, hikers, and nature lovers of all kinds. Vancouver is ideally located for getaways to the nearby ski resorts of Whistler and Blackcomb, and is a gateway to the scenic Gulf Islands.

ATHLETICS & EXTRACURRICULAR ACTIVITIES

The Department of Athletics and Intramurals offers a variety of activities for the student population, from intercollegiate athletics to campus recreation. Langara competes in the BC Colleges Athletic Association (BCAAA) in men's and women's badminton, basketball, soccer and volleyball. Students attending Langara full-time are entitled to try out for intercollegiate teams.

The intramural activities offered at the college provide opportunities for students to participate in activities, including aerobics, basketball, badminton, outdoor soccer, softball, tennis and volleyball, in a friendly environment. Individual day lockers, shower facilities and towel service are available.

The college's theatre, Studio 58, stages public performances of four full-length plays between October and April.

STUDENT SUPPORT SERVICES

The Langara College Counselling Department has been established to respond to the needs of currently enrolled and prospective students and to encourage personal growth and development. The counsellors are able to provide student support and counselling for personal, educational and career concerns. The department also provides a career and resource centre, which includes a collection of college and university calendars, occupational literature and information on labour market trends. In addition to counselling services, the department offers a variety of free workshops each semester to promote student success. These include such topics as study skills, stress management, self-esteem, resume writing and career planning.

First Nations students at Langara have access to a variety of services arranged by the First Nations Education Coordinator and the First Nations Liaison Counsellor, including a college orientation session, individual counselling, advocacy support and general advice on student life.

College Recognition

- Member of ACCC
- Member of ACRAO
- Member of NAFSA

International Students

College Enrolment: 435

% of College Enrolment: 3%

Countries of Origin: Langara students come from approximately 25 countries including China and Japan.

NORTH ISLAND COLLEGE BRITISH COLUMBIA

College Mission

...to provide high-quality, comprehensive educational services that are current, relevant and accessible

Student Voice:

I researched other colleges but given the campus, facility and the costs, North Island College was way better. The instructors are terrific and provide lots of one-on-one support. The training I received has opened lots of doors and it is exciting to think about future possibilities.

Aaron Ball
Graphic Design
Fine Arts Diploma Program

CONTACT INFORMATION
North Island College
3699 Roger Street
Port Alberni, British Columbia
Canada V9Y 8E3
PH 1-250-724-8734
FAX 1-250-724-8700
EMAIL internationaled@nic.bc.ca
INTERNET http://www.nic.bc.ca

COLLEGE OVERVIEW

North Island College (NIC) has been a community college since 1975, serving the educational and training needs of the residential and international students on north Vancouver Island and the Central Coast. The college has three campuses and 13 centres serving a total population of 160,000 people. NIC has nearly 50 programs, including: academics, health & human services, tourism, trades & technology, upgrading and general education.

Certificate & Diploma Programs

NIC offers numerous certificate and diploma programs. The majority of students complete the certificate programs in one year (two semesters), full-time; some programs require students to fulfil a semester of cooperative education, which can lengthen the amount of time required to complete the program. Generally, certificate programs require students to complete between 13.5 to 21 units of study.

Diploma programs require between 30 and 33 units and usually can be completed in two years (four semesters) of full-time study.

Associate Degrees

Associate degrees are granted for two years of university-level study in art, science and environmental studies. The general requirements for an associate degree are 30 units of first- and second-year university-level courses; at least 15 must be completed at NIC (the remaining units may be from accredited institutions).

Work Experience Programs

NIC offers an optional cooperative education programs in business administration, computer science & technology, and office administration. Interested students should complete an application form and consult the Cooperative Education Office for additional requirements. Co-op applicants should generally achieve and maintain an above-average academic standing (C+ average) and demonstrate the motivation and potential to pursue a professional career.

The apprenticeship program is offered in cooperation with the Apprenticeship Board of British Columbia. During each year of a four-year apprenticeship, students attend a mandatory 10-week training program and complete laboratory training.

Highlights

- Three main campuses and 13 college centres covering 80,000 square kilometres of northern Vancouver Island
- Offers full-, half- and part-time study options
- Cooperative education program options
- Largest number of campuses/centres of any college in British Columbia

College Statistics

Year Founded: 1975
Academic Options:
diploma/certificates/associate degrees
Calendar Year: fall semester (Sept-Dec); winter semester (Jan-Apr)

ACADEMIC PROGRAMS

Academics: University Studies; Associate Degrees (Arts, Science, Environmental Studies); Fine Arts; Business Administration (Accounting, General); Computer Science & Technology; Humanities; Social Sciences

Health & Human Services: Continuing Care; CPR & First Aid; Early Childhood Care & Education; Human Service Worker; Nursing

Tourism: Coastal Adventure Tourism; Cook Training (professional); Food & Beverage Management; Resort/Hotel Management; Short Entry-Level; Travel Counselling

General Education & Uprgrading: Adult Basic Education; Adult Special Education; ESL; GED Tests; Grade 12 Completion; Study & Reading Skills; Workers with Disabilities

Trades & Technology: Professional Diving; Drafting; Electricity; Electronics (Electronics Technician, Industrial Electronics Specialty); Heating Technician; Marine Training; Industrial Mobile Training; Journeyman Upgrading; Mechanics; Motor Vehicle Operating Skills; Office Administration; Renewable Resources (Aquaculture & Fisheries Technician, Salmon Farm Production Skills, Environmental); Welding (Levels A,B & C, Fabricator); Wood Products Technology

ADMISSIONS CRITERIA & PROCEDURES

All students must complete an application form and provide official transcripts of their secondary and postsecondary education. Some students may be required to take NIC's assessment test.

Canadian applicants must meet one of the following criteria: be at least 18 years of age; have graduated from secondary school; be a Canadian citizen or a landed immigrant; or be a participant in an exchange program. Admission requirements are program specific; students should consult the college calendar for further details.

International applicants should be at least 18 years of age and meet all Canadian immigration standards; international students must have maintained a C average (or equivalent) in secondary school academics and have evidence of medical insurance coverage in Canada. International applicants do not need to supply TOEFL or SAT scores; instead, they will take NIC's assessment test (with C$50 assessment fee) and be placed in an appropriate academic level. Students who do not meet the college's English language requirements may be admitted to their desired program conditionally provided they enrol in NIC's ESL program.

Admissions at a Glance

Minimum GPA: no set minimums

Minimum English Requirements: TOEFL score not required; students are placed based on NIC's assessment test

Application Fee: C$25 (Canadian), $100 (international)

Application Deadlines: vary for each program

ACADEMIC FACILITIES

NIC has four campus libraries with reference and circulating materials, journals, popular magazines and video- and audiotapes. Each library has a computerized catalogue list of the complete holdings of NIC and provides access to the library catalogues of all British Columbia postsecondary libraries, British Columbia public libraries and the index/reference databases of the provincial Electronic Library Network. Materials that are not available within NIC libraries may be borrowed through an interlibrary loan, usually from the University of Victoria.

Students can access NIC computer facilities on a limited basis; priority is given to those students for whom computer use is a course requirement. Campuses with more extensive computer facilities may have computers available on a regular basis for students not fulfilling course requirements; students should ask local staff about this possibility.

Student & Faculty Profile

Total Enrolment: 10,600

Full-Time Enrolment: 2,000

# of Faculty: 147

Student/Faculty Ratio: 21:1

Male/Female Students: 43%/57%

Academic Class Sizes: 18-34

Enrolment by Program Type:

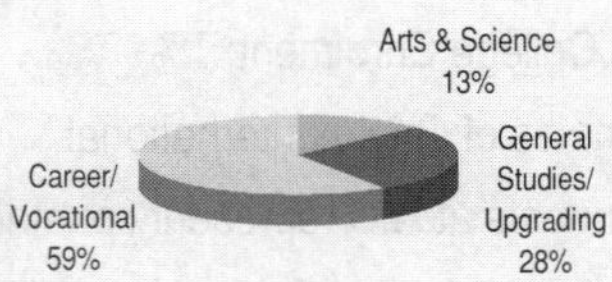

SCHOLARSHIPS & FINANCIAL ASSISTANCE

Financial aid may be available to Canadian students to help alleviate the cost of tuition, books, food, lodging and transportation. Canadian students are eligible to apply for several provincial and national postsecondary grants and financial assistance programs. NIC also supports a work-study program designed to provide on-campus work for students requiring financial assistance while attending NIC. The program is only open to British Columbia residents studying at participating universities, colleges and institutes in British Columbia.

Unfortunately, at this time, NIC cannot provide grants or financial assistance to international students.

Expenses at a Glance

Tuition (full-time):

- In-Province: C$1,186/year
- Out-of-Province: C$1,186/year
- International: C$1,800/year

Fees, Books, Materials: C$500/year (approx)

Accommodation:

- Private: C$400-600/month
- Residence: C$375/month
- Homestay: C$684/month

Health Insurance: not available through the college

CAMPUS & LOCATION

City Population:	160,000 (combined)
Cost of Living:	medium
Climate Range:	0° to 26°C
Campus Setting:	rural
# of Students in Residence:	not available

NIC's three campuses cover an 80,000-square-kilometre region of northern Vancouver Island from Desolation Sound to Swindle Island. The college's regional campuses are located in Port Alberni, Comox Valley and Campbell River and serve a number of smaller college centres including Bamfield, Tofino, Ucluelet, Ahousat, Gold River, Tahsis, Port Hardy, Port McNeill, Port Alice, Alert Bay, Bella Coola and Sointula. North Vancouver Island enjoys a temperate coastal climate with mild winters and warm summers, providing ample opportunity for outdoor activities.

The Port Alberni campus offers a privately owned and operated residence hall located directly adjacent to the campus. The Kildonan Hall is part of the Pacific Rim Residences and provides accommodation in a traditional residence setting. The other communities offer a large variety of reasonably priced private accommodation.

ATHLETICS & EXTRACURRICULAR ACTIVITIES

The North Island Students' Association (NISA) is a member of the Canadian Federation of Students (CFS), an alliance of over 70 college and university associations nationwide. The NISA organizes a number of extracurricular activities on campus, and all students are encouraged to participate. Clubs, sports and recreational opportunities are organized by individual campuses/centres.

College Recognition

- Former NIC students rated NIC highly for teaching quality and satisfaction with studies in BC Colleges & Institutes: 1997 Student Outcome Indicators

STUDENT SUPPORT SERVICES

NIC provides professionally trained counsellors to advise students in career or educational matters; advisers and counsellors are available at the campuses. Counsellors also provide workshops in areas such as time management, study skills, job interview skills, resume writing and stress management.

Assessment Services aims to help students be successful in their academic studies at NIC. To do this, the service offers skill testing on a regular basis to ensure that students have the necessary skill level for the courses or programs they have chosen.

International Students

College Enrolment: 10

% of College Enrolment: 1%

Countries of Origin: International students at NIC represent countries including Japan, China, Korea, Hong Kong and the US.

Institutes

IN

British Columbia

BRITISH COLUMBIA INSTITUTE OF TECHNOLOGY BURNABY, BRITISH COLUMBIA

Institute Mission

...to provide British Columbians with world-class, job-ready skills for career success

Student Voice:

At BCIT I worked with such diverse groups of people that I learned quickly how to interact and fit in. Teamwork and communication skills are essential.

Jacqueline Ramirez
Engineering Diploma Graduate

CONTACT INFORMATION
British Columbia Institute of Technology
3700 Willingdon Avenue
Burnaby, British Columbia
Canada V5G 3H2
PH 1-604-434-5734
FAX 1-604-687-2488
EMAIL inforeg@bcit.bc.ca
INTERNET http://www.bcit.bc.ca

INSTITUTE OVERVIEW

Founded in 1964 by the Government of British Columbia, the British Columbia Institute of Technology (BCIT) aims to produce well-trained, job-ready graduates for business, industry and health care organizations. BCIT's focus on career training has meant that in the past more than 80 per cent of technology and trades graduates were employed nine months after they graduated.

BCIT prides itself on approachable instructors who bring extensive real-world work experience to the classroom. Many BCIT programs are set up around student groups that allow students to spend all or most of their time at BCIT with the same small peer group. A group will typically include a wide range of students from recent high school graduates to students returning from the work force.

Part-time and distance education courses allow students who are currently employed to upgrade their skills without having to return to school full-time. Students across Canada and around the world are registered in BCIT's distance education programs.

Highlights

- Knowledgeable faculty with real-world work experience
- Career-oriented education with many cooperative education programs
- Expansive institute with four campuses

Institute Statistics

Year Founded: 1964
Academic Options: certificate/diploma/undergraduate/graduate
Calendar Year: varies

Courses and Programs at BCIT

BCIT offers programs leading to certificates, diplomas and undergraduate degrees, as well as a graduate degree program. Many programs lead to professional certification and some provide course exemptions that allow graduates to write qualifying exams for professional designations.

BCIT offers a variety of career programs in eight operating units: business; computing; construction; electrical & electronic; health sciences; manufacturing & industrial/mechanical; processing energy & natural resources; and transportation.

BCIT also has degree-granting status and offers Bachelor of Technology degrees in accounting, computer systems technology, construction management, environmental engineering technology, environmental health, management, manufacturing, medical imaging and specialty nursing. Most bachelor of technology programs are offered on a part-time basis.

Not all programs are offered every year and students should check with BCIT for the programs being offered in their prospective year.

Cooperative Education at BCIT

BCIT enjoys a strong relationship with industry, which helps support the institute's cooperative education program.

A number of technology and trades programs offer co-op at BCIT. Co-op combines academic and vocational studies with paid work experience and is offered in electronic engineering technology, robotics & automation and renewable resources programs. In some trades programs, cooperative education is an integral part of the program. Each co-op has specific entry requirements.

DISCIPLINES/MAJORS OFFERED

Business: Broadcast Communications, Financial Management, Human Resource Management, International Trade & Transportation, Management, Management Systems, Marketing Management, Operations Management

Computing: Computer Systems

Construction: Building Engineering Technology, Civil & Structural Engineering Technology; Several Trades Specializations Available

Electrical & Electronics: Automation & Instrumentation Technology, Computer Control Technology, Electronic Engineering Technology, Power Technology, Telecommunications Technology; Several Trades Specializations Available

Health Sciences: Biomedical Engineering, Electroneurophysiology, Environmental Health, Medical Laboratory, Medical Radiography, Nuclear Medicine, Nursing, Occupational Health & Safety, Prosthetics & Orthotics

Manufacturing & Industrial/Mechanical: CAD Programming, Mechanical Engineering Technologies, Plastics Technology, Robotics & Automation, Technology Teacher Education, Wood Products Manufacturing; Several Trades Specializations Available

Processing Energy & Natural Resources: Biotechnology, Chemical Sciences Technology, Food Technology, Geomatics Technology, Mining Technology, Petroleum & Natural Gas Technology, Renewable Resources Technology

Transportation: Several Trades Specializations Available

ADMISSIONS CRITERIA & PROCEDURES

Application forms and official supporting documentation should be submitted as early as possible to BCIT's admissions department, due to the limited space available in most programs. Applicants must supply all relevant documents, including a work history (where applicable), with their application package. For admission, most programs require grade 12 graduation, with specific grade 11 and 12 prerequisite courses. Grade 10 is the minimum entrance requirement for some courses; however, employers generally require a grade 12 level of education for employment. BCIT may take appropriate combinations of employment and education into consideration during the admission process. Priority consideration for admission goes to Canadian British Columbia residents. International students should apply for fall courses by October 1 of the previous year.

An applicant who has not graduated from a senior secondary school may be considered for admission as a mature student based on their personal and occupational experience.

For more information students may access the BCIT website at http://www.bcit.bc.ca or contact registration & information by phone 1-604-433-1610.

Admissions at a Glance

Minimum GPA: varies

Minimum English Requirements: varies, TOEFL 500-580 or equivalent

Application Fee: C$30 (Canadian); $200 (international)

Application Deadlines: varies; October 1 (international)

ACADEMIC FACILITIES

The BCIT libraries include the main library of the Burnaby campus and specialized branch libraries at the Pacific Marine Training campus and the Sea Island campus. The main library has a wide variety of books, periodicals, technical reports, video and maps, as well as specialized collections of legal material, standards, Statistics Canada publications and more. The main library also has the latest in computerized information technologies including Internet access and several CD-ROM databases; the ground floor microcomputer centre is for student use in preparing reports and spreadsheets. The Pacific Marine Training Campus library specializes in nautical, marine engineering, marine emergency, radar simulation and ship operations material. The Sea Island library collection specializes in aircraft maintenance and repair, and avionics material. The libraries are also wheelchair accessible and have special needs facilities such as a print-to-voice machine for the visually challenged.

BCIT offers a number of unique facilities including a fire simulation theatre, a fully operational pulp mill, a planetarium, a demonstration forest, a modern radio and television studio, a commercial aircraft hanger with aircraft training facilities and an automated manufacturing robotics lab.

Student & Faculty Profile

Total Enrolment: 44,277

Undergraduate Enrolment: 15,134

# of Faculty: 1,197

Student/Faculty Ratio: 20:1

Male/Female Students: 74%/26%

First-Year Class Sizes: not available

Undergraduate Acceptance Rate: not available

Undergraduate Enrolment by Discipline:

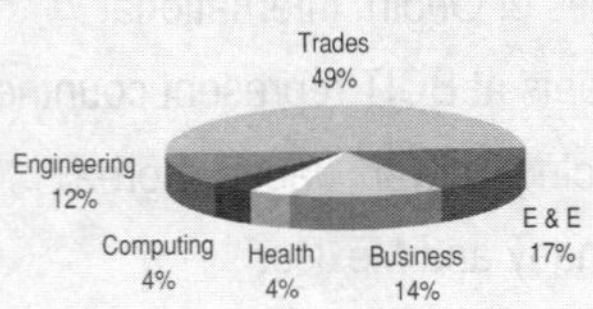

SCHOLARSHIPS & FINANCIAL ASSISTANCE

The British Columbia Student Assistance Program (BCSAP) is the major source of financial aid available to British Columbia residents attending postsecondary study full-time. Students should apply early as it may take up to three months to process applications.

Part-time positions for up to 10 hours a week are available to eligible students who have applied for the BCSAP. Work-study jobs are advertised by the BCIT Employment Placement Services starting in mid-August.

Up to 60 President's Entrance awards are presented annually to students entering BCIT directly from secondary school. The college offers several other types of scholarships. Interested students should contact the Financial Aid and Awards Office for more information.

Expenses at a Glance

Tuition (undergraduate, full-time):

- In-Province: C$2,338/year*
- Out-of-Province: C$2,338/year*
- International: C$4,350/term

Fees, Books, Materials: C$200-2,000/year

Accommodation:

- Private: C$5,650/year
- Residence: C$570/month
- Homestay: C$600/month

Health Insurance: not available

CAMPUS & LOCATION

City Population:	3,000,000
Cost of Living:	high
Climate Range:	0° to 22°C
Campus Setting:	urban
# of Students in Residence:	336

While most students attend classes at the main campus only, BCIT is spread across the Lower Mainland of British Columbia. Burnaby is home to the BCIT's main campus, while Vancouver is home to BCIT's smaller downtown campus. Two specialized campuses, the Sea Island Vancouver International Airport and Pacific Marine Training campuses, are located in Richmond and North Vancouver respectively.

The Burnaby campus is centrally located in the lower mainland, away from the higher density of downtown Vancouver. The Burnaby campus is home to BCIT's residence hall, conveniently located within a five-minute walk from the classrooms. A wide variety of apartments, shared accommodations, basement suites and room and board housing options are also available in the area.

The downtown Vancouver campus is located in the heart of the city's business, entertainment and shopping districts. It is equipped with advanced telecommunications equipment and provides career upgrading and industry training programs. The campus features a research and development facility, an entrepreneurial centre and a computer-aided language lab.

Burnaby, Vancouver, North Vancouver and Richmond are part of the Greater Vancouver Regional District, the largest urban centre on Canada's west coast. Vancouver offers a wide range of occupational and educational opportunities for students seeking to diversify or update their career training. The area is multicultural and cosmopolitan, and offers a wide variety cultural opportunities including art galleries, theatre and excellent shopping. An expanding and modern city, Vancouver is also nestled among outstanding natural surroundings and outdoor enthusiasts will appreciate the easy access to the local forests and mountains.

ATHLETICS & EXTRACURRICULAR ACTIVITIES

The institute's recreation and athletic services offers facilities and programs to help students maintain a balance between the healthy body and the healthy mind. More than 1,200 students participate in eight intramural team sports, use the campus gym, weight and exercise room, and racquetball, squash and tennis courts. BCIT also participates in intercollegiate athletics on teams including badminton, and men's and women's soccer and volleyball.

STUDENT SUPPORT SERVICES

BCIT offers several resources and support services to its large and diverse student population.

BCIT International develops and coordinates international activities with industry, government agencies and other agencies to provide international professional development and study opportunities for students and faculty. BCIT International is also committed to internationalizing the BCIT campus.

The NOW Project coordinates BCIT's services and programs for Youth Works and Welfare to Work program participants and others receiving income assistance. BCIT attempts to offer personal and financial support to students pursuing their career goals.

The First Nations Office provides culturally-appropriate initiatives for aboriginal students to enhance and increase their participation at BCIT.

In addition, BCIT offers services including daycare for three to five year olds, counseling services, a resource centre for students with disabilities and an alumni association. BCIT holds workshops each year on time management, study skills and stress management to aid students returning to study after a long period in the work place.

Institute Recognition

- 80% of technology and trades graduates were employed nine months after graduation
- Provides most of the apprenticeship training in the province of British Columbia

International Students

Institute Enrolment: 611

% of Institute Enrolment: 2%

Countries of Origin: International students at BCIT represent countries including Taiwan, Japan, Korea, Germany and Mexico.

Emily Carr Institute of ART + DESIGN

EMILY CARR INSTITUTE OF ART & DESIGN VANCOUVER, BRITISH COLUMBIA

Institute Mission

...to fuel and nurture

individual and collective

creativity and to make a vital

contribution to society

Student Voice:

Everything you need is here—supportive staff, helpful instructors, facilities and students who come from a wide variety of backgrounds and interests. But Emily Carr is what you make of it—your explorations, your processes and your experiments.

Sylvain Provencher, Design Student

CONTACT INFORMATION

Emily Carr Institute of Art & Design
1399 Johnston Street
Vancouver, British Columbia
Canada V6H 3R9
PH 1-604-844-3800
FAX 1-604-844-3089
EMAIL admissions@eciad.bc.ca
INTERNET http://www.eciad.bc.ca

INSTITUTE OVERVIEW

Emily Carr Institute of Art & Design (Emily Carr) is an intimate, progressive institute offering programs that lead to Bachelor of Fine Arts (BFA), Bachelor of Media Arts (BMA) and Bachelor of Design (BDes) degrees and four-year diplomas.

Programs at Emily Carr begin with a Foundation year, which provides students with a common knowledge and skill base. This general training is followed by three years of specialized study in the School of Design, the School of Media Arts or the School of Visual Arts.

Emily Carr students are encouraged to take creative risks, to experiment with ideas and materials, and to engage themselves in contemporary art, media and design issues. Courses in critical studies encourage students to formulate an informed perspective on their professional practice. Critical Studies courses are offered in the history and theory of art, media or design; cultural studies; humanities; social sciences; and sciences.

Emily Carr also offers noncredit courses and programs through the School of Continuing & Networked Education. The school is currently developing curricula in international cyberexchanges, online credit course delivery and networked art, media and design access.

In addition, Emily Carr offers internships, co-ops and directed studies on a limited basis.

Highlights

- Personalized teaching environment; student-to-faculty ratios of about 15 to one
- Students are encouraged to experiment with interdisciplinary projects and ideas
- Beautiful and convenient campus close to all Vancouver amenities

Institute Statistics

Year Founded: 1925

Academic Options: diploma/undergraduate

Calendar Year: September-April; summer term (Jun-Aug)

School of Visual Arts

Programs in this school allow students to explore the diversity of contemporary art practices, and provide students with an awareness of historical precedents. The school emphasizes the development of technical proficiency and the importance of the theoretical aspects of artistic processes and production.

School of Media Arts

Media arts students are encouraged to develop an innovative and experimental media practice that includes time-based image and sound, performance and installation, or electronic, digital, and film-based technologies.

School of Design

Design students research current and emerging design issues, and develop skills in all phases of the design process through the use of advanced media, methodologies and technologies. Individual initiative and collaborative teamwork are encouraged.

International Focus

Emily Carr welcomes applicants from other countries and also has exchange agreements with 25 art and design schools in North America, Europe and Australia. Second-year students may apply to spend one semester of their third year at an overseas institute, working towards transferable credits for their Emily Carr degree program.

ACADEMIC PROGRAMS

School of Continuing & Networked Education: Certificate Programs; Networked Education; Professional Development; Transition Program in the Arts

School of Design: Communication Design; Industrial Design

School of Foundation & Critical Studies: Cultural Studies; English; First-Year Studio Courses; History and Theory of Art, Media and Design; Humanities; Science; Social Sciences

School of Media Arts: Animation; Integrated Media (Film, Intermedia, Video); Photography

School of Visual Arts: Visual Arts (Ceramics, Drawing, Painting, Printmaking, Sculpture)

ADMISSIONS CRITERIA & PROCEDURES

Candidates for admission to Emily Carr must include in their application dossier a completed application form, a C$30 application fee, official transcripts of all secondary and postsecondary schools attended, and a 250-word essay describing employment and educational history as it relates to their interests in art, media and/or design. The portfolio must be submitted no later than the deadline indicated on the application form. Students applying to the School of Foundation & Critical Studies must submit a portfolio of 15 to 20 pieces and a special project. Foundation students are not interviewed. If applicants are applying to transfer to second or third year they must submit a portfolio of 20 to 25 pieces and may be invited to attend an admission interview.

Applications for full-time study beginning in September must be submitted by March 1, with portfolio submission before May 1; applications for part-time study beginning in January must be submitted by October 15. International applicants wishing to begin full-time study in September may submit applications and portfolios as early as the preceding November 1 and receive an early admissions decision (normally by January 31).

General admission requires a high school GPA of at least 2.5, with an English requirement for international students of TOEFL 570 (paper-based), or 230 (computer-based). Effective 2000-2001 British Columbia high school applicants will require a C+ average on four grade 12 subjects including grade 12 English and one additional provincially examinable course.

There is no quota on international admissions at Emily Carr; each applicant is assessed based on their admissions portfolio and academic background.

Emily Carr will consider admission under a mature student category if applicants are 21 years of age or older and have been away from formal education for at least one year.

It is now possible to apply to Emily Carr online through BC's postsecondary system application system at http://www.pas.bc.ca.

Admissions at a Glance

Minimum GPA: 2.5 (for year 2000)

Minimum English Requirements:

TOEFL 570 (paper-based); TOEFL 230 (computer-based)

Application Fee: C$30 (Canadian and international)

Application Deadlines: October 15 (January admission, part-time); March 1 (September admission)

Student & Faculty Profile

Total Enrolment: 1,600

Undergraduate Enrolment: 945

# of Faculty: 123

Student/Faculty Ratio: 15:1

Male/Female Students: 40%/60%

First-Year Class Sizes: 15 (studio classes); 30 (academic)

Undergraduate Acceptance Rate: 33%

Undergraduate Enrolment by Discipline:

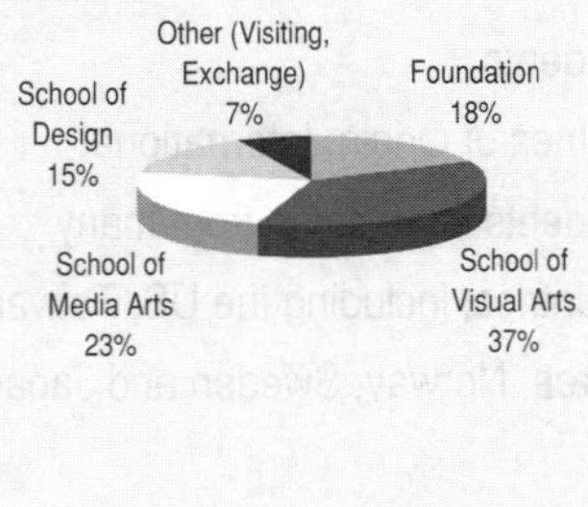

ACADEMIC FACILITIES

Emily Carr is equipped with modern facilities in a broad range of technological and art/media/design-related areas. Facilities include design, printmaking, ceramics, and painting studios; a new library; computer and photography labs; indoor and outdoor sculpture areas; woodshops; and galleries. The galleries offer students the opportunity to show their work to the general public, and to assemble and maintain functional and professional gallery space.

SCHOLARSHIPS & FINANCIAL ASSISTANCE

Students who have completed one full term at Emily Carr are eligible to compete for available scholarships. The scholarship program is administered by the Financial Awards Office in Student Services. Eligible students may participate in Emily Carr's co-op program, earning paid work experience while completing their degrees.

Expenses at a Glance

Tuition (undergraduate, full-time):

In-Province: C$2,520/year

Out-of-Province: C$2,520/year

International: C$9,222/year

Fees, Books, Materials: C$2,000/year

Accommodation:

Private: C$1,000/month

Residence: n/a

Homestay: n/a

Health Insurance: C$35/month (approx)

CAMPUS & LOCATION

City Population:	2,000,000
Cost of Living:	high
Climate Range:	0° to 32°C
Campus Setting:	urban
# of Students in Residence:	n/a

Emily Carr is located in two modern buildings with large, light-filled painting studios, a new library, computer labs, exceptional photography labs, printmaking studios, a ceramics studio, indoor and outdoor sculpture areas, woodshops, design studios, classrooms and galleries.

There is no student housing at Emily Carr; the city of Vancouver offers extensive housing options, with apartments, suites and shared housing readily available in the nearby downtown area, as well as in quieter residential areas accessible by the city's first-rate transportation system. Student Services offers assistance to applicants seeking housing.

The campus of Emily Carr is situated on popular Granville Island in the False Creek harbour, in view of the Northshore mountains and the downtown skyline. Granville Island is home to a bustling market, and a variety of restaurants and theatres

Vancouver is the unofficial capital of western Canada, and offers a cosmopolitan mix of recreational and cultural activities. Located on the edge of both the Pacific Ocean and the Coastal mountains, the city is perfect for skiers, hikers and nature lovers of all types. Vancouver has become a shopping mecca, and offers world-class art galleries, restaurants, cafes, theatres and the renowned Museum of Anthropology. Vancouver's ideal location on the Pacific Rim lends to easy international travel; situated only an hour from the US border, Vancouver also offers convenient access to Seattle, Washington.

ATHLETICS & EXTRACURRICULAR ACTIVITIES

Students at Emily Carr regularly participate in extracurricular field trips, attend artist lectures, mount and maintain exhibits, attend gallery showings and host performance nights.

Students at Emily Carr have access to the athletic opportunities and recreational amenities of downtown Vancouver. The Aquatics Centre is adjacent to Granville Island; nearby Vanier Park offers scenic, relaxing walking trails; Stanley Park's 10 kilometres of seawall provides a refreshing break and stunning vistas.

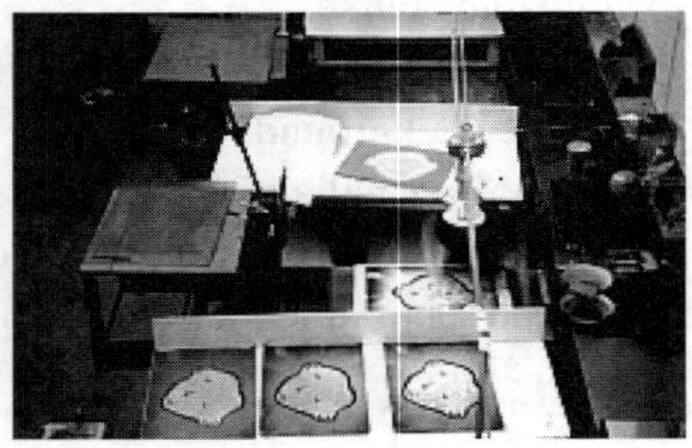

STUDENT SUPPORT SERVICES

Emily Carr staff assist students with academic, personal and career-related issues and questions. The institute has an on-site counsellor to deal with student concerns and to advise students who need help with their academic performance. The institute also has a Prior Learning Assessment Coordinator who can help accepted students earn credit for nonformal education and experience.

A Learning Centre provides assistance to students seeking to develop their essay writing skills. Student Services offers advising to students with disabilities, First Nations students and international students.

As there is no student housing at the campus, Emily Carr's Student Services helps new international students find accommodation in the city.

Students at Emily Carr are represented by the Students' Union Association which supports many student activities and lobbies for student interests on both a local and national level.

Emily Carr students publish Planet of the Arts, a monthly newspaper with information and articles of interest to the student body and to the general public.

Institute Recognition

- Funded by the provincial government of British Columbia
- Mandated by the British Columbia government to grant Bachelor of Fine Arts, Bachelor of Media Arts and Bachelor of Design degrees
- Associate member of the Association of Independent Colleges of Art & Design (AICAD) in North America

International Students

Institute Enrolment: 45

% of Institute Enrolment: 5% of full-time students

Countries of Origin: International students have come from many countries, including the US, Taiwan, Korea, Norway, Sweden and Japan.

PROFILES OF Universities & Colleges IN The Prairie Provinces

Universities

IN

The Prairie Provinces

BRANDON UNIVERSITY
BRANDON, MANITOBA

University Mission

...to provide a personalized learner-centred environment, offering high-quality programs of teaching and research; to prepare students for academic, career and personal success

Student Voice:

I decided to attend Brandon University because the education program had an excellent reputation. Because of the size, I have found that professors are always willing to take time to help students and it is easy to meet fellow students in your class.

Cheri Hassleer
Education Program
Fifth-year student

CONTACT INFORMATION
Admissions Office
Brandon University
270-18th Street
Brandon, Manitoba
Canada R7A 6A9
PH 1-204-727-9784
FAX 1-204-725-2143
EMAIL admissions@brandonu.ca
INTERNET http://www.brandonu.ca

UNIVERSITY OVERVIEW

Brandon University (BU) is a coeducational, nondenominational, government-supported institution and a member of the Association of Universities & Colleges of Canada. BU was founded in 1899 by the Baptist Convention of Manitoba as Brandon College, and was chartered in 1967 on the occasion of the visit of Her Royal Highness Princess Alexandra.

As a small university, BU offers personalized classes (between 10 and 50 students per class) with a student-to-teacher ratio of 10 to 1. BU has made notable contributions to agriculture, athletics, business, the professions and government, and is a national leader in the fields of adult, First Nations and distance education.

Academic Programs

The Faculties of Arts, Science and Education and the Schools of Music and Health Studies offer over 40 major and minor programs. Most undergraduate degrees require the successful completion of 90 credit hours or three years of study, though a few undergraduate programs are four or five years in duration. BU also offers two-year postdiploma programs in nursing & mental health.

Students pursuing graduate-level studies may earn a Master of Music, Education or Rural Development.

Preprofessional Programs

BU offers preprofessional programs in agriculture, chiropractic studies, dentistry, dental hygiene, engineering, journalism, law, management studies, medicine, occupational therapy, optometry, pharmacy, physiotherapy, recreation studies, rehabilitation medicine, social work, speech therapy and veterinary medicine. BU has a high placement rate into graduate and professional schools.

General Studies

Recognizing the need for program flexibility in baccalaureate studies, BU has developed a Bachelor of General Studies (BGS). The program's objective is to provide greater accessibility to the university through diversification, innovation and transferability. The BGS program was established in 1972 and is three years in length (90 credit hours). The BGS program has no major or minor requirements, no required liberal education curriculum and (with some exceptions) no limits upon the academic area or specific faculties in which courses may be taken.

International students with an International Baccalaurate (IB) degree may transfer up to 30 credit hours towards their BGS degree.

Highlights

- Low student-to-teacher ratio
- A safe community
- Personalized instruction
- An English for Academic Purposes program offered
- Comprehensive student services
- Exchange programs

University Statistics

Year Founded: 1899 (chartered in 1967)

Academic Options: undergraduate/graduate

Calendar Year: fall term (Sept-Dec); spring term (Jan-Apr)

DISCIPLINES/MAJORS OFFERED

Faculty of Arts: Aboriginal & Visual Arts, Anthropology, Business Administration, Canadian Studies, Classical & Modern Languages (French, German, Native Languages and others), Drama, Economics, English, Geography, History, Native Studies, Philosophy, Political Science, Psychology, Religion, Rural & Community Studies, Sociology, Women's Studies

Faculty of Education: Early Years/Childhood Education, Middle Years, Native Education, Senior Years (High School), Teaching English as a Second Language

Faculty of Science: Botany, Chemistry, Computer Science, Geography, Geology, Mathematics, Physics & Astronomy, Psychology, Zoology

School of Health Studies: Nursing, Mental Health, Psychiatric Nursing

School of Music: Applied Music, General Music, Music Education

ADMISSIONS CRITERIA & PROCEDURES

All applicants must complete an application form and return it to the Admissions Office, accompanied by the C$35 nonrefundable application fee; applications should include official copies of all secondary and, if applicable, postsecondary transcripts.

Students whose first language is not English are required to submit minimum TOEFL scores of 550, MELAB scores of 80 or IELTS scores of 6.5. International students should supply notarized English translations of all documents, where applicable. International visa students must also provide evidence of sufficient funds to cover their first year of university costs.

Admissions at a Glance

Minimum GPA: Manitoba: high school diploma; others: 60-65% avg

Minimum English Requirements:

TOEFL 550, MELAB 80 or IELTS 6.5

Application Fee: C$35 (Canadian and international)

Application Deadlines: rolling admissions

ACADEMIC FACILITIES

The John E. Robbins Library houses books, journals, microforms, sound and video recordings, and other nonprint materials. The library is a depository for both national and provincial government publications. The library catalogue, while enabling students to access the library's holdings, also acts as a gateway (via the Internet) to other campus libraries' catalogues, databases and information sources.

BU has 160 PCs in public access labs, providing students with modern computer facilities and personalized accounts. BU's network serves as a gateway to the Internet and the World Wide Web, to which students have unlimited access. Students use up-to-date software packages to operate their email accounts. Available software ranges from word-processing packages to statistical and office automation packages.

A learning skills specialist is available to address a wide range of topics that are directly related to students' success at university: taking lecture notes, organizing study, reading (or processing) text materials, creating conceptual maps, and preparing for and taking tests and examinations.

The university offers a peer-tutoring service that may provide students with a faculty-approved tutor for most first- and second-year courses.

The Writing Centre helps students with the following writing activities: learning and practising different stages of the essay research, writing and referencing process; developing and rehearsing basic writing skills; and completing course assignments.

Many departments and schools provide additional learning resources specific to their discipline, ranging from language laboratories, to computer equipment and software, to greenhouses, to seminars and tutorials.

Student & Faculty Profile

Total Enrolment: 2,605

Undergraduate Enrolment: 2,555

# of Faculty: 200

Student/Faculty Ratio: 10:1

Male/Female Students: 37%/63%

First-Year Class Sizes: 10-50

Undergraduate Acceptance Rate: 80%

Undergraduate Enrolment by Discipline:

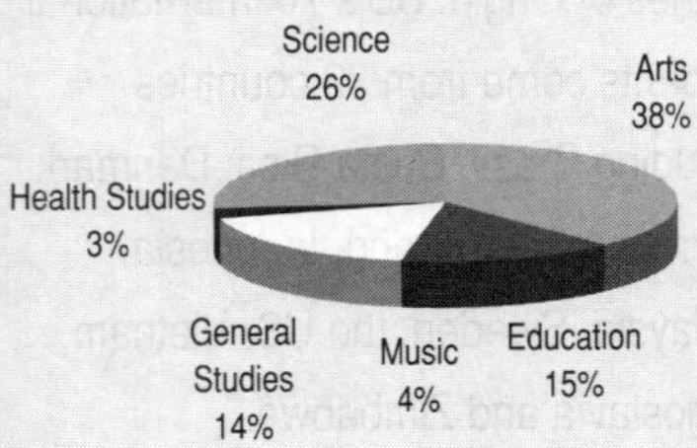

SCHOLARSHIPS & FINANCIAL ASSISTANCE

A number of entrance scholarships, bursaries and loans are available for Canadian students at BU. University entrance awards are open to all students graduating from an accredited Canadian high school who have a minimum 80 per cent average upon graduation. Scholarships, awards and bursaries are intended to alleviate the financial stress of university tuition, books and fees during the regular academic sessions.

International students studying in Canada are not eligible for student loans offered by the Canadian government. After their first year at BU, international students may become eligible for university scholarships, awarded on the basis of academic performance.

Expenses at a Glance

Tuition (undergraduate, full-time):

In-Province: C$2,808-3,050/year

Out-of-Province: C$2,808-3,050/year

International: C$4,914/year

Fees, Books, Materials: C$900/year

Accommodation:

Private: C$500+/month

Residence: C$3,400-4,100/year

Homestay: C$550/month

Health Insurance: C$350/year

CAMPUS & LOCATION

City Population:	40,000
Cost of Living:	low
Climate Range:	-24° to 26°C
Campus Setting:	suburban
# of Students in Residence:	300

The city of Brandon has the safe, community feeling of a small town with the convenience and amenities of a large city. Brandon is located in the southwestern corner of Manitoba, in central Canada. Manitoba experiences four distinct seasons with hot, sunny summers and snowy winters. BU is situated on a landscaped campus among some of Brandon's most attractive residential neighbourhoods and scenic avenues.

For those international students who want to learn as much as possible about Canada and the English language, BU's homestay program provides students with the option of living with a Canadian family in Brandon.

BU provides residences for 300 undergraduate students in three separate residence halls including McMaster (coeducational), Darrach (men) and Flora Cowan (women). All three residence halls are connected to the main dining room by glass-enclosed links; the majority of the rooms are double occupancy.

ATHLETICS & EXTRACURRICULAR ACTIVITIES

BU's intercollegiate teams are known as the Bobcats; currently, these teams compete in hockey and women's and men's basketball. BU participates in interconference and international competitions in the US and other countries, and as a member of the Canadian Inter-University Athletic Union can compete at the national level in a variety of sports.

BU's Campus Recreation (BUCR) provides a wide variety of recreational activities for students, faculty, staff and BUFIT members. BUCR's structured activities include coed slow pitch baseball, volleyball, basketball, floor hockey and badminton; men's touch football and ice hockey; and women's soccer and handball. Informal fitness activities such as swimming, skating, racquetball, aerobics and exercising in the hydra or fitness gyms are all available.

STUDENT SUPPORT SERVICES

Personal, academic and career counselling are available to all students at BU. The personal and academic counselling services provide professional support to those students in need of assistance with their personal or educational relationships. The career counselling service helps students decide on a major, and provides advice regarding higher education planning. The Careers Planning & Placement Office posts employment opportunities on its job board, holds resume- and cover letter–writing workshops, and provides a resource centre with job market information.

BU offers a 12-week immersion English for Academic Purposes (EAP) program that is designed to benefit international students who are preparing to study at an English language university. It also offers advanced levels of study for students who want to improve their writing and speaking skills for professional or personal reasons. The EAP classes help students prepare for the TOEFL, MELAB or IELTS proficiency exams.

University Recognition

- Accredited by the Association of Universities & Colleges in Canada (AUCC) and the Association of Commonwealth Universities (ACU)
- A national leader in the fields of adult, First Nations and distance education
- One of the most affordable universities in North America

International Students

University Enrolment: 70

% of University Enrolment: 3%

Countries of Origin: BU's 70 international students come from 32 countries including Brazil, Costa Rica, Denmark, Germany, Hong Kong, Indonesia, Malaysia, Sweden, the US, Vietnam, Yugoslavia and Zimbabwe.

University of Alberta
Edmonton, Alberta
Canada

UNIVERSITY OF ALBERTA EDMONTON, ALBERTA

University Mission

...to serve our community by the dissemination of knowledge through teaching and the discovery of knowledge through research

Student Voice:

I will remember my time at the University of Alberta by the friends that I made, many of whom will be friends for life.

Kevin Barr
Law Student

CONTACT INFORMATION
Office of the Registrar & Student Awards
University of Alberta
120 Administration Building
Edmonton, Alberta
Canada T6C 2M7
PH 1-403-492-3113
FAX 1-403-492-7172
EMAIL registrar@ualberta.ca
INTERNET
http://www.registrar.ualberta.ca

UNIVERSITY OVERVIEW

The University of Alberta (U of A) takes pride in its 90 year history of creating and disseminating knowledge. It is building upon its tradition of excellence with the view "to be indisputably recognized, nationally and internationally, as one of Canada's finest universities." U of A's priorities are to attract and retain outstanding scholars, to attract and develop outstanding students and to maintain and expand a first-class learning environment.

Study at the University of Alberta

In most U of A programs students will pursue a major area of concentration within their chosen program; some programs also offer minor areas of concentration. In addition to regular academic programs, U of A offers many professional programs which require a year or more of preprofessional study.

Graduate programs are available at both the master's and doctoral levels.

Graduate degrees are offered by 62 of the university's departments in almost 200 fields of study.

Off-Campus Options

Offering the only French language university degree programs west of Manitoba, Faculté St-Jean is a self-contained academic community for students pursuing undergraduate arts, science and education programs. Faculté St-Jean offers the first two years of the Bilingual BCom program, which enables students to develop fluency in both of Canada's official languages while earning a business degree.

Research Capabilities

Since 1988, the university has attracted more than C$777 million in research funding from external sources. In addition, it stands third in the nation among postsecondary institutions attracting grants from the Natural Sciences & Engineering Council and is among the top five in funding from the Medical Research Council.

International Focus

U of A students can add an international dimension to their education through the International Centre, which organizes overseas study terms. Students can spend either a term or a year studying overseas while paying U of A tuition and fees.

Highlights

- A comprehensive research institution attracting more than C$777 million in outside research funding
- Over 5,000 classes offered per year
- The second largest university library system in Canada
- U of A participates in all 14 of the Canadian Networks of Centres of Excellence

University Statistics

Year Founded: 1906
Academic Options: undergraduate/graduate
Calendar Year: fall semester (Sept-Dec); winter semester (Jan-Apr); spring/summer (May-Aug)

DISCIPLINES/MAJORS OFFERED

U of A offers more than 300 undergraduate degree programs, including programs in the following areas.

Faculty of Agriculture, Forestry & Home Economics
Faculty of Arts
Faculty of Business
Faculty of Education
Faculty of Engineering
Faculty of Extension
Faculty of Graduate Studies & Research
Faculty of Law
Faculty of Medicine & Dentistry
Faculty of Nursing
Faculty of Pharmacy & Pharmaceutical Sciences
Faculty of Physical Education & Recreation
Faculty of Rehabilitation Medicine
Faculty of Science
Faculté St-Jean
School of Native Studies

ADMISSIONS CRITERIA & PROCEDURES

Admissions to undergraduate programs at U of A are divided into two categories: direct entry programs and programs requiring preprofessional study. Eligible students may be admitted to direct entry programs without previous postsecondary experience. Programs requiring preprofessional study are generally started after at least one year of preprofessional study in courses specified in the professional course's admissions regulations. Admissions requirements may vary considerably by program; students are advised to consult the U of A calendar or the Office of the Registrar & Student Awards for more information on specific programs.

Students whose first language is not English may be required to submit a minimum TOEFL score of 580 (paper-based) or 237 (computer-based) depending on their educational history. Applicants to the Faculté St-Jean must demonstrate French language proficiency.

Application deadline for admission to programs beginning in the fall semester is generally May 1, but may vary by faculty. Few faculties at U of A admit new students for the winter semester or intersession; the application deadlines for those faculties that do admit students at these times are November 15 and March 1 respectively. All faculties accept applications via the Internet at http://www.registrar.ualberta.ca/admissions/undergrad.

Admissions at a Glance

Minimum GPA: varies (65-70%)

Minimum English Requirements:
- TOEFL 580 (paper-based), 237 (computer-based)

Application Fee: C$60 (Canadian and international)

Application Deadlines: fall semester (May 1); winter semester (November 15); intersession (March 1)

ACADEMIC FACILITIES

U of A's library system is the second largest in Canada, with a total collection of more than five million volumes, over one million maps and more than 26,000 serial subscriptions; a vast array of audiovisual resources and research materials in microform are also available. The collection is spread across 10 libraries, which house general or specific collections.

The university's Computing & Network Services issues computing accounts to students and offers 20 computer labs equipped with nearly 600 computers. Most computer labs are available for general student use; several specialized workstations are also available for advanced work. U of A is implementing several initiatives to develop and exploit new information and telecommunication technologies.

Student & Faculty Profile

Total Enrolment: 30,000

Undergraduate Enrolment: 25,000

# of Faculty: 2,239

Student/Faculty Ratio: 15:1

Male/Female Students: not available

First-Year Class Sizes: 15-250

Undergraduate Acceptance Rate: varies

Undergraduate Enrolment by Discipline:

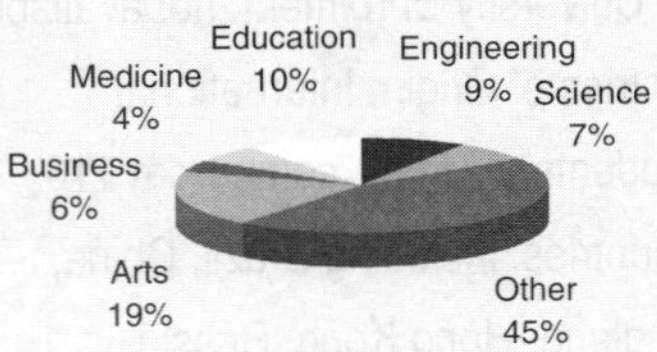

SCHOLARSHIPS & FINANCIAL ASSISTANCE

Six types of scholarships are available at U of A for entering undergraduates. These include academic excellence scholarships, international baccalaureate diploma scholarships and academic entrance scholarships. There are over 5,500 scholarships, valued at over C$8 million, available annually to undergraduates at the U of A.

Students at U of A can seek financial assistance through provincial and federal student loans by applying before May 31 for assistance beginning in the fall term. The Financial Aid & Information Centre can help students with student loan concerns or financial questions.

Expenses at a Glance

Tuition (undergraduate, full-time):
- In-Province: C$3,700/year
- Out-of-Province: C$3,700/year
- International: C$7,400/year

Fees, Books, Materials: C$800/year

Accommodation:
- Private: C$200-450/month
- Residence: C$375/month
- Homestay: n/a

Health Insurance: required

CAMPUS & LOCATION

City Population:	850,000
Cost of Living:	medium
Climate Range:	-15° to 25°C
Campus Setting:	urban
# of Students in Residence:	2,400

The University of Alberta's 89-hecare main campus borders the North Saskatchewan River and is located 3 kilometres southwest of downtown Edmonton. There are almost 100 buildings on campus, and parking is available for 7,500 vehicles. The university holds an additional 5,000 hectares of land for research and conservation activities.

U of A is just minutes from the Ribbon of Green, North America's longest system of parks and trails, where Edmontonians can be found cycling, jogging, walking and relaxing. The university is connected to all areas of the city by an extensive system of buses and Light Rail Transit (LRT). Edmonton, the capital of Alberta, has been identified as one of the Canada's "Smart Cities" and offers students a wide variety of cultural events, including the Edmonton Folk Festival and the largest Fringe Festival in Canada. The city is home to the largest shopping and entertainment complex in Canada, the West Edmonton Mall.

Edmonton is centrally located in the province and is easily accessed via the Edmonton International Airport. Edmonton is just a few hours' drive from the spectacular Rocky Mountains and its countless opportunities for outdoor recreation.

ATHLETICS & EXTRACURRICULAR ACTIVITIES

All U of A students are eligible to participate in the university's wide variety of recreation programs. Over 20,000 students and staff register annually in Campus Recreation programs, which include skating, swimming, soccer, snooker and a long list of other activities. Men's, women's and co-ed intramural programs are available in sports such as inner-tube water polo, basketball, volleyball and others. Noncredit classes are offered in subjects ranging from dance to weight training. The Campus Outdoor Centre allows students to take advantage of a wide range of outdoor goods for rent including equipment for camping, mountaineering, water sports, cross-country skiing, in-line skating or cycling. The Campus Outdoor Centre also maintains the U of A Climbing Wall, which is available for use at an hourly rate.

U of A has 17 intercollegiate teams that all full-time students are welcome to try out for. The U of A Pandas (women's teams) and Golden Bears (men's teams) compete in basketball, hockey, football, soccer, track & field, cross-country, swimming, volleyball and wrestling. Students can also choose to participate in any number of U of A's 250 student clubs, including academic, cultural, recreational, public service, fraternity, sport and special interest clubs.

University Recognition

- U of A holds the highest number of 3M Teaching Award winners in the country
- U of A stands third in the nation in attracting grants from the Natural Sciences & Engineering Research Council
- First place in the CIAU Academic All-Canadian Standing

STUDENT SUPPORT SERVICES

The International Centre provides support for international students through a variety of services. Centre staff contact international students upon admission, mail predeparture information packages, and arrange a student orientation upon arrival. The centre provides ongoing financial, academic and personal advice and support for international students.

In addition to its services for international students, U of A offers career and placement services, several student advisers, native student services, services for students with disabilities, student counselling services, a university health centre and an academic support centre.

International Students

University Enrolment: not available

% of University Enrolment: not available

Countries of Origin: International students at U of A come from 110 countries, including Brazil, China, England, Hong Kong, Russia, Singapore and the USA.

UNIVERSITY OF CALGARY
CALGARY, ALBERTA

University Mission

...to seek truth and to disseminate knowledge...to combine the best of long-established university traditions with the freshness, originality and independence of the Calgary environment

Student Voice:

I really enjoyed the professors here. They see you more as colleagues than students. There can be great two-way dialogues and exchanges of ideas.

Yvan Botteron
Master's Student, Electrical Engineering

CONTACT INFORMATION

Prospective Student Office
University of Calgary
Room 135, MacKimmie Library Block
2500 University Drive NW
Calgary, Alberta
Canada T2N 1N4
PH 1-403-220-6920
FAX 1-403-210-0043
EMAIL uofcinfo@acs.ucalgary.ca
INTERNET http://www.ucalgary.ca

UNIVERSITY OVERVIEW

Established as a degree-granting institution in 1966, University of Calgary (U of C) is recognized for its innovative teaching and research activities. Its award-winning faculty, of which 29 members have been elected to the prestigious Royal Society of Canada, attracted nearly C$80 million in research funding in 1998.

Academic Programs

U of C's 16 faculties contain more than 60 academic departments and major program areas. At the undergraduate level, students choose from bachelor's degrees in arts, commerce, community rehabilitation, fine arts, general studies, kinesiology, music, nursing, science and social work. With the exception of the Bachelor of General Studies, all bachelor's degrees require students to complete a minimum of 20 full courses, normally over a four-year period.

Programs offered by the Faculty of Education leading to certification as an elementary or as a secondary school teacher are normally restricted to students who already possess an undergraduate degree, preferably with at least three years of study in the liberal arts or sciences.

In addition to its undergraduate programs, U of C offers more than 70 programs leading to master's degrees and over 40 doctoral programs as well as professional programs in medicine, law and environmental design.

Co-op and internship programs are offered in more than 35 areas of study and typically extend studies by one year.

Interdisciplinary Study

Collaborative programs include kinesiology & fine arts (dance studies), and environmental & earth sciences. Students may combine a BComm with a BSc in actuarial sciences or with a BA in humanities or social sciences. The Faculty of Engineering offers joint degrees with the Faculties of Fine Arts, Humanities, and Social Sciences, leading to a BSc/BA.

General Studies

The Faculty of General Studies offers first- and second-year students the opportunity to explore their academic options before transferring to a program in science, social work, social sciences, management, or humanities. Students may also opt to complete a three-year non-major degree.

Internationalism

Students from over 80 countries attend U of C. The university also has agreements with hundreds of universities worldwide and offers its students study-abroad and exchange programs in most areas of study.

Highlights

- Young university with a dynamic and innovative approach to learning
- More than 150 exchange programs with universities worldwide
- Wide variety of programs at both undergraduate and graduate levels

University Statistics

Year Founded: 1966
Academic Options: undergraduate/graduate
Calendar Year: fall semester (Sept-Dec); winter semester (Jan-Apr); spring session (May-Jun); summer session (Jul-Aug)

DISCIPLINES/MAJORS OFFERED

Faculty of Education: Community Rehabilitation; Early Childhood Educ; Elementary; Secondary

Faculty of Engineering: Chemical; Civil; Electrical; Geomatics; Manufacturing; Mechanical, Oil & Gas Production

Faculty of Environmental Design

Faculty of Fine Arts: Art Educ; Art History; Dance; Dev't Art; Drama

Faculty of General Studies: Cdn Studies; Communication; Dev't Studies; Law & Society; Leisure & Tourism; Science & Tech; Urban Studies; Women's Studies

Faculty of Graduate Studies

Faculty of Humanities: Ancient & Medieval History; Ethics; Early Christian Study; Classics; English; French; German; Russian; Spanish; Philosophy; Religious Studies

Faculty of Kinesiology: Biomechanics; Exercise & Health Physiology; Mind Sci; Outdoor Pursuits; Pedagogy

Faculty of Law

Faculty of Management: Accounting; Finance & Operations; Organizations & HR; Info Systems; Marketing; Policy & Env

Faculty of Nursing

Faculty of Science: Astrophysics; Bio Science; Botany; Chem; Comp Sci; Earth Sci; Ecology; Env Sci; Geology; Geophysics; Math & Stats; Physics; Zoology

Faculty of Social Sciences: Anthropology; Archaeology; Economics; Geography; History; Linguistics; Political Science; Psychology

Faculty of Social Work

ADMISSIONS CRITERIA & PROCEDURES

Students who wish to apply to U of C should contact the Prospective Student Office or visit the university's website for an application form. High school applicants must show satisfactory standing in five appropriate grade 12 subjects or their equivalents from other provinces or countries. The Faculty of General Studies requires an average of at least 70 per cent in these five subjects. Transfer applicants are considered for admission based primarily on their previous performance at a university or college. Applicants who wish to transfer from another postsecondary institution may be eligible to receive credit towards their U of C degrees; consideration is on a course-by-course basis. Higher averages may be required for programs with limited enrolment. Students interested in science, social work, social sciences, management or humanities begin in the general studies program and enter their chosen program or major in their second or third year. Applicants interested in fine arts, nursing, kinesiology or engineering should apply directly to those faculties; admission averages vary according to faculties. International students' grades will be equated to an Alberta standard; students must meet an English proficiency requirement of TOEFL 560 (or TOEFL 550 with a minimum 5.0 TWE) or an IELTS 7.0. International students must submit their applications by April 1; all official transcripts must be forwarded to the Office of the Registrar no later than May 31. Foreign students should direct enquiries to the International Admissions Officer in the Registrar's Office. Students will receive application packages for residence in their notification of acceptance to U of C.

Admissions at a Glance

Minimum GPA: 65-80%

Minimum English Requirements:
TOEFL 560, IELTS 7.0

Application Fee: C$65 (Canadian and international)

Application Deadlines: January 15 (outdoor pursuits); April 1 (international students; all applicants to dance & music); May 1 (engineering, kinesiology); June 1 (fine arts, general studies, nursing)

ACADEMIC FACILITIES

MacKimmie Library at U of C is one of the largest university libraries in Canada. It contains more than two million books, journals and other print materials, and 2.7 million microforms. The university also houses libraries that specialize in geology & geophysics, law, management, medicine and teaching resources. Computing facilities for U of C include seven mainframe computers that support more than 5,000 terminals, as well as several dozen computer labs throughout the campus. Computing Services provides an extensive support system for its users. The university also has a large biological field station and an astrophysical observatory.

Student & Faculty Profile

Total Enrolment: 23,638

Undergraduate Enrolment: 20,472

# of Faculty: 1,754

Student/Faculty Ratio: 15:1 (approx)

Male/Female Students: 47%/53%

First-Year Class Sizes: 25-100

Undergraduate Acceptance Rate: 75%

Undergraduate Enrolment by Discipline:

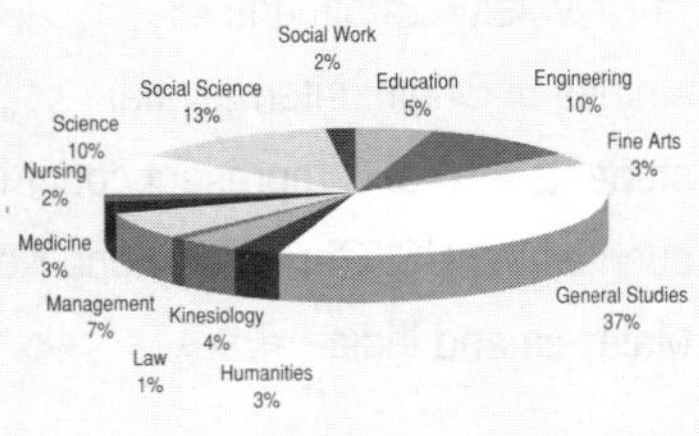

SCHOLARSHIPS & FINANCIAL ASSISTANCE

U of C awards over C$4 million to undergraduate students every year. Some entrance scholarships are awarded based on students' outstanding academic achievement and exceptional contributions to their high schools and communities; other awards are based on the academic merit and financial need of entering high school students, as well as transfer and continuing students. In addition, more than C$1 million in bursaries is offered to help control student debt. International students may compete for scholarships on the basis of academic merit after their first year of studies. Students should contact the Student Awards & Financial Aid Office for further information.

Expenses at a Glance

Tuition (undergraduate, full-time):
In-Province: C$3,841/year*
Out-of-Province: C$3,841/year*
International: C$7,682/year*

Fees, Books, Materials: C$1,200/year

Accommodation:
Private: C$500-800/month
Residence: C$2,045-5,180/year
Homestay: n/a

Health Insurance: C$408/year (int'l)

CAMPUS & LOCATION

City Population:	828,500
Cost of Living:	medium
Climate Range:	-16° to 23°C
Campus Setting:	suburban
# of Students in Residence:	1,400

University of Calgary's 123-hectare campus comprises 18 modern academic buildings, most of which are connected by covered walkways. U of C's campus offers beautiful vistas of the snow-capped Rocky Mountains and boasts a wide selection of excellent facilities, many of which were built for the 1988 winter Olympics. Among U of C's on-campus facilities are art studios, theatres, a concert hall, a museum, an art gallery and a daycare centre.

Residence services include 1,600 spaces in seven traditional and apartment-style residence halls, 250 townhouse family units and accommodation for students with disabilities. Students in residence may choose from four different meal plans. Students who choose to live off campus may take advantage of Calgary's efficient, reliable public transportation.

Calgary, with its population of 800,000 people, is safe, friendly, multicultural and cosmopolitan. The petroleum capital of Canada, Calgary is a rapidly growing, high-technology city offering a wide array of cultural facilities. The city's four distinct seasons support superb outdoor recreational opportunities. Calgary's proximity to the majestic Rocky Mountains and Banff National Park provides students with year-round natural beauty and access to world-class skiing, hiking, photography, fishing and camping. Calgary is also renowned for its annual Stampede, which celebrates the city's western heritage and attracts thousands of tourists each year.

ATHLETICS & EXTRACURRICULAR ACTIVITIES

U of C has one of the most competitive varsity programs of all Canadian universities. The U of C Dinosaurs compete in both the Canada West University Athletic Association (CWUAA) and the Canadian Interuniversity Athletic Union (CIAU). Teams have won countless conference titles and 24 national championships in sports such as hockey, football, swimming, volleyball and women's basketball.

As a result of the 1988 Winter Olympics, U of C has the finest combined athletic facilities in Canada, including the country's only covered speedskating oval, two hockey rinks, tennis courts, a triple gymnasium, a racquet ball centre, an Olympic-sized swimming pool, weight rooms, a fitness centre, jogging tracks, an indoor climbing wall and a large sports stadium. All registered U of C students are invited to take full advantage of the many on-campus facilities. The university also supports many student clubs and organizations with a range of academic, cultural, religious and political themes.

University Recognition

- Research funding of nearly $80 million per year makes U of C the most research-intensive university in Alberta and among the top 10 in Canada
- Distinguished faculty includes 29 Royal Society of Canada members and three 3-M Teaching Fellowship recipients
- U of C boasts one of Canada's top athletic programs with 24 national championships

STUDENT SUPPORT SERVICES

All entering students receive an introduction to university life in a required four-day orientation program, U of C 101. A detailed listing of available accommodation is maintained by the Off-Campus Housing Registry. The International Student Centre offers information and assistance regarding opportunities to study, travel or work abroad; provides advising assistance to visiting foreign students; and supports a volunteer program that encourages social interaction between overseas and Canadian students. Other services include a counselling centre for students with academic, career and personal concerns as well as for students with disabilities. University Health Services provides both regular and emergency health care. Aboriginal students receive support in the Native Centre, and Career Services assists students in their career searches.

International Students

University Enrolment: 900

% of University Enrolment: 4%

Countries of Origin: International students at U of C represent countries such as the US, Germany, Hong Kong, Malaysia and India.

University of Lethbridge
Lethbridge, Alberta

University Mission

...to cultivate humane values; to foster intellectual growth, social development, aesthetic sensitivity, personal ethics and physical well-being; to cultivate the transcendental dimension of the scholar's personality

Student Voice:

The personal attention and instruction that University of Lethbridge students receive from our professors is amazing.

Kyla Thompson
Fourth year BA (Co-op) student
Sociology

CONTACT INFORMATION

Admissions Office
University of Lethbridge
4401 University Drive
Lethbridge, Alberta
Canada T1K 3M4
PH 1-403-320-5700
FAX 1-403-329-5159
EMAIL Inquiries@uleth.ca
INTERNET http://home.uleth.ca

UNIVERSITY OVERVIEW

The University of Lethbridge (UL) was founded in 1967 and began instruction with 638 students; that number has now grown to approximately 5,500 students. UL offers bachelor's and master's degrees, certificate and diploma programs, as well as nine preprofessional programs. Most first-year students are first admitted into the Faculty of Arts & Science, with the exception of nursing and certificate students for business management and health sciences. UL also offers cooperative education programs for all majors, allowing student to enhance their theoretical education with paid work experience in an area related to their field of study.

Degree Programs

UL's degree programs are divided into three main faculties and two schools: the Faculty of Arts & Science, the Faculty of Education, the Faculty of Management, the School of Fine Arts and the School of Health Sciences.

The Faculty of Arts & Science offers over 30 degree programs leading to a BA, a BSc, a joint BA/BSc degree, or a number of postdiploma programs. The Faculty of Education offers both bachelor's and master's degrees in education and various combined degrees in the arts, fine arts and music. The Faculty of Management's certificate and postdiploma programs lead to bachelor's degrees in management. The School of Fine Arts offers Bachelor of Fine Arts (BFA) degrees in art, the dramatic arts and multidisciplinary arts subjects; Bachelor of Music degrees; as well as many postdiploma programs leading to these degrees. UL also supports a four-year Bachelor of Nursing degree in cooperation with Lethbridge Community College through the School of Health Sciences. This school also offers a bachelor's degree in health sciences additions, as well as postdiploma program in nursing and a certificate in palliative care.

UL provides the opportunity for students to undertake one of eight combined cross-disciplinary degrees leading to master's degrees in arts and science. In addition, a Bachelor of Social Work (BSW) is offered in cooperation with the University of Calgary at UL's campus.

Cooperative Education

UL provides co-op and internship programs in the Faculty of Arts & Science (humanities, social sciences and sciences) and the Faculty of Management for qualified students to enrich their regular academic programs. The co-op program offers students the opportunity to obtain hands-on paid work experience in their specialized fields of interest.

Highlights

- Cooperative education/internship programs available in arts, science and management
- Part-time and full-time options available in most programs
- UL's programs are diversified by participation with nearby universities and other postsecondary institutions in cooperative programs and activities

University Statistics

Year Founded: 1967
Academic Options: undergraduate/graduate
Calendar Year: fall semester (Sept-Dec); spring semester (Jan- Apr)

DISCIPLINES/MAJORS OFFERED

Faculty of Arts & Science: Agricultural Biotechnology; Agricultural Studies; Anthropology; Art; Biochemistry; Biological Sciences; Canadian Studies; Chemistry; Computer Science; Dramatic Arts; Economics; English; Environmental Studies; Exercise Science; Geography; History; Independent Study; Kinesiology; Mathematics & Computer Science; Modern Languages; Music; Native American Studies; Neuroscience; Philosophy; Physical Education; Physics; Political Science; Psychology; Recreation & Leisure Studies; Religious Studies; Sociology; Special Studies; Urban & Regional Studies; Women's Studies

Faculty of Education: Art; Biological Sciences; Career & Technology Studies; Drama; English/Languages/Arts; Mathematics; Modern Languages; Music; Native; Physical; Science; Social Studies;

Faculty of Management: Accounting; Business Enterprises & Self-Governing Systems of Indian, Inuit & Metis Peoples; Computer Science; Economics; Finance; General Management; Human Resources Management & Organization Studies; International Management; Labour Relations; Management Information Systems; Marketing; Mathematics; Political Science; Public Administration

School of Fine Arts: Art; Dramatic Arts (Theatre); Music; Multidisciplinary

School of Health Sciences: Nursing; Health Sciences Additions; Palliative Care

ADMISSIONS CRITERIA & PROCEDURES

Undergraduate candidates must submit their completed application forms to the Registrar's office, along with the nonrefundable application fee of C$50. Students whose primary language is not English are required to submit TOEFL scores of 550; evidence of successful completion of an advanced level ESL program; IELTS scores of 6.0 with no individual score less than 5.5; or a passing grade in an approved English for Academic Purposes (EAP) program (UL offers one on campus). Application forms are available through the Registrar's office; students may also complete the online form on UL's website.

Applicants should arrange to have their official secondary and postsecondary transcripts from all institutions attended forwarded to the Registrar's Office. Applicants seeking guaranteed admission need to prove an academic average of 65 per cent or higher; transfer students must have a GPA of 2.0 (on a 4.0 scale) and more than three transferable courses. Individual programs may require additional admissions documents. Students should consult the UL calendar for more information. Applications must be received by June 1 for admission to the fall semester and November 15 for the spring semester.

Admissions at a Glance

Minimum GPA: 2.0-2.75 on a 4.0 scale (varies according faculty)

Minimum English Requirements: TOEFL 550, IELTS 6.0

Application Fee: C$50 (Canadian and international)

Application Deadlines: June 1 (fall semester); November 15 (spring semester)

ACADEMIC FACILITIES

The UL campus has many modern buildings and facilities that serve over 5,500 full- and part-time students. The University Centre of the Arts features a versatile 406-seat theatre, a 203-seat recital hall & film theatre, as well as the University Art Gallery, classrooms, practice rooms and studios. The Physical Education building offers students extracurricular activities in its fitness centre, sauna, gymnasium and steam room. There is an Olympic-size swimming facility with a 50-metre pool and separate diving tank in the 250-seat Max Bell Regional Aquatic Centre.

Student & Faculty Profile

Total Enrolment: 5,503

Undergraduate Enrolment: 5,289

# of Faculty: 300

Student/Faculty Ratio: 19:1

Male/Female Students: 44%/56%

First-Year Class Sizes: 35-180

Undergraduate Acceptance Rate: 77%

Undergraduate Enrolment by Discipline:

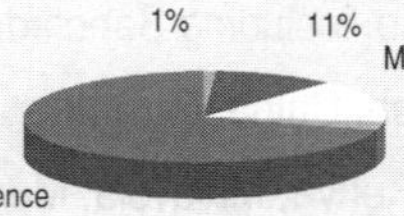

SCHOLARSHIPS & FINANCIAL ASSISTANCE

UL offers approximately 300 entrance scholarships for students entering first-year studies at UL. Another approximately 100 awards are available for students transferring to UL from other postsecondary institutions. Scholarships and bursaries are also available for students continuing their undergraduate studies at UL. Awards range in value up to C$5,000 and can be used for tuition, books and fees at the university. Students should consult the university calendar for further details on applications, academic requirements and specific dollar values of each scholarship.

Expenses at a Glance

Tuition (undergraduate, full-time):
- In-Province: C$1,680/semester
- Out-of-Province: C$1,680/semester
- International: C$3,360/semester

Fees, Books, Materials: C$500+/month

Accommodation:
- Private: C$420/month
- Residence: not available
- Homestay: not available

Health Insurance: C$240/year

CAMPUS & LOCATION

City Population:	66,000
Cost of Living:	low
Climate Range:	-20° to 23°C
Campus Setting:	urban
# of Students in Residence:	452

The University of Lethbridge is situated on more than 180 hectares overlooking the Oldman River. Over 400 students at UL live in the popular on-campus residences. The university offers two different styles of housing: traditional residences for first- and second-year students, and apartments for mature students. Aperutre Residential Park is the main residence for first- and second-year students; there are 150 guaranteed spaces for first-year students in the Kainai and Piikani houses. All apartments are fully furnished and the building has views of both the Oldman River and the Canadian Rocky Mountains.

Lethbridge, located in the southwestern corner of Alberta, is situated only 145 kilometres from the Rocky Mountains and 95 kilometres from the US border. This small city combines the comfort and safety of a small-town community with the convenience of the third largest concentration of retail in Alberta and the attraction of many historical sites, including Indian Battle Park.

Alberta's four distinct seasons, including hot summers and snowy winters, support various outdoor activities such as camping, hiking, fishing and tobogganing.

ATHLETICS & EXTRACURRICULAR ACTIVITIES

Recreation Services offers athletic programs for UL students of all ages and levels in classes including aerobics, yoga, self-defense, dance, gymnastics, kayaking, scuba diving and karate. There are also many athletic clubs and intramural sports that students can join such as kickboxing, rugby, fencing, rockclimbing, and coed basketball, volleyball, slo-pitch softball, floor hockey, flag football, indoor soccer and badminton.

UL has basketball, soccer, hockey, judo, swimming, and track & field teams that compete with most other universities in western Canada. The Intercollegiate Athletics program at UL has represented the province nationally and internationally, benefiting from the combined professional experience of the coaching staff.

University Recognition

- Campus design, by architect Arthur Erickson, has received international acclaim for its originality and functional design
- Member of the Association of Commonwealth Universities (ACU) and the Association of Universities and Colleges in Canada (AUCC)
- UL is consistently rated first for small universities in Canada for its student services and medical/science research

STUDENT SUPPORT SERVICES

The Career Resources Centre (CRC), located on the UL campus aids in linking students with potential employers in areas related to the students' fields of study. Within the CRC are three separate programs: Career & Employment Services, Applied Studies and Cooperative Education & Internships. These programs offer students opportunities to gain relevant skills and to network with interested companies in preparation for graduation.

UL has an on-campus language centre for students who need additional help with their English language skills. The centre offers advanced, upper intermediate and low intermediate EAP programs.

UL also has a Counselling Centre, advising program, Student Health Centre, International Centre, Peer Support Centre and other services.

International Students

University Enrolment: 214

% of University Enrolment: 4%

Countries of Origin: The international students at UL come from 31 countries worldwide, including Bangladesh, Cameroon, China, Colombia, Gambia, Ghana, Kenya, Malaysia, Mexico, Portugal, South Korea, Sweden, Tanzania, the US, Venezuela and Zimbabwe.

UNIVERSITY OF REGINA

UNIVERSITY OF REGINA
REGINA, SASKATCHEWAN

University Mission

...to continue the preservation, transmission, interpretation and enhancement of the cultural, scientific and artistic heritage of the human race, and the acquisition and expansion of new knowledge and understanding

Student Voice:

The University of Regina is a place where I can be educated and then apply what I learn along with my life experiences to a business setting.

Tracy Romphf
Cooperative Education Program
Second-Year Business Administration

CONTACT INFORMATION
Admissions Office
University of Regina
3737 Wascana Parkway
Regina, Saskatchewan
Canada S4S 0A2
PH 1-306-585-4591
FAX 1-306-585-5203
EMAIL admissions.office@uregina.ca
INTERNET http://www.uregina.ca

UNIVERSITY OVERVIEW

The University of Regina (UR) became an independent university in 1974 after serving for 50 years as the University of Saskatchewan's second campus. Since then, UR has expanded around a historic campus that began as a Methodist high school in 1911, and today offers students programs leading to bachelor's, master's and doctoral degrees in nine faculties and 22 departments. Unique and highly recognized programs in areas such as aboriginal education, cooperative education, teacher training, systems engineering and training for human services careers, exemplify UR's commitment to innovative and progressive postsecondary education.

Academic Programs

Fields of study available to undergraduate students at UR include administration, arts, fine arts, education, engineering, human justice, journalism, physical activity studies, science and social work. Most degrees can be completed in four years, with the exception of programs such as the cooperative education and combined degree programs, which can require up to six years to complete.

UR also provides university courses to over 60 communities throughout Saskatchewan through the University Extension program. This program televises university classes for students who are not able to leave home to attend UR. The first year of the arts and sciences programs can be completed off campus and courses in social work, administration and education, as well as several graduate studies options, are also available.

Cooperative Education

UR's cooperative education (co-op) programs allow students to apply the academic knowledge learned at university in a real-world work environment. Students must complete one academic year (two four-month semesters) before being eligible to alternate four month salaried work terms with their academic study terms at the university. Co-op jobs are located primarily in western Canada; there are also a number of opportunities to work overseas. Students gain practical experience in workplaces that typically include consulting or accounting firms, banks, oil companies, laboratories, federal, provincial and municipal governments and computer hardware companies. Co-op programs are available to students in the administration, engineering, physics, mathematics, computer science and chemistry departments.

Highlights

- Offers a cooperative education program in six different fields of study
- University Extension program allows Saskatchewan residents to complete their first year of study from home
- UR's Language Institute offers intensive instruction in 13 languages

University Statistics

Year Founded: 1974
Academic Options: undergraduate/graduate
Calendar Year: fall semester (Sept-Dec); winter semester (Jan-Apr)

DISCIPLINES/MAJORS OFFERED

Faculty of Administration

Faculty of Arts: Anthropology, Economics, English, French, Geography, Germanic Studies, History, Indian Languages, Philosophy & Classics, Political Science, Psychology, Religious Studies, School of Human Justice, School of Journalism, Sociology & Social Studies, Women's Studies

Faculty of Education: Elementary, Secondary, French & Indian Teacher, Education Program, Arts, Vocational Technical

Faculty of Engineering: Environmental Systems, Electronic Information Systems, Industrial Systems & Petroleum Systems

Faculty of Fine Arts: Film & Video, Music, Indian Fine Arts, Theatre, Visual Arts

Faculty of Graduate Studies & Research

Faculty of Physical Activity Studies: Adapted Physical Activity, Fitness & Lifestyle, Recreation Administration, Sport Administration

Faculty of Science: Biology, Computer Science, Chemistry, Geology, Mathematics & Statistics, Physics & Astronomy

Faculty of Social Work

ADMISSIONS CRITERIA & PROCEDURES

All candidates must complete an application form and submit it to UR along with the C$50 nonrefundable application fee. Candidates must also arrange to have official copies of all secondary and postsecondary transcripts sent directly from their previous institutions to UR's Admission Office; transcripts will not be accepted when sent by students. Most programs require a minimum average of 65 per cent in prerequisite work for admission. All students must provide proof of English language proficiency; students who have not taken the equivalent to Canadian high school grades 10, 11 and 12 English must submit a TOEFL score of 550, a Michigan Test of English Proficiency (MTEP) score of 85 or a Regina Test of English Proficiency score of 80 (may be taken at UR).

Individual faculties set their application deadlines for fall, winter and spring/summer semesters; students are advised to consult the university calendar for more information.

Admissions at a Glance

Minimum GPA: 65%

Minimum English Requirements:
- TOEFL 550, MTEP 85, RTEP 80 or CELT 60%

Application Fee: C$50 (Canadian and international)

Application Deadlines: varies by faculty

ACADEMIC FACILITIES

The two UR campuses comprise more than 20 buildings connected on each campus by a system of indoor walkways; the campuses house almost 600 classrooms and offer over 150,000 square metres of interior space. There are six libraries at UR housing a collection that includes more than two million volumes, over 3,500 periodical and journal subscriptions, and an array of government documents, audio and film items, microform materials and CD-ROM-based reference resources.

The Language Institute at UR comprises L'Intstitut de formation linguistique (L'Intstitut), the Saskatchewan Centre for International Languages (SCIL) and the ESL Centre. L'Istitut offers both anglophone and francophone residents of Saskatchewan instruction in French. L'Institut offers both credit and noncredit programs in French, including a one year certificate program and a Bachelor of Arts degree in French-Canadian studies. The Language Institute building houses a library, language laboratory, multimedia centre, social centre, cafeteria and a student residence. The SCIL is also situated in the Language Institute building and offers intensive language training during the spring and summer study sessions at UR. The program's emphasis is on oral fluency, which is supported by reading, writing, social and cultural activities. Languages currently offered through the program are Arabic, Cree, German, Hindi, Italian, Japanese, Korean, Mandarin, Russian, Spanish and Ukrainian. The ESL program at UR offers part- and full-time English language in three different programs, English for Academic Purposes, Individual Skill Areas and Specific Purposes.

Student & Faculty Profile

Total Enrolment: 11,625

Undergraduate Enrolment: 10,716

\# of Faculty: 452

Student/Faculty Ratio: 16:1

Male/Female Students: 41%/59%

First-Year Class Sizes: 25-100

Undergraduate Acceptance Rate: not available

Undergraduate Enrolment by Discipline:

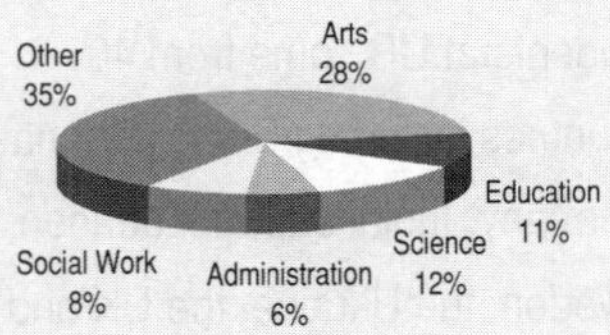

SCHOLARSHIPS & FINANCIAL ASSISTANCE

In 1996, UR enrolled 112 of Saskatchewan's most academically accomplished high school graduates in the UR Scholars program, which provides full tuition remission to graduating students with the highest average in each province. UR offers almost C$600,000 in undergraduate scholarships every year. While international students are not eligible for entrance scholarships, there are academic awards and bursaries available to them after their first semester at UR.

Expenses at a Glance

Tuition (undergraduate, full-time):
- In-Province: C$2,812/year
- Out-of-Province: C$2,812/year
- International: C$5,625/year

Fees, Books, Materials: C$1,500/year

Accommodation:
- Private: C$600-800/month
- Residence: C$740-2,000/semester
- Homestay: C$475/month

Health Insurance: C$320/year (for additional coverage, recommended)

City Population:	200,000
Cost of Living:	low
Climate Range:	-22° to 26°C
Campus Setting:	urban
# of Students in Residence:	620

CAMPUS & LOCATION

The University of Regina's is located in Regina, the capital of Saskatchewan, on 920 hectares of land known as Wascana Centre, the largest urban park in North America. UR has two main campuses, both conveniently located just outside the city centre.

In addition to the university proper, UR has three federated colleges on its campus, Campion College (of Jesuit affiliation), Luther College (of Lutheran affiliation) and the Saskatchewan Indian Federated College (secular). Enrolling through one of the federated colleges enables students to earn a UR degree while living and learning in the small community atmosphere of the federated college. All UR classes are available to federated college students and UR students may study at the federated colleges; however, each college has its own unique character and purpose.

UR has three different on-campus residences for students to choose from, including College West, Luther College and the Language Institute. College West houses 340 students in private and semi-private accommodations with shared showers and kitchen facilities. College West offers both one- and two-storey apartments with single and double bedrooms, and the residence complex includes television and recreational lounges, a music practice room and laundry rooms. The Luther College residence houses 214 students, with floors divided into male and female residents; all rooms house single occupants only and each has its own bathroom. Lutheran College residents must choose a meal plan prepared by Luther Food Services. The Language Institute accommodates 67 residents in either single or double rooms. Each floor has its own lounge area with a television, VCR and laundry facilities.

ATHLETICS & EXTRACURRICULAR ACTIVITIES

UR campus recreation programs attract over 60 per cent of the full-time student population, making it the largest extracurricular program on campus. The recreation program provides a variety of options to all students such as competitive leagues for volleyball, ice hockey, basketball, soccer, slow pitch softball, and touch football; noncompetitive activities including aerobics, fitness classes and sports clubs; and weight room, a swimming pool and several gyms for more informal activities. In addition, UR participates in 13 sports at the interuniversity level including men's and women's basketball, hockey, swimming, track & field, volleyball and wrestling; and men's football.

The Faculty of Fine Arts encourages interested students to attend or participate in the theatre performances, concert choirs, chamber orchestra, concert band, jazz ensembles, opera workshops and film productions the faculty coordinates throughout the year.

The are many other student-run clubs and organizations on campus for students to join.

STUDENT SUPPORT SERVICES

UR provides many different services for international students in order to make the transition to Canadian life and campus culture easier. The services available to international students include a campus orientation, counselling services, and organized educational and recreational activities both on and off campus. The Office of Student Affairs & International Student Services also provides students with information and advice regarding health insurance, immigration matters and international student exchange programs.

Academic advising and career counselling are available to all students in need of advice regarding the choices and options before them. Students in their last year of high school are encouraged to participate in the Spend-a-Day Program, which allows high school students to shadow a university student for a day on the UR campus.

University Recognition

- All engineering disciplines accredited by Canadian Engineering Accreditation Board
- Faculty of Social Work is accredited by the Canadian Association of Schools of Social Work Accreditation Board

International Students

University Enrolment: 347

% of University Enrolment: 3%

Countries of Origin: International students at UR come from 40 countries including China, Ghana, Germany, India, Japan, Lebanon, Sweden, the Ukraine, the UK and the USA.

University of Saskatchewan
Saskatoon, Saskatchewan

University Mission

...to be a model of scholarly enquiry, a place where all who contribute to its achievement—students, faculty and staff—can take pride in their commitment to this centre of excellence

Student Voice:

One of the best in North America, the University of Saskatchewan has very famous professors and very powerful equipment related to my major.

Reza Ahrabian
Computer Science Major

CONTACT INFORMATION
Office of the Registrar
University of Saskatchewan
105 Administration Place
Saskatoon, Saskatchewan
Canada S7N 5A2
PH 1-306-966-6450
FAX 1-306-966-6730
EMAIL registrar@usask.ca
INTERNET
http://www.usask.ca/registrar

UNIVERSITY OVERVIEW

Founded in 1907, the University of Saskatchewan (U of S) is a publicly funded, medium-sized research institution. U of S enjoys a reputation for excellence in both teaching and research and prides itself on delivering innovative programs in a comfortable learning environment.

Academic Programs

U of S offers a wide variety of programs. There are more than 100 programs at the undergraduate or graduate level offered through the Colleges of Agriculture, Arts & Science, Commerce, Dentistry, Education, Engineering, Graduate Studies & Research, Law, Medicine, Nursing, Pharmacy & Nutrition, Kinesiology, and Veterinary Medicine as well as the School Physical Therapy. Most undergraduate degree programs can be completed in three to four years.

U of S allows first-year arts & sciences courses to be completed at several affiliated colleges located throughout Saskatchewan.

Internationalism

U of S takes pride in its large international student body. The university believes in the need for a global outlook and has created the University of Saskatchewan International, which coordinates all international programs, research projects and contracts that U of S maintains.

University of Saskatchewan International offers a number of academic student exchanges and study abroad programs with universities in countries including Australia, Germany, Mexico, Thailand, Sweden, Guatemala, the US and the Ukraine.

Practical Experience

U of S understands how important practical experience is in a modern education. Class sizes are kept small to ensure that students can work closely with professors; a variety of experiential learning activities, such as field studies and research, are incorporated into many university programs. Many programs include optional co-op or internship placements, which provide students with valuable hands-on training.

Excellence in Research

U of S researchers attract more than C$51 million in research funding per year. Research conducted at the U of S has resulted in the first genetically engineered vaccine for animals, the first Canadian experiment undertaken aboard a space shuttle and the introduction of over 100 new crop varieties.

Highlights

- More than 100 programs of study
- World renowned for its research
- International study abroad and exchange programs available
- Saskatoon has one of the lowest costs of living in Canada
- Free provincial medical and health insurance

University Statistics

Year Founded: 1907
Academic Options: undergraduate/graduate
Calendar Year: term I (Sept-Dec); term II (Jan-Apr)

DISCIPLINES/MAJORS OFFERED

College of Agriculture: Ag Bio, Ag Chem, Ag Econ, Agronomy, Animal Sci, Applied Microbio, Crop Sci, Env Sci, Food Sci, Horticulture Sci, Mech Ag, Plant Ecology, Rangeland Res, Soil Sci

College of Arts & Sciences: Anatomy, Ancient History & Classical Culture, Anthropology & Archaeology, Art History, Biochem, Bio, Chem, Classical & Near Eastern Archaeology, Classics, Comp Sci, Drama, Econ, English, Env Earth Sci, Food Sci, French, Geography, Geology, Geophysics, German, History, Int'l, Land Use & Env, Linguistics, Mathematical Physics, Math, Microbio, Music, Native, Palaeobio, Phil, Pharmacology, Physics, Physiology, Poli, Psych, Public Admin, Regional & Urban Dev't, Religious, Russian, Spanish, Stats, Studio Art, Ukrainian, Women's & Gender

College of Commerce: Acc, Dev't of IS, Bus Econ, Finance, Gen Bus, HR Mgmt, Mktg, Prod & Ops Mgmt

College of Education: Elementary/Middle Years or Secondary; 5-yr combined degree (Music & Ed, Physical Ed & Ed)

College of Engineering: Ag & Biores, Chem, Chem, Civil, Electrical, Eng Physics, Mech

Additional Program Offerings:

Additional programs are also offered in the following colleges and schools:
College of Dentistry
College of Graduate Studies & Research
College of Kinesiology
College of Law
College of Medicine
College of Nursing
College of Pharmacy & Nutrition
School of Physical Therapy
Western School of Veterinary Medicine

ADMISSIONS CRITERIA & PROCEDURES

Generally, undergraduate admission to U of S is open to students who have completed the highest level of study in their region's secondary school program, or equivalent. Individual programs may require specific secondary school course prerequisites. Additional admission requirements may include submission of standardized test scores, a personal statement, portfolio or an audition. Further information regarding specific programs can be obtained by contacting the Office of the Registrar.

A completed application form must be accompanied by a C$50 application fee. Official transcripts are normally required directly from the educational institutions attended. The application deadlines, unless otherwise noted, are April 1 for term I and September 1 for term II. There are enrolment restrictions for several U of S programs and students are encouraged to apply early.

The admissions process for international students is handled by the International Admissions Office. International students whose native language is not English must submit one of the following: a TOEFL score of 550, a MELAB score of 85, an IELTS band of 6.0 or CanTEST band of 4.5. Students who do not meet the minimum requirement may enrol in ESL classes offered by U of S's Centre for Second Language Instruction.

Applicants to graduate-level programs should contact the College of Graduate Studies & Research directly.

Admissions at a Glance

Minimum GPA: 65% or C average

Minimum English Requirements:

- TOEFL 550 (paper-based), 213 (computer-based); MELAB 85; IELTS 6.0; CanTEST 4.5

Application Fee: C$50 (Canadian and international)

Application Deadlines: April 1 (term I); September 1 (term II)

ACADEMIC FACILITIES

U of S boasts some of the finest academic facilities in the country, including one of the largest and most successful university-related research parks, outstanding computing facilities and highly specialized engineering and agricultural laboratories. The university has made an effort to incorporate the latest technological teaching aids into every program. All students have Internet and email accounts, as well as access to numerous computing facilities, some of which are open 24 hours a day. In addition, the U of S library is recognized as one of the finest in the country, with more than 500,000 books, 8,000 periodicals and 2.5 million microform items. Other notable facilities on campus include greenhouses, the Saskatchewan Linear Accelerator, the Cancer Clinic and a number of art studios.

Student & Faculty Profile

Total Enrolment: 17,078

Undergraduate Enrolment: 15,290

# of Faculty: 967

Student/Faculty Ratio: 29:1

Male/Female Students: 45%/55%

First-Year Class Sizes: 70 (average)

Undergraduate Acceptance Rate: not available

Undergraduate Enrolment by Discipline:

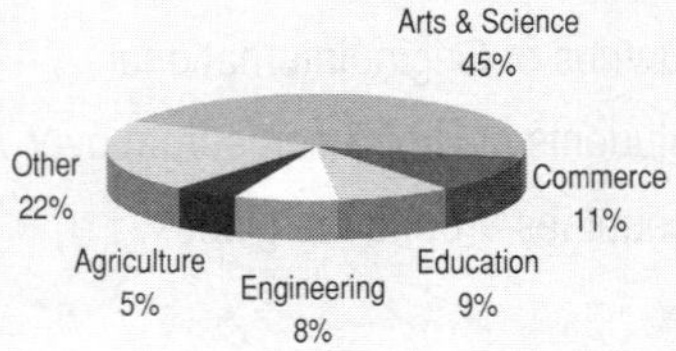

SCHOLARSHIPS & FINANCIAL ASSISTANCE

The U of S offers only a limited number of entrance scholarships to international students in good academic standing whose economic hardship would make it difficult for them to attend university in Canada, and whose intention it is to return to their home countries. The entrance awards are open to international students who are citizens of developing countries as defined by the International Awards Committee.

International students who have successfully completed at least one year of full-time study at the U of S are eligible to compete for a number of awards for continuing students.

Federal and provincial student loan programs are not available to international students.

Expenses at a Glance

Tuition (undergraduate, full-time):

- In-Province: C$3,000-3,780/year*
- Out-of-Province: C$3,000-3,780/year*
- International: C$6,450-8,901/year*

Fees, Books, Materials: C$750-1,000/year*

Accommodation:

- Private: C$400/month*
- Residence: C$450/month*
- Homestay: C$500/month*

Health Insurance: n/a

CAMPUS & LOCATION

City Population:	210,000
Cost of Living:	low
Climate Range:	-30° to 35°C
Campus Setting:	urban
# of Students in Residence:	1,430

U of S rests on 755 hectares, which are occupied by the campus and Innovation Place, Canada's largest operating research park, as well as the university's farm and experimental plots. Recently named one of the 20 most beautiful places in Canada by Canadian Living Magazine, the U of S campus is home to several original buildings, adorned with carved gargoyles, that were built out of greystone drawn from the Saskatchewan River's banks. The campus also houses several art galleries and museums, including the Museum of Natural Science. The university is located in the heart of Saskatoon, on the scenic South Saskatchewan River.

Saskatoon, Saskatchewan has more hours of sunshine than any other major city in Canada. Its landscape is marked by more than 120 hectares of riverbank parkland. The city boasts all the amenities of a large metropolitan area, including theatre companies and a symphony, yet maintains the friendliness and charm of a small town. It is safe and clean and has one of the lowest costs of living in North America. The surrounding landscape includes forests, wheat fields and valleys of wildflowers. Saskatchewan enjoys four distinct seasons with warm summers and brisk winters, and offers a wide variety of recreational activities and opportunities.

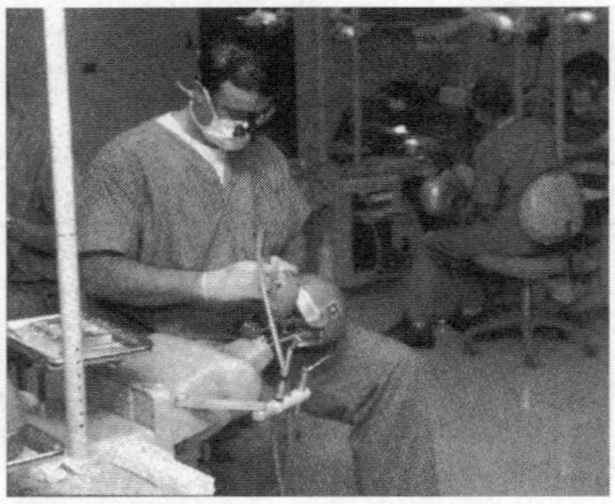

ATHLETICS & EXTRACURRICULAR ACTIVITIES

U of S encourages all students to participate in the extracurricular activities available on campus. With a wide variety of athletic, social and cultural programs, the university strives to provide a comprehensive and positive learning environment.

The College of Kinesiology offers a variety of programs to all students. Students can participate at the varsity, intramural or recreational level. U of S competes in eight men's and six women's sports at the varsity level. Intramural activities encourage sportsmanship and fellowship, and both co-ed and gender-based activities are available. U of S also offers a number of recreational and instructional programs ranging from aerobics to Tae Kwon Do. Athletic facilities on campus include a swimming pool, multi-purpose gymnasia, weight training facilities, outdoor playing fields and racquet courts.

There are many student cultural, academic and social organizations on campus. The student body supports a student-run newspaper. The Department of Music organizes several concerts during the year and students are encouraged to take advantage of the university's museums and art galleries.

University Recognition

- U of S has produced Nobel Prize winners and 11 Rhodes Scholars
- U of S researchers pioneered the use of radiation in cancer treatment
- College of Engineering ranked in the top 20 by 1996 Gorman Report
- Department of Computer Science ranked number one in Canada in term of scientific impact of its research
- Only university in Western Canada with all five health science colleges

STUDENT SUPPORT SERVICES

All registered students have access to the personal and academic counselling available through Student Counselling Services. The Student Employment & Career Centre offers comprehensive job search and employment services. Other supports services include the Student Health Centre, Campus Day Care Centre and the information desk.

International students will find that U of S provides a wide variety of services through its International Student Advisor's Office. The office organizes a two-day orientation program, an International Friendship program and an informal Oral English program. The office also offers assistance with immigration, housing, as well as cultural and academic concerns, and provides free airport reception service to newly arrived students.

International Students

University Enrolment: 698

% of University Enrolment: 4%

Countries of Origin: International students at U of S come from over 70 countries around the globe.

THE UNIVERSITY OF WINNIPEG
WINNIPEG, MANITOBA

University Mission

...to remain committed to excellence in postsecondary education by striving to offer a community that appreciates, fosters and promotes values of human dignity, equality, non-discrimination and tolerance of diversity, and to view both accessibility and excellence as important goals

Student Voice:

The professors and staff are very flexible; they can always help you whatever your situation is.

Miguel Rueda, Mexico
BA Economics
1997

CONTACT INFORMATION
The University of Winnipeg
515 Portage Avenue
Winnipeg, Manitoba
Canada R3B 2E9
PH 1-204-786-9159
FAX 1-204-786-8656
EMAIL adm@uwinnipeg.ca
INTERNET http://www.uwinnipeg.ca

UNIVERSITY OVERVIEW

The University of Winnipeg (UW) was developed from the United College in 1967 and now provides nonsectarian education in the urban centre of Winnipeg. UW offers undergraduate degrees in 34 majors, and has an enrolment of approximately 6,500 students. The main downtown campus is supported by affiliated colleges and programs, including Concord College and the Continuing Education Division.

A Small, Personal University

UW aims to provide top-quality education that is accessible to all students. UW's small class sizes ensure students benefit from a close, comfortable learning environment, and receive personalized instruction from UW's highly qualified faculty. The wide variety of programs offered by the university combine with its central location to offer flexible course scheduling options to the diverse student body. UW has recently introduced three full academic terms per year, enabling students to complete their degrees in a shorter period of time. Students enrolled in undergraduate programs are required to fulfil an academic writing requirement through credit courses in academic English and rhetoric.

Programs Offered

UW specializes in providing undergraduate education, offering a variety of arts, science, education, theology and preprofessional programs in a total of over 400 courses. The preprofessional programs (which vary from one to three years in length) are designed to prepare students for admission to fields such as law and medicine.

The university's main focus is on the liberal arts. Undergraduate programs are offered in the form of three-year, four-year and honours programs leading to Bachelor of Arts (BA) and Science (BSc), Bachelor of Education (BEd) and Bachelor of Theology degrees. At the graduate level, the university offers a Master of Arts (MA) degree in History and Religious Studies; a Master of Public Administration (MPA) degree in Political Science; and a number of master's degrees through the Faculty of Theology. UW's Faculty of Theology reflects the university's heritage as, originally, a Methodist and United college.

UW also offers English language and continuing education programs and courses. The 14-week English language program is offered three times a year, with courses starting in January, May and September.

Highlights

- Small classes and personalized contact with professors
- Centrally located in downtown Winnipeg
- Primarily undergraduate university, offering 34 major areas of study

University Statistics

Year Founded: 1967

Academic Options: undergraduate (joint diploma)/graduate

Calendar Year: fall semester (Sept-Dec); winter semester (Jan-Apr); spring semester (May-Aug)

DISCIPLINES/MAJORS OFFERED

Faculty of Arts: Academic Writing, Administrative Studies, Anthropology, Business Computing, Classics, Conflict Resolution Studies, Developmental Studies, Economics, English, Environmental/Urban Studies, French Studies, Geography, German Studies, History, History of Art, International Development Studies, Justice & Law Enforcement, Mathematics, Mennonite Studies, Music, Philosophy, Physical Activity & Sport Studies, Political Science, Psychology, Religious Studies, Sociology, Statistics, Theatre & Drama, Women's Studies

Faculty of Education

Faculty of Sciences: Biochemistry, Biology, Business Computing, Chemistry, Environmental Studies/Urban Studies, Geography, Mathematics, Physics, Statistics

Faculty of Theology

Preprofessional Programs: Prechiropractic, Pre-Dental Hygiene, Predentistry, Pre-Environmental Design (Pre-architecture), Pre-Interior Design, Prejournalism, Prelaw, Premanagement, Premedicine, Pre-Medical Rehabilitation, Pre-Optometry, Prepharmacy, Pre-Recreation Studies, Pre-Social Work, Pre-Veterinary Medicine

ADMISSIONS CRITERIA & PROCEDURES

In general, applicants from other provinces and countries required qualifications comparable to Manitoba senior matriculation. A minimum grade average of 60 per cent is normally required. However, UW reserves the right to set a level of academic proficiency to determine acceptance.

All international students must provide evidence of English language proficiency, and must submit one of the following minimum English language test scores: TOEFL 570; Can TEST 4.5; IELTS 6.5; or evidence of successful completion of the Academic Preparation Program (APP).

Application deadlines are August 7 for fall term for Canadian students, and May 31 for international students.

Admissions at a Glance

Minimum GPA: 60% or special approval

Minimum English Requirements:
- TOEFL 570, Can TEST 4.5, IELTS 6.5, APP completion

Application Fee: C$35 (Canadian), $60 (international)

Application Deadlines: Aug 7 (fall term);
- December 1 (winter term); April 3 (spring term); May 31 (international students, fall term)

ACADEMIC FACILITIES

The library at UW holds over 600,000 books, journals and microforms. The library is also part of an interlibrary system which allows students access to libraries across North America. The reference department offers five online bibliographic services and 26 CD-ROM databases. The downtown location of the university also allows students easy access to the main branch of the Winnipeg Public Library, the Winnipeg Art Gallery and the Museum of Man and Nature.

UW provides computer facilities for students, including UPLINK, an open online computer lab.

SCHOLARSHIPS & FINANCIAL ASSISTANCE

The activities of the Awards & Financial Aid Office at UW provide many possible financial resources for students, ranging from awards for academic excellence to emergency assistance for basic necessities. The Awards program consists of entrance, undergraduate, collegiate, theology and athletic scholarships and bursaries, a graduate fellowship, and administration of awards by other authorities. Over one half of all full-time students at the university receive provincial or federal student loans.

UW has no bursary program for international students. However, students admitted on the basis of academic credentials earned outside Manitoba are eligible for academic awards after they have completed at least 30 credit hours or 5.0 UW full courses.

Students in Canada on student authorizations are not eligible for government assistance. It is the student's responsibility to ensure that they have enough funds to cover all probable expenses.

Student & Faculty Profile

Total Enrolment: 6,500

Undergraduate Enrolment: 7,000

# of Faculty: 450

Student/Faculty Ratio: 15:1

Male/Female Students: 66%/34%

First-Year Class Sizes: 25-50

Undergraduate Acceptance Rate: 85%

Undergraduate Enrolment by Discipline:

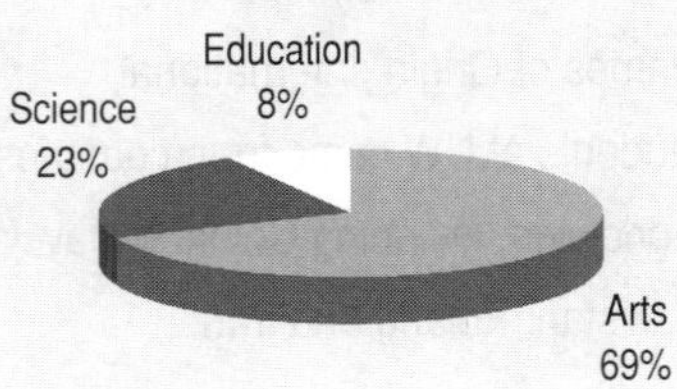

Expenses at a Glance

Tuition (undergraduate, full-time):
- In-Province: C$3,300/year
- Out-of-Province: C$3,300/year
- International: C$5,778/year

Fees, Books, Materials: C$800/year

Accommodation:
- Private: C$500-700/month
- Residence: n/a
- Homestay: C$450/month

Health Insurance: C$453/month

CAMPUS & LOCATION

City Population:	700,000
Cost of Living:	low
Climate Range:	-30° to 30°C
Campus Setting:	urban
# of Students in Residence:	n/a

The University of Winnipeg's campus is composed of a series of interconnected buildings nestled into the business and recreational centre of Winnipeg. The campus boasts a variety of facilities including a new C$4 million student centre, an extensive library, a concert hall, an athletic centre, computer facilities and two bookstores.

UW is located in downtown Winnipeg, providing students with easy access to all of the urban amenities of Manitoba's capital. Winnipeg's population comprises a blend of over forty ethnic groups; the city's cultural life reflects the diversity of its inhabitants. Winnipeg is home to a national football team, two orchestras, a zoo, and an art gallery which houses the world's largest collection of Inuit art. Many historic sites highlight the city's history as an early transportation and trade hub of the country.

The cost of living in Winnipeg is the second lowest in Canada, making it the perfect city to experience on a student budget.

Winnipeg has a continental climate with wide seasonal variations in temperature, providing opportunities for varied outdoor activities such as ice-skating, skiing, boating and golf.

ATHLETICS & EXTRACURRICULAR ACTIVITIES

Duckworth Centre, a recreation & sports facility, is designed to accommodate the needs of the entire university. A variety of instructional programs are offered at the centre, including aerobics, badminton, fitness classes, jogging, karate, racquetball, squash, and tae-kwon-do. UW also offers students the chance to compete in a variety of team sports, including coed volleyball and basketball. The university is represented in the Canadian Inter-University Athletic Union (CIAU) by the Wesmen athletic teams in men's and women's basketball, and men's and women's volleyball.

The centre also offers an indoor two-lane track, a weight room and racquetball and squash courts. It also houses one of the best athletic therapy centres in any Canadian university.

University Recognition

- In 1997, UW ranked in the top 10 for its undergraduate programs in Maclean's Canada-wide survey

STUDENT SUPPORT SERVICES

The university supports many campus groups and clubs which provide opportunities for student participation in a social and public capacity. Many groups provide lounge and study space, including the Women's Centre, the First Nations Student Council, Lesbian/Gay/Bisexual Student's Centre, Mature/Part-Time Students' Association and the International Students' Resource Centre.

Counselling services are available for all interested students with academic or personal issues. Vocational counsellors, personal counsellors and native student services counsellors all provide advice and assistance to UW students.

UW childcare facilities are available for children between the ages of 18 months and six years.

International Students

University Enrolment: 250

% of University Enrolment: 4%

Countries of Origin: International students at UW come from countries worldwide, including China, Malaysia, Pakistan, Poland and Iran.

University Colleges

IN

The Prairie Provinces

AUGUSTANA UNIVERSITY COLLEGE CAMROSE, ALBERTA

University College Mission

...to prepare men and women intellectually, morally and spiritually for leadership and service in church and society, liberating and inspiring them with the Christ-like model of the leader as servant

Student Voice:

I've attended several postsecondary institutions and Augustana offers the very best variety of courses with top-rate instruction.

Curtis Nelson
Augustana Student
Edmonton, Alberta

CONTACT INFORMATION
Augustana University College
4901-46 Avenue
Camrose, Alberta
Canada T4V 2R3
PH 1-403-679-1132
FAX 1-403-679-1132
EMAIL admissions@augustana.ab.ca
INTERNET http://www.augustana.ab.ca

UNIVERSITY COLLEGE OVERVIEW

Founded in 1910, Augustana University College (Augustana) is a residential liberal arts & science institution providing high-quality education within the context of the Christian tradition. In 1983, Augustana became the first private college in Alberta to receive degree-granting authority under the provisions of revised provincial legislation. Originally known as Camrose Lutheran College, Augustana University College took its present name in 1991.

Augustana is a small institution that specializes in teaching at the undergraduate level. Students benefit from small class sizes and the opportunity for personal relationships with professors. All students under the age of 21 are required to live in residence during their first year of studies.

Academic Programs

Augustana University College offers Bachelor of Arts (BA) and Bachelor of Science (BSc) degree programs which may be completed in either three or four years. The four-year special programs consist of 120 credits, including at least 55 arts credits for the BA and at least 66 science credits for the BSc. The three-year general programs consist of 90 credits, including at least 43 arts credits for the BA and at least 48 science credits for the BSc.

Degrees earned at Augustana can be used as foundation studies for a number of specific vocational interests, including agriculture, dentistry, law and veterinary medicine.

Additional Programs

The Centre for Continuing Education (CCE) offers one-year certificate and two-year diploma business programs such as computing, accounting, administrative assistant or personal care practitioner. A full range of academic upgrading programs, from basic education to university readiness, prepare students for workforce entry or further education. As well, the CCE operates customized programs for business and industry, offering work skills and career development programs.

International Programs

Augustana offers a range of innovative international programs that supplement and enhance the liberal arts and sciences experience while enabling students to add a valuable global dimension to their education. Participating countries include Cuba, Mexico, Germany, France and Norway. As well, study tours in art and classical studies provide students with opportunities to study art, architecture and archaeology onsite in Europe and the Middle East.

Highlights

- Wide range of university transfer, career developmental and continuing education programs
- Specialization in undergraduate-level programs
- Emphasis on a warm, community-style campus atmosphere

University College Statistics

Year Founded: 1910

Academic Options: certificate/diploma/undergraduate

Calendar Year: fall term (Sept-Dec); winter term (Jan-Apr)

ACADEMIC PROGRAMS

Biology and Chemistry Division: Biology, Chemistry

Fine Arts Division: Art, Drama, Music

History, Sociology & Political Studies Division: Crime & Community, History, Political Studies, Sociology

Humanities Division: Classical Studies, English, Philosophy, Religious Studies, World Literatures

Interdisciplinary Studies & International Programs Division: Canadian Studies, Developmental Studies, Environmental Studies, General Studies, Interdisciplinary Studies, Language Studies, Women's Studies

Mathematical Sciences Division: Computing Science, Mathematics, Physics, Statistics

Modern Languages Division: French, German, Scandinavian Studies, Spanish

Physical Education Division: Physical Education

Psychology, Economics & Geography Division: Business, Economics, Education, Geography, Psychology

ADMISSIONS CRITERIA & PROCEDURES

Augustana University College begins to process applications one year before the start of the term. Applicants should apply as early as possible, as acceptance is based on a first-come, first-served basis, until 80 per cent capacity has been reached. The final 20 per cent of students are accepted based on previous academic standing. Applications received after deadlines may be considered but will be assessed a C$20 late fee. An early admission policy enables qualifying students to be accepted while still completing grade 12.

Along with a completed application form, all application packages must include a C$30 application fee, a signed declaration of agreement to comply with stated university regulations, and official secondary or postsecondary transcripts. Once applications for admission are received, students are sent a residence application form. All first-year students under 21 years of age must live in residence; completed residence application forms must be accompanied by a C$100 nonrefundable deposit. Certain students may be required to provide a nonrefundable tuition deposit; these students will be notified in writing.

International students are advised to apply at least three months in advance. In addition to meeting general admission requirements, international students must submit a TOEFL score of 550 or higher and provide three deposits: C$50 for the application evaluation fee, C$100 for residence deposit and a tuition deposit of C$250 within six weeks of acceptance. The residence deposit and tuition deposit are refundable only if the student is unable to obtain a student visa.

Students should contact the Office of Admissions for further information or visit Augustana's website at http://www.augustana.ab.ca for an electronic application form.

Admissions at a Glance

Minimum GPA: 2.5 on 4.0 scale; 5.0 on 9.0 scale; 60% or C (avg)

Minimum English Requirements:
- TOEFL 550

Application Fee: C$30 (Canadian); $50 (international)

Application Deadlines: Canadian: August 1 (fall term); December 1 (winter term); international: June 1 (fall term); October 1 (winter term)

ACADEMIC FACILITIES

The Augustana Library houses a collection of approximately 80,000 volumes and 500 periodical subscriptions, maintained to support the research needs of undergraduate liberal arts & sciences students. As well, students have access to NEOS, a central Alberta library consortium which has collaborated to create and maintain a shared online catalogue, as well as to provide user services such as reference assistance, interlibrary loan privileges and a document delivery service. Augustana University College is currently fund-raising for a new library building.

Student & Faculty Profile

Total Enrolment: 848

Undergraduate Enrolment: 742

# of Faculty: not available

Student/Faculty Ratio: 15:1 (full-time students)

Male/Female Students: 45%/55%

First Year Class Sizes: 25 (average)

Undergraduate Acceptance Rate: not available

Undergraduate Enrolment by Discipline:

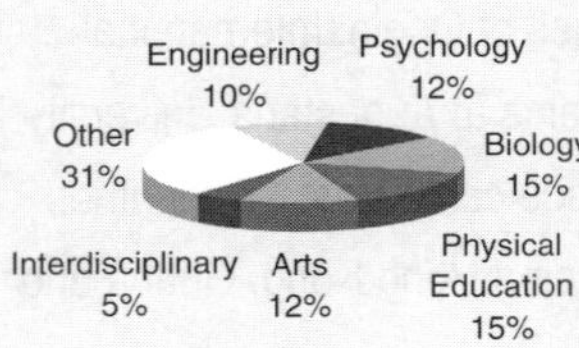

SCHOLARSHIPS & FINANCIAL ASSISTANCE

Augustana University College has one of the most generous financial aid programs in western Canada, providing assistance beyond government loans and awards. In the 1998-99 academic year, Augustana's program provided C$500,000, with an average per-student award of more than $1,400. Numerous academic scholarships, awards and grants are also available, as are a limit of 12 supplemental assistance grants to international students.

Approximately 40 per cent of Augustana students receive financial aid from the university.

Expenses at a Glance

Tuition (undergraduate, full-time):
- In-Province: C$4,695/year
- Out-of-Province: C$4,695/year
- International: C$6,260/year

Fees, Books, Materials: C$885/year (approx)

Accommodation:
- Private: C$400/month
- Residence: C$3,994/year
- Homestay: n/a

Health Insurance: C$36/month (int'l)

CAMPUS & LOCATION

City Population:	14,000
Cost of Living:	low
Climate Range:	-15° to 25°C
Campus Setting:	rural
# of Students in Residence:	420

Built in 1912, Founders' Hall is Augustana University College's landmark and an Alberta designated historic site; the hall houses university administration and faculty offices. In the belief that the largest impact outside the classroom takes place in residence, Augustana students are encouraged to live on campus. The first-year residence complex contains traditional dormitory-style rooms connected to a main hallway, a social lounge, a study lounge, laundry facilities and classrooms. The senior student residence complex provides semi-private dormitories. Over 150 scheduled programs and activities happen in residence each year.

Augustana University College is located in Camrose, a small city in central Alberta about one hour's drive southeast of Edmonton, the provincial capital city. Camrose offers many of the amenities of a larger city while maintaining a small town's friendliness and security. Camrose's close proximity to Edmonton provides students with convenient access to the shopping, dining, entertainment and recreation opportunities of a major centre.

ATHLETICS & EXTRACURRICULAR ACTIVITIES

Augustana University College is a founding member of the Alberta Colleges Athletic Conference (ACAC). Its varsity Vikings take part in ACAC competitions in basketball, hockey (men only), cross-country skiing, curling, canoeing and cross-country running. The ACAC is the premier competitive collegiate hockey conference in Canada. Augustana University College hosts the Viking Cup hockey tournament every second year; in alternate years its team members travel to Europe.

STUDENT SUPPORT SERVICES

The Faith and Life Centre is the focal point of student activities; the centre contains the students' union, student services, campus ministry offices, the career resource centre, a bookstore, a chapel, a coffee house, a student lounge and two classrooms. The chapel, a setting for choral concerts and instrumental recitals, houses the Lede Memorial Organ, a 750-pipe, handcrafted natural oak organ constructed in London, Ontario, by master-builder Gabriel Kney.

Augustana's annual calendar is filled with social, religious, cultural and athletic events. Students are encouraged to participate in extracurricular activities, to compete on athletic teams, to perform in dramatic productions, to sing in a choir or become student leaders.

Through the campus ministry, students are invited to involve themselves in a variety of philanthropic opportunities throughout the year, such as chapel services, retreats, and visitation in local care facilities and prisons and in inner-city Edmonton.

University College Recognition

- Augustana University College is a member of the Association of Universities and Colleges of Canada
- Degree programs offered at Augustana are approved and authorized by the Government of Alberta on the recommendation of the Private Colleges Accreditation Board
- Augustana University College was the first private college in Alberta to receive degree-granting authority under the new provincial legislation in 1983

International Students

University College Enrolment: 38

% of University College Enrolment: 5%

Countries of Origin: International students at Augustana University College come from 17 countries including Hong Kong, Ghana and Jordan.

Colleges

IN

The Prairie Provinces

BOW VALLEY COLLEGE
CALGARY, ALBERTA

College Mission

...to provide academic foundations, English as a second language and career-entry programs of one year or less in the health, business and service industries

Student Voice:

My decision to attend Bow Valley College was one of the best of my life. I went from being computer illiterate to being prepared to tackle any computer project. The instructors were not only my teachers but also my mentors and friends.

Rhandi Tyssen
Office Careers Program graduate
PCL Construction

CONTACT INFORMATION
Bow Valley College
332-6 Avenue SE
Calgary, Alberta
Canada T2G 4S6
PH 1-403-297-4040
FAX 1-403-297-4081
EMAIL info@bowvalleyc.ab.ca
INTERNET
http://www.bowvalleyc.ab.ca

COLLEGE OVERVIEW

For over 30 years, Bow Valley College has offered flexible, responsive and innovative programs that address the needs of individuals, nonprofit organizations, governments and the business community.

Formerly known as the Alberta Vocational College–Calgary, the college took its new name in 1998. Areas of specialization include one-year career programs, practical health-care training, academic foundations, English as a Second Language (ESL) and assessment services.

Career-Related Programs

Bow Valley College responds to labour market conditions by delivering customized programs and assisting corporations, small businesses, community groups and government agencies in determining training needs. Current career-related programs include accounting assistant, administrative assistant, arborist, dental receptionist, hairstyling, hospital unit clerk, hospital admitting clerk, legal secretary, medical office assistant, office careers, practical nurse and surveying.

Part-time certificate programs allow students to continue full-time employment while upgrading their skills. Certificate programs are designed for training, professional development and preparation for the changing workforce.

Health & Community Care Programs

The Health & Community Care Department delivers customized, specialized programs as requested by private and public sector organizations. Past participants include Educational Consortia, Regional Health Authorities, Alberta Health, Family & Social Services and individual health-care organizations.

Students may choose from a variety of career entry programs in the health and community service industries. More than 90 per cent of graduates obtain employment in their chosen area.

ESL Programs

With one of the best ESL programs in Canada, Bow Valley College is renowned for its progressive teaching methods, alternative delivery expertise, care and attention to individual student needs, and dynamic classroom atmosphere. Bow Valley College's ESL certificate program offers nine levels and serves more than 2,000 ESL students per year.

The ESL department offers intercultural and language tours for groups. International partnerships have been established with business and educational organizations; clients include immigrants, employees of international companies, student exchange groups and international visa students.

Highlights

- Key programs include academic foundations, career programs and ESL
- Flexible scheduling; classes are held in mornings, afternoons and evenings
- Options include full-time, part-time, self-paced and home study programs

College Statistics

Year Founded: 1965

Academic Options: high school diploma/GED/certificate

Calendar Year: varies according to program

ACADEMIC PROGRAMS

Academic Foundations: Adult Basic Education, Tutored Literacy Programs, Speech Assisted Reading & Writing (SARAW), Personal Employability & Academic Competencies, High School Credit Courses, Apprenticeship Math & Science, Customized Academic Programs (Artstream, Women in Science & Technology, Deaf & Hard-of-Hearing Literacy)

Aboriginal Programs: Adult Upgrading & Pre-employment Training, Aboriginal Bridge & Literacy

English as a Second Language (ESL): General ESL, Intermediate to Advanced ESL, ESL for Academic Purposes, Tutored Small Group ESL, Language Instruction for Newcomers to Canada (LINC), ESL for International Students

Career-Related Programs: Applied Accounting, Computer Skills, Hairstyling, Landscaping & Arboriculture, Legal, Office Careers, Private Investigation, Real Estate, Surveying, Teaching English Abroad

Health & Community Care: Child Care, Dental Receptionist, Hospital Admitting Clerk, Hospital Unit Clerk, Personal Care Attendant, Practical Nursing, Medical Office Assistant

Training for Business: The Assessment Centre, Essential Skills Needs Assessment, Communicating Across Cultures, Business Client English Language & English in the Workplace, Customized Computer Training

ADMISSIONS CRITERIA & PROCEDURES

Applicants are encouraged to apply as soon as possible; qualified students are admitted on a first-come, first-served basis, upon receipt of tuition payment. Individuals may register if they are 18 years or older, or are able to demonstrate to the registrar the maturity to benefit from a selected program of study. Prerequisites and registration dates vary by program; students should consult Bow Valley College's current calendar or contact the registrar's office. Student eligibility is determined by reviewing assessments, transcripts and medical information, when applicable. Applicants for Personal Care Attendant, Hospital Unit Clerk, Hospital Admitting Clerk and Practical Nurse programs are required to provide a security clearance (evidence of no criminal record).

Certain programs may require an assessment of the student's abilities. Assessments are scheduled by the registrar's office and are subject to a nonrefundable fee that may vary by program. Tuition for all programs must be paid in full at the time of registration.

Registration for most courses can be done by mail, by phone or by fax. International students should send completed application forms (registration and homestay placement) along with fees of C$100 for registration, C$100 for homestay placement and C$45 for airport pickup (optional); tuition may be paid in advance or upon arrival in Calgary. Groups interested in intercultural exchange tours should contact the International Recruitment & Marketing Officer at ncroft@bowvalley.ab.ca.

Admissions at a Glance

Minimum GPA: n/a

Minimum English Requirements: n/a

Application Fee: n/a (Canadian); C$100 (international)

Application Deadlines: varies by program

ACADEMIC FACILITIES

Bow Valley College's Learner Support Services is a fully integrated service area designed to help students in their studies by providing a wide range of resource materials, from computer and Internet access to resource books and tutors. Students have access to learning professionals for assistance in one-on-one and small group settings. These professionals are accessible on a drop-in or appointment basis from Monday through Saturday.

Areas of assistance include computer-managed learning, study skills, instructional technology, services for special needs students and tutorial assistance. ESL students may receive individualized help before and after class through the ESL Tutorial Centre.

Student & Faculty Profile

Total Enrolment: 10,520

Full-Time Enrolment: 3,258

\# of Faculty: 269

Student/Faculty Ratio: 15:1

Male/Female Students: 35%/65%

Academic Class Sizes: varies

Enrolment by Program Type:

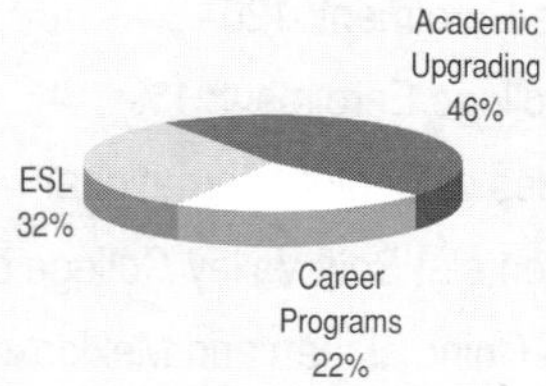

SCHOLARSHIPS & FINANCIAL ASSISTANCE

Depending on the chosen course, the registrar's office will refer students to potential sponsoring agencies.

Assistance is available to both full- and part-time learners. Individuals may want to apply for a student loan and/or grants from the Alberta Students' Finance Board. Application forms are available through the Bow Valley College Registrar's Office.

Expenses at a Glance

Tuition (full-time):
- In-Province: varies
- Out-of-Province: varies
- International: C$1,500 (full-time ESL)

Fees, Books, Materials: varies

Accommodation:
- Private: C$550-800/month
- Residence: n/a
- Homestay: C$300-550/month (ESL students only)

Health Insurance: C$36/month (international)

CAMPUS & LOCATION

City Population:	830,000
Cost of Living:	medium
Climate Range:	-16° to 23°C
Campus Setting:	urban
# of Students in Residence:	n/a

Bow Valley College runs 17 community learning centres in Calgary and southern Alberta. Most programs are offered at the main campus in downtown Calgary, a city famous as the home of the world's largest rodeo, the Calgary Stampede. The main campus location has convenient access to the downtown C-train and transit routes and is just a five minute walk from the Bow River Valley. There are two other campuses within the city of Calgary.

Additional campuses in southern Alberta are located in Airdrie, Canmore, Drumheller and Strathmore.

One of Alberta's two major cities, Calgary is located just an hour's drive from Banff and the Rocky Mountains. The city offers numerous recreational and cultural activities, including tennis, horseback riding, swimming and live theatre. Calgary is also home to many golf courses and green parks, as well as Canada Olympic Park, the site of the 1988 Winter Olympics.

ATHLETICS & EXTRACURRICULAR ACTIVITIES

The Student's Association is available to work with students from all programs at the college to help meet recreational, cultural and student community needs. Passes for use of YWCA athletic facilities across the street are available at a reasonable cost to students in full-time programs. Students may also purchase a discounted membership at Fitness on 5th, another health & fitness club nearby the campus; facilities include an indoor swimming pool, nautilus equipment and fitness classes.

Through the ESL program, full-time international students participate in two day trips per 10-week term. These trips may include destinations such as Banff or Kananaskis Country; activities often involve skiing or hiking.

STUDENT SUPPORT SERVICES

Bow Valley College offers on-campus daycare, student counselling services, free health services, a cafeteria, a bookstore and the Family Resource Centre.

The daycare facility provides care for children aged two to six years; a full-time ECS (kindergarten) program is available on site. Counselling Services helps students resolve educational, career and personal concerns as well as providing assistance with job search skills, relaxation and stress management techniques and study skills. The cafeteria, located on the second floor, is open Monday to Friday. Textbooks are available at the Bow Valley College bookstore, located on the ground floor of the college.

ESL students have access to a student adviser for assistance with personal issues, cultural adjustment, and official forms and procedures. Staff interpreters speak more than 25 languages, so assistance may be available to international students in their first language.

College Recognition

- Member of the Council of Second Language Programs of Canada, the Association of Canadian Community Colleges, the Canadian Bureau of International Education and the Alberta Centre for International Education

International Students

College Enrolment: 120

% of College Enrolment: 1%

Countries of Origin: International students at Bow Valley College come from China, Japan and Mexico.

MOUNT ROYAL COLLEGE
CALGARY, ALBERTA

A Mount Royal Education

College Mission

...to be Canada's leading

undergraduate college, educating

and training individuals for success

in the new economy

Student Voice:

There is a real sense of community at Mount Royal. Instructors really go out of their way to ensure that students are well prepared, not only for the work force, but a life filled with learning.

Jeff Breckenridge
Bachelor of Applied Communication

CONTACT INFORMATION
Mount Royal College
4825 Richard Road S.W.
Calgary, Alberta
Canada T3E 6K6
PH 1-403-240-6111
FAX 1-403-240-6698
EMAIL admissions@mtroyal.ab.ca
INTERNET http://www.mtroyal.ab.ca

COLLEGE OVERVIEW

Mount Royal College (MRC) is the oldest and largest college in Alberta. Founded in 1910, MRC continues to meet the needs of the community through its skill upgrading and career development programs.

MRC offers three applied degree programs—in communications, interior design and small business & entrepreneurship—as well as a joint degree program in nursing with the University of Calgary. The college also offers university transfer, diploma and certificate programs, many of which feature workterm opportunities.

Applied Degree and Degree Programs

MRC now offers three applied degree programs—applied communications, with specializations in journalism, public relations and technical writing; interior design; and applied small business & entrepreneurship. All programs require students to complete two terms of paid work experience. In conjunction with the University of Calgary, MRC also offers a four-year degree program in nursing.

Diplomas and Certificates

MRC offers a wide range of one- and two-year full-time certificate and diploma programs, preparing students for immediate career employment. Several of these certificates are advanced certificates adding to the existing skills of nurses and athletic therapists. Many of the diplomas and certificates are transferable to university degree programs for further study.

University Transfer

Students who complete the first two years of a university degree at MRC pay less tuition and enjoy individual attention from instructors and small class sizes. Students can pursue majors in arts, commerce, computer science, education, engineering, physical education, science and general studies.

Workterm Experience

Cooperative education and workterm experiences help bridge the transition from the classroom to the workplace. Co-op education opportunities are in place for students in business administration and general insurance. Students in applied degree programs must complete two terms of paid work experience.

Additional Programs

The Centre for Health Studies offers courses in Forensic Studies via the Internet for nurses and law enforcement professionals who deal with victims of violence. The Small Business Training Centre prepares individuals to start and operate small businesses.

Highlights

- Three applied degree programs
- Over 50 credit programs, including university transfers
- Full- and part-time study options
- City campus location is home to the Languages Institute and Office of International Education

College Statistics

Year Founded: 1910

Academic Options: certificate/diploma/applied degree

Calendar Year: fall semester (Sept-Dec); winter semester (Jan-April); spring semester (May-June); summer semester (Jul-Aug)

ACADEMIC PROGRAMS

Faculty of Arts & Communications: Anthro, Archaeology, Broadcasting, Econ, Ed, English, Journalism, Languages, Poli Econ, Poli Sci, Professional Writing, Psych, PR, Sociology, Tech Writing

School for Business & Entrepreneurial Studies: Aviation & Airflight Training; Bus Admin (Accounting & Financial Mgmt, Gen Bus, HR, Mktg Mgmt), Gen Insurance & Bus Admin

Faculty of Community Studies: Crim (Corrections, Law Enforcement), Physical Ed & Rec Studies (Athletic Therapy, Community Rec, Outdoor Pursuits, Physical Activity & Sport Administrations, Therapeutic Rec), Social Services (Child & Youth Care, Community Rehab, Early Childhood Ed, Social Work)

Centre For Health Studies: Calgary Conjoint Nursing, Critical Care Nursing, Mental Health Nursing, Gerontology, Child Health Care, Forensic Health

Faculty of Science & Technology: Chem, Bio & Environmental Sci (Environmental Tech, Biochem, Biology, Chem, Microbio, Natural Science, Zoology), Comp Sci & IS, Earth Sci (Geog, Geology), Math, Physics & Eng (Astro, Math, Eng, Physics)

The Mount Royal College Conservatory: Music Performance, Music, Speech, Theatre Arts

Faculty of Continuing Education & Extension: Small Business Training Centre

ADMISSIONS CRITERIA & PROCEDURES

Enquiries relating to admission should be directed to the Advising Centre at the Office of the Registrar (1-403-240-0148). Program information is available on the website: http://www.mtroyal.ab.ca. Applications can be accessed through MRC's Internet site, the Office of the Registrar or a high school counsellor's office. Candidates must submit a completed application form and the C$30 nonrefundable application fee as soon as possible, since the college receives far more qualified applications than there are spaces available each year.

To be eligible for admission, applicants must have graduated from an Alberta high school or a recognized secondary school, or be 18 years of age or older. All transcripts must be submitted to the admissions office, regardless of whether or not the applicant has received a high school diploma. International applicants must have their transcripts certified by a school official. Applicants who have insufficient entrance requirements may enrol in credit-free courses to upgrade their status.

Applicants whose first language is not English and who have not received two years of secondary school instruction in English must demonstrate English proficiency by submitting a TOEFL score of 560 or higher, or by proving successful completion of MRC's ESL program. International applicants are accepted for the fall semester only, and all students must submit a completed medical history form.

Admissions at a Glance

Minimum GPA: equivalent to Alberta high school diploma

Minimum English Requirements: TOEFL 560 or completion of ESL program

Application Fee: C$30 (Canadian and international)

Application Deadlines: priority application period: Dec 1-Jan 31 (fall semester); Canadian: Nov 20 (winter semester), July 15 (fall semester); international: April 1 (fall semester)

ACADEMIC FACILITIES

The Learning Skills Centre offers four main services—workshops, individual assistance, peer tutoring and services for students with disabilities—to help students succeed at their academic studies. To foster teaching excellence and innovation, the Academic Development Centre provides a variety of services such as curriculum development and media production.

The library houses over 120,000 books, 1,200 periodicals, computers with Internet access and many other items all accessible for student and faculty research. An additional smaller library is located at the City Centre campus. Four computer laboratories are available to full- and part-time students; these labs provide students with Internet access and free email accounts.

Student & Faculty Profile

Total Enrolment: 21,453

Full-Time Enrolment: 5,443

# of Faculty: 519

Student/Faculty Ratio: 17:1

Male/Female Students: 40%/60%

Academic Class Sizes: 24 (average)

Enrolment by Program Type:

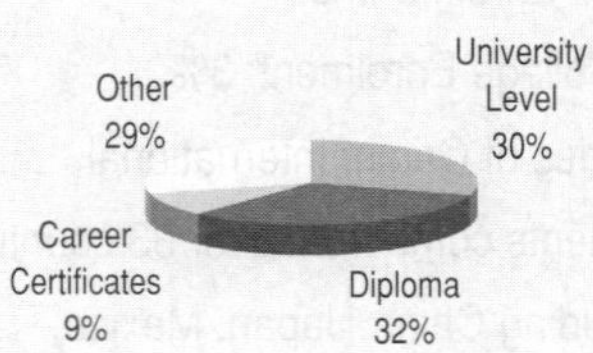

SCHOLARSHIPS & FINANCIAL ASSISTANCE

MRC offers a variety of scholarships for entering, new and continuing students. Residents of Alberta are eligible to apply for 25 entrance awards and 10 entrance bursaries each year. Scholarship applications for new and continuing students are available from the Student Awards Office; the application deadline is the end of October. In addition to the numerous entrance scholarships, students may apply for financial assistance through the Canada Student Loans Plan, the Province of Alberta Assistance or maintenance grants (available to financially disadvantaged students). For more information, students should contact Financial Aid and Student Awards (1-403-240-6223).

Expenses at a Glance

Tuition (full-time):

- In-Province: C$2,800-3,000/year
- Out-of-Province: C$2,800-3,000/year
- International: C$6,168/year

Fees, Books, Materials: C$800/year

Accommodation:

- Private: C$450-675/month
- Residence: C$2,104-3,280/year
- Homestay: C$500-575/month

Health Insurance: C$81/semester

CAMPUS & LOCATION

City Population:	828,500
Cost of Living:	medium
Climate Range:	-16° to 23°C
Campus Setting:	urban
# of Students in Residence:	438

Mount Royal College is located in Calgary, the site of the 1988 Winter Olympics. The main campus, Lincoln Park, is situated in southwest Calgary; the satellite City Centre campus lies in the heart of the downtown core. In 1989, the Lincoln campus underwent a C$73-million facility expansion and renovation to ensure that the college would maintain an edge on current technology and meet the needs of its growing student population.

In the same year as the campus expansion, a C$12-million student residence townhouse complex opened at the Lincoln Park campus, providing housing for more than 435 students. All rooms are fully furnished, and each townhouse provides laundry facilities.

Calgary was founded in 1875 as a small North West Mounted Police post; today it ranks second in Canada as a corporate home base and is known as Canada's gateway to the majestic Rocky Mountains. Calgary, with its population of 800,000 people, is safe, friendly, multicultural and cosmopolitan. Calgary's spectacular natural setting, near Banff National Park, provides students with year-round outdoor recreational opportunities. Calgary is also renowned for its annual Stampede, which celebrates the city's western heritage and attracts thousands of tourists each year.

ATHLETICS & EXTRACURRICULAR ACTIVITIES

MRC's Cougar sports teams have won many titles over the years. In 1997 to 1998, the college won four Canadian Colleges Athletic Association (CCAA) titles in men's volleyball, hockey and soccer, and in women's badminton doubles, as well as national silver medals in women's basketball and men's badminton doubles.

Recreational sports are available through intramural and clubs; activities include ice hockey, volleyball, rodeo and soccer. Recreational facilities for students and faculty use include the 800-seat main gymnasium, a smaller gymnasium with a rock-climbing wall, a 25-square-metre saltwater pool and a fitness centre. Campus Recreation offers a wide range of courses and drop-in activities during the school year, including Step classes, yoga and power pacing.

MRC also has three performance theatres: the 300-seat Leacock Theatre is used primarily for music and speech events; full theatrical lighting and sound equipment make the 250-seat Wright Theatre ideal for theatrical performances; and the smaller 183-seat Nickle Theatre is also ideal for performing arts activities.

College Recognition

- 96% of graduates in 1997 were satisfied with their MRC education
- MRC's new interior design degree is the only degree of three in Canada that offers work experience
- MRC has the only applied degree in small business & entrepreneurship in Canada
- The applied degree in communications, specialization public relations, is one of only two in Canada

STUDENT SUPPORT SERVICES

To ensure student success, MRC offers many student support services: the Advising Centre for initial and continuing help in program selection; the Counselling Centre for help with school and personal issues; Health Services for medical concerns; Career Services for assistance in career selection; the Learning Skills Centre for help in managing courses and exams; and an on-site chaplaincy. The Students' Association runs student clubs, sponsors events and provides student support services. New students are strongly encouraged to attend MRC's New Student Orientation Program, designed to introduce students to the various services available on campus, as well as to give a general overall introduction to the college.

International Students

College Enrolment: 567

% of College Enrolment: 3%

Countries of Origin: International students come from over 33 countries, including China, Japan, Mexico, Tanzania, the US, the UK and Taiwan.

RED DEER COLLEGE
RED DEER, ALBERTA

College Mission

...to provide students with a foundation of knowledge and skills which enables them to develop to their fullest potential

Student Voice:

RDC is a very friendly atmosphere...you really get to know your instructors and fellow students.

Beth Cowper
Student, Biological Sciences Technology

CONTACT INFORMATION
Red Deer College
PO Box 5005
Red Deer, Alberta
Canada T4N 5H5
PH 1-403-342-3300
FAX 1-403-340-8940
EMAIL registrar@admin.rdc.ab.ca
INTERNET http://www.rdc.ab.ca

COLLEGE OVERVIEW

Red Deer College (RDC) was founded in 1963 and offers diploma, certificate, transfer credit, and apprenticeship programs.

University Transfer Programs

RDC offers 32 two-year transfer programs, developed in consultation with local universities (particularly the University of Alberta), in the areas of arts, commerce, education, education & science, fine arts, kinesiology & sports studies, recreation administration, science (25 programs), nursing, prechiropractic, predentistry, premedicine, pre-optometry, prepharmacy and preveterinary. RDC has transfer agreements with universities in Alberta and outside the province. Students may earn up to two years of credit towards bachelor's degrees.

Four degree completion programs are offered by RDC: Bachelor of Arts (BA) from the University of Calgary, Bachelor of Education (BEd) and Bachelor of Science in Nursing (BScN) from the University of Alberta, and Bachelor of Science (BGS) from Athabasca University. These programs enable students to complete full baccalaureate degrees at the RDC campus.

Career, Certificate and Diploma Programs

RDC enjoys a close relationship with the local business community, and designs course curricula in anticipation of its needs. RDC career, certificate and diploma programs are designed for students who wish to advance their careers. The programs give students specific skills and practical experience. Over 90 per cent of students graduating from these programs are employed within nine months of graduation.

Other Programs

RDC offers numerous other programs including continuing education courses, extension courses, Certified General Accountants of Canada (CGA) and Society of Management Accountants (CMA) courses and ESL courses.

Extension Services offers a variety of on-site training programs as well as workshops, seminars and noncredit courses for professionals who wish to acquire new skills or increase their knowledge in a specific field.

The Adult Basic Education (ABE) program offers small classes in reading, writing and math skills. Levels range from elementary to grade nine.

Highlights

- 32 university transfer programs to choose from
- Over 90% of diploma/certificate graduates have found employment within 9 months of graduation
- Close ties with local business community
- Degree completion available

College Statistics

Year Founded: 1963
Academic Options: diploma/certificate/undergraduate
Calendar Year: fall term (Sept-Dec); winter term (Jan-Apr); spring term (May-Aug); summer term (Jul-Aug)

ACADEMIC PROGRAMS

University of Transfer Programs: Agriculture, Agriculture/Food Business Management, Arts, Biochemistry, Biological Sciences, Chemistry, Commerce, Computing Science, Education, Engineering, Environmental & Conversation Sciences, Fine Arts, Forestry, General Science, Geography, Geophysics, Human Ecology, Kinesiology & Sports Studies, Math & Economics, Mathematics, Meteorology, Nutrition & Food Sciences, Physics, Physiology, Prechiropractic, Predentistry, Premedicine, Pre-optometry, Prepharmacy, Pre-Veterinary Medicine, Psychology, Recreation Administration, Science & Education, Statistics

Certificate, Diploma & Career Programs: Biological Sciences Technology, Business Administration, Career & Academic Preparation, Chemical Technology, Computer Systems Technology, Early Childhood Development, General Studies, Hospitality & Tourism, Kinesiology & Sports Studies, Legal Assistant, Music, Nursing, Office Administration, Pharmacy Technician, Rehabilitation Services, Social Work, Teacher Assistant, Theatre Studies in Performance (Technology, Costume Cutting and Construction), Transitional/Vocational Program, Visual Arts

Apprenticeship Programs: Automotive Service Technician, Carpenter, Electrician, Heavy Equipment Technician, Locksmith, Plumber, Sprinkler System Installer, Water Well Driller, Welder

ADMISSIONS CRITERIA & PROCEDURES

Students wishing to attend RDC should submit a completed application form to the Access Centre. Individuals are eligible for general admission if they have graduated from an Alberta secondary school, or its equivalent, or are 19 years of age and have been out of school for over one year. Mature students may be required to take equivalency classes before being admitted to their desired program. Eligible applicants are accepted on a first-come, first-served basis. Students are encouraged to apply early for limited enrolment programs.

All students wishing to enter university transfer diploma programs must graduate from secondary school with a minimum average of 60 per cent and no mark below 50 per cent. Individual programs have their own specific prerequisites and course requirements. Students wishing to enter career and academic preparation programs are required to take placement tests before registering for classes.

International students are eligible for all academic programs at RDC. Students from abroad are required to submit a TOEFL score of 550 or higher and notarized transcripts of all academic documents in order to be considered for admission. International applications must include a C$50 application fee.

The application fee for Canadian students is C$40.

Admissions at a Glance

Minimum GPA: n/a

Minimum English Requirements: TOEFL 550

Application Fee: C$40 (Canadian), $50 (international)

Application Deadlines: December 1 (fall term); April 1 (winter term); August 1 (spring term)

ACADEMIC FACILITIES

The Red Deer College Library holds over 130,000 items. Students have access to a variety of learning materials including CD-ROMs, online databases and periodicals. RDC is also a member of NEOS, a central Alberta library consortium, giving students access to over four million items.

The Audio Visual Centre is equipped with a variety of media equipment. The centre offers workshops throughout the year on how to effectively use technology.

Computing Services has a collection of VAX microcomputers to meet high-end computing needs. All students have email and Internet access. Computer workstations are available in designated labs and the library.

The Learning Assistance Centre is available for those students wishing to improve fundamental skills in reading, writing and mathematics. Students may attend workshops and class presentations, use self-instructional materials or arrange for individual appointments.

Student & Faculty Profile

Total Enrolment: 10,309

Full-Time Enrolment: 5,800

# of Faculty: 320 (total)

Student/Faculty Ratio: 18:1 (full-time)

Male/Female Students: 40%/60%

Academic Class Sizes: 25 (average)

Enrolment by Program Type:

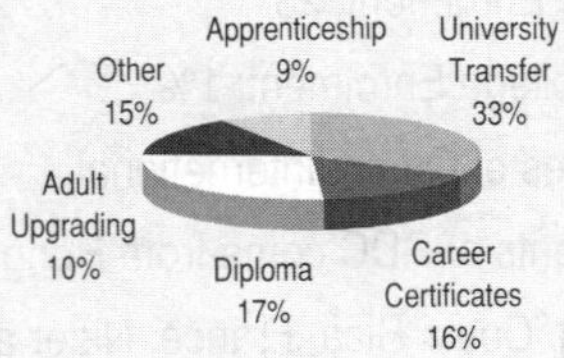

SCHOLARSHIPS & FINANCIAL ASSISTANCE

The Student Financial Aid & Awards Office can assist students with applications to federal and provincial loan programs, as well as provide information concerning college grants, bursaries and scholarships. There are a variety of merit-based, need-based and athletic awards available through RDC. Students are encouraged to apply early for all financial assistance and awards since competition is high.

Expenses at a Glance

Tuition (full-time):

- In-Province: C$2,564-3,495/year
- Out-of-Province: C$2,564-3,495/year
- International: C$7,511-8,422/year

Fees, Books, Materials: C$800/year (average)

Accommodation:

- Private: C$400-500/month
- Residence: C$475/month
- Homestay: n/a

Health Insurance: not available

CAMPUS & LOCATION

City Population:	60,000
Cost of Living:	low
Climate Range:	-16° to 24°C
Campus Setting:	suburban
# of Students in Residence:	210

The main campus of Red Deer College is located in the city of Red Deer. With an extensive river valley park system providing over 50 kilometres of walking trails, the modern campus is a focal point of the city. The college's Literary & Learning Centre and Community & Workplace Development Training Centre are located downtown. The college's renowned Art Centre offers a variety of cultural opportunities, including art exhibits, live performances and readings.

Red Deer has a population of 60,000, an ideal size combining a friendly, safe, small community with the conveniences of a larger city. The city is centrally located, within two hours of the major metropolitan centres of Edmonton and Calgary as well as Banff National Park. Red Deer is home to many competitive sports teams and is a popular choice for many athletic tournaments due to its central location. The outdoor recreational activities abound in the area, including skiing, swimming, hiking and skating.

ATHLETICS & EXTRACURRICULAR ACTIVITIES

RDC is a member of the Alberta College Athletic Conference (ACAC). Both men and women may participate in sporting activities such as badminton, basketball, cross-country skiing, golf, hockey, soccer and volleyball. On a less competitive level, the college has a large intramural recreation program that encourages students to become involved in the school outside the classroom. A variety of programs, including noncredit instructional courses, drop-in activities and activity clubs are available. The coeducational intramural programs can include activities such as slo-pitch baseball, floor hockey, volleyball and curling.

On-campus recreational facilities include two full-service gymnasia, a weight room and racquetball courts. The Kevin Sirois Fitness Resource Centre helps students to become more involved and to maintain active, healthy and well-rounded lifestyles. Services include fitness testing, nutrition counselling and massage therapy. The Department of Music offers a number of concerts throughout the year, many of which are free to students.

College Recognition

- Recipient of the National Council for Staff, Program & Organizational Development Award for Excellence
- Awarded the Alberta Tourism, Parks & Recreation Association Merit Award
- Frequent winner of the Alberta Colleges Athletic Conference Supremacy Award (13 times in 25 years)

STUDENT SUPPORT SERVICES

RDC students have access to a variety of support services. The Career, Counselling & Enrollment Support Centre provides assistance through academic, career and personal counselling, as well as by offering many workshops throughout the year in areas such as communication skills and career decision making. Employment Assistance Services helps students find employment during and after studies.

There are a variety of social services offered on campus including a child care centre, a chaplaincy and a health centre. RDC strives to create a positive environment for all of its students.

The International Students Advising Office assists and supports international students who have concerns regarding immigration issues, health care, housing, academic issues and cultural adaptation.

International Students

College Enrolment: 23

% of College Enrolment: 1%

Countries of Origin: International students at RDC come from Hong Kong, Costa Rica, France, Niger and Trinidad, Tobago.

Institutes

IN

The Prairie Provinces

SOUTHERN ALBERTA INSTITUTE OF TECHNOLOGY CALGARY, ALBERTA

Institute Mission

...to be an innovative organization equipping people to compete successfully in the changing world of work by providing relevant, skill-oriented education

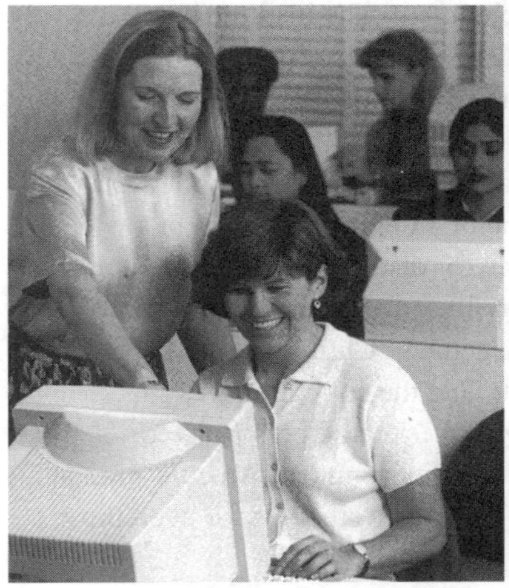

Student Voice:

I like the hands-on training you get at SAIT and the instructors really take the time out to help you.

Lisa Nasrin
Printing Management Technology

CONTACT INFORMATION
Southern Alberta Institute of Technology
1301 - 16 Avenue NW
Calgary, Alberta
Canada T2M 0L4
PH 1-403-284-7114
FAX 1-403-284-7163
EMAIL international@sait.ab.ca
INTERNET http://www.sait.ab.ca

Institute Overview

Southern Alberta Institute of Technology (SAIT) was founded in 1916, and is the oldest polytechnic institute in Canada. SAIT is a public, coeducational institution which today offers over 87 programs, providing training in business, industry, technology, trades and applied arts.

Academic Programs

SAIT's approach to career-oriented education combines theoretical knowledge with practical skills development. The institute has continually improved programs to meet the changing demands of the working world. SAIT currently offers certificate, diploma and applied bachelor's degree programs in a wide variety of disciplines such as avionics technology and hotel & restaurant management. Class sizes are kept small, and the college strives to provide a friendly, personalized learning environment. An education at SAIT prepares students for even more specialized training. There are many post-diploma certificate programs designed to complement the core programs available. The college has study and transfer agreements with many universities in Canada and the US.

Practical Experience

SAIT understands how important practical experience is to successful entry into the workforce. Many of the institute's certificate and diploma programs have optional co-op programs which provide students with opportunities for meaningful work experience. Students can also obtain practical training in a variety of other ways, such as fieldwork and group projects, or through participation in the one of the five Centres for Applied Technology, supported by SAIT in partnership with national and local industry. SAIT currently has 91 partnerships within various businesses and industries. Most instructors are hired from industry so that students benefit directly from their wisdom and experience.

Internationalism

There is a growing commitment towards global education at SAIT. The institute's large international student body represents a mere fraction of the foreign students trained by SAIT. Through innovations in teaching technology, SAIT has been able to offer distance education and career-training to more than 47,000 students worldwide. The institute has executed technology transfer and training services in both the public and private sector with more than 25 different countries. The Business Development & International Training department handles all international operations.

Highlights

- Diploma, certificate and degree programs offered in a variety of disciplines
- Close partnerships with business and industry
- 95 per cent employment rate within six months of graduation
- Located in Canada's fastest growing city

Institute Statistics

Year Founded: 1916

Academic Options: certificate/diploma/undergraduate

Calendar Year: fall term (Aug-Dec); winter term (Jan-Apr); summer term (May-Aug)

ACADEMIC PROGRAMS

Applied Degrees: Applied Information Systems, Applied Petroleum Eng

Aviation: Aeronautical Eng, Aircraft Maintenance Engineers, Avionics

Business: Bus Admin (Accounting, General Mgmt, Marketing, Financial Services, Automotive Marketing); Hotel & Restaurant Mgmt; Legal Assistant; Office Administration; Office Assistant; Travel Counselling

Communications: Cinema; Television, Stage & Radio; Journalism; Library & Information; Multimedia; Printing Mgmt

Engineering & Technology Diploma Programs: Allied Studies, Aeronautical Eng, Arch , Avionics, Broadcast, Building Mech Systems, Chem Eng, Chem, Civil Eng, Comp Eng, Comp, Electrical Eng, Electronics Eng, Electronics, Energy & Natural Resources, Eng Design & Drafting, Ind Instrumentation, Machinist, Mech Eng, Mech, Operations Mgmt, Petroleum Eng, Power Eng, Process Operations, Surveying & Mapping, Telecommunications, Welding Eng, Wood Eng

Health: Animal Health, Dental Assistant, Emergency Med Responder, Emergency Med - Ambulance, Emergency Med - Paramedic, Food & Nutrition Mgmt, Health Record, Med Lab Assistant, Med Transcriptionist, Nuclear Medicine, Respiratory Therapy, Sterile Processing & Distribution

ADMISSIONS CRITERIA & PROCEDURES

To be granted admission to SAIT, applicants must possess an Alberta High School Diploma (AHSD), or its equivalent, and must satisfy the academic prerequisites of the individual program. Prerequisites vary from program to program, but the general requirements are senior-level mathematics and English. Entry to some programs may be competitive; the admissions committee may consider such criteria as GPA, related work experience or a portfolio submission. Students entering engineering programs must write a placement test to determine the level at which they enter the program. Students with lower scores may be required to enrol in upgrading courses.

Canadian students should send completed applications, along with a C$25 application fee, to the Admissions Office at SAIT. International students whose native language is not English must submit a TOEFL score of 560 or higher to be considered for direct entry into programs. International students who cannot meet this or other requirements may choose to enrol in the International Academic Upgrading program which is designed to provide students with the English language, mathematics and science prerequisites necessary to proceed into regular programs at SAIT. All international applications should be sent to the Business Development & International Training Office and must be accompanied by a C$500 application fee, which includes a C$425 deposit for the first semester of studies.

Applicants who do not have an AHSD, or its equivalent, may be considered for admission provided they are over 21 years of age and meet other minimum requirements.

Admissions at a Glance

Minimum GPA: no set minimum

Minimum English Requirements:
TOEFL 560

Application Fee: C$25 (Canadian), $500 (international)

Application Deadlines: June 1 (fall term); December 1 (winter term); April 1 (spring term)

ACADEMIC FACILITIES

SAIT prides itself on providing students with a positive, modern learning environment. There are numerous high-quality academic facilities on campus, including a library, a resource centre and several computer laboratories, which encourage students to incorporate computer use into their daily routine. All SAIT students have email accounts and Internet access.

A technological institute, SAIT strives to be ahead of current trends by providing comprehensive research and experimental testing facilities containing the latest scientific equipment. Notable scientific laboratories include a wind tunnel, a fluid mechanics lab and a computer-aided design (CAD) lab. The Learning Skills Centre offers additional academic assistance to students who need to improve fundamental learning skills. The centre offers group workshops and individual tutorials in a variety of fields.

Student & Faculty Profile

Total Enrolment: 8,800

Undergraduate Enrolment: 8,800

# of Faculty: 650

Student/Faculty Ratio: 13:1

Male/Female Students: 60%/40%

First-Year Class Sizes: 30-35

Undergraduate Acceptance Rate: not available

Undergraduate Enrolment by Discipline:

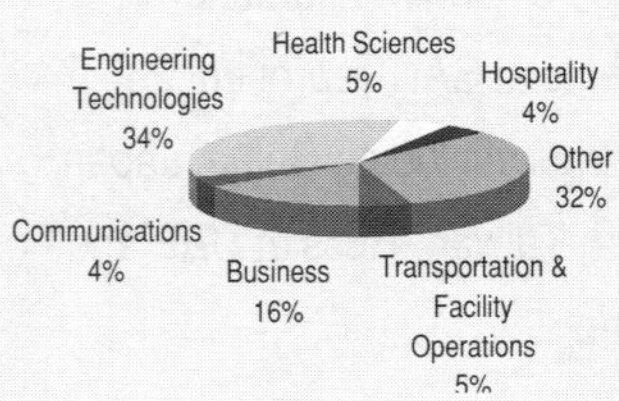

SCHOLARSHIPS & FINANCIAL ASSISTANCE

There are several forms of financial assistance available to Canadian students, including government loans, grants, scholarships and bursaries. Government grant and loans are need-based awards of a maximum value of C$9,000 per year. SAIT administers an extensive variety of scholarships to encourage superior academic achievement and bursaries to worthy students in need of financial aid. Students will be automatically considered for most scholarships.

While there are no entrance scholarships for first-year international students, returning students are eligible for tuition reduction scholarships.

Expenses at a Glance

Tuition (undergraduate, full-time):
In-Province: C$1,780-3,033/year
Out-of-Province: C$1,780-3,033/year
International: C$8,500-9,500/year

Fees, Books, Materials: C$600-800/year

Accommodation:
Private: C$525-575/month
Residence: C$550/month
Homestay: C$550/month

Health Insurance: C$104/year

CAMPUS & LOCATION

City Population:	828,500
Cost of Living:	medium
Climate Range:	-16° to 23°C
Campus Setting:	urban
# of Students in Residence:	491

The main campus of the Southern Alberta Institute of Technology is located on 40 hectares of land in north-central Calgary and comprises 139 classrooms, 137 laboratories and 71 workshops housed in 12 buildings. The urban campus offers students a quiet place to study, secluded from the bustle of the city. With many tree-filled areas and tranquil settings, the campus provides the best of both worlds. Across the street from SAIT is a shopping complex with retail shops, banks, supermarkets and a professional medical clinic. The SAIT II campus, located in northwest Calgary and housed in one building, is home to students enrolled in apprenticeship trades. Owasina Hall, a 22-storey high residence facility, offers 204 self-contained apartments for students.

Calgary is located in the southern part of Alberta and is the fastest growing city in Canada. A multicultural city that is well-known for its friendliness and hospitality, Calgary has become a popular destination for international students. The city is renowned for its natural beauty and is close to the majestic Rocky Mountains; Calgary hosted the Winter Olympics in 1988. The city is also home to the world-renowned Calgary Stampede as well as numerous other cultural opportunities including galleries, museums, the symphony and theatre. Students can enjoy the many recreational activities the region has to offer including skiing, hiking, fishing, horseback riding and cycling.

ATHLETICS & EXTRACURRICULAR ACTIVITIES

SAIT believes that student activities provide educational, cultural and social experiences which contribute to a positive learning environment. SAIT currently competes in eight intercollegiate sports. The Campus Centre houses all of the college's recreational facilities, including a fully equipped gymnasium, squash and racquetball courts, a weight room, a 35-metre swimming pool and a hockey arena. All students are encouraged to participate in the many intramural sports the college has to offer such as badminton, basketball, volleyball and hockey. SAIT also organizes a variety of instructional programs to complement academic life such as aerobics, martial arts and ballroom dancing.

There are numerous social and cultural activities available. The Campus Centre is the hub of all student activity and is home to the study government which runs a weekly newspaper and organizes many social events throughout the year. The centre also houses a 341-seat theatre, large cabaret facility, a games room and several student lounges. There are many social and cultural student organizations meeting on campus including a multicultural club and numerous departmental clubs.

Institute Recognition

- Programs accredited by organizations including the Alberta Ministry of Education; Canadian Council of Technicians & Technologists; Canadian Medical Association; Transport Canada; Hotel & Catering International Management Association

STUDENT SUPPORT SERVICES

The Advising Centre for Counselling & Employment Services is designed to handle most of the student services on campus. Within the centre, students can find personal counselling, career advice and workshops, an employment centre and a chaplaincy. SAIT's health services program is administered through Campus Health.

International students benefit from SAIT's International Student Centre and international advisers who strive to assist students with a variety of academic and personal issues, such as immigration and cultural concerns, housing information and setting up a bank account.

International Students

Institute Enrolment: 250

% of Institute Enrolment: 3%

Countries of Origin: International students at SAIT represent 26 countries, including China, Japan, Korea, Taiwan, Russia, UAE and Ireland.

PROFILES OF Universities & Colleges IN Ontario

Universities

IN

Ontario

CARLETON UNIVERSITY
OTTAWA, ONTARIO

University Mission

...to foster the pursuit of knowledge; to provide students with the opportunity to realize their intellectual, social, cultural and athletic potential

Student Voice:

I found my time and education at Carleton to be an extremely positive experience. Because of its location in the national capital, no other school can offer the kind of hands-on experience and education available [at Carleton].

Jim Watson
BA Honours in Mass Communication
Mayor of Ottawa

CONTACT INFORMATION
Admission Services
Carleton University
1125 Colonel By Drive
Ottawa, Ontario
Canada K1S 5B6
PH 1-613-520-3663
FAX 1-613-520-3847
EMAIL liaison@carleton.ca
INTERNET http://www.carleton.ca

UNIVERSITY OVERVIEW

Founded in 1942 as Carleton College, Carleton University (Carleton) is a medium-sized, public, coeducational institution offering both undergraduate and graduate degrees in more than 50 areas of study, and supporting over 90 research centres. Carleton has earned a reputation as one of the foremost universities in the nation in the fields of high technology and public affairs & management.

Academic Programs

Carleton offers 63 undergraduate programs through the Faculties of Arts & Social Sciences, Public Affairs & Management, Engineering & Design and Science. Most undergraduate degree programs take four years to complete.

The university offers 50 graduate-level programs in a wide variety of disciplines, from neuroscience to film studies. There are also six certificate programs: English Language & Composition, Public Services Studies, Teaching English as a Second Language (TESL), Law Enforcement Studies, French Language Studies and French Translation Studies.

Carleton takes pride in its innovative curricula and high quality of instruction: the university has won more 3M Teaching Awards than any other institution in Ontario. The focus of all programs is to provide students with the critical, analytical and communications skills that enable graduates to be vibrant, essential citizens of the global environment.

Practical Experience

Students have the opportunity to gain practical experience in over 30 disciplines. The university understands how important hands-on training is. In particular, Carleton's cooperative education program for engineering and science allows students in 14 different programs to work in the largest concentration of high-technology companies in the nation. Ideally situated in the nation's capital, Carleton enjoys close relationships with both the public and private sectors. Internships, practica and work placements in areas as diverse as management and computer science also provide students with real-world experience. In addition, the 90 research centres on campus enable students to work closely with faculty members on important projects.

Internationalism

Carleton has ties with more than 50 universities in over 30 countries. Students can take advantage of such programs as a parliamentary internship exchange in the UK or study abroad in countries such as Spain, France and China.

Highlights

- Location in nation's capital gives Carleton strong connections with both public and private sectors
- Co-op programs, work placements, practica and internships in more than 30 disciplines
- Exchange agreements with nearly 50 universities in more than 30 countries around the globe

University Statistics

Year Founded: 1942

Academic Options: undergraduate/graduate

Calendar Year: fall term (Sept-Dec); winter term (Jan-Apr)

DISCIPLINES/MAJORS OFFERED

Faculty of Arts & Social Sciences: Anthropology, Architecture & Art History, Art & Culture, Art History, Biology, Canadian Studies, Child Studies, Cognitive Science, Directed Interdisciplinary Studies, English, Environmental Studies, Film Studies, French, Geography, History, Humanities, Linguistics & Applied Language Studies, Music, Philosophy, Psychology, Religion, Sociology, Women's Studies

Faculty of Public Affairs & Management: Commerce, Criminology & Criminal Justice, Economics, European & Russian Studies, International Business, Journalism, Law, Mass Communication, Political Science, Public Affairs & Policy Management, Social Work

Faculty of Engineering & Design: Aerospace, Architectural Studies, Civil, Communications, Computer Systems, Electrical, Engineering Physics, Environmental, Industrial Design, Mechanical, Software

Faculty of Science: Applied Physics, Biochemistry, Biology, Biotechnology, Chemistry, Computational Chemistry, Computer Mathematics, Computer Science, Computer Statistics, Environmental Science, Geography, Geology, Integrated Science Studies, Mathematics, Neuroscience, Operations Research, Psychology, Statistics

ADMISSIONS CRITERIA & PROCEDURES

The Admission Services handles all admissions decisions. The general requirement for admission to Carleton is an Ontario Secondary School Diploma, including six OACs, or its equivalent. Grade and prerequisite requirements vary from program to program. Applications from students whose grades do not meet the requirements in a given year are considered individually. These students may have to take a qualifying university year in order to improve appropriate academic skills.

A completed application form must be accompanied by official academic transcripts and a nonrefundable C$80 application fee. All applications are to be sent to the Ontario Universities' Application Centre (OUAC) at 650 Woodlawn Road West, PO Box 1328, Guelph, Ontario, Canada, N1H 7P4. Information about additional requirements, such as portfolios, interviews and auditions, can be obtained by contacting Admission Services. The application deadline varies from program to program. Students applying to programs in architectural studies and social work should submit applications before February 1. Potential music or humanities students must submit applications before March 1. All international students not applying for the above programs, or those students applying from overseas, must submit completed applications before April. The general application for all other Canadian students is June 1.

International students whose native language is not English can meet the English requirements at Carleton with one of the following: a TOEFL score of 580 or higher; an adequate score on the Carleton Academic English Language Assessment test; or four years of study in a Canadian secondary school.

Admissions at a Glance

Minimum GPA: 2.8-3.2 (on a 4.0 scale)

Minimum English Requirements:
- TOEFL 580

Application Fee: C$80 (Canadian, OUAC), $95 (international, OUAC), $75 (students applying directly to Carleton)

Application Deadlines: February 1 (architecture and social work; early admission for all other programs); April 1 (international); June 1 (Canadian, general)

ACADEMIC FACILITIES

MacOdrum Library's collection includes approximately three million books, periodicals, government documents, microforms and rare books. The library offers a wide variety of services to assist students in their studies, such as an orientation program and an interlibrary loan program. Research assistants are readily available to help students with their work. Computing & Communication Services, located in Robertson Hall, is the main computing centre on campus. Students have access to several UNIX workstations as well as a number microcomputer networks. All students have Internet and email access through the school's award-winning CHAT system. The Writing Tutorial Service offers individual and small group tutorials to students who need assistance writing academic essays.

Student & Faculty Profile

Total Enrolment: 17,445

Undergraduate Enrolment: 15,084

# of Faculty: 620

Student/Faculty Ratio: 28:1

Male/Female Students: 54%/46%

First-Year Class Sizes: 82 (average)

Undergraduate Acceptance Rate: 26%

Undergraduate Enrolment by Discipline:

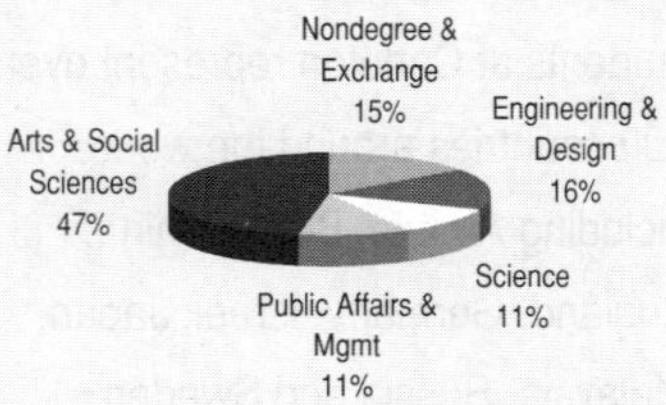

SCHOLARSHIPS & FINANCIAL ASSISTANCE

Carleton awards more than C$3 million in scholarships and bursaries to over 3,000 new and returning students. One-third of students in the 1997 entering class were scholarship recipients. Most scholarships are awarded on the basis of superior academic performance.

Canadian students may apply for assistance to both federal and provincial loan programs. Further scholarship and loan information can be obtained by contacting the Awards Office at 1-613-520-3600.

Expenses at a Glance

Tuition (undergraduate, full-time):
- In-Province: C$3,822-4,432/year
- Out-of-Province: C$3,822-4,432/year
- International: C$10,202-11,242/year

Fees, Books, Materials: C$800-1,700/year

Accommodation:
- Private: C$621-746/month
- Residence: C$850/month
- Homestay: C$600/month

Health Insurance: C$579/year

CAMPUS & LOCATION

City Population:	1,026,900
Cost of Living:	high
Climate Range:	-16° to 27°C
Campus Setting:	suburban
# of Students in Residence:	1,666

Carleton's 29 buildings occupy a picturesque 62-hectare campus situated between the Rideau River and the Rideau Canal, just a 10-minute drive south of Parliament Hill. All buildings are connected by an extensive underground tunnel system, and the campus is conveniently linked to the rest of the city by bus. The university's location in Ottawa, Canada's capital city, gives students access to unique resources unavailable to many other Canadian medium-sized institutions. These include the Parliament Buildings, embassies and national organizations. Museums, art galleries and libraries also abound in the area. Ottawa itself is an historic city of more than one million people, offering a rich perspective on Canadian political life. The city is also home to many high-technology companies.

Ottawa has a lively blend of English, French and international communities within small, quaint neighbourhoods with bustling outdoor markets. The city is clean and safe. There are numerous recreational activities available year-round, including rafting and cycling in the summer and skiing and ice skating on the Rideau Canal in the winter.

Residences at Carleton house approximately 1,700 students. The six residence buildings accommodate a variety of living styles while providing an environment conducive to study and high-quality scholarship.

ATHLETICS & EXTRACURRICULAR ACTIVITIES

A variety of student clubs, an undergraduate student government, a student newspaper, a radio station and a theatre company, as well as first-rate athletic facilities and university sports teams, add many dimensions to enrich Carleton's campus life.

Carleton has a proud tradition in athletics, with nine women's and eight men's varsity teams. The university also has a strong intramural system. Recreational facilities include a 50-metre swimming pool with a 10-metre diving platform, a fitness centre, squash and tennis courts, a football and soccer stadium and a double-gymnasium used for various sports such as basketball and volleyball. There are fitness and instructional programs to satisfy nearly all students' interests including canoeing, ballet, karate and rock-climbing.

There are more than 100 student clubs and organizations meeting on campus including several cultural and international student organizations. The university encourages all students to participate in making Carleton a vibrant and diverse campus.

University Recognition

- One out of every 10 recruits for the federal government's foreign service officer program graduated from Carleton
  CU is the leading supplier of graduates to Canada's premier high technology corporation, Nortel
- Carleton has won more 3M Teaching Awards than any other university in Ontario

STUDENT SUPPORT SERVICES

Carleton strives to provide all the resources and assistance students may need to enjoy a fruitful learning experience. Each academic department offers academic advising to its registered students. Career Services assists students with honing and realizing their career goals through workshops, on-campus recruiting and an alumni referral service, among other services. Student Life Services offers a wide range of programs and services designed to assist first-year students in their adjustment to academic life.

A full-time International Student Advisor (ISA) assists students year-round in all aspects of their transition to life at Carleton. An orientation program is held every August and January, and the ISA can offer advice on a variety of personal and academic issues.

International Students

University Enrolment: 893

% of University Enrolment: 5%

Countries of Origin: International students at Carleton represent over 100 countries around the world, including Austria, Brazil, China, England, Germany, Israel, Japan, Malaysia, Russia and Sweden.

COLLEGE MILITAIRE ROYAL DU CANADA KINGSTON, ONTARIO

Énoncé de Mission

...éduquer et former des élèves-officiers et des officiers qui se destinent à faire carrière dans les Forces canadiennes

INFORMATION DE RENSEIGNEMENT

Secrétaire général
College Militaire Royal du Canada
CP 17000, Succursale Forces
Kingston, Ontario
Canada K7K 7B4
TÉLÉPHONE 1-613-541-6000 poste 6302 ou 6652
TÉLÉCOPIEUR 1-613-542-3565
COURRIER ÉLECTRONIQUE registrar@rmc.ca
INTERNET http://www.rmc.ca

Voix de l'étudiant:

Je ne dirai pas «J'ai étudié au CMR.» Je dirai probablement «J'ai vécu le CMR.»

ÉLOF Jay Steele
Baccalauréat ès Sciences, 1997

For the English version of this profile, please see page 213.

SURVOL DE L'UNIVERSITÉ

L'éducation au College Militaire Royal du Canada (RMC) consiste de 4 "piliers," chacun étant important dans la vie des Élèves Officiers (ÉLOFS): l'académique, l'entraînement militaire, l'éducation physique, et l'enseignement de la langue seconde. Les programmes d'études ressemblent beaucoup à ceux d'autres universités. Toutefois, les programmes sont différents en raison des matières supplémentaires que les ÉLOFS doivent suivre: un cours de psychologie militaire et de leadership, pendant chaque année de leurs études.

Afin d'élargir la sphère des connaissances des étudiants pour leur donner les moyens de répondre aux besoins uniques d'un officier des Forces canadiennes, les étudiants en sciences et en génie doivent suivre des cours d'arts; les étudiants en arts doivent suivre des cours de sciences.

La vie militaire d'un ÉLOF commence par le cours élémentaire d'officier (CEO), dont la première partie a lieu juste avant la première année universitaire. La seconde partie du CEO comprend l'instruction militaire dispensée durant la première année et un cours d'immersion dans la seconde langue entre la première et la deuxième années. Durant les étés qui suivent la deuxième et la troisième années, les ÉLOFS continuent leur formation militaire.

Le programme obligatoire d'éducation physique et de sports de quatre ans, permet à chaque ÉLOF d'atteindre une excellente forme physique et d'acquérir des aptitudes satisfaisantes en sports. Le programme accentue la forme physique, les connaissances élémentaires dans plusieurs sports et l'administration sportive. Les ÉLOFS passent des tests d'aptitude physique régulièrement et doivent atteindre la norme en matière d'endurance, d'agilité et de force.

L'enseignement de la langue seconde permet aux étudiants de s'exprimer dans les deux langues officielles et de comprendre les principes du bilinguisme. L'étudiant est placé dans une petite classe à son niveau et progresse à son propre rythme. Il reçoit cinq périodes de cours par semaine, durant la journée. Ceux qui n'ont pas atteint le niveau fonctionnel obligatoire de bilinguisme la première année suivent un programme d'immersion de dix semaines pendant l'été.

Le CMR étant un établissement bilingue, les ÉLOFS peuvent étudier en anglais ou en français. Aussi, les ÉLOFS de première année sont deux par chambre, un francophone et un anglophone.

En Vedette

- La seule université militaire au Canada
- Offre une éducation bilingue de renommée et une carrière stimulante
- Une des seules univerisités au Canada dotée de son propre réacteur nucléaire, utlilisé aux fins de recherches par les étudiants et les professeurs

Statistiques Universitaires

Année fondée: 1876

Options académiques: baccalauréat/études supérieures

Année scolaire: premier semestre (sept-déc); deuxième semestre (jan-avr)

DISCIPLINES OFFERTES

Administration des affaires

Études militaires et stratégiques

Génie: chimique & des matériaux, civil, électrique, informatique, mécanique

Lettres et sciences humaines: anglais, français, histoire

Science spatiale

Sciences: chimie, mathématique & informatique, physique, sans spécialisation

Sciences sociales: politique, économique

CRITÈRES & PROCÉDURES D'ADMISSION

L'étudiant se présente au Centre de recrutement des Force canadiennes le plus proche (1-800-856-8488). La procédure inclut un examen médical, des tests d'aptitudes et physiques et une entrevue.

Il existe deux programmes d'admission: le Programme de formation des officiers de la Force régulière (PFOR), le programme d'admission en vertu les frais de scolarité sont payés, et le Programme de formation (Intégration à la Réserve) (PFIR) pour lequel les étudiants doivent payer des droits. Les deux programmes fournissent la même instruction et formation.

Quand les ÉLOFS du PFOR terminent le programme d'études, ils reçoivent leur baccalauréat et leur brevet d'officier et doivent servir un minimum de cinq ans dans la Force régulière (plein temps) des Forces canadiennes. Les ÉLOFS du PFIR doivent aussi suivre l'instruction d'été, pour laquelle ils reçoivent une solde et des indemnités.

Les candidats devraient présenter leur demande dès le début de la dernière année scolaire au secondaire. Pour l'année universitaire débutant en septembre 1999, l'échéance est le 12 février 1999 pour ceux souhaitant devenir pilotes et le 12 mars 1999 pour les autres métiers. Les étudiants sont conseillés de consulter le centre de recrutement pour recevoir encore plus de détails.

Tout candidat admissible doit être citoyen canadien (les immigrants ayant le droit d'établissement peuvent se porter candidats au PFIR); satisfaire aux normes médicales minimales; obtenir la note de passage aux tests de sélection; et obtenir la note de passage au cours élémentaire d'officier.

Les admissions en bref

Notes minimum: 75-80%

Niveau de français minimum requis: n/a (aisance dans une des langues officielles)

Frais de demande: n/a

Dates d'échéance: le 12 février 1999 (ceux souhaitant devenir pilote), le 12 mars 1999 (toutes autres demandes)

ÉTABLISSEMENTS ACADÉMIQUES

La Bibliothèque Massey (collection lettres et humanités) et la Bibliothèque des Sciences et Génie contiennent environ 300,000 volumes, y inclus la plus grande collection de volumes en Science militaire au Canada, 18,000 microfiches, un grand nombre de cassettes audio et vidéo, à peu près 1,100 revues couvrant tous les sujets d'étude, les archives et une collection spéciale importante de matériaux militaires et autres. Les étudiants peuvent aussi pleinement accéder les ressources de recherche tels CD-ROMS, Telnet, les Bibliothèques de l'Université Queens.

Les installations informatiques incluent des postes Windows NT ou Sun Solaris situés de par le campus. Tous utilisent les technologies Pentium et/ou SPARC. Il existe aussi des classes multimédias, des classes vidéoconférences et des installations audiovisuelles à l'usage des étudiants.

Enfin les étudiants en sciences et génie ont accès à des laboratoires complets, incluant un réacteur nucléaire disponible pour la recherche par les étudiants et les professeurs.

Profil des étudiants et du corps enseignant

total d'étudiants: 1,100

Étudiants au niveau du baccalauréat: 900

d'enseignants: 160

Rapport étudiants/enseignants: 6:1

Rappport hommes/femmes: 72%/28%

d'élèves dans les cours de première année: 35 (moyenne)

Taux d'acceptation au niveau du baccalauréat: 55%

Inscriptions au niveau baccalauréat, par discipline:

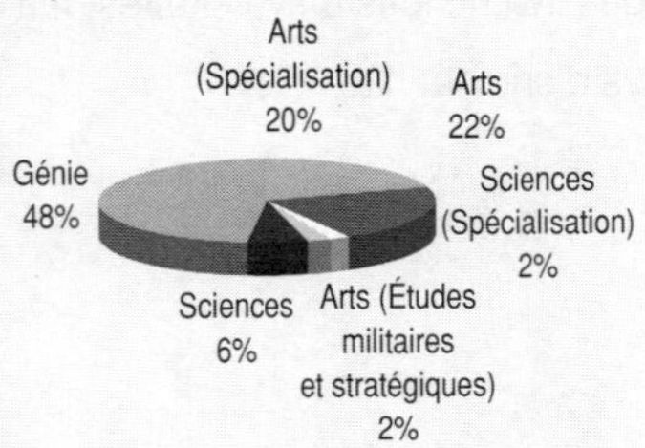

BOURSES & AIDE FINANCIÈRE

Le Département de la défence nationale parraine la plupart des cadets dans le PFOR.

Dans le PFIR, les membres paient une partie des frais de scolarité. Ils peuvent faire demande pour certaines bourses auxquelles ont accès les étudiants dans les universitiés canadiennes. De plus, les membres du PFIR peuvent recevoir des bourses au niveau provincial. Le secrétaire général peut fournir de plus amples renseignements.

Les frais en bref

Frais de scolarité (niveau baccalauréat, plein temps):
- En-province: C$1,524/année scolaire
- Hors-province: C$1,524/année scolaire
- International: n/a

Frais, livres, matériaux: C$107/année scolaire (font partie des frais de scolarité annuels)

Vivres et logements:
- Privés: n/a
- Résidence: C$2,400/année scolaire

Assurance santé: n/a

CAMPUS & EMPLACEMENT

Population de la ville:	140,000
Coût de la vie:	moyen
Échelle du climat:	-8° à 24°C
Emplacement du campus:	banlieue
# d'étudiants en résidence:	900

Le CMR se trouve à Pointe Frederick, une petite péninsule située à l'est de la municipalité de Kingston, en Ontario. Ce lieu pittoresque, à la jonction du Lac Ontario et du fleuve Saint-Laurent, a une grande importance historique. Ce site militaire a été occupé activement depuis 1789, et durant la guerre de 1812, il s'agissait de la principale station navale du Haut-Canada. Les navires de la Royal Navy y étaient construits et basés, et c'est grâce à eux que l'armée britannique a pu empêcher les Américains d'occuper le Haut-Canada.

Plusieurs édifices de la Royal Navy, datant de l'époque qui suit immédiatement la guerre de 1812, existent encore sur le campus, et des fortifications érigées des années plus tard, comme le fort Frederick et le fort Henry, qui est tout à côté, ajoutent à l'ambiance militaire du collège.

Les ÉLOFS doivent vivre dans le logement qui leur est attribué à l'intérieur de l'escadre des élèves-officiers. Rien n'empêche les candidats qui sont mariés et ceux qui ont des personnes à charge de poser leur candidature, mais le programme du CMR exige un engagement de 24 heures sur 24 de la part de chaque élève-officier et leurs familles et personnes à charge ne peuvent pas vivre sur le campus.

ACTIVITÉS ATHLÉTIQUES & RÉCRÉATIVES

Le collège a des représentants intercollégiaux dans plusieurs sports.

Le collège a trois gymnases, des pistes intérieures, une salle de poids et haltères et six terrains de squash. Il est aussi doté d'une patinoire et d'une piscine intérieures, cinq terrains de tennis en plein air, des pistes cendrées, plusieurs terrains de sports, une salle de tir au fusil et au pistolet, et d'installations excellentes pour la voile et la navigation de plaisance et de compétition. Il fournit le matériel nécessaire. Les élèves-officiers utilisent aussi des installations voisines, telles un terrain de golf (18 trous) et une patinoire de curling.

Plusieurs clubs permettent aux élèves-officiers de pratiquer des sports sans participer à des compétitions. On peut se livrer à bon nombre de loisirs et d'occupations, y inclus un mess des ÉLOFS, une cantine comportant un casse-croûte pour les ÉLOFS et le personnel, et un petit magasin d'articles personnels et de souvenirs. Il y a d'autres clubs non sportifs, comme par exemple l'astronomie, la musique, l'équitation, les débats oratoires, le théatre et autres.

Reconnaissance de l'université

- Programmes en génie accrédités par le Conseil canadien des ingénieurs professionels
- A chaque année, plusieurs diplômés reçoivent des bourses NSERC d'études supérieures
- Plusieurs diplômés ont déjà reçu les bourses prestigieuses Rhodes et Athlone-Vanier

SERVICES D'APPUI AUX ÉTUDIANTS

Afin de mieux faire leur choix de carrières, les étudiants sont assistés au centre de recrutement où ils posent leur candidature.

Les aumôniers (protestant et catholique) célèbrent des offices religieux tous les dimanches. Les groupes de discussion, les dîners débats et l'heure de l'aumônier offrent aux élèves-officiers l'occasion d'échanger des vues avec les aumôniers sur les questions d'éthique, de morale et de religion. Les aumôniers sont toujours à la disposition des élèves-officiers pour leur donner des conseils.

Les étudiants ont accès aux services médicaux et dentaires.

Étudiants internationaux

Inscriptions universitaires: n/a

% des inscriptions universitaires: n/a

Pays d'origine: n/a

Lakehead
UNIVERSITY

LAKEHEAD UNIVERSITY
THUNDER BAY, ONTARIO

University Mission

...to remain committed to excellence and innovation in undergraduate and graduate teaching, service, research and scholarly activity....to educate graduates who demonstrate leadership, independent critical thinking, and social and environmental responsibility

Student Voice:
The University offers an unbeatable combination of quality education plus one of the most beautiful locations in Canada.

Larysa Turko
Bachelor of Arts
1998

CONTACT INFORMATION
Office of the Registrar
Lakehead University
955 Oliver Road
Thunder Bay, Ontario
Canada P7B 5E1
PH 1-807-343-8500 (Cdn);
1-807-343-8133 (int'l)
FAX 1-807-343-8023 (Cdn);
1-807-346-7829 (int'l)
EMAIL liaison@lakeheadu.ca (Cdn);
International.Activities@lakehead.ca (int'l)
INTERNET http://www.lakeheadu.ca

UNIVERSITY OVERVIEW

Established in 1965, Lakehead University (Lakehead), one of Ontario's newest universities, is dedicated to achieving excellence in teaching, research, scholarship and service. With a campus backyard that includes the Canadian Shield and Lake Superior, programs such as biology, forestry, geography, geology, outdoor recreation, and parks and tourism take advantage of a natural laboratory in and around the university. The relatively small class sizes, participatory programs and comfortable learning environment allow students to develop the analytic, practical and interpersonal skills required in the modern world. Lakehead welcomes students from across Canada and around the world.

Variety

Lakehead, the only university in the northwestern Ontario region, offers a wide variety of programs and courses in more than 35 departments. Lakehead has developed an extensive range of options from two-year diploma courses to graduate programs.

Highlights

- Diploma, undergraduate and graduate programs available
- Many courses take advantage of expansive natural environment of northwestern Ontario
- Cooperative education available
- International opportunities

University Statistics

Year Founded: 1965
Academic Options: diploma/undergraduate/graduate
Calendar Year: fall term (Sept-Dec); winter term (Jan-Apr); spring/summer (May-Aug)

Participatory Education

Lakehead believes in the value of a participatory and practical education that allows students to gain hands-on experience and knowledge.

The university tries whenever possible to combine its coursework with fieldwork that takes advantage of the environments available around Thunder Bay; fieldwork is prevalent in the Departments of Outdoor Recreation, Forestry, Geology, Biology and Geography.

The Student Placement & Cooperative Education Centre administers its Co-op Program in association with several Lakehead departments and provides employment counselling services that include instruction on job search techniques, resume composition and developing interview skills.

International Activities

The Department of International Activities provides a focal point for all international students at Lakehead. Through the university's extensive exchange programs, Lakehead students have an opportunity to travel and study abroad. Lakehead prepares students for the increasing globalization, and the various challenges facing the world during the next millennium.

Distance Education

Lakehead offers an extensive range of programs and courses (undergraduate, graduate, diploma and certificate) through Distance Education. Courses are delivered using various distance education formats, including: print packages, audio/videocassettes, audioconferencing, videoconferencing, computer conferencing, World Wide Web and other Internet services. Courses begin in January, February, May and September.

DISCIPLINES/MAJORS OFFERED

Lakehead offers programs in the following areas:

Anthropology
Biology
Business/Commerce
Chemistry
Computer Science
Economics
Education (Concurrent)
Education (Consecutive)
Engineering
English
Environmental Science
Environmental Studies
Integrated Forest Resources Management Diploma
Forestry
French/Language
Geography
Geology/Earth Science
Gerontology
History
Indigenous Learning
Kinesiology
Library & Information Studies Diploma
Mathematical Sciences
Music
Natural Science
Northern Studies
Nursing
Outdoor Recreation
Philosophy
Physics
Political Science
Psychology
Religious Studies
Social Work
Sociology
Visual Arts
Women's Studies

ADMISSIONS CRITERIA & PROCEDURES

Students apply to Lakehead using the General Application form for Ontario universities, available from the Ontario Universities' Application Centre, the Office of the Registrar at Lakehead or from high schools around Ontario. The application form requires applicants to specify the program and major applied to, and whether the applicant will be studying on a full- or part-time basis.

Admissions requirements vary by department and program. Applicants are encouraged to contact Lakehead regarding specific program requirements. Generally applicants are expected to have completed an Ontario Secondary School Diploma (OSSD) with an overall average of 65 per cent or its equivalent; this is the basic criteria for admission to all degree and most diploma programs. Certain degree and diploma programs require specific course prerequisites for admission.

International students seeking admission to regular study are normally required to have a TOEFL score of 550. International enquiries should be addressed to the Department of International Activities.

Admissions to the cooperative education programs are more selective due to the limited number of positions within the programs. Admissions decisions for co-op programs are based on academic standing and background information which points to a competency level and background experience appropriate to the co-op positions.

Admissions at a Glance

Minimum GPA: 65%

Minimum English Requirements:

TOEFL 550

Application Fee: C$80 (Canadian), $90 (international)

Application Deadlines: July 1 (fall term); may vary by program

ACADEMIC FACILITIES

The University Library consists of the Chancellor Norman M. Paterson Library and the Education Library. Together these libraries serve the needs of students and faculty on campus as well as those students taking courses at off-campus locations and by distance education. The University Library collection contains 696,499 books, journals and other documents as well as over 354,500 microform volumes; several online resources are provided through the library's webpage. Access to the collection is provided through the multiLIS automated library management system. The library has an ERL server that provides university access to some of its CD-ROM databases. The library also offers computerized literature searching and interlibrary loan service. Library staff are available help students take full advantage of all library resources.

Lakehead has become a centre of research in the northwestern Ontario region. Facilities relevant to environmental and scientific research and study have benefited not only the forestry and environmental studies but also the inhabitants of Thunder Bay and the area in general.

Student & Faculty Profile

Total Enrolment: 6,600

Undergraduate Enrolment: 6,267

# of Faculty: 240

Student/Faculty Ratio: 20:1

Male/Female Students: 47%/53%

First-Year Class Sizes: 50-100

Undergraduate Acceptance Rate: not available

Undergraduate Enrolment by Discipline:

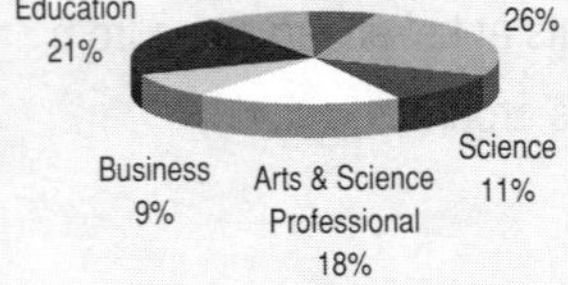

SCHOLARSHIPS & FINANCIAL ASSISTANCE

Residents of Ontario who are Canadian citizens or permanent residents of Canada may qualify for financial assistance through the Ontario Student Assistance Program (OSAP); further information is available online at http://osap.gov.on.ca.

International students are not eligible to apply for OSAP if they are studying at Lakehead on a student visa. Although international students are normally not eligible for entrance scholarships, bursaries and awards, they are eligible to apply for these forms of assistance once they are registered as full-time students.

Students are encouraged to contact the Financial Aid Office at 1-807-343-8206.

Expenses at a Glance

Tuition (undergraduate, full-time):

In-Province: C$2,345-$3,550/year

Out-of-Province: C$2,345-$3,550/year

International: C$4,850-$7,000/year

Fees, Books, Materials: C$750-$2,400/year

Accommodation:

Private: C$600-850/month

Residence: C$4,882/year

Homestay: n/a

Health Insurance: C$579/year*

City Population:	125,000
Cost of Living:	medium
Climate Range:	-13° to 20°C
Campus Setting:	suburban
# of Students in Residence:	1,140

CAMPUS & LOCATION

Lakehead is situated on approximately 150 hectares of wooded land overlooking the city of Thunder Bay. Most of the university's administrative and instructional buildings are grouped around Lake Tamblyn; the residence buildings are located along the McIntyre River. The Student Centre is a focal point of campus life and provides an assortment of student facilities including banking services, restaurants and campus stores. Many of the campus's buildings are connected by underground tunnels that allow for comfortable walking between classes during cold winter days. In addition to its academic facilities, Lakehead has provided a number of scenic paved trails on and around the campus for walking, jogging, biking or cross-country skiing in the winter. The campus is within walking distance of the edge of the city, and is serviced regularly by public transit services.

Thunder Bay, with a population of about 125,000 people, is located on the northern shore of Lake Superior, the world's largest lake, making Thunder Bay Canada's largest inland port. Thunder Bay is the commercial, educational and recreational centre of the northwestern Ontario area, and offers as examples historic Old Fort William and the Thunder Bay Symphony Orchestra. Thunder Bay and its surrounding areas provide an array of outdoor recreational opportunities. Three local ski resorts and many other activities such as fishing, boating, swimming are readily available. Although self-contained, Thunder Bay is within a day's driving time of Winnipeg, the capital of Manitoba.

ATHLETICS & EXTRACURRICULAR ACTIVITIES

Lakehead is proud to offer excellent recreational and sporting facilities, as part of the student fees, to all its students. Students have access to the university pool, saunas, fitness centre, courts, gymnasium and track.

Lakehead's varsity teams are members of the CIAU interuniversity league and compete in men's basketball, women's basketball, women's volleyball, track & field, cross-country running and wrestling. The university is the three-year host (1997-99) of the CIAU Women's National Basketball Championship. Lakehead's curling, rowing and Nordic skiing teams compete at the provincial level.

Lakehead students are also active in cultural and artistic pursuits, as is evident in the extensive variety of clubs, societies and organizations available on campus.

STUDENT SUPPORT SERVICES

The Counselling & Career Centre is home to the university chaplain, two student counsellors and a career information library. Students can receive personal and career counselling at the centre any time throughout the year. The centre organizes a series of seminars on a variety of topics.

The Learning Assistance Centre is available to help students experiencing academic difficulties. Tutoring is available in a variety of subjects, and students with special needs can arrange for additional support services. The Learning Assistance Centre assists students in maximizing their academic potential at Lakehead.

The International Student Advisor provides information and support counselling to graduate and undergraduate international students.

The Health Centre provides a comprehensive health promotion program and offers students information and print material on a variety of subjects.

University Recognition

- Professor Emerita Margaret R. Page named a member of the Order of Canada

International Students

University Enrolment: 115

% of University Enrolment: 2% (approx)

Countries of Origin: International students at Lakehead come from nations around the world.

Laurentian University Université Laurentienne

LAURENTIAN UNIVERSITY
SUDBURY, ONTARIO

University Mission

...to offer accessible and excellent academic programming, teaching and research, which reflects the region it serves with an environmentally sound approach to human development and the universal quest for knowledge

Student Voice:

Challenging programs, friendly people, small classes, great varsity athletics, a tri-cultural environment, and lots to do—who could ask for anything more?

Amy Bateman
BA English
Graduating April 1999

CONTACT INFORMATION
The Office of Admissions
Laurentian University
935 Ramsey Lake Rd
Sudbury, Ontario
Canada P3E 2C6
PH 1-705-675-1151 ext. 3915
FAX 1-705-675-4891
EMAIL
admissions@nickel.laurentian.ca
INTERNET http://www.laurentian.ca

UNIVERSITY OVERVIEW

Founded in 1960 by an Act of the Ontario Legislature, Laurentian University (Laurentian) is northeastern Ontario's most comprehensive institution of higher learning. Laurentian includes three federated universities and two affiliated university colleges.

Academic Programs

A strong commitment to its students and the community has enabled Laurentian to develop innovative and relevant programs that combine theoretical knowledge, analysis and practical experience. The university offers several unique bachelor's program such as those in sports administration, forensic biology and extractive metallurgical engineering as well as a wide variety of traditional programs. Over 100 academic programs are offered in the humanities, social sciences, science & engineering as well as professional and graduate studies.

Highlights

- Laurentian is the largest bilingual provider of distance education courses in Canada
- Many unique programs offered such as Forensic Biology, Sports Administration and Native Prelaw
- Home to renowned research facilities including the Sudbury Neutrino Observatory

University Statistics

Year Founded: 1960
Academic Options: undergraduate/graduate
Calendar Year: fall semester (Sept-Dec); winter term (Jan-Apr)

English and French are the official languages of study at Laurentian.

Practical Experience

Many programs at Laurentian offer co-op and internship opportunities, which provide students with valuable hands-on training in jobs related to their field of study. The university's six research centres also provide students with the opportunity to gain real-world experience through projects coordinated with faculty members and the community.

Federated Universities and Affiliated Colleges

Laurentian includes three federated universities which offer unique educational opportunities to students. The University of Sudbury is a bilingual, Roman Catholic institution operating in the Jesuit tradition and offers programs in religious studies, philosophy, native studies and folklore.

Huntington University College is a college of arts and sciences, offering programs at the bachelor's level, including concentrations in music, religious studies and gerontology.

Thornloe University College is an Anglican institution providing Laurentian with its Department of Classical Studies and other programs in areas such as religious studies, theatre arts and women's studies.

These institutions offer housing to Laurentian students and the opportunity to learn in a small, personalized environment.

Laurentian is also affiliated with two university colleges: Le Collège universitaire de Hearst and Algoma University College.

DISCIPLINES/MAJORS OFFERED

Humanities Programs: Classical Studies, Computer Science, Education (French only), English, Ethics Studies, French, Italian, Mathematics, Modern Languages, Music, Native Studies, Philosophy, Religious Studies, Spanish, Theatre Arts, Women's Studies

Social Science Programs: Anthropology, Earth Science, Economics, Geography, History, Law & Justice, Political Science, Psychology, Sociology

Science & Engineering Programs: Anthropology, Behavioural Neuroscience (Integrated, Biomedical, Conservation & Restoration, Ecology, Forensic Biology, Wildlife & Habitat Ecology, Zoology) Biochemistry, Biology, Biomedical Physics, Chemistry, Computer Science, Environmental Earth Science, Extractive Metallurgical Engineering, Geology, Liberal Science, Mathematics, Mining Engineering, Physics

Professional Schools Programs: Administration des affaires, Commerce Administration, Education (French only), Health Promotion, Kinesiology, Native Human Services, Nursing, Outdoor Adventure Leadership, Sport & Physical Education, Profession de sage-femme, Social Work, Sports Administration, Translators & Interpreters

Graduate Programs

ADMISSIONS CRITERIA & PROCEDURES

Admission to Laurentian is open to those students who have completed the highest level of secondary education in their region; students with an International Baccalaureate are also eligible. Ontario residents must have a minimum grade average of 60 per cent on six OAC's. Quebec residents must have completed year one of a CGEP program. International students typically require above-average academic grades. The minimum averages required for entry may vary by program. Additional admissions criteria for individual programs may include subject prerequisites, auditions or submission of a portfolio. Students should contact the Office of Admissions for further details.

Candidates interested in applying for full-time study in an undergraduate degree program must submit their application to the Ontario Universities' Application Centre. Completed applications must be accompanied by official academic transcripts, any additional information requested by Laurentian and an application fee. The application fee for Canadian students is C$85; the application fee for international students is C$95. The general deadline for domestic applications is June 1; international applications must generally be submitted by April 1.

International students whose native language is not English or French must submit adequate TOEFL, MELAB or CELA scores. All documents not in English or French must be officially translated.

Admissions at a Glance

Minimum GPA: varies

Minimum English Requirements:
TOEFL 550, MELAB 90, CELA 60

Application Fee: C$85 (Canadian), $95 (international)

Application Deadlines: June 1 (Canadian); April 1 (international)

ACADEMIC FACILITIES

Laurentian strives to provide the latest teaching technologies and maintains modern laboratories and research facilities for its students and faculty.

There are three libraries on Laurentian's campuses with combined holdings of over one million books and journals. All students have Internet and email access through the university's Nickel network. There are a number of computer labs open to all students as well as many department-specific laboratories with specialized hardware and software. The Distance Education program incorporates electronic classrooms and interactive computer-based learning into its curricula.

The university is a partner in many world-class independent research projects through its six research centres, including the Centre in Mining & Mineral Exploration Research and the renowned Sudbury Neutrino Observatory, the first facility of its kind in the world.

Student & Faculty Profile

Total Enrolment: 6,384

Undergraduate Enrolment: 6,026

# of Faculty: 370

Student/Faculty Ratio: 17:1

Male/Female Students: 41%/59%

First-Year Class Sizes: 39 (average)

Undergraduate Acceptance Rate: 30%

Undergraduate Enrolment by Discipline:

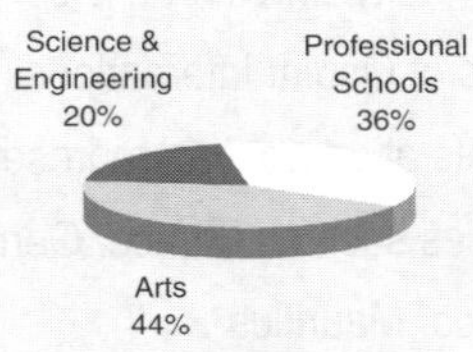

SCHOLARSHIPS & FINANCIAL ASSISTANCE

The Student Awards Office is responsible for the administration of all forms of financial assistance for undergraduate students. There are numerous forms of financial assistance available, including loans, bursaries, scholarships, medals and prizes. Both federal and provincial need-based loan programs are available to domestic students. Bursaries are also typically need-based awards. Students do not need to apply for most merit-based scholarships because admissions applications will be used in the selection process. Awards and prizes are typically merit-based.

International students may be eligible for certain merit-based awards.

Expenses at a Glance

Tuition (undergraduate, full-time):
In-Province: C$3,486/year
Out-of-Province: C$3,486/year
International: C$7,560/year

Fees, Books, Materials: C$600-1,000/year

Accommodation:
Private: C$425-575/month
Residence: C$2,225-2,800/year
Homestay: n/a

Health Insurance: C$578/year

City Population:	92,059
Cost of Living:	moderate
Climate Range:	-18° to 24°C
Campus Setting:	urban
# of Students in Residence:	1,200

CAMPUS & LOCATION

Laurentian University's main campus is located in Sudbury on 300 hectares overlooking five lakes. The land the campus sits on rises in an arc of hills and offers many scenic views and hiking trails. The campus provides a tranquil, tree-filled environment for students to study and relax. Some buildings on campus are connected by underground walkways, allowing for indoor passage between classes in the colder months of winter. To the east and southeast of the main campus are the residences of Huntington, Thorneloe, Sudbury universities. The main campus is located 11 kilometres from downtown Sudbury.

The city of Sudbury is located in northeastern Ontario on the Canadian Shield, one of Canada's most beautiful natural areas. Nearby Lake Ramsey offers plenty of outdoor recreational opportunities including boating, fishing and swimming and outdoor enthusiasts will find a great many other activities to enjoy in the region. The city's location on the Canadian Shield has made it the mining capital of North America, as well as a thriving centre for high-technology industries. The region is home to many festivals and celebrations and the city enjoys a long tradition of community involvement. Students can take advantage of the many museums, galleries, a symphony orchestra and a thriving theatre community. The city is known for its charming shops and friendly citizens, and Sudbury has the largest French population west of Quebec.

ATHLETICS & EXTRACURRICULAR ACTIVITIES

Laurentian provides a wide variety of athletic and extracurricular activities to its students. The university has a proud tradition in interuniversity athletics and competes in sports such as women's basketball, swimming, cross-country, track & field, and Nordic skiing, and men's basketball, soccer, ice hockey, volleyball, swimming, cross-country, track & field, and Nordic skiing. The university's Department of Active Living also organizes an array of recreational and intramural activities on campus. The intramural program on campus includes activities such as bowling, golf, soccer and ultimate Frisbee. In addition, Laurentian students have access to a wide range of athletic facilities including a gymnasium, weight training facilities, an Olympic-sized swimming pool, ski trails, tennis courts and outdoor playing fields.

The university has two full-time students associations and more than 160 students organizations, covering a wide variety of interests, meeting at Laurentian. A student newspaper and radio station keep students informed and entertained, and offer students the chance to gain additional practical experience while studying. There are many concert performances organized by the music department as well as theatre productions organized through the university. Students can also take advantage many social activities organized by Student Affairs.

University Recognition

- The Canadian Foundation for Innovation has ranked Laurentian 4th in applied research out of 35 small and medium-sized universities in Canada
- One of only two institutions to offer Forensic Biology, Sports Administration and Native Prelaw Certificate programs
- Over the past 27 years, the Laurentian Lady Vees basketball team has competed in the national tournament 26 times

STUDENT SUPPORT SERVICES

The university provides a comprehensive support system for its students. Counselling Services meets with every Laurentian student to discuss academic and career planning. Counselling Services can also offer personal advice and assistance. The Language Centre offers language instruction (English and French) to those students who need to improve their academic language skills. Other services at Laurentian includes two day cares, a chaplaincy and health services.

The Placement Centre provides career counselling and employment resources to all Laurentian students. Individuals can search for an internship placement, summer employment or a full-time career opportunity using the centres resources.

International Students

University Enrolment: 137

% of University Enrolment: 2%

Countries of Origin: International students at Laurentian represent countries such as France, Germany, Morocco, Mauritius

McMaster University
Hamilton, Ontario

University Mission

..to inspire creativity, innovation and excellence in our teaching, research and scholarship

Student Voice:

McMaster has been everything I thought it would be and more…my residence was great, my courses were interesting and my professors were supportive.

Rosanne Aleong
Honours Biology & Psychology

Contact Information

Office of International Affairs (int'l)
McMaster University
1280 Main Street West
Hamilton, Ontario
Canada L8S 4L8
PH 1-905-525-9140 ext. 24211 (int'l)
FAX 1-905-527-1105
EMAIL
inadin@mcmail.cis.mcmaster.ca (int'l)
INTERNET
http://www.mcmaster.ca/oia (int'l)

UNIVERSITY OVERVIEW

Founded in 1887, McMaster University (McMaster) is a medium-sized, research institution offering 135 undergraduate and 65 graduate degree programs. McMaster is dedicated to creating a diverse and exciting educational environment.

Academic Programs

McMaster strives to be a leader in developing new and innovative programs. Through its Faculties of Business, Engineering, Health Sciences, Humanities, Sciences and Social Sciences, McMaster provides its undergraduate students with a broad-based education in several disciplines, as well as the analytical and practical skills needed for more specialized study. Third- and fourth-year Theme Schools, act as centres for interdisciplinary learning, and encourage students to explore outside the boundaries of a more traditional education. McMaster understands that its role is to facilitate the quest for knowledge. Programs are designed to be ahead of current trends and students play an active role in many of the research projects taking place on campus. McMaster's extensive research activity is supported by over C$79 million in grants and contracts.

Students pursuing graduate studies may earn a Master of Arts, Business Administration, Engineering, Science, Social Work or a PhD. McMaster also offers distance education programs to students around the globe.

Global Perspective

McMaster has become increasingly involved around the world in exchange agreements, institutional partnerships and collaborative research. The university has 58 educational agreements with universities in 26 countries including the UK, France, Japan and Germany. Students can study abroad for up to one year and experience the global environment firsthand. McMaster is also home to international students representing 78 countries worldwide who help create a diverse learning environment on campus.

Many programs incorporate global issues into their curricula; the Globalization, Social Change & Human Experience Theme School addresses a wide range of international subjects and relationships.

Practical Experience

McMaster understands the importance of practical experience and hands-on training. Many of the programs at the university have optional co-op placements in the public and private sectors. Co-op students engage in meaningful and relevant work while earning credit towards their degree. Practical experience can also be gained through internships, work study programs and field studies.

Highlights

- A leader in developing innovative and challenging programs
- Theme Schools promote in-depth interaction across disciplines
- Supported by more than C$79 million in grants and research contracts

University Statistics

Year Founded: 1887
Academic Options: undergraduate/graduate
Calendar Year: fall/winter session (Sept-Apr); spring/summer session (May-Aug)

DISCIPLINES/MAJORS OFFERED

Faculty of Business: Accounting, Finance, Human Resources, Information Systems, Marketing, Production/Operations

Faculty of Engineering: Chemical, Civil, Computer, Electrical, Engineering Physics, Manufacturing, Materials, Mechanical, Software

Faculty of Science: Astrophysics, Biochemistry, Biological Chemistry, Biology, Biology & Psychology, Chemistry, Computer Science, Geo-Science, Environmental Science, Geography, Geology, Life Science, Materials Science, Mathematical Science, Mathematics, Medical & Health Physics, Molecular Biology & Biotechnology, Neural Computation, Physics, Physical Science, Psychology, Statistics

Faculty of Health Sciences: Medical Program, Occupational Therapy/Physiotherapy Nursing, Midwifery

Faculty of Social Sciences: Anthropology, Economics, Gerontological Studies, Geography, Kinesiology, Labour Studies, Political Science, Psychology, Religious Studies, Social Work, Sociology

Faculty of Humanities: Art, Art History, Classics, Comparative Literature, English, French, History, Japanese Studies, Latin American Studies, Linguistics, Modern Languages (German, Italian, Russian, Spanish), Music, Philosophy, Women's Studies

ADMISSIONS CRITERIA & PROCEDURES

McMaster seeks out those students who display academic promise, leadership skills and a wide variety of interests. The general admission requirement for admission to McMaster is an OSSD with at least six OACs, or its equivalent. Individual program requirements, prerequisites, minimum grade averages and related information can be obtained by contacting the Admissions Office. Additional admissions criteria may include a portfolio submission, an interview or a letter of recommendation. International applicants may be admitted to McMaster with satisfactory completion of the International Baccalaureate Diploma program with a grade of at least 28 overall or by acquiring a GCE in five subjects, two of which must be Advanced Level.

In addition to the above, international students whose native language is not English must also submit a TOEFL score of 560 or higher to gain direct entry into academic programs. Students who do not meet this requirement but have achieved a TOEFL score between 530 and 539 may be eligible for admission. International students who need to improve English language skills may enrol in McMaster's English Qualifying University Intensive Programme. All academic transcripts not in English must be accompanied by officially translated copies.

International students must submit completed applications by May 1 and have all supporting documents in by June 1. The deadline for general Canadian admission to the fall semester is July 15.

Admissions at a Glance

Minimum GPA: varies

Minimum English Requirements:

TOEFL 560

Application Fee: C$80 (Canadian), $95 (international)

Application Deadlines: February 1 (limited enrolment); June 1 (Canadian); May 1 (international)

ACADEMIC FACILITIES

McMaster's diverse academic programs are supported by many high-quality facilities. The University Library contains over 1.7 million volumes and 12,000 periodicals. The library has an extensive special collections section which includes the Bertrand Russell Archives, consisting of many 18th Century documents.

Facilities for individual programs include modern language laboratories, music rehearsal rooms, art studios, sophisticated science laboratories, a nuclear accelerator and one of the few university-operated nuclear reactors in the nation. The campus features a broad range of classrooms to facilitate learning environments that vary from small seminar rooms to large lecture auditoriums. There are four general computer laboratories including numerous microcomputer and UNIX workstation clusters. The entire university is networked through a coaxial cable network known as McABLEnet. All students have 24-hour access to McMaster's systems through the Internet.

Student & Faculty Profile

Total Enrolment: 17,019

Undergraduate Enrolment: 11,861

# of Faculty: 1,131

Student/Faculty Ratio: 23:1

Male/Female Students: 46%/54%

First-Year Class Sizes: 40 (average)

Undergraduate Acceptance Rate: not available

Undergraduate Enrolment by Discipline: not available

SCHOLARSHIPS & FINANCIAL ASSISTANCE

McMaster strives to attract the most promising students from around the globe, and therefore, rewards more than 10 per cent of the entering student body with academic and extracurricular scholarships. Canadian students may also apply for financial assistance from either the federal or provincial government. Students receiving government loans also qualify for university-administered bursaries. McMaster's Faculty Deans set aside five scholarships for entering international students with a high level of academic achievement. These one-time scholarships range from C$2,000-4,000 which goes towards first-year tuition.

Expenses at a Glance

Tuition (undergraduate, full-time):

In-Province: C$3,900/year

Out-of-Province: C$3,900/year

International: C$12,000/year

Fees, Books, Materials: C$850/year

Accommodation:

Private: C$625-750/month

Residence: C$625-700/month

Homestay: n/a

Health Insurance: C$575/year

CAMPUS & LOCATION

City Population:	350,000
Cost of Living:	medium
Climate Range:	-10° to 25°C
Campus Setting:	suburban
# of Students in Residence:	2,780

The university's main campus rests on 12 hectares, bordered by the Royal Botanical Gardens, Lake Ontario and the streets of Hamilton. The attractive main campus is located on the west side of the city, surrounded by beautiful residential areas. The campus is home to several cultural facilities including the Museum of Art. Less than an hour from Toronto, and neighbouring other major Canadian cities, Hamilton is a part of southern Ontario's Golden Horseshoe region. The multicultural nature of Hamilton and the surrounding areas ensures that international students are comfortable at McMaster.

Approximately 350,000 people live in Hamilton. Historically known for its heavy industry and steel companies, it is also a cultural and recreational centre. The Royal Botanical Gardens are a major area attraction. The rural areas around the city have long been known for abundant fruit crops. An hour's drive through current and former fruit-growing areas leads to Canada's famous Niagara Falls. Lake Ontario, one of the Great Lakes, offers many recreational opportunities including boating, swimming and ice-skating in the winter.

ATHLETICS & EXTRACURRICULAR ACTIVITIES

McMaster strives to provide students with a well-rounded learning experience that extends outside the world of academics. Students are encouraged to take advantage of the many extracurricular activities that take place on campus. The recreation, fitness and intramural programs offer more than 30 different sports in which over 6,000 students participate. The university competes in 16 varsity sports for men and 14 for women. Notable athletic facilities include a 50-metre swimming pool, all-weather track, tennis and squash courts, a modern weight training facility known as Pulse, several gymnasia and the Sports Medicine Clinic. There are countless instructional programs offered throughout the year in a wide variety of interests, including areas as diverse as flamenco dancing and wall climbing.

The student body at McMaster is able to enjoy a vibrant and fulfilling life outside of the classroom. With over 100 social and cultural student clubs and organizations meeting on campus, students can find like-minded peers as well as expand their own interests. McMaster students are served by a student newspaper and an FM radio station.

STUDENT SUPPORT SERVICES

Students can receive academic counselling from faculty members throughout the year. In addition, the Centre for Student Development (CSD) assists students with personal, family and social problems, and provides skill-development and writing workshops. The Career Planning & Employment Centre helps students implement career strategies and find employment; the centre aggressively promotes its students. The McMaster Student Union sponsors a host of services for students including an information centre, walk safe program and a health education centre.

The Office of International Students' Advisor (OISA) acts as a liaison between students from abroad and McMaster. OISA can assist students in a variety of ways, including offering advice concerning immigration and cultural issues. OISA is also responsible for organizing social and cultural activities that promote diversity on campus.

University Recognition

- McMaster is home to the 1997 Nobel Prize for Physics
- Ninety-seven per cent of the faculty hold the highest degree in their field

International Students

University Enrolment: 240

% of University Enrolment: 2%

Countries of Origin: International students at McMaster represent 78 countries including Japan, Korea, the UK, Brazil and Germany.

QUEEN'S UNIVERSITY KINGSTON, ONTARIO

University Mission

...to build on the strength that is Queen's—students, faculty, staff and alumni—to be among the best of internationally known universities in Canada

Student Voice:

When I decided to come to Queen's, my decision was based on the notion that I would receive a quality education and while doing so, have a fun and rewarding experience. Since arriving at Queen's I feel that I have grown not just intellectually, but personally and emotionally.

Perry Lao,
Biochemistry, 1999
Engineering Chemistry 2001

CONTACT INFORMATION
Admission Services
Queen's University
Victoria School Building
110 Alfred Street
Kingston, Ontario
Canada K7L 3N6
PH 1-613-533-2218
FAX 1-613-533-6810
EMAIL admissn@post.queensu.ca
INTERNET http://www.queensu.ca/

UNIVERSITY OVERVIEW

Queen's University (Queen's) was founded by a royal charter in 1841. With an emphasis on teaching and first-class research, Queen's offers distinguished undergraduate and graduate curricula through 15 faculties and schools. The university maintains a relatively small student body to ensure close interaction with faculty and a strong sense of community. In a recent national survey of high school guidance counsellors, academic administrators and CEOs of major corporations, Queen's was ranked as highest in quality and as having the best overall reputation in Canada.

Innovation and Flexibility

Queen's strives to offer the most innovative and progressive programs available. Small class sizes and the numerous research centres on campus create an exceptional learning environment. Many schools and faculties offer dual degree programs, which allow students to study in more than one area of interest. Students gain the broad-based knowledge and analytical and problem-solving skills that are vital in today's global environment.

Queen's recognizes how important practical experience is to a modern education. The university's internship program, in cooperation with more than 50 companies, offers students the opportunity to apply the skills learned in the classroom in a real-world setting.

Internationalism

Queen's is keeping pace with the ever-changing global environment by offering several opportunities for its students to study abroad. Queen's own and operates the International Study Centre (ISC) at Herstmonceux, East Sussex, UK. The ISC offers programs featuring a focus on British and European Studies combined with Integrated Field Studies to sites of historic, cultural and economic importance in Britain and continental Europe. Students may choose a first-year university program offering courses in the arts, humanities and social sciences or an upper-year university program offering courses in the arts, humanities, commerce, law, social sciences and strategic policy planning. An innovative ESL Plus program is available for high-intermediate and advanced-level ESL learners who wish to complement their English-training with content-based learning in subjects of interest.

Queen's has international study agreements with more than 50 universities around the globe, providing students with the opportunity to learn firsthand about the global environment. The student exchange program allows students to study in countries such as Australia, Chile, France, Germany, Mexico, Sweden, Italy, Japan, USA and Singapore.

Highlights

- Receives more than C$70 million in research grants each year
- International exchange programs with more than 50 universities around the world and an international study centre in England
- Programs integrate practical experience in a theoretical framework

University Statistics

Year Founded: 1841

Academic Options: undergraduate/graduate

Calendar Year: fall term (Sept-Dec); winter term (Jan-Apr)

DISCIPLINES/MAJORS OFFERED

Faculty of Arts & Science: Applied Economics; Art History; Astrophysics; Biochemistry; Biology; Canadian Studies; Chemical Physics; Chemistry; Classical Studies; Cognitive Science; Commonwealth Studies; Computing & Information Science; Communication, Culture & Information Technology; Computing & Information Science; Development Studies; Drama; Economics; English; Environmental Science; Environmental Studies; Film; Fine Arts; French Studies, Geography, Geological Sciences, German, Greek; Health; History; Italian; Jewish Studies; Language & Linguistics; Latin; Life Sciences; Mathematical Physics; Mathematics; Medieval Studies; Music; Philosophy; Physical & Health Education; Physics; Political Studies; Psychology; Religious Studies; Sociology; Spanish; Stage & Screen Studies; Statistics; Women's Studies

Faculty of Applied Science: Engineering: Chemical; Civil; Computer; Electrical; Geological; Mechanical; Materials & Metallurgical; Mining; Engineering Physics; Engineering Chemistry; Mathematics & Engineering

School of Business: Commerce

School of Nursing: Nursing Science

Faculty of Education

Faculty of Law

School of Rehabilitation Therapy: Occupational Therapy; Physical Therapy

ADMISSIONS CRITERIA & PROCEDURES

Admission to Queen's is highly competitive. Applications must be submitted through the Ontario Universities' Application Centre (OUAC), Box 1328, Guelph, Ontario N1H 7P4. Generally, admission is based on successful completion of secondary school. The minimum grade average for admission is 70 per cent or equivalent; however, because all degree programs have limited enrolment, the actual minimum average may be considerably higher. Additional admissions requirements such as portfolios, standardized test scores and interviews may be required for certain programs. Students should contact Admission Services for further details. Applicants will be contacted after receipt of application and asked to provide two official transcripts of academic records and a completed personal information form, which requests information on students' extracurricular activities and work experience. The application deadline for the fall term, when most programs begin, is February 24 for the Faculty of Education and February 26 for all others. Students will normally receive an admissions decision by the middle of May. The application fee for Canadian students is C$85. International students must pay a C$95 application fee.

In addition to the above, international students whose native language is not English must submit a TOEFL score of 580, MELAB score of 90 or IELTS score of 7.0 to be considered for admission. Students who wish to improve their English language skills may enrol in the on-campus English for Academic Purposes program, offered by the School of English.

Admissions at a Glance

Minimum GPA: 70% (may vary)

Minimum English Requirements:
TOEFL 580, MELAB 90, IELTS 7.0

Application Fee: C$85 (Canadian), $95 (international)

Application Deadlines: February 24 (fall term) Faculty of Education; February 26 (fall term) all other faculties and schools

ACADEMIC FACILITIES

Queen's provides its students with exceptional academic facilities. Classrooms and laboratories are continually updated and renovated to incorporate the latest teaching and research technologies. Information Technology Services operates several computer labs and assists with the university-wide network. Internet and email access is readily available throughout the campus. The Stauffer and Douglas Libraries, together with two departmental libraries, hold more than five million items including books, periodicals, maps, microfilms and newspapers. Queen's supports 14 federal and provincial research centres, as well as 23 of its own research groups. Other notable Queen's facilities include the Biological Station, an 1,800-hectare outdoor laboratory and the new Biosciences Complex. The Writing Centre provides a comprehensive program of tutorials, workshops and courses for students who wish to improve their academic communication skills.

Student & Faculty Profile

Total Enrolment: 12,982

Undergraduate Enrolment: 10,998

# of Faculty: 965

Student/Faculty Ratio: 11:1

Male/Female Students: 44%/56%

First-Year Class Sizes: varies

Undergraduate Acceptance Rate: 57%

Undergraduate Enrolment by Discipline:

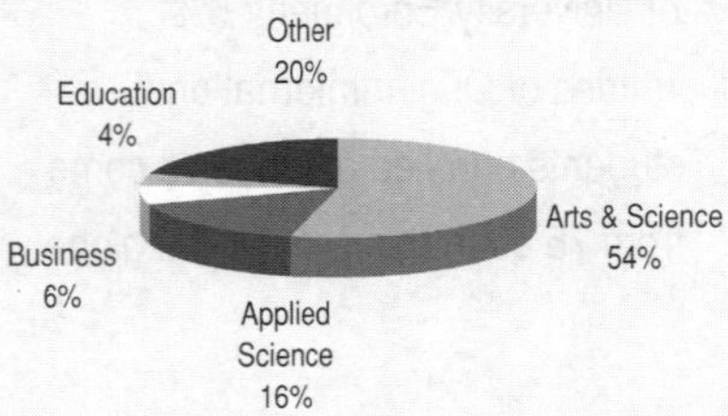

SCHOLARSHIPS & FINANCIAL ASSISTANCE

Queen's is committed to attracting the brightest and most promising students and, therefore, offers more than 450 entrance awards and nearly 2,000 undergraduate scholarships each year. Entrance awards are granted to domestic students who have displayed a high level of academic achievement. Many awards and scholarships require additional applications. After students have completed one year of studies, they are eligible for a wide range of scholarships, regardless of citizenship. Federal and provincial loan programs are also available for Canadian students. Recent studies show that the percentage of Queen's students receiving awards and the average amount of money awarded per student are the among the highest in Ontario.

Expenses at a Glance

Tuition (undergraduate, full-time):
In-Province: C$3,551-3,915/year*
Out-of-Province: C$3,551-3,915/year*
International: C$10,000-16,300/year*

Fees, Books, Materials: C$1,000/year*

Accommodation:
Private: C$500-700/month*
Residence: C$625-725/month*
Homestay: C$600/month*

Health Insurance: C$209/term*

CAMPUS & LOCATION

City Population:	120,000
Cost of Living:	medium
Climate Range:	-6° to 28°C
Campus Setting:	urban
# of Students in Residence:	3,000

Queen's University's 100 buildings are situated on a 40-hectare main campus and a 24-hectare West Campus. The main campus is a 10-minute walk of downtown Kingston. The main campus offers a blend of fully restored, stately historic buildings and modern, bright, contemporary structures in a tree-filled setting. Queen's International Study Centre (ISC) is situated on the historic 200-hecatre Herstmonceux Castle Estate in East Sussex, UK (100 kilometres south of London).

Kingston, with a population of 120,000, is home to a number of institutions of higher learning, making it a true college town. It is also an historic site, having once been Canada's capital city for a brief period in the 1840s. The city hugs the northeastern shore of Lake Ontario, a freshwater sailing haven in the heart of the Thousand Island resort region. Over one million tourists visit the region each year. It is conveniently accessible from Toronto, Ottawa and Montreal. The city's strategic location and intellectual resources have attracted many high-profile businesses such as Alcan, Bombardier and Du Pont. A culturally diverse city, Kingston boasts many theatre groups, the Kingston Symphony and a world-renowned busking festival.

ATHLETICS & EXTRACURRICULAR ACTIVITIES

Queen's offers a wide variety of recreational and cultural activities to provide students with a varied and fulfilling educational experience.

The university offers an array of athletic programs to its students. Students can participate at the recreational, instructional, intramural or interuniversity level. There are more than 45 intramural activities available including ball hockey, badminton and tennis. Queen's enjoys notable success at the interuniversity level (41 teams), and each year its students claim numerous national titles. The Physical Education Centre is the hub of all athletic activity on campus. The centre includes three multipurpose gymnasia, 10 indoor racquet courts, a swimming pool, two weight rooms, an arena and a newly renovated cardio-fitness area.

Students are active in more than 200 student clubs and organizations addressing a wide variety of interests including professional and cultural clubs. The student-run newspaper and radio station make the campus a lively and informed forum for debate and the exchange of ideas. The university's Agnes Etherington Art Centre is the third largest gallery in the province.

University Recognition

- 44 Queens graduates have won prestigious Rhodes scholarships
- Maclean's magazine consistently ranks Queen's 1st in terms of reputation for quality of its programs
- Queen's is acknowledged to have the highest admission standards in the entire country
- Member of the Association of Commonwealth Universities

STUDENT SUPPORT SERVICES

Queen's provides a comprehensive support system to address all issues or concerns that students may have. Individual academic counselling is given by informed faculty members who meet with students throughout the year. Career Services organizes workshops and placement programs and provides one-on-one career planning. The John Deutsch University Centre houses many of the student government offices and services for students.

The International Centre at Queen's promotes the academic and personal development of the foreign community at Queen's by organizing a range of social, cultural, educational and orientation activities throughout the year.

International Students

University Enrolment: 763

% of University Enrolment: 6%

Countries of Origin: International students enrolled at Queen's come from 75 countries around the globe.

Royal Military College of Canada
Kingston, Ontario

University Mission

...to educate and train officer cadets and commissioned officers for careers of effective service in the Canadian Forces

Student Voice:

I'm not going to look at it as "I went to RMC." I'm probably going to look at it as "I lived RMC."

OCdt Jay Steele
Bachelor of Science, '97

Contact Information

Registrar
Royal Military College of Canada
PO Box 17000, Station Forces
Kingston, Ontario
Canada K7K 7B4
PH 1-613-541-6000 ext. 6302 or 6652
FAX 1-613-542-3565
EMAIL registrar@rmc.ca
INTERNET http://www.rmc.ca

For the French version of this profile, please see page 193.

UNIVERSITY OVERVIEW

An education at Royal Military College (RMC) consists of four "pillars," each playing an important role in the life of a cadet: academics, military training, physical education and second language training. The academic program is much like that at any other university, although RMC programs differ from those offered elsewhere because of additional subjects studied by cadets: all cadets take a course in military psychology and leadership during each of their four years of study.

To broaden their education to meet the unique needs of an officer in the Canadian Forces, students in science and engineering must take arts courses, and those in arts must take science courses.

A cadet's military life begins with the Basic Officer Training Course (BOTC), the first part of which is completed just prior to the first academic year. The second part of the BOTC includes military training during the first year and an immersion course in the cadet's second language between the first and second years. During summers following the second and third years, cadets receive further military training.

RMC's mandatory four-year program in physical education and athletics allows cadets to attain a high level of physical fitness and a satisfactory level of sports skills. The program emphasizes fitness, basic knowledge in many sports, and the administration of athletics. Cadets are tested periodically and must meet fitness standards in stamina, agility and strength.

Second language training develops the ability to communicate in both official languages and an understanding of the principles of bilingualism.

Students are placed in small classes at their own level and progress at their own rate. There are five periods of instruction per week during normal class hours. As well, cadets who are not yet functionally bilingual (a mandatory standard) attend a 10-week immersion program during the second summer.

Since RMC is a bilingual institution, cadets can study in either English or French as a matter of choice. Also, each first-year cadet rooms with a cadet proficient in the other official language.

Highlights

- The only military university in Canada
- Offers both a renowned bilingual education and a challenging career
- One of only a small number of universities in Canada with its own nuclear reactor, used for study purposes by both staff and students

University Statistics

Year Founded: 1876
Academic Options: undergraduate/graduate
Calendar Year: first term (Sept-Dec); second term (Jan-Apr)

DISCIPLINES/MAJORS OFFERED

Business Administration

Engineering: Chemical & Materials, Civil, Computer, Electrical, Mechanical

Humanities: English, French, History

Military & Strategic Studies

Science: Chemistry, General, Mathematics & Computer Science, Physics

Social Sciences: Politics & Economics

Space Science

ADMISSIONS CRITERIA & PROCEDURES

Students apply at their local Canadian Forces Recruiting Centre (1-800-856-8488). The process includes medical, aptitude and physical fitness testing, as well as an interview.

There are two admission plans: the Regular Officer Training Plan (ROTP), which provides a fully subsidized education, and the Reserve Entry Training Plan, for which cadets are required to pay fees. Both programs provide the same education and training.

Upon successful completion of the ROTP program, cadets are awarded their degrees and granted commissions as officers in the Canadian Forces, and must serve at least five years in the regular (or full-time) component of the Canadian Forces.

RETP cadets must also take summer training, for which they receive pay and allowances.

Applications are best initiated early in the student's final year of high school. For the school year beginning in September 1999, the deadline is February 12, 1999 for students wishing to be pilots, or March 12, 1999 for all other career choices. Students should consult the local Recruiting Centre for more details.

In order to qualify for admission, a candidate must be a Canadian citizen (landed immigrants may be eligible under the Reserve Entry Training Plan); meet the medical standards required for enrolment; pass pre-enrolment tests; and pass the Basic Officers Training Course.

Admissions at a Glance

Minimum GPA: 75-80%

Minimum English Requirements: n/a; students are expected to be fluent in at least one official language

Application Fee: n/a

Application Deadlines: Feb 12 (applicants who wish to be pilots), Mar 12 (all other applicants)

ACADEMIC FACILITIES

RMC's two libraries, Massey Library (housing the arts & humanities collection) and the Science & Engineering Library, contain approximately 300,000 volumes, including Canada's largest collection of military science volumes, 18,000 microfiches and a large number of video- and audiotapes, and approximately 1,100 journals in all fields of study. The libraries also house the RMC archives and an extensive special collection of military and other materials. Students have full access to library research resources like CD-ROMs and Telnet and access to the Queen's University Library.

RMC's computing facilities include Windows NT and Sun Solaris workstations located all over the campus, all of which use Pentium and/or SPARC technologies. Furthermore, the campus has multimedia classrooms, videoconferencing classrooms and audiovisual facilities for the use of students.

Students in our science and engineering departments have access to fully developed laboratory facilities, which include a nuclear reactor used for study by both students and staff.

Student & Faculty Profile

Total Enrolment: 1,100

Undergraduate Enrolment: 900

# of Faculty: 160

Student/Faculty Ratio: 6:1

Male/Female Students: 72%/28%

First-Year Class Sizes: 35 (average)

Undergraduate Acceptance Rate: 55% (after screening by recruiting centre)

Undergraduate Enrolment by Discipline:

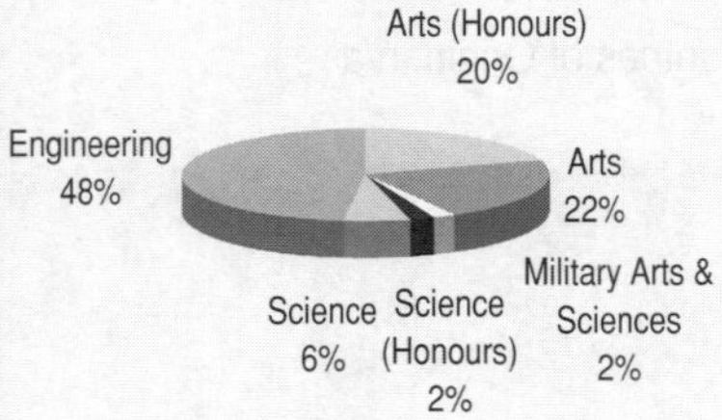

SCHOLARSHIPS & FINANCIAL ASSISTANCE

The Department of National Defence sponsors most cadets under ROTP.

Reserve Entry Training Plan (RETP) members pay for part of the costs of their education. They may be eligible for some scholarships and bursaries that are available to students at Canadian universities. Also, RETP members may receive awards under the Provincial Student Awards Programmes. The registrar can provide details.

Expenses at a Glance

Tuition (undergraduate, full-time):
- In-Province: C$1,524/year
- Out-of-Province: C$1,524/year
- International: n/a

Fees, Books, Materials: C$107/academic year (included in tuition)

Accommodation:
- Private: n/a
- Residence: C$2,400/academic year
- Homestay: n/a

Health Insurance: n/a

CAMPUS & LOCATION

City Population:	140,000
Cost of Living:	medium
Climate Range:	-8° to 24°C
Campus Setting:	suburban
# of Students in Residence:	900

The RMC campus is situated on Point Frederick, a small peninsula just to the east of the city of Kingston, Ontario. This scenic location, at the junction of Lake Ontario and the St. Lawrence River, is one of great historic importance. It has been occupied as an active military site since 1789 and during the War of 1812 it served as the major naval station in Upper Canada. Ships of the Royal Navy were built and based here and it was because of these ships that Upper Canada was preserved from American occupation.

Several Royal Navy buildings, from the immediate post–War of 1812 period, still exist on campus, and later fortifications, such as Fort Frederick and the immediately adjacent Fort Henry, add to the military ambience of the college.

Cadets are required to live in an assigned dormitory on the campus. Married applicants and those with dependants are not precluded from making application; however, the RMC program is designed to demand a 24-hour-a-day commitment from all cadets and their spouses and families cannot live on the campus.

ATHLETICS & EXTRACURRICULAR ACTIVITIES

The college competes, at an intercollegiate level, in many representative sports.

Athletic facilities at the college include three gymnasia, indoor running tracks, a weight-training area and six squash courts. The college has an indoor artificial ice arena, an indoor swimming pool, five outdoor tennis courts, running tracks, many sports fields and a rifle and pistol range, as well as excellent facilities for recreational and competitive sailing and boating. All sports equipment is provided. Students also use nearby military specialized athletic facilities, such as an 18-hole golf course and a curling rink.

A number of intramural sports clubs provide cadets with an opportunity to participate in sports that do not involve representative competition. There is also a wide range of recreational and other activities available, including a Cadet Mess and College Canteen with a snack bar for cadets and staff, and a small store for personal articles and souvenirs.

Other clubs provide for special interests, such as astronomy, band, equitation, debating and theatre.

University Recognition

- Engineering programs accredited by the Canadian Council of Professional Engineers
- Each year, several RMC graduates are given NSERC Post Graduate Study Awards
- Several graduates have been awarded prestigious Rhodes and Athlone-Vanier scholarships

STUDENT SUPPORT SERVICES

Students are assisted in their career choices by staff at the Recruiting Centre where they apply.

At RMC, the Chaplains—Protestant and Roman Catholic—conduct regular Sunday Services of Divine Worship. Discussion groups, dialogue dinners and Padre's Hour provide opportunities for interchange with the chaplains on ethical, moral and religious issues. The chaplains are always available for individual counselling.

The students have access to full medical and dental services.

International Students

University Enrolment: n/a

% of University Enrolment: n/a

Countries of Origin: n/a

TRENT UNIVERSITY

TRENT UNIVERSITY PETERBOROUGH, ONTARIO

University Mission

...to be Canada's outstanding small university known for its commitment to liberal undergraduate education in the humanities, social sciences and natural sciences

Student Voice:

It was easy to make friends in the colleges, and small class sizes and approachable professors make the academic experience challenging yet stimulating.

Rhian Holder, Jamaica

CONTACT INFORMATION

Trent University
1600 West Bank Drive
Peterborough, Ontario
Canada K9J 7B8
PH 1-705-748-1215
FAX 1-705-748-1629
EMAIL liaison@trentu.ca
INTERNET http://www.trentu.ca

UNIVERSITY OVERVIEW

Trent University (Trent) is one of Canada's smallest universities, renowned for its emphasis on small-group teaching and interdisciplinary studies.

Trent's interdisciplinary approach exposes students to courses in a wide variety of subject areas, encouraging them to develop a broad base of academic knowledge. Trent offers undergraduate programs in 30 subject areas, and allows single- and joint-major programs, giving students hundreds of possible combinations. Trent also offers several programs at the graduate level, including anthropology.

Student-Centred Education

Three-quarters of classes at Trent contain fewer than 25 students. In most cases, lectures are supplemented by small-group tutorials or lab sections that provide more intimate learning environments. Seminars and labs are usually led by professors rather than teaching assistants. Maclean's magazine ranked Trent number one for small class sizes among primarily undergraduate universities in Canada.

International Opportunities at Trent

Trent offers an International Program, designed to provide students with the opportunity to develop a global perspective, to pursue a special emphasis in International Studies, or to participate in one of the university's popular international exchange opportunities.

Trent encourages students to spend a year studying outside of Canada. Students can apply to participate in an exchange program in the United Kingdom, Japan, Korea or the US, or in one of Trent's study-abroad programs in countries such as Russia, Israel, Poland, Spain and South Africa. Students studying Modern Languages can sign up to spend a year abroad in France, Germany or Mexico.

The Comparative Development Studies programs in Ecuador and Ghana, and the Native Studies program in Thailand, combine academic courses with work placement. Students receive full credit at Trent for all courses successfully completed while studying abroad.

Highlights

- Emphasis on interdisciplinary and international studies
- Award-winning architecture
- A small, intimate campus with a focus on student-centred learning

University Statistics

Year Founded: 1963

Academic Options: undergraduate/graduate

Calendar Year: fall term (Sept-Dec); spring term (Jan-Apr)

DISCIPLINES/MAJORS OFFERED

Undergraduate Programs: Administrative Studies, Ancient History & Classics, Anthropology, Biology, Canadian Studies, Chemistry, Comparative Development Studies, Computer Studies, Cultural Studies, Economics, Education, English Literature, Environmental & Resource Studies, Environmental Chemistry, Geography, History, International Studies, Mathematics, Modern Languages, Native Studies, Philosophy, Physics, Political Studies, Psychology, Sociology, Women's Studies

ADMISSIONS CRITERIA & PROCEDURES

Canadian applicants for full-time studies at Trent should submit completed application packages directly to Trent or to the Ontario Universities' Application Centre (OAC). All international applicants should contact Trent directly. Applicants for part-time study should also contact Trent, and submit their applications directly to the Department of Part-Time Studies. Admission is based on successful completion of an Ontario Secondary School Diploma (OSSD) program. An OAC- or senior-level English credit is required for admission to all courses of study. Applicants should be aware that there are additional requirements for specific subject areas, and are encouraged to contact Trent for further information.

All new students admitted to Trent are guaranteed a residence room. College and residence application forms should be submitted along with the C$300 deposit as early as possible, no later than April 1.

Admissions at a Glance

Minimum GPA: 2.5

Minimum English Requirements:
- TOEFL 550 (paper-based), 213 (computer-based)

Application Fee: no application fee for students applying directly to Trent

Application Deadlines: April 1 (teacher education); June 11 (general admission)

ACADEMIC FACILITIES

Trent is served by the Thomas J. Bata Library, located in the heart of the campus. Designed by Canadian architect Ron Thom and opened in 1969, the library has an abundance of research material, including 470,000 volumes, 260,000 microforms, 190,000 government documents, 100,000 maps and air photos, and 2,500 current serial subscriptions. A wide range of audiovisual materials is also available at the library for student use. The online TOPCAT database helps students locate materials quickly and easily.

The university offers extensive computer services, including PC and Macintosh labs and six NCD workstations. Students also receive free email accounts and access to the Internet.

SCHOLARSHIPS & FINANCIAL ASSISTANCE

All students are automatically considered for scholarships when they apply for admission to Trent. There is more than C$1.5 million in scholarships available for academically distinguished students. New undergraduate students automatically receive applications for bursaries by post; the Financial Aid Office awards bursaries in July of each year. Students with financial need are encouraged to apply for aid through the Ontario Student Assistance Program (OSAP). All students are eligible to apply for in-course bursaries, primarily available for emergency situations. These bursaries are usually awarded in the second semester, and are based on students' financial need and satisfactory academic achievement.

Student & Faculty Profile

Total Enrolment: 5,160

Undergraduate Enrolment: 3,800

# of Faculty: 200

Student/Faculty Ratio: 19:1

Male/Female Students: 60%/40%

First-Year Class Sizes: 25 (average)

Undergraduate Acceptance Rate: 80%

Undergraduate Enrolment by Discipline:

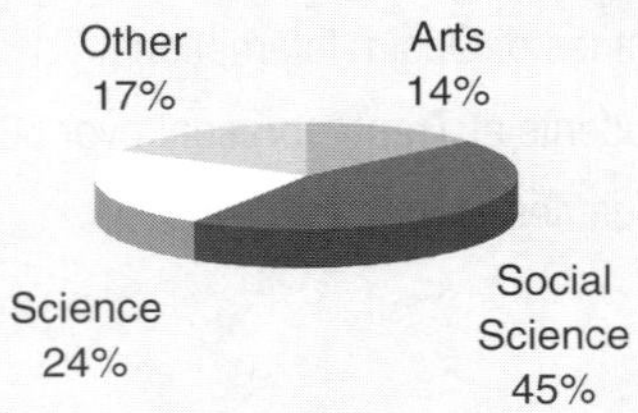

Expenses at a Glance

Tuition (undergraduate, full-time):
- In-Province: C$4,231/year*
- Out-of-Province: C$4,231/year*
- International: C$10,796/year (includes fees)*

Fees, Books, Materials: not available

Accommodation:
- Private: C$350-550/month*
- Residence: C$662-706/month*
- Homestay: n/a

Health Insurance: C$461 (international)*

CAMPUS & LOCATION

City Population:	68,000
Cost of Living:	medium
Climate Range:	-11° to 27°C
Campus Setting:	suburban
# of Students in Residence:	1,100

Trent's campus, comprising five colleges, offers dramatic architecture and close proximity to natural settings. The university is proud of its unique residential college system and its commitment to providing strong student support. The college system at Trent strongly promotes students' active participation in their education. A large percentage of Trent students live on campus in one of the five colleges; over 80 per cent of college residences are single rooms. Students benefit from an intellectual and social environment intimate enough to provide ample opportunity for development and meaningful interaction. This ethic is most evident at Champlain College where the award-winning architecture brings office, living quarters, and seminar spaces into interchanging spaces. Students living in residence have many opportunities to encounter professors and visitors informally and personally.

The campus is located on 580 hectares, with nature areas making up over half of the campus plot. These areas are composed of a diverse range of habitats and are home to white-tailed deer, porcupines, squirrels, rabbits, herons and hawks.

Trent is located in the city of Peterborough, in the Kawartha Lakes tourist area of Ontario, between Toronto and Ottawa. Peterborough offers residents a small-town ambience with cosmopolitan opportunities close by. Peterborough is also close to many lakes, beaches, conservation areas and hiking & ski trails. Peterborough offers a variety of restaurants, shops, art galleries, museums and a performing arts centre. Trent students, faculty and staff are active in community activities, such as the Peterborough Symphony, theatre groups and choirs.

ATHLETICS & EXTRACURRICULAR ACTIVITIES

The university offers a fully equipped Athletic Centre, featuring a 25-metre pool, a gymnasium, squash courts, weight-training areas and saunas, a floodlit playing field, a 400-metre track, tennis courts, rowing shells, and cross-country skiing & biking trails. Trent also supports both competitive intercollegiate sports and intramurals, including the largest long-distance rowing regatta in Canada. Varsity sports include skiing, volleyball, soccer, curling, rugby, fencing, golf, basketball, swimming, field hockey, running and squash. The university also organizes the annual Trent Triathlon, an intercollegiate sprint triathlon combining biking, running and swimming.

Trent supports many student-run clubs and organizations.

STUDENT SUPPORT SERVICES

To help international students ease their transition to Canada, Trent's International Program Office offers counselling in such areas as health insurance, immigration information, employment, finances, scholarships and academic programs. Throughout the year, the office organizes a variety of social and cultural activities with an international theme.

The Academic Skills Centre can provide individual counselling as well as group workshops on essay writing, efficient and critical reading, study techniques, note-taking and examination writing. It also offers tutoring in mathematics and French, as well as additional help for special needs students and non-native speakers of English.

The Counselling & Careers Centre provides students with personal counselling and assistance in finding part-time, summer, or full-time employment.

The Special Needs Office provides support and advocacy services for students with physical, sensory or learning disabilities.

University Recognition

- Ranked number one for class size in first- and second-year classes by Maclean's magazine
- Ranked number one for number of faculty awards out of primarily undergraduate schools by Maclean's magazine

International Students

University Enrolment: 135

% of University Enrolment: 6%

Countries of Origin: International students at Trent represent over 50 countries around the globe.

UNIVERSITY OF GUELPH
GUELPH, ONTARIO

University Mission

...to serve society and to enhance the quality of life through scholarship . . . to put the learner at the centre of all [the university] does, recognizing that research and teaching are intimately linked and that learning is a lifelong commitment

Student Voice:

Guelph has all the facilities of a large university, but the feel of a smaller one. . . . The opportunities at the University of Guelph are endless.

Eri Yamada
Bachelor of Arts
International Development

CONTACT INFORMATION

Admission Services
University of Guelph
50 Stone Road East
Guelph, Ontario
Canada N1G 2W1
PH 1-519-821-2130
FAX 1-519-766-9481
EMAIL jphippen@registrar.uoguelph.ca
INTERNET http://www.uoguelph.ca/

UNIVERSITY OVERVIEW

The University of Guelph (U of G) is rich in tradition, its roots extending back more than 120 years to the Ontario Agricultural College, the Ontario Veterinary College and the Macdonald Institute. Officially founded in 1964, U of G is recognized as one of Canada's most research-intensive universities, receiving more than C$82 million each year in research funding. The university's distinguished alumni include Canada's first female astronaut, Roberta Bondar, and world-renowned economist, John Kenneth Galbraith.

Academic Programs

U of G offers over 80 undergraduate and more than 45 graduate degree programs. Students may choose from Bachelors of Applied Science, Arts, Commerce, Landscape Architecture and Science. The Bachelor of Science program is divided into studies focused on agriculture, engineering and environmental sciences. The university offers a Doctor of Veterinary Medicine program and an extensive co-op program in over 25 disciplines.

U of G currently offers 44 master's and 28 doctoral programs in arts, business administration, engineering, fine arts, landscape architecture and veterinary medicine.

Areas of study for one- and two-year associate diplomas include agriculture, equine studies, food & nutrition management, horticulture and veterinary technology.

Under U of G's three-semester system, undergraduate students can expect to study for two to four years, depending on the program and the amount of summer study undertaken.

Overseas Study

With students from over 75 countries and more than 80,000 alumni in 115 countries, U of G has a strong international focus. Over 300 U of G students each year study at foreign institutions, while paying tuition and earning credit at U of G. There are 65 study-abroad and exchange programs in more than 30 countries worldwide.

Distance Education

U of G offers a broad range of degree and nondegree programming through the Office of Open Learning. The distance education program allows foreign students to begin studies in their home countries before applying to the university. It also gives Canadian students the flexibility to study at their own time, place and pace. Nondegree distance education students who choose to shift to a degree program may apply credit from their part-time studies. There are over 60 degree-credit courses available through distance education.

Highlights

- Over 80 undergraduate programs offer many academic options
- Excellent student support, including special programs for first-year and international students
- Overseas study with 65 partner institutions in over 30 countries

University Statistics

Year Founded: 1964
Academic Options: undergraduate/graduate
Calendar Year: fall semester (Sept-Dec); winter semester (Jan-Apr); summer semester (May-Aug)

DISCIPLINES/MAJORS OFFERED

College of Arts: Art History; Classical (Languages, Studies); Drama; English; European Studies; French; History; Music; Philosophy; Spanish; Studio Arts; Women's Studies

College of Biological Science: Biological Sci; Biomedical Sci; Ecology; Human Kinetics; Biology (Marine & Freshwater, Molecular & Genetics, Plant, Wildlife); Microbiology; Nutritional Sci; Zoology

College of Physical & Engineering Science: Applied Math & Stats; Biochem; Biological Eng; Biophysics; Chem Physics; Chem; Comp & Info Sci; Eng Systems & Comp; Env Eng; Env Monitoring & Analysis; Environmetrics; Math; Physical Sci; Physics; Stats; Theoretical Physics; Water Res Eng

College of Social & Applied Human Sciences: Anthropology; Applied Human Nutrition; Canadian Studies; Criminal Justice & Public Policy; Env Geography; Family & Social Relations; Geography; Gerontology; Hotel & Food Admin; Housing & Real Estate Mgmt; Information Systems & Human Behaviour; Int'l Dev't; Mgmt Econ; Mgmt Econ in Industry & Finance; Marketing Mgmt; Math Econ; Poli Sci; Psych; Rural & Dev't Sociology; Sociology

Ontario Agricultural College: Ag (Business, Economics); Agroecosystem Mgmt; Agronomy; Animal Bio; Animal Sci; Horticultural Sci & Bus; Biomedical Toxicology; Earth & Atmosphere Sci; Env Econ & Policy; Env Protection; Earth Surface Sci; Env Bio; Env Toxicology; Food Sci; Landscape Arch; Natural Resources Mgmt

Ontario Veterinary College

ADMISSIONS CRITERIA & PROCEDURES

Students who wish to apply to the University of Guelph should contact Admission Services. Admission to the first year of any degree program is normally available in the fall semester only. In some cases, winter and spring admission may be granted for students applying to the Bachelor Arts, Bachelor of Science and Bachelor of Commerce programs. All applicants must submit official copies of transcripts from secondary and postsecondary institutions previously attended; all transcripts should be sent directly to Admission Services by the issuing institution.

Normally, a 70 per cent average is required for admission consideration. Some programs, such as landscape architecture and most sciences, may require higher averages. Students who wish to switch from Office of Open Learning courses to regular, on-campus degree programs must have an average of 60 per cent. Normally, the average required for co-op programs is higher than 70 per cent.

Students whose first language is not English and who have less than four years of full-time secondary or postsecondary study in an English language school system must have a minimum score of TOEFL 600 (with a minimum of TWE 5.0 and TSE of 50), IELTS 6.5 (no band less than 6.0) or MELAB 85 (composition score of 83 and oral test score of 3). Students with a TOEFL score of 550 or higher may be considered for admission. Francophone Canadian citizens educated in Canada and international students who have completed the International Baccalaureate diploma where English was the language of instruction are not required to meet proficiency requirements.

Admissions at a Glance

Minimum GPA: 60-79%

Minimum English Requirements:
TOEFL 600 (TWE 5.0, TSE 50 [TOEFL 550 for consideration]), IELTS 6.5 (no band < 6) or MELAB 85 (composition 83, oral 3)

Application Fee: C$60 (Canadian and international)

Application Deadlines: Feb 1 (Veterinary Medicine); Apr 1 (BComm [Hotel & Food Admin], BLA); Jun 15 (all other programs)

ACADEMIC FACILITIES

McLaughlin Library at U of G has received a 94 per cent satisfaction rating from its users. The library is home to more than 100 computers; 2.8 million volumes of books, periodicals, films and government documents; 12,000 audiovisual and archival materials; and over 70,000 maps. All students enjoy access to email and the World Wide Web, and those who live in residence can be connected to the campus fibre-optic network. Over 1,000 microcomputers are available for students' use at various locations around the campus, and training and support are provided for those who need it.

The Research Park Centre provides excellent research facilities and a link between U of G researchers and scientists from research-intensive companies.

Student & Faculty Profile

Total Enrolment: 13,746

Undergraduate Enrolment: 12,192

# of Faculty: 612 (full-time)

Student/Faculty Ratio: 21:1

Male/Female Students: 62%/38%

First-Year Class Sizes: 20-250+

Undergraduate Acceptance Rate: 51%

Undergraduate Enrolment by Discipline:

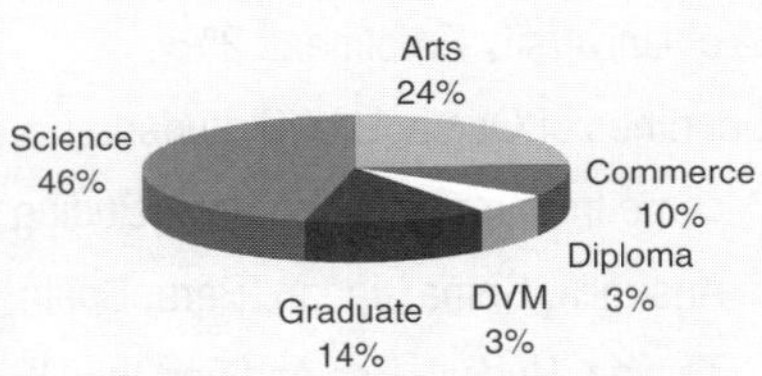

SCHOLARSHIPS & FINANCIAL ASSISTANCE

For information about scholarships and financial assistance, students should contact Student Financial Services at 1-519-824-4120, ext. 2868. U of G awards over C$6 million every year in entrance scholarships, bursaries and scholarships for academic excellence. Both Canadian and international students are automatically considered for most entrance awards when they apply to U of G. Student Financial Services also administers government loans for the Ontario Student Assistance Program. Other financial opportunities for both Canadian and international students include work-study and other part-time work.

Expenses at a Glance

Tuition (undergraduate, full-time):
In-Province: C$3,223-3,500*
Out-of-Province: C$3,223-3,500*
International: C$5,140-8,380*

Fees, Books, Materials: C$1,300/year*

Accommodation:
Private: C$550-700/month*
Residence: C$2,381-3,061/semester*
Homestay: n/a

Health Insurance: C$570/year (int'l)

CAMPUS & LOCATION

City Population:	95,000
Cost of Living:	medium
Climate Range:	-20° to 30°C
Campus Setting:	suburban
# of Students in Residence:	4,600

The University of Guelph is located in the city of Guelph in southwestern Ontario. The 330-hectare campus features modern and traditional architecture, including Victorian turrets, brick walkways and landscaped plazas. The campus boasts a 165-hectare arboretum, with 2,900 species of trees and shrubs, as well as many trails for walking or jogging.

With room for 4,600 students, U of G offers a living environment to suit every taste. The 13 residences include coed and traditional housing; modern facilities and comfortable older residences; suites for six to 12 people; and rooms for one, two or three students. Demand is high for the 340 family housing units. All first-year and international students are guaranteed housing if they apply by the June 1 deadline. Off-campus students may purchase a campus meal plan. The campus has 13 eateries including vegetarian and ethnic restaurants, a sports lounge and a coffee house.

With a population of 95,000, the city of Guelph offers small-community living with many conveniences. Toronto, one of the world's top financial and cultural cities, is only a one-hour drive away. Guelph offers many cultural events such as folk, classical and jazz music festivals; recreational activities include hiking and excellent on- and off-road cycling.

ATHLETICS & EXTRACURRICULAR ACTIVITIES

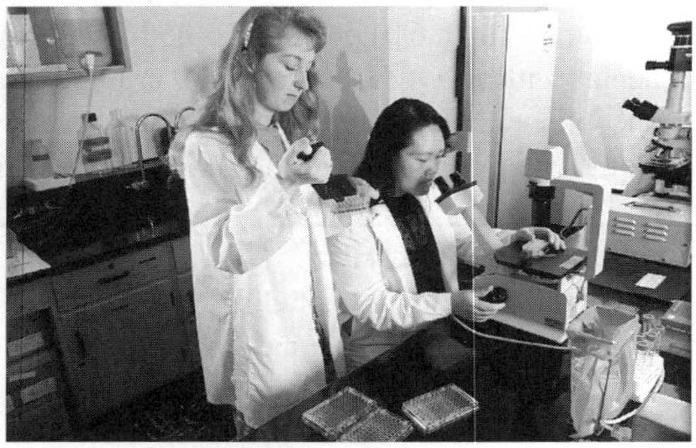

Most of U of G's athletic facilities were built or renovated in the last 10 years. Men's and women's varsity teams, the Gryphons, compete in 13 team and individual sports in the Ontario University Athletics (OUA) as well as the Canadian Inter-university Athletics Union (CIAU). In 1996-97, the men's hockey team won the national championship. The women's rugby team has won five straight provincial championships and currently holds the national title. The intramural program offers male, female and coed teams sports such as softball, soccer, football, ice hockey, basketball, volleyball and inner-tube water polo. Free-time activities such as swimming, gymnasium activities, and fitness and weight training are also available. About half of the over 100 student clubs and organizations involve academics or student government; the rest accommodate practically every imaginable interest. The Central Student Association can help set up a group not yet represented. Already existing clubs include performing arts, media, cultural, religious and political groups.

University Recognition

- Recognition for excellence for over 100 faculty including nine 3-M Teaching, one of Canada's top teaching honours
- Rated by Maclean's among the top two comprehensive universities in Canada in three categories: educational quality, producing leaders and best overall university; and rated the number one comprehensive university for the portion of students who graduate

STUDENT SUPPORT SERVICES

Students receive academic advice from program counsellors and departmental advisers. In addition, the Counselling & Student Resource Centre helps students with both learning and personal development issues. Counselling Services offers professional counselling, and the Campus Ministry represents all of the world's major religions. Student Health Services' staff of male and female doctors offers regular weekday and 24-hour emergency services. The Career Centre helps students with career choices and resume writing, and advertises part-time and summer jobs. The Centre for International Programs helps overseas students with transportation, accommodation and immigration, and offers many counselling services. The university also offers a LINK program, which pairs international students with other U of G students who act as guides to both the university and the community.

International Students

University Enrolment: 224

% of University Enrolment: 2%

Countries of Origin: U of G students come from many countries, including Australia, China, Japan, Peru, Spain, Taiwan, Russia, England and the US.

Université d'Ottawa
University of Ottawa

UNIVERSITY OF OTTAWA
OTTAWA, ONTARIO

University Mission

...to learn and grow in an exceptional environment distinguished by the quality of interaction and understanding between different cultures and disciplines

Student Voice:

Right from when I arrived at UO, I could feel the energy in this unique place. You get to know the campus and make friends in an incredible atmosphere....There's something for everyone.

Jason Bett
First-Year Student

CONTACT INFORMATION
Office of the Registrar
University of Ottawa
550 Cumberland, PO Box 450, Station A
Ottawa, Ontario
Canada K1N 6N5
PH 1-613-562-5700 (Cdn);
1-613-562-5847 (int'l)
FAX 1-613-562-5323 (Cdn);
1-613-562-5100 (int'l)
EMAIL admission@uottawa.ca (Cdn);
intl@uottawa.ca (int'l)
INTERNET http://www.uottawa.ca

Université d'Ottawa
University of Ottawa

UNIVERSITY OVERVIEW

Since its establishment in 1848, the University of Ottawa (UO) has remained committed to innovation in education and research. Today, approximately 23,000 students are registered in over 200 academic and professional programs at the undergraduate and graduate levels offered in both official languages—French and English.

The academic year runs from September to the end of April. Spring and summer sessions are offered from May through mid-August. The Second Language Institute offers semi-intensive and intensive ESL and FSL courses and the possibility of writing the CANtest instead of the TOEFL.

Academic Programs

UO offers 5,000 undergraduate courses in a wide variety of fields, including administration, arts, education, engineering, law, science, health sciences, social sciences and medicine.

Undergraduate students can choose from nearly 120 majors (Honours) and minors (Concentrations). Concentration programs run three years, with at least a third of the courses taken in one subject area or in closely related disciplines. Honours programs usually require four or five years to complete and at least half the courses are taken in the area of specialization. Only undergraduates with honours standing can pursue a graduate degree.

Cooperative Education Programs

The cooperative education program at UO is rated among the top three in Ontario and is the second largest in Canada. A co-op option is offered in 26 academic programs within the faculties of administration, arts, engineering, science and social sciences faculties. Co-op placements are usually four or eight months (one to two sessions); some programs such as engineering and computer science offer co-op placements that are 12 months long. Although co-op programs are optional, they are highly recommended. Entry into the program is very competitive and students are chosen on the basis of academic merit.

Special Programs

UO offers national and international exchange programs that can enrich a student's academic experience through study at another university in Canada, in another country or another language. UO has 140 international exchange agreements with countries around the world.

Canadian students graduating from a secondary school or a CGEP may apply for the House of Commons Page Program. The program allows bilingual students who have an excellent overall academic average to experience Canadian politics on Parliament Hill. Pages are responsible of collecting and distributing official documents and maintaining links between MPs and their offices on Parliament Hill.

Highlights

- Over 5,000 undergraduate courses offered in English or French
- Co-op opportunities in 26 academic programs
- International exchange agreements with 140 institutes around the world

University Statistics

Year Founded: 1848
Academic Options: undergraduate/graduate
Calendar Year: fall session (Sept-Dec); winter session (Jan-Apr)

DISCIPLINES/MAJORS OFFERED

Administration: Admin, Commerce, Acc, Entrepreneurial Mgmt, Finance, HR Mgmt, Int'l Mgmt, Mgmt IS, Mktg, Prod-Mgmt Sci, Public Policy & Public Mgmt

Arts: Arts (General), Arts Admin, Canadian Studies, Classical Studies, Communication, English, Env Studies, French, Geography, German, History, Italian, Latin & English Studies, Lettres françaises, Linguistics, Math, Medieval Studies, Second Language Teaching, Slavic Languages & Literature, Spanish, Theatre, Translation (English, French & Spanish), Visual Arts, Women's Studies

Social Sciences: Criminology, Econ, Leisure Studies, Poli Sci, Psych (Arts, Science), Sociology

Engineering: Biotech, Chem (Env Eng & Eng Mgmt), Civil (Structural & Geotechnical Eng), Comp, Comp Sci, Comp Tech (with Civil, Elect, or Mech), Info & Mgmt Systems, Mechanical, Software

Science: Biochem, Biochem (Nutrition), Bio, Biotech, Chemistry, Computational Physics, Environmental Science, Geology, Geology (Physics), Math, Math & Stats, Math Sci, Physics, Physics (Mathematics), Sci (General), Sci/Education (French only)

Health Sciences: Human Kinetics, Nursing, Occupational Therapy (French only), Physiotherapy (French only)

Medicine: Medical Sciences, Physiology

Law: Droit Civil, Common Law, National Program (combined program)

ADMISSIONS CRITERIA & PROCEDURES

Both Canadian and international applicants must complete an application for admission form and submit it to the Ontario Universities' Application Centre or directly to UO. All required documentation must be submitted to the Office of the Registrar by April 30 to be considered for fall admission and November 1 to be considered for winter admission. All applicants must submit official copies of their academic records and any examination results, certificates or diplomas earned; international students are required to submit certified translations in English or French of all documentation, where applicable.

Applicants whose first language is not English or French are required to provide evidence of English or French language proficiency. The minimum language requirement varies depending upon the program of studies; however, the minimum requirement can usually be met by submitting a TOEFL score of 550-580 (paper-based) or 213-237 (computer-based); a MELAB score of 85 to 90; a minimum IELTS score of 7.0; a minimum CANtest score of 4.5; or a pass grade of C on the Cambridge Certificate of Proficiency in English.

Admissions at a Glance

Minimum GPA: B- (70%)

Minimum English Requirements:
TOEFL 550-580 (paper) or 213-237 (comp), MELAB 85-90, IELTS 7.0, CANtest 4.5, Cambridge CPE Pass

Application Fee: C$85 (Canadian), $95 (international)

Application Deadlines: April 30 (fall session); November 1 (winter session)

ACADEMIC FACILITIES

UO's library network includes the three main libraries: the Morisset Library (arts, social sciences, science and engineering), the Law Library and the Health Sciences Library. UO also has a number of specialized libraries, a music library and a map library. Library collections total nearly 1.5 million books, more than 10,000 periodicals and include numerous microform items, government publications and documents. The ORBIS electronic catalogue allows students to access the library's resource information and indices from their personal computers, and allows students to reference files and borrow books from the National Archives, the Library of Parliament and Ottawa's public libraries.

UO students have access to more than 15 computer laboratories on campus and over 1,500 work stations linked to the university's main network. Labs are equipped with IBM and Macintosh PCs and UNIX workstations, running current software applications. Students are provided with a computer account upon registration that allows them access to UO's networks and databases, email, and the Internet. Computer workshops are also offered to students who wish to update their skills in a variety of different applications.

Student & Faculty Profile

Total Enrolment: 22,695

Undergraduate Enrolment: 19,345

# of Faculty: 1,432

Student/Faculty Ratio: 20:1

Male/Female Students: 42%/58%

First-Year Class Sizes: 25 (average)

Undergraduate Acceptance Rate: 45-55%

Undergraduate Enrolment by Discipline:

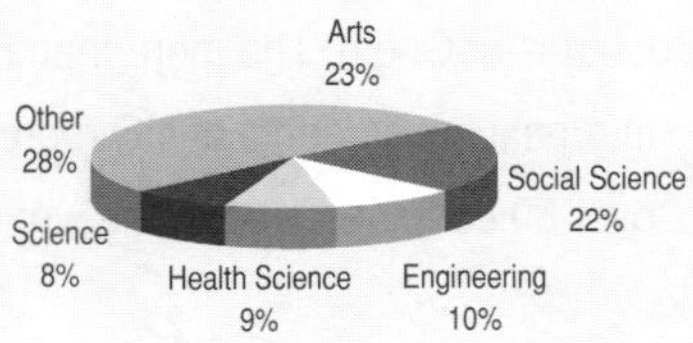

SCHOLARSHIPS & FINANCIAL ASSISTANCE

The Financial Aid & Awards Service (FAAS) offers support to qualified Canadian applicants through scholarships in recognition of academic merit. The FAAS also offers loans or bursaries to domestic students in association with all the provinces and the federal government.

The FAAS offers several types of entrance scholarships including the Rector's Scholarship, Admission Scholarships, Merit Scholarships and Professional Training Scholarships. The yearly value of scholarships ranges from C$500 to $4,000 and are to be used towards tuition, fees, books and course materials or living expenses. Scholarship candidates should have outstanding academic and extracurricular records and be Canadian citizens or permanent residents.

Expenses at a Glance

Tuition (undergraduate, full-time):
In-Province: C$3,653-5,003/year
Out-of-Province: C$3,653-5,003year
International: C$8,005-8,778/year

Fees, Books, Materials: C$620-1,475/year

Accommodation:
Private: C$450-600/month
Residence: C$3,549-4,130/year
Homestay: n/a

Health Insurance: C$570/year

UNIVERSITY OF OTTAWA, OTTAWA, ONTARIO

CAMPUS & LOCATION

The University of Ottawa was founded in 1848 as the College of Bytown. It is located in the heart of Ottawa, Canada's capital, and its one kilometre by one half a kilometre campus borders the picturesque Rideau Canal. Ottawa is known for its clean air, safe parks, hot summers, snowy winters and its large variety of cultural activities. Ottawa is also only a few hour's drive from the major centres of Montreal and Toronto. UO is the largest bilingual university in the country. Its bilingual character in a multicultural society is one of the university's key strengths. This strength can be seen in the university's unique program options and interesting combinations of teaching and research programs in both official languages.

City Population:	1,000,000
Cost of Living:	medium
Climate Range:	-20° to 33°C
Campus Setting:	urban
# of Students in Residence:	2,400

Approximately 2,400 UO students live on campus. Most first-year students are housed in shared rooms in traditional residences (LeBlanc, Marchand, Thompson or Stanton). Second-year students have a wider variety of residential housing choices, including single room, traditional residence-style, family and couples housing.

ATHLETICS & EXTRACURRICULAR ACTIVITIES

Sports and physical activities are open to all students; students become members of the Sports Service when they register and have access to all recreation facilities at no extra charge. UO's sports complex houses three gymnasia, a 50-metre pool with diving boards and a 10-metre diving tower, an aerobics and dance studio, a fitness centre, a martial arts room, as well as racquetball and squash courts.

The university has 27 sports teams competing at the interuniversity level, as well as a wide variety of men's, women's and coed intramural sports including hockey, soccer, volleyball, basketball and broomball. Students who wish to participate in less competitive sports can join instructional or recreational activities such as ballet, fencing, karate, women's self defense and skating. Sports Service also offers aerobic dancing, aqua-fitness, step aerobics, weight training, swimming, synchronized swimming, kayaking and scuba diving programs.

University Recognition

- UO is Canada's oldest and largest bilingual university
- UO Heart Institute is a leader in transplant surgery
- UO professors have received major awards, including the Royal Society of Canada Medal, the Hoffman-LaRoche Award of the Canadian Society of Chemistry for Medicinal Chemistry (1997), the Distinguished Psychologist Award of the American Psychology Association (1997), and the Hans Schneider Prize from the International Linear Algebra Society (1997)

STUDENT SUPPORT SERVICES

InfoService is an information centre that provides details on admission procedures and tuition fees, assigns identification cards, parking permits, and can provide copies of transcripts, timetables and diplomas, as well as receipts for services rendered.

UO provides a range of intensive English or French courses through the Second Language Institute. The Career & Employment Centre (CEC) provides brochures and calendars from universities all around the world, employer and association directories and information on job opportunities to students of the university. The centre also gives advice on resume and interview preparation and organizes a career fair each year. The CEC also offers a variety of workshops designed to help students improve their study skills, including workshops on time management, note taking, essay writing and examination preparation.

International Students

University Enrolment: 800

% of University Enrolment: 3%

Countries of Origin: The more than 800 international students at UO represent over 80 countries around the world.

UNIVERSITY OF TORONTO
TORONTO, ONTARIO

University Mission

...to be an internationally significant research university, with undergraduate, graduate and professional programs of excellent quality

Student Voice:
As a research university of international stature, the University of Toronto offers you the opportunity to exceed your expectations.

Robert Chang
Computer Engineering
Class of 2001

CONTACT INFORMATION
University of Toronto
315 Bloor Street West
Toronto, Ontario
Canada M5S 1A3
PH 1-416-978-2190
FAX 1-416-978-7022
EMAIL ask@adm.utoronto.ca
INTERNET http://www.utoronto.ca

UNIVERSITY OVERVIEW

As the largest university in Canada, the University of Toronto (U of T) offers the widest range of programs of any Canadian university. U of T's 14 faculties deliver 300 bachelor's, 148 master's and 95 doctoral degree programs. U of T has been ranked as the top research university in the nation by Maclean's magazine five years in a row.

Flexibility and Focus

U of T supports nine arts and science colleges on three campuses, offering diverse lifestyle options. Whether students decide to study in the hallowed halls of Trinity College or in the modern environment of New College, they benefit from the close interaction fostered by the small college concept, while enjoying the amenities of a large university.

U of T is renowned for academic innovation. Students can choose up to three majors and are encouraged to personalize their studies to meet their career goals. The university prides itself on its flexibility, offering many multidisciplinary programs such as Cognitive Science, Neuroscience & Management.

Practical Experience

Many programs at U of T offer practica, fieldwork, internship and co-op programs that allow students to practise the skills learned in the classroom and to make important career contacts. Co-op programs are available in five areas: arts management, computer science, environmental science, international development studies and management/management & economics. Internships offered through the Professional Experience Year program are also available for arts and science, and engineering students

The Research Opportunities Program provides students with the opportunity to work with professors in the development of their research. Students work in some of the finest laboratories in the country in areas such as the humanities, science and social science. The Professional Experience Year is an internship program which places students in study-related positions in the public and private sectors.

Global Perspective

U of T offers more than 40 language programs. With an international student body representing more than 100 countries, U of T supports a global learning environment. There are numerous programs with an international perspective in a variety of disciplines, from ethics and business to culture studies and arts. U of T's Study Elsewhere Program enables students to spend a semester or a year in a university abroad, in countries including Australia, Austria, England, Japan, Mexico, Scotland, Sweden, the US and Wales.

Highlights

- The largest university in Canada, situated in the nation's biggest city
- More than 300 undergraduate programs of study
- Co-op, internship, practicum and research opportunities available
- U of T houses the fifth largest library in North America

University Statistics

Year Founded: 1827
Academic Options: undergraduate/graduate
Calendar Year: fall semester (Sep-Dec); winter semester (Jan-Apr); summer sessions (May-Aug)

DISCIPLINES/MAJORS OFFERED

U of T offers more than 300 programs of study, including programs in the following disciplines:

Architecture, Landscape & Design
Applied Science & Engineering
Biomedical Communications
Dentistry
Economics, Commerce & Management
Education
Forestry
Graduate Studies
Humanities & Social Science
Information Studies
Law
Life Sciences (including psychology)
Mathematical, Physical & Computer Science
Medicine
Music
Nursing
Occupational Therapy
Pharmacy
Physical Education and Health
Physical Therapy
Radiation Sciences
Social Work
Theology

ADMISSIONS CRITERIA & PROCEDURES

Admission to U of T is competitive. Applicants from outside of Ontario may obtain applications from the University of Toronto Admissions & Awards Office or from the Ontario Universities' Application Centre (OUAC). Electronic applications for international applicants only are available through the OUAC via the Internet at http://www.ouac.on.ca. Only those students who have obtained a very high level of academic achievement are admitted. Overseas students must also submit a completed application form by the appropriate program deadline (listed to the right); supporting documentation, such as TOEFL scores and academic records, must be received by June 1.

The admission requirements vary from program to program. Students should contact the Admissions & Awards office for further details. Generally, academic requirements are six Ontario Academic Courses (OAC), or equivalent high school matriculation. The 1998 entering class had a senior average of 85 per cent. Other admission requirements may include entrance examinations, portfolios and auditions. There is a C$95 OUAC application fee; a C$60 U of T application fee must also be included.

For students whose first language is not English, the university's minimum English requirement is a MELAB score of 90, an IELTS score of 6.5 or a TOEFL score of 600, with a minimum score of 5.0 on the TWE. All application documents not in English must be officially translated.

Admissions at a Glance

Minimum GPA: no set minimum

Minimum English Requirements: TOEFL 600 with TWE 5.0, IELTS 6.5, MELAB 90

Application Fee: C$95 (OUAC, Cdn and int'l), $60 (U of T, Cdn and int'l)

Application Deadlines: March 1: Cdn all programs; int'l for Applied Science, Engineering, Arts & Science, Music, Physical Education and Health. February 1 int'l for Nursing, Occupational Therapy, Physical Therapy and Radiation Sciences

ACADEMIC FACILITIES

U of T has world-class research and academic facilities that include scientific laboratories in areas as diverse as microbiology and thermodynamics, with the latest experimental equipment. U of T is considered Canada's premier research university.

There are a variety of learning environments available at U of T, ranging from small seminar rooms to large multimedia lecture halls.

There are over 50 libraries at U of T that boast a collection of over 10 million items including books, microfilms, periodicals, audiovisual materials and government documents. There are numerous computing facilities available on campus, including department-specific and university-wide laboratories. Every student has Internet access and a free email account. Other notable academic services include Math Aid Centres, Writing Centres and Study Skills Centres, all of which provide additional academic assistance.

Student & Faculty Profile

Total Enrolment: 54,000

Undergraduate Enrolment: 30,484

# of Faculty: 6,000

Student/Faculty Ratio: 9:1

Male/Female Students: 46%/54%

First-Year Class Sizes: 70

Undergraduate Acceptance Rate: 50%

Undergraduate Enrolment by Discipline:

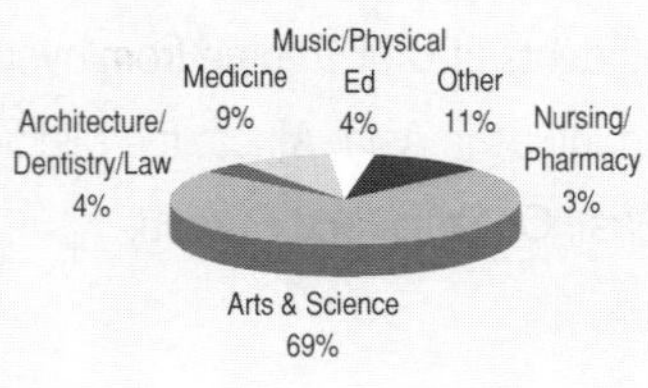

SCHOLARSHIPS & FINANCIAL ASSISTANCE

U of T has established a C$240 million endowment for student financial assistance. The university is committed t o the principle that no student admitted to a program will be unable to enrol due to lack of funding. There are three forms of financial assistance available to Canadian residents: loans, scholarships and grants. Both federal and provincial loans are awarded to students on the basis of need. Students should contact Admissions & Awards for further details.

Most scholarships are awarded to students who have displayed a high level of academic achievement; Canadian and international students are automatically considered for most scholarships and do not need to apply.

Expenses at a Glance

Tuition (undergraduate, full-time):
- In-Province: C$3,516-5,808/year
- Out-of-Province: C$3,516-5,808/year
- International: C$8,320-11,345/year

Fees, Books, Materials: C$500-1,000/year

Accommodation:
- Private: C$350-1,000/month
- Residence: C$680-800/month
- Homestay: n/a

Health Insurance: C$579/year

CAMPUS & LOCATION

City Population:	4,338,400
Cost of Living:	high
Climate Range:	-11° to 27°C
Campus Setting:	urban
# of Students in Residence:	4,500

The three campuses of the University of Toronto are the St. George Campus, located in the heart of the city; the U of T at Missausauga, 33 kilometres west of downtown; and the U of T at Scarborough, 33 kilometres east of the city core. Students on each campus enjoy a distinctive learning environment and sense of community within the larger university context.

Residential, family and private housing are available on or near each campus. All new, first-year undergraduate students who are offered admission to their program of studies by July 1 and who have applied for residence are accommodated. Most residences are associated with one of the nine U of T colleges: benefits include personal and academic counselling and extracurricular activities.

Toronto's clean, efficient transportation system, which includes an extensive subway system, makes all parts of this vibrant, multicultural city accessible to U of T students. Canada's business centre, Toronto is also rich in culture and sport, with live theatre, ballet, opera, a science centre, a zoo and professional baseball, hockey, basketball and football teams. Its international airport is located about a 45-minute drive from the St. George campus. The peaceful parklands of the Toronto Islands offer a nearby escape from the bustle of urban life.

ATHLETICS & EXTRACURRICULAR ACTIVITIES

There are numerous opportunities for students to participate in athletic programs at U of T. With more than 43 men's and women's intercollegiate teams and an extensive intramural system on each campus, U of T strives to provide students with a rich and varied life. Intramural sports include such diverse interests as ball hockey, basketball, rowing, beach volleyball and table tennis. The recreation program also offers a wide variety of instructional courses in areas such as aerobics, various martial arts, tennis, scuba diving and swimming. Each campus has comprehensive athletic and recreational facilities including gymnasia, weight rooms, tennis and squash courts, outdoor playing fields, swimming pools, dance studios, jogging trails and fitness-therapy rooms.

There are 175 student organizations that meet on U of T campuses, including international groups such as the Chinese Students Association, International Students Association and the Indo-Caribbean Students Association. Students also benefit from student-run newspapers, a university radio station and numerous on-campus festivals.

University Recognition

- Ranked as top research university for the last five years in Maclean's magazine's annual survey
- Since 1980, U of T's staff, comprising 7% of the nation's professorate has won nearly 25% of the major research fellowships
- U of T has had more Rhodes Scholarship winners than any other Canadian university

STUDENT SUPPORT SERVICES

Students will find that U of T offers support services for nearly every imaginable aspect of academic and personal life. Counselling Services assists students with the adjustment to living on campus by offering personal counselling with peers or professionals. Each campus has a comprehensive Career Centre, providing job search assistance and workshops in areas such as interview skills and resume writing. Other services include a family care adviser & resource centre, a food & clothing bank, health & housing services, a student affairs office and women's centres.

The on-campus International Student Centre (ISC), at St. George, promotes and supports international education and intercultural communication. ISC offers assistance to international students in a variety of ways including an orientation program, an ESL program, a reception service, and advice and assistance concerning immigration, personal counselling and employment.

International Students

University Enrolment: 3,168

% of University Enrolment: 6%

Countries of Origin: International students at U of T come from over 100 countries in Asia, Africa, the Middle East, Oceania, and Europe.

UNIVERSITY OF WATERLOO
WATERLOO, ONTARIO

...to continue pushing the limits of knowledge through innovation and academic excellence, preparing a community of learners for a future as leaders

Student Voice:

The University of Waterloo's excellent reputation translates into so many benefits—innovative programs, a quality education, great facilities, fantastic professors and excellent job prospects after graduation. I know that when I graduate, my degree will be highly respected.

Cam Neil
Fourth-Year Student
Psychology

CONTACT INFORMATION
Office of the Registrar
University of Waterloo
200 University Avenue West
Waterloo, Ontario
Canada N2L 3G1
PH 1-519-888-4567 ext. 3614
FAX 1-519-746-8088
EMAIL
watquest@nh1adm.uwaterloo.ca
INTERNET http://www.uwaterloo.ca

UNIVERSITY OVERVIEW

The University of Waterloo (UW), founded in 1957, became a full degree-granting institution in 1959. Since then, it has built a reputation as one of Canada's foremost universities, attracting professors committed to excellence in teaching and research. Today, UW receives more than C$50 million in research funding from public and private sources.

UW has been ranked number one by Maclean's national reputational survey of Canadian universities for the past seven years.

Academic Programs

The list of programs offered at UW is extensive, with over 100 areas of study leading to undergraduate degrees through six faculties and four affiliated and federated institutions. In addition, the university offers 49 master's and 28 doctoral degrees.

Undergraduate students may earn a Bachelor of Applied Science, Architecture, Arts, Environmental Studies, Independent Studies, Mathematics or Science. Bachelor of Social Work and Doctor of Optometry degrees are also available. Through the Graduate School, students can earn a Master of Accounting, Arts, Applied Environmental Studies, Applied Science, Environmental Studies, Fine Arts, Mathematics, Science or Taxation, or a Doctor of Philosophy.

UW offers one of the most extensive distance education programs in Canada. Students can earn Bachelor of Arts, Environmental Studies or Science degrees without attending classes on campus.

On campus, UW offers late afternoon and evening credit courses for part-time students. There are also many noncredit personal and professional development courses scheduled in the evening, on weekends or as full-day workshops.

Co-op Program

UW pioneered cooperative education in Canada by implementing a cooperative engineering program in 1957. Today, UW's co-op program continues as the world's largest and most acclaimed.

Students in the co-op program alternate between periods of study and paid work experience. Accounting, applied studies, architecture, biotechnology/economics and engineering programs include a mandatory co-op component. The co-op fee per school term is C$411.

To be considered for admission into the co-op program, students must be Canadian citizens or hold permanent residence status in Canada.

Highlights

- UW has the highest co-op enrolment in the world
- Over 100 areas of study
- One of the most extensive distance education programs in Canada

University Statistics

Year Founded: 1957
Academic Options: undergraduate/graduate
Calendar Year: fall term (Sept-Dec); winter term (Jan-Apr); spring term (May-Aug)

DISCIPLINES/MAJORS OFFERED

Faculty of Applied Health Sciences: Health; Kinesiology; Pre-Health Professions, Recreation & Leisure

Faculty of Arts: Acc; Anthropology; Canadian; Classical; Cultural Mgmt; Drama; Econ; English; Fine Arts; French & French Teaching; Geography; German; History; Hons Applied; Hons Arts; Hons Arts & Business; Int'l Trade; Medieval; Music; Philosophy; Poli Sci; Psych; Religious; Rhetoric & Professional Writing; Russian & Slavic; Social Development; Sociology; Spanish; Speech Comm; Women's

Faculty of Engineering: Chem; Civil; Comp; Electrical; Env (Chem, Civil); Geological; Mech; Systems Design

Faculty of Environmental Studies: Architecture; Env & Resource; Geography; Planning

Faculty of Mathematics: Acc; Actuarial Sci; Applied Math; Bus Admin; Combinatorics & Optimization; Comp Sci; Math; Operations Research; Pure Math; Stats; Teaching

Faculty of Science: Biochem; Biology; Biotech/Chartered Acc; Biotech/Econ; Chem Physics; Chem; Earth Sci; Env Chem; Env Prog; Geochem; Geology; Optometry; Physics; Pre-Optometry/Pre-Health; Psych; Sci & Bus; Sci Teaching

Independent Studies

Interdisciplinary Programs: Career Dev't Practitioner; Cognitive Sci; Env Econ; Fine & Performing Arts; Gerontology; HR Mgmt; Int'l Studies; Legal & Criminology; Mgmt; Middle East; Peace & Conflict Studies; Print Journalism; Russian & East European; Society, Tech & Values; Personality & Religion; Sexuality, Marriage & the Family

Social Work

ADMISSIONS CRITERIA & PROCEDURES

All undergraduate applications to UW are processed by the Ontario Universities' Application Centre (OUAC). Ontario high school students must complete and submit an OUAC 101 form; applicants not registered in an Ontario high school must submit an OUAC 105D form for Canadian students or a 105F form for international students available from either UW's admissions office or the OUAC in Guelph. All applicants should be aware that they must meet the prerequisites set by each program.

Ontario secondary school applicants must submit proof of an Ontario Secondary School Diploma (OSSD), indicating that they have completed a minimum of six Ontario Academic Courses (OACs), with an overall minimum average of 70 per cent, including required OACs.

International applicants must provide all academic transcripts for each year of studies undertaken at a secondary or postsecondary level institution, showing the grades received and the courses taken. Certificates equivalent to an OSSD include an International Baccalaureate, a General Certificate of Education from Britain and the Hong Kong Certificate of Education. Notarized English translations must accompany all documents, where applicable. Potential students whose first language is not English must provide one of the following minimum test scores: TOEFL 600 (paper-based) or 250 (computer-based), with TSE 50 and TWE 5.0; or IELTS 7.5; or MELAB 90. The Faculties of Applied Health Sciences, Mathematics and Science will consider, on an individual basis, talented applicants with lower test scores.

Applicants who can offer clear evidence of their ability to undertake and manage university studies, and who have been away from formal education for at least two years may be considered for mature student admission. Applicants interested in part-time study should contact admissions services; those interested in distance education should contact the Distance Education Office for more information.

Admissions at a Glance

Minimum GPA: 70%

Minimum English Requirements:
- TOEFL 600 (paper-based) or 250 (computer-based), with TSE 50 and TWE 5.0; IELTS 7.5; or MELAB 90

Application Fee: C$80 (Cdn), $90 (int'l)

Application Deadlines:
- Apr 30 (fall term); Nov 1 (winter term); Feb 29 (spring term)

ACADEMIC FACILITIES

The University Library system comprises the Dana Porter Library, which houses over 2.5 million items in support of social sciences, humanities, fine arts and environmental studies; the Davis Centre Library, which has a collection of 486,000 items to support engineering, mathematics and science; the University Map & Design Library; and the Optometry Learning Resource Centre. UW's computing services are extensive. Each faculty has its own computer resource centre equipped with specialized software. A central facility on campus maintains the campus network, providing all students with access to email and the Internet. Four federated and affiliated institutions, all located on campus, offer additional specialized resources to UW students.

Student & Faculty Profile

Total Enrolment: 18,125

Undergraduate Enrolment: 16,300

# of Faculty: 1,240

Student/Faculty Ratio: 20:1

Male/Female Students: 51%/49%

First-Year Class Sizes: 90 (average)

Undergraduate Acceptance Rate: not available

Undergraduate Enrolment by Discipline:

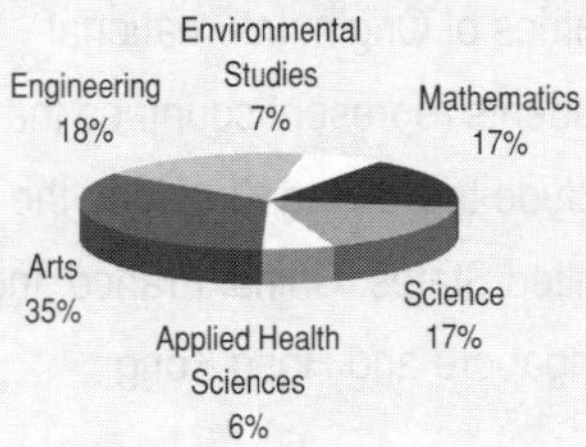

SCHOLARSHIPS & FINANCIAL ASSISTANCE

First-year students with outstanding grades may be eligible for university entrance scholarships offered by UW. Financial assistance for Ontario students is available through the Ontario government. Canadian students who are applying from provinces other than Ontario should approach the provincial assistance authority in their home province concerning the possibility of assistance from that source. For more information, students should contact the Student Awards Office.

Expenses at a Glance

Tuition (undergraduate, full-time):
- In-Province: C$3,454-4,858/year*
- Out-of-Province: C$3,454-4,858/year*
- International: C$12,174-20,848/year*

Fees, Books, Materials: C$1,200-1,900/year*

Accommodation:
- Private: C$500-700/month*
- Residence: C$5,000-5,500/year*
- Homestay: n/a

Health Insurance: C$209/term* (int'l only)

CAMPUS & LOCATION

City Population:	275,000
Cost of Living:	medium
Climate Range:	-6° to 26°C
Campus Setting:	urban
# of Students in Residence:	3,358

Located in the city of Waterloo, the University of Waterloo spans 404 hectares and is housed in 45 teaching and research buildings. First-year students at UW are given priority for on-campus accommodation. Two student villages, four university college residences and a townhouse residence house 3,358 students. Many residence rooms have access to the campus network and the Internet. Students wishing to live off campus or who are on co-op work terms may make use of the services provided by the Off Campus Housing Office, which provides lists of affordable accommodation within Waterloo and across the province. Students can explore the campus online through the Virtual Tour on the UW website.

Waterloo is situated in Canada's technology trade triangle and is one of the key centres in the area. The city is only an hour's drive from Toronto's International Airport. As a mid-sized, active city, Waterloo has more than 400 hectares of parkland and trails, which may be used for a variety of recreational activities such as hiking and biking.

ATHLETICS & EXTRACURRICULAR ACTIVITIES

UW offers extensive athletic programs and facilities to its students, staff and faculty. The Physical Activities Complex is available to everyone on campus and includes multipurpose gymnasia, fully equipped weight & training rooms, squash courts and a pool. A nine-hole practice golf course, numerous outdoor fields, and the Columbia Icefield recreational complex also provide recreational opportunities to the UW community.

Students can participate in organized sports, including 32 varsity athletic teams for both men and women, and intramural leagues. Various instructional classes, certification courses and campus recreational clubs are offered through the Campus Recreation program, the largest such program in Canada. Students interested in journalism and photography can volunteer at Imprint, the student-run campus newspaper. The Student Life Centre is the community meeting place of UW's student population. Open 24 hours a day, year-round, the centre provides an information booth, a games area, meeting spaces, eating places and retail stores. Over 40 student clubs and organizations are active at UW with focuses ranging from amateur radio to business administration.

STUDENT SUPPORT SERVICES

UW operates a full medical clinic, and counsellors are available to help students with academic and personal concerns. Career Services assists students with career planning and the Mature Student Services helps students who have been away from school adjust to campus life. University chaplains are also available to provide spiritual guidance. The Office for Persons with Disabilities helps make UW one of the most accessible campuses in the country.

The International Student Organization (ISO) arranges a fall orientation session for international students and operates several additional programs and events, both on campus and in the local community. The ISO's SHADOW program is an ongoing support program that pairs foreign students with UW students to provide peer guidance.

UW offers several English language support and upgrading programs including English conversation classes, a writing clinic and an intensive English training summer session at Renison College.

University Recognition

- 25% of UW faculty members are Fellows of the Royal Society of Canada, the country's most prestigious scholarly society
- Ranked "Best Overall" in Maclean's national reputational survey since 1992
- UW students win a higher percentage of national awards than students at any other comprehensive university in Canada

International Students

University Enrolment: 428

% of University Enrolment: 2%

Countries of Origin: International students represent countries that include the United Kingdom, the United States, China, France, India, Singapore and Hong Kong.

The University of Western Ontario
London, Ontario

University Mission

...to provide an environment of free and creative inquiry within which critical thinking, humane values, and practical skills are cultivated and sustained. By pursuing these objectives, the university endeavours to serve the interests of society

Contact Information

Admissions Services

The University of Western Ontario

Room 165

Stevenson-Lawson Building

London, Ontario

Canada N6A 5B8

PH 1-519-661-2100

FAX 1-519-661-3710

EMAIL reg-admissions@julian.uwo.ca

INTERNET http://www.uwo.ca

Student Voice:

Western takes care of its students.

Jocelyn Sylvester

UNIVERSITY OVERVIEW

Originally the Western University of London, The University of Western Ontario (Western) is one of the oldest universities in Canada. Western received its charter in 1878 and is now a long-established academic community. The university currently consists of 17 faculties and professional schools that deliver programs to over 26,000 students. More than 200 individual and combined three-year general and four-year honours degree are offered.

A Broad Knowledge Base

Students can choose from more than 60 programs in their first year of study. Students are not required to declare an intended area of concentration until their second year. Most students initially apply to a general faculty and take first-year courses from inside and outside that faculty. First-year students complete a wide cross-section of courses, acquiring a broad base of knowledge; students must take five introductory courses covering at least four different subjects from two or more of the Faculties of Arts, Social Science and Science.

Degree Choices

Western offers the following degree choices: a three-year Bachelor of Arts (BA) or Bachelor of Science (BSc) with one area of concentration; a four-year honours BA or BSc; or a combined honours program that provides students with the opportunity to pursue concentrated work in two subjects. Western also offers selected graduate degrees.

Individualized & Study-Abroad Programs

For students with averages of 90 per cent or above, Western offers the Scholar's Electives Program. The Scholar's Electives Program is designed for highly committed and academically excellent students who want to create their own course of study throughout their degree. Theme areas allow students to combine subjects and create their own specialized degree options.

Western sponsors students who wish to study at an international study centre at Herstmonceux Castle in England.

Affiliated Colleges

Western is affiliated with three colleges. Students enrolled at the colleges obtain a degree from Western and can take some courses from the main campus. Brescia College is a Catholic liberal arts university college for women; Huron College offers small classes and an intimate environment in the arts and social sciences; and King's College is a Catholic coed liberal arts college which also offers small classes.

Highlights

- Western's Scholar's Electives Programs allows selected students to personalize their curriculum
- Study abroad program in England
- Main campus and three affiliated colleges

University Statistics

Year Founded: 1878
Academic Options: undergraduate/graduate
Calendar Year: fall term (Sept-Dec); winter term (Jan-Apr); summer term (May-Aug)

DISCIPLINES/MAJORS OFFERED

Faculty of Arts: Classical Studies, Comparative Literature & Civilization, English, Film, French, German, Greek, Latin, Modern Eastern Civilizations, Philosophy, Polish, Religious Studies, Russian, Spanish, Visual Arts, Women's Studies

Faculty of Science: Actuarial Science, Applied Mathematics, Astronomy, Biochemistry, Biology, Biophysics, Cell Biology, Chemistry, Computer Science, Earth Sciences, Genetics, Geology, Geophysics, Mathematics, Pharmacology & Toxicology, Physics, Physiology, Plant Sciences, Zoology

Faculty of Social Science: Administrative Studies, Anthropology, Economics, Geography, History, Political Science, Psychology, Sociology, Women's Studies

Additional Programs: Business, Clothing, Textiles & Design, Engineering Science, Foods & Nutrition, Health Sciences, Human Ecology, Kinesiology, Media, Information & Technoculture, Music, Nursing, Occupational Therapy (MSc), Physical Therapy, Social Work

ADMISSIONS CRITERIA & PROCEDURES

Applications can be obtained by contacting the Ontario Universities' Application Centre (OUAC) in Guelph, Ontario. The deadline for Canadian citizens or permanent residents residing in Canada or abroad is June 1; international applications must be submitted by May 15. Along with the required transcripts and materials, applicants may submit a supplementary application form outlining extracurricular involvement in the school or community. Applicants must enclose an application fee of C$80 for Ontario students, $85 for Canadian applicants outside of Ontario; and $90 for international applicants.

Non-native English speakers who have not been studying in an English institution for the past three years, must submit proof of English proficiency. Applicants must submit TOEFL, MELAB or IELTS test scores for consideration.

Admission to residence is guaranteed for all students entering university based on secondary school qualifications.

Admissions at a Glance

Minimum GPA: B or 75% average

Minimum English Requirements: evaluated on a case-by-case basis

Application Fee: C$80 (Ontario); $85 (Canadian); $90 (international)

Application Deadlines: June 1 (Canadian); May 15 (international)

ACADEMIC FACILITIES

The Western Library is the sixth largest academic library system in Canada. The six libraries provide resources in both print and electronic format, and hold approximately 2.2 million books and 3.3 million items in audio, visual or microform format. The library has approximately 15,000 journal, magazine and newspaper subscriptions.

Material not available at the Western libraries can be ordered from other libraries through Interlibrary Loans Service.

SCHOLARSHIPS & FINANCIAL ASSISTANCE

Western offers more than C$6 million in financial aid, in addition to the amount available to prospective students through the Ontario Student Assistance Program (OSAP) or other similar provincial programs. Western also offers one of the most extensive scholarship programs in Ontario. Students must be Canadian citizens or permanent residents to be eligible for an admission scholarship or award, and must be applying to the Western main campus for first-year studies. Eligibility is based on mid-year average as calculated for admission purposes. International students are eligible for some upper-year scholarships.

Applications are submitted in October for awards and bursaries valued between C$250 and $4,000. Students are advised to get their applications in early as the deadline for most awards and bursaries is October 31.

Funding programs are available in home provinces of those applying from provinces other than Ontario; applicants should also contact Western for information.

Student & Faculty Profile

Total Enrolment: 26,538

Undergraduate Enrolment: 23,572

# of Faculty: 1,500

Student/Faculty Ratio: 18:1

Male/Female Students: 50%/50%

First-Year Class Sizes: less than 50

Undergraduate Acceptance Rate: not available

Undergraduate Enrolment by Discipline:

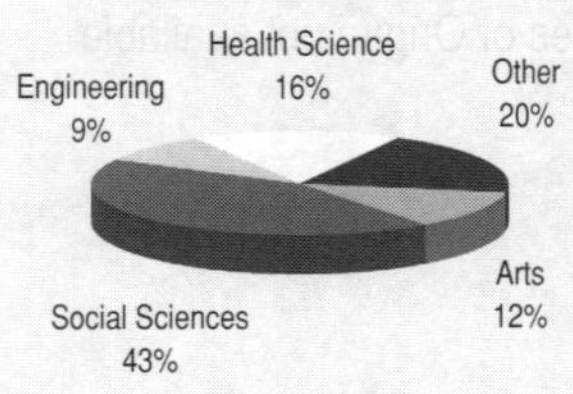

Expenses at a Glance

Tuition (undergraduate, full-time):

In-Province: C$4,200/year

Out-of-Province: C$4,200/year

International: C$10,000/year (approx)

Fees, Books, Materials: C$800/year

Accommodation:

Private: C$2,560/eight months

Residence: C$5,191/year

Homestay: n/a

Health Insurance: C$570/year (international)

CAMPUS & LOCATION

City Population:	412,600
Cost of Living:	medium
Climate Range:	-11° to 26°C
Campus Setting:	urban
# of Students in Residence:	3,440

As one of Canada's oldest and largest universities, The University of Western Ontario is renowned for its teaching and research excellence, and for its professional schools of business, dentistry, engineering, law and medicine. Situated in picturesque southwestern Ontario between Windsor and Toronto, Western is ideally located to provide students with a comfortable, relaxed learning environment. Western's main campus is centrally located near downtown London, giving students convenient access to the amenities of the city; all undergraduate students can make use of the city's public transportation system with their student bus passes, paid for through their student fees.

With the Thames River running through it, and its many parks and trails, London supports many outdoor activities. London also has a rich cultural life, while maintaining its small town appeal. Students seeking an urban environment will find that London, with a population of over 400,000, has much to offer. The metropolitan advantages of Toronto, Ontario, and Detroit, Michigan, are only two hours away by car.

ATHLETICS & EXTRACURRICULAR ACTIVITIES

Western prides itself on its varsity teams, the Mustangs. Last year, 21 of the 35 teams finished in the top three spots in the province; seven teams won gold medals. All full-time students are invited to try out for the varsity teams, which include badminton, basketball, cross-country, curling, fencing, field hockey, figure skating, football, golf, hockey, indoor hockey, rowing, rugby, nordic skiing, soccer, squash, swimming, synchronized swimming, tennis, track & field, volleyball, waterpolo and wrestling.

Thousands of participants and hundreds of teams at Western make up the largest university intramural program in Canada. Many students also participate in Western's sports clubs. Intramural sports include: aerobics, Aikido, aquatic masters, badminton, ball hockey, basketball, beach volleyball, broomball, cross-country skiing, curling, cycling, downhill skiing, equestrian, fencing, hap ki do, hockey, inner-tube waterpolo, judo, karate, kayaking, rollerblading, sailing, scuba, slo-pitch, soccer, squash, swimming, table tennis, tae kwon do, tennis, touch football, triathlon, ultimate frisbee and volleyball.

University Recognition

- Member of the Association of Universities and Colleges of Canada (AUCC)
- Western has produced two Rhodes Scholars in the last two year
- Over 20 faculty members were recognized with awards for excellence in teaching and research in 1997

STUDENT SUPPORT SERVICES

The main headquarters for leisure and extracurricular learning pursuits at Western is the University Community Centre. Approximately 20,000 students use its facilities and services every day.

The Student Development Centre provides Western students with many support services and workshops. Services are available in a wide variety of areas, including career counselling and First Nations Services.

International students are offered the services of the International Student Office, which can provide individual or group counselling, reception and orientation, assistance with immigration, help with housing and referral or tutorial services in English as a second language.

International Students

University Enrolment: not available

% of University Enrolment: not available

Countries of Origin: not available

University of Windsor
Windsor, Ontario

University Mission

...to provide an atmosphere fostering creativity, discovery, application, critical thinking, service, and communication in a collegial environment, in which people can work together in ways conducive to personal growth and embodying the principles of equity, accessibility, mutual respect and understanding

Student Voice:
Windsor's program gave me both a solid academic foundation and lots of practical work experience through the co-op education program.

Priya Sreedharan, Engineering
1997 winner of the Award for Excellence in Research & Technology

CONTACT INFORMATION
Office of the Registrar
University of Windsor
Windsor, Ontario
Canada N9B 3P4
PH 1-519-253-3000
FAX 1-519-971-3653
EMAIL registr@uwindsor.ca
INTERNET http://www.uwindsor.ca

UNIVERSITY OVERVIEW

The University of Windsor (UW) was established in 1963 from an affiliation between Assumption College and Essex College, the first provincially-assisted public institution of higher education in Ontario.

UW currently has over 11,000 students in attendance, including 400 international students from 70 countries worldwide. UW offers some programs in a part-time format, providing students with flexible study options.

Academic Programs

UW offers a broad range of undergraduate, graduate and professional programs. The university delivers 100 undergraduate programs through four colleges: the College of Arts & Human Sciences; the College of Business Administration, Education & Law; the College of Engineering & Sciences; and the College of Graduate Studies & Research.

Highlights

- Co-op program offered in six undergraduate programs
- Part-time study options available
- Unique cross-border partnerships with US universities

University Statistics

Year Founded: 1963
Academic Options: undergraduate/graduate
Calendar Year: fall semester (Sept-Dec); spring semester (Jan-Apr)

Cooperative Education

UW offers co-op programs in undergraduate business, computer science, earth sciences, engineering, environmental biology, kinesiology and at the graduate level in the MBA program. Both Canadian and international students may apply to participate in UW's co-op program, earning valuable paid work experience, developing business contacts and integrating theoretical knowledge into practical settings.

Partnerships & Research

The university maintains many progressive partnerships with Canadian business and industry, including agreements with Chrysler Canada Ltd. With strong support from the automobile industry, UW is able to offer students many opportunities for co-op placements and internships.

Because of its unique southerly location just minutes from the US border, UW has also formed many cooperative agreements with American universities. These partnerships provide students with cross-border learning opportunities and access to diverse teaching expertise, research facilities and libraries.

UW is home to the London Life Great Lakes Environmental Research Centre, one of the foremost freshwater research centres in North America.

DISCIPLINES/MAJORS OFFERED

College of Arts & Human Sciences: Art History, Asian/Oriental Studies, Classical Civilization, Dramatic Art, English & Creative Writing, General Arts & Human Sciences, Intercultural Studies, Kinesiology, Multicultural Studies, Music (Academic or Performance Studies), Philosophy, Visual Arts

College of Business Administration, Education & Law: Business (Accounting, Administration, Commerce), Education, Law

College of Engineering & Sciences: Biology, Biochemistry, Chemistry, Computer Science, Environmental Science, General, Geography, Geology, Mathematics, Nursing, Physics, Statistics

College of Graduate Studies & Research: Master's and doctoral programs in most areas of study in each college.

ADMISSIONS CRITERIA & PROCEDURES

All candidates for full-time, undergraduate studies should apply through the Ontario Universities' Application Centre (OUAC); part-time applicants can apply through the Office of the Registrar at the university itself.

Canadian students are required to submit their secondary and postsecondary transcripts with their application form. The minimum admission requirement for all programs is an average of 60 per cent on six Ontario Academic Courses (OAC) or its equivalent. UW has additional individual admission requirements for each college and school; students should consult the UW calendar for more information.

Students whose first language is not English are required to take either the MELAB, IELTS or TOEFL and submit the scores along with their application. International applicants should send the official documents of their secondary school education indicating courses taken and grades achieved; certified translations of all documents should be included, if necessary. International students must complete the equivalent to Ontario grade 12 secondary course requirements.

Admissions at a Glance

Minimum GPA: 2.75 (B-)

Minimum English Requirements:
- TOEFL 550 (paper-based), 213 (computer-based)

Application Fee: C$95 (Canadian and international)

Application Deadlines: Canadian: July 1 (fall semester), December 1 (spring semester); international: March 1 (all semesters)

ACADEMIC FACILITIES

UW's Computer Centre provides a complete range of facilities and services for students through its Computing Services. Many of the computer labs on campus are conveniently open for student use at least 20 hours per day. Computer labs are equipped with the UNIX server that links all the terminals on the UW campus. Student have access to the Internet and receive email accounts; both IBM and Macintosh computers are available.

The UW library system includes the Leddy Library and the Paul Martin Law Library. Together, these libraries house a collection of 2.2 million volumes, 776,000 microform items, 350,000 government documents and 8,000 current periodical titles. The Leddy Library, the main branch, supports over 1,200 users in both open and closed carrel seating facilities.

The Academic Writing Centre offers support for UW students in need of assistance in writing university papers and essays. The centre also offers writing workshops, individual tutorials and diagnostic assessments.

Student & Faculty Profile

Total Enrolment: 12,500

Undergraduate Enrolment: 11,900

# of Faculty: 450

Student/Faculty Ratio: 25:1

Male/Female Students: 42%/58%

First-Year Class Sizes: 30 (average)

Undergraduate Acceptance Rate: not available

Undergraduate Enrolment by Discipline:

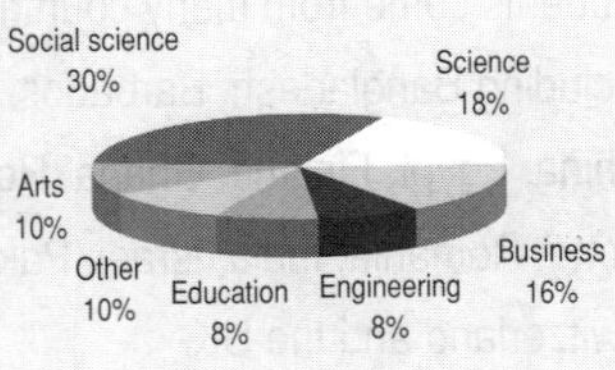

SCHOLARSHIPS & FINANCIAL ASSISTANCE

There are 36 university-endowed entrance scholarship awards, ranging from C$500 to C$12,000. Scholarship candidates are generally required to have at least a B (70%) standing in the subjects required for admission; students are advised that some scholarships have additional requirements and they should consult the university calendar for further details. Students may also apply for 11 other entrance scholarships that are not administered by UW. More than two-thirds of students entering first year receive some form of financial assistance.

Expenses at a Glance

Tuition (undergraduate, full-time):
- In-Province: C$1,725-1,874/sem
- Out-of-Province: C$1,725-1,874/sem
- International: C$4,572-5,947/sem

Fees, Books, Materials: C$700/year

Accommodation:
- Private: C$800-1,000/month (3-bedroom house)
- Residence: C$3,178-6,900/year
- Homestay: n/a

Health Insurance: included in tuition

CAMPUS & LOCATION

City Population:	290,000
Cost of Living:	medium
Climate Range:	-9° to 28°C
Campus Setting:	urban
# of Students in Residence:	1,400

The University of Windsor's 52-hectare campus is situated in the heart of Windsor, Ontario, at the foot of the Ambassador Bridge between Canada and the US. First-year students at UW are guaranteed housing in one of the seven on-campus residences; first-year students are generally housed in either the Clark, Electa, Huron or Tecumseh Halls. UW offers students many housing options, ranging from traditional residences to townhouse- and apartment-style quarters. All of the residence halls are close to the university and its students services. Affordable off-campus housing is also readily available to students in the university area.

Windsor, Ontario, is a city with a population of nearly 300,000. Windsor lies on the most southerly point of Canada, sharing the same latitude as Northern California. The city offers a wide variety of high-quality hotels, restaurants and retail areas. Windsor enjoys a temperate climate with warm summers and mild winters, which supports ample opportunities for outdoor activities such as swimming and boating in Canada's Great Lakes region or visiting the nearby Niagara Falls.

UW's proximity to the US offers convenient travel opportunities to American cities such as Detroit and Chicago.

ATHLETICS & EXTRACURRICULAR ACTIVITIES

UW supports many interuniversity athletics and recreational activities. The UW Lancers compete in the Ontario University Athletics (OUA) conference and the Canadian Interuniversity Athletic Union (CIAU). The men's interuniversity teams include basketball, cross-country, indoor track & field and volleyball. The women's teams include basketball, cross-country, ice hockey, soccer, indoor track & field and volleyball.

For students who wish to participate in instructional activities, Campus Recreation provides classes including weight-training, fitness, swimming, martial arts, tai chi and dance. Intramural sports offer activities such as volleyball, basketball, slo-pitch, badminton, floor & ice hockey, soccer, and water polo, in levels from novice to experienced.

There are many different clubs and organizations that operate on the UW campus, including student government, theatre groups, course and student unions, and cultural clubs.

University Recognition

- Provincial and national awards for equity policies and implementation
- National awards for the development of industrial partnerships
- Nine national track & field championships in the 1990s

STUDENT SUPPORT SERVICES

The International Students' Centre offers assistance, advice and information regarding campus orientation, personal counselling and Canadian immigration matters. The centre provides a social lounge for international students to hold meetings or to relax with other students; the centre also houses the International Students' Society (ISS).

The Academic Advisory Centre at UW provides assistance to students through support programs and professional advising. Assistance is directed to students with academic concerns.

Through workshops, career counselling, and resume-writing, job search and interview techniques, the Office of Co-op Education & Student Placement prepares students for entry to the job market. Job postings for on- and off-campus positions, part-time, full-time, summer, and overseas employment are continually updated on the office's job board.

International Students

University Enrolment: 400

% of University Enrolment: 4%

Countries of Origin: International students come from many countries including Bangladesh, Barbados, China, Egypt, Finland, Ghana, Hong Kong, Romania, India, Israel, Pakistan, Switzerland and the UK.

WILFRID LAURIER UNIVERSITY WATERLOO, ONTARIO

University Mission

...to educate a community of life learners, spark their creativity and develop their expertise in a diverse, supportive environment

Student Voice:

My stay at Laurier has been valuable and enjoyable. Everybody has been extremely helpful and friendly.

Adrian Katzew
Business Student
Mexico

CONTACT INFORMATION
Office of the Int'l Student Advisor - Debbie King
Wilfrid Laurier University
75 University Avenue West
Waterloo, Ontario
Canada N2L 3C5
PH 1-519-884-0710 ext. 3784
FAX 1-519-883-8127
EMAIL dking@wlu.ca
INTERNET http://www.wlu.ca

UNIVERSITY OVERVIEW

Wilfrid Laurier University (Laurier) began in 1911 as the Evangelical Lutheran Seminary of Canada. Over time, the school has gradually evolved from a private, denominational school into a publicly funded, secular centre for teaching and research. Today, Laurier has an enrolment of more than 6,000 students from across Canada and around the world studying in a wide variety of undergraduate and graduate programs. Laurier has a reputation for academic excellence.

Academic Programs

Laurier extends program choices to students through its Faculties of Arts, Science, Business & Economics, Music, Science and Social Work.

Undergraduate students may earn a Bachelor of Arts, Science, Music or Business Administration. The university also offers two-year diplomas in accounting, financial planning, business administration, chamber music, opera and performance.

Graduate students may earn a master's-level degree in business administration, business economics, English, environmental studies, geography, history, political science, psychology religion & culture or social work; doctoral programs are offered in social work, geography and history.

Co-op Programs

Laurier offers an extensive cooperative education program has been developed to provide an alternative to the standard structure of an academic degree. Placement in the co-op program is competitive and is open to honours students in the arts & science and business & economics faculties. The co-op option allows students to combine the skills learned in class with hands-on training in a workplace.

Study Abroad

In an effort to instil an international and cultural awareness on campus and within its students, Laurier developed Laurier International. Created in 1994, the international office handles most international activities, including student exchanges with other postsecondary institutions around the world. Undergraduate students in their third or fourth years of study may study in another country or enrol at Laurier from other institutions. Students will earn course credit while paying their respective university tuition fees.

Distance Education

Distance Education at Laurier is a growing program with over 3,000 course registrations per year. Students may earn a Laurier General BA through home study, or through a mix of on campus and distance courses; more than 70 degree-credit courses are available. Each course provides a resource binder and, where applicable, textbooks, video- and audiotapes, and other supplies; an increasing number of courses are offered over the Internet (http://www.wlu.ca/~wwwconte).

Highlights

- Laurier ranked among the top 5 four-year Canadian universities in Maclean's 1998 survey
- Many co-op and study abroad opportunities
- Part-time studies available in selected programs

University Statistics

Year Founded: 1910
Academic Options: undergraduate/graduate
Calendar Year: fall term (Sept-Dec); winter term (Jan-May)

DISCIPLINES/MAJORS OFFERED

Faculty of Arts & Science: Anthropology, Archaeology, Canadian Studies, Chemistry, Classical Studies, Communication Studies, Computing, Development & International Studies, Economics, English, Fine Arts, French, Geography & Environmental Studies, German, Greek, History, Kinesiology & Physical Education, Latin, Mathematics, Philosophy, Physics, Political Science, Psychology, Religion & Culture, Sociology, Spanish, Statistics, Theatre, Women's Studies

School of Business & Economics: Business Administration, Economics, Economics & Accounting, Economics & Financial Management

Faculty of Music: Music

Faculty of Graduate Studies

ADMISSIONS CRITERIA & PROCEDURES

All applicants are required to complete an application form from the Ontario Universities' Application Centre (OUAC) and submit it to the OUAC for processing. Applicants currently not attending an Ontario secondary school must have official secondary and postsecondary school transcripts (in English, where applicable) sent from all schools attended sent directly to Laurier's Admissions Office. Enquiries concerning admissions should be made to Laurier's Admissions Office.

Applicants to Laurier should have earned a secondary school diploma in a university preparatory curriculum, including six Ontario Academic Credits or equivalent, with a minimum overall average of 70 per cent; the minimum requirements vary for each program. Applicants may also submit additional personal information that may be useful in the admissions decision.

The admissions requirements for international students are normally based upon the minimum requirements for equivalent Ontario universities. Applicants from the UK and other Commonwealth countries are eligible for admission provided they have completed a General Certificate of Secondary Education in at least five or six subjects and at least two of the subjects are at an advanced level with acceptable standing. Applicants from the US typically require a Grade 12 diploma and an SAT score of 1000 (with a minimum 500 verbal, 500 mathematics). Applicants holding an International Baccalaureate diploma must demonstrate passing grades in a minimum of six subjects, three of which must be at a higher level.

International applicants whose first language is not English must submit proof of English proficiency through a minimum paper-based TOEFL score of 560, computer-based TOEFL score of 220, IELTS score of 7.0 or MELAB score of 90.

Admissions at a Glance

Minimum GPA: 70%

Minimum English Requirements:
- TOEFL 560 (paper) or 220 (computer), IELTS 7.0 or MELAB 90

Application Fee: C$90 (Cdn & int'l)

Application Deadlines: fall semester: April 1 (Cdn), April 30 (int'l); spring semester: Dec 1 (Cdn), Nov 1 (int'l)

ACADEMIC FACILITIES

The Laurier library collection consists of more than one million items, including 544,000 periodical publications and 128,000 government documents. A new, modern library information systems connects the Laurier library with the Universities of Guelph and Waterloo, and offers students access to the resources of all three libraries.

All students have access to the various computing facilities located throughout the campus; these facilities provide access to a variety of both popular and highly specialized software applications, and provide Internet access. Each student is issued a personal email account that may be accessed on or off campus.

Student are encouraged to participate in the many clubs, organizations and sporting activities offered at Laurier. Recently, the Athletics & Recreation Department was reorganized, increasing the number of Laurier varsity contenders in national competitions.

Student & Faculty Profile

Total Enrolment: 6,000

Undergraduate Enrolment: 5,200

# of Faculty: 600

Student/Faculty Ratio: 20:1

Male/Female Students: 47%/53%

First-Year Class Sizes: 25 or fewer (in 49% of classes)

Undergraduate Acceptance Rate: 33%

Undergraduate Enrolment by Discipline:

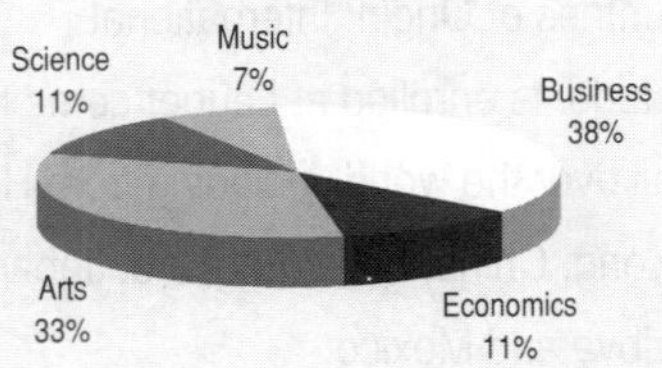

SCHOLARSHIPS & FINANCIAL ASSISTANCE

Laurier has been working hard to put more money into students' hands through bursaries and scholarships. These are awarded on a competitive basis. Students should consult the Laurier calendar or the website for details

International students should note that entrance scholarships are not available at this time for international students. Laurier is committed to keeping international student fees reasonable. Tuition fees for international students have not changed for three years.

Expenses at a Glance

Tuition (undergraduate, full-time):
- In-Province: C$3,300/year
- Out-of-Province: C$3,300/year
- International: C$7,000/year

Fees, Books, Materials: C$2,000/year

Accommodation:
- Private: C$400-550/month
- Residence: C$450-520/month
- Homestay: C$350-520/month

Health Insurance: included in student fees for Cdn; C$590/yr (int'l)

CAMPUS & LOCATION

City Population:	275,000 (Kitchener-Waterloo)
Cost of Living:	medium
Climate Range:	-15° to 32°C
Campus Setting:	suburban
# of Students in Residence:	1,500

The province of Ontario is Canada's industrial heart and contains about one-third of Canada's population. The combined population of Waterloo and its adjoining city, Kitchener, is approximately 275,000. Waterloo is about one hour by car from Toronto's Pearson International Airport, about two hours by car from Niagara Falls and Buffalo, New York, and three hours by car from Detroit, Michigan. Waterloo is further south than Paris, Berlin and several American states. The Great Lakes have a moderating effect on the climate, so winters are milder in southern Ontario than in states such as Minnesota and Wisconsin. A normal winter temperature in Waterloo in January is about -10 degrees Celsius (it can be colder or warmer) and a normal July temperature is about 25 degrees Celsius, though it can get as hot as 35 degrees Celsius.

More than 1,100 students live in eight main residence buildings on campus, which offer dormitory-style and apartment-style residences and include both all-male or all-female and coed options. The apartment residence buildings house four students per apartment, while the dormitories house two students per room. A university meal plan is required, except for those students living in the apartment-style Bricker Residence. Students wishing to live off campus can access housing option lists through the Laurier Housing office or online through the Kitchener Record (regional newspaper) prior to their arrival.

The campus is only 2 kilometres from neighbouring University of Waterloo and close to Waterloo Park, a local park and zoo. The city of Waterloo is in one of southwestern Ontario's more prosperous rural areas and is only 90 kilometres from Toronto. Waterloo is also only 40 minutes from the Stratford Festival, a renowned festival of Shakespearean theatre. The city offers a variety of cultural and recreational activities, all in a safe, clean environment.

ATHLETICS & EXTRACURRICULAR ACTIVITIES

Laurier is famous for the support it gives its sports teams, regardless of whether they win or lose. A recent survey showed that more than 30 per cent of Laurier's graduates attended at least one of their teams' home games a year (double the national average).

Exceptional sports teams are an ongoing part of the Laurier tradition. The Golden Hawks football team has a strong winning tradition, the women's soccer team is always a contender at the provincial and national levels, and the men's hockey team has consistently ranked in the top 10 teams in Canada for over decade.

Everyone at Laurier benefits from the university's Athletic Complex, which provides recreational and competitive sports facilities, including six squash courts, a weight & exercise room, saunas and three gymnasia that provide seating for 2,500 spectators. The outdoor facilities are just as extensive, including a fully lit practice football and soccer field, several tennis courts and a 5,000-seat stadium with the only artificial-turf playing field at an Ontario university.

Dozens of student clubs and organizations meet on campus, covering areas of interest that vary from chess to politics. Those interested in writing, photography and publishing can involve themselves with a number publications including the student newspaper.

University Recognition

- In 1998, Maclean's magazine ranked Laurier third in "highest quality" and "most innovative" categories
- The Faculty of Music has a national reputation for excellence and offers a unique degree in music therapy
- Through a highly respected archaeology program, students are working in Jordan in conjunction with Saskatchewan and Quebec archaeology programs

STUDENT SUPPORT SERVICES

Laurier offers an extensive range of support services to its students. Not only does tuition pay for courses, but all Laurier students have access to services including Student Counselling, Chaplains Office, Career Services, Special Needs Office, Housing, Athletics & Recreation and the Writing Clinic. The International Student Advisor is available to address the concerns of international students.

International Students

University Enrolment: 200

% of University Enrolment: 3%

Countries of Origin: International students enrolled at Laurier come from all over the world, including from Hong Kong, China, India, England, Japan, Libya and Mexico.

York University
Toronto, Ontario

University Mission

...to pursue, preserve, and disseminate knowledge in a context of social diversity, life-long education, bilingualism, and multiculturalism

Contact Information

Office of Admissions

York University

Room 150 Atkinson,

4700 Keele Street

Toronto, Ontario

Canada M3J 1P3

PH 1-416-736-5100 (Cdn);
1-416-736-5825 (int'l)

FAX 1-416-736-5100 (Cdn);
1-416-650-8195 (int'l)

EMAIL admenq@yorku.ca;
intlenq@yorku.ca

INTERNET http://www.yorku.ca

Student Voice:

It has been extremely satisfying to study at a university built on academic, creative and social exploration.

Jonathon Page

UNIVERSITY OVERVIEW

York University (York), located in Toronto, is home to approximately 37,000 undergraduate and graduate students. Since the university's founding in 1959, professors and students have dedicated themselves to excellence in scholarship. York is recognized nationally and internationally for its innovative research and award-winning teaching. Students from more than 140 countries have chosen to study at York.

York is proud to be able to offer two different environments for its students. The York Campus in Toronto's north end offers a modern learning environment and extensive facilities, including a bookstore, a variety of restaurants, a retail mall, an athletics complex, on-campus housing, and hundreds of on-campus events and cultural activities. At the York Campus, aside from language-based courses, all programs are offered in English. The Glendon Campus, in mid-town Toronto, is a small liberal arts college with a close-knit community where classes are taught in both English and French.

Programs Offered

The York Campus houses nine faculties: the Faculties of Arts (humanities and social sciences), Pure Applied Science, Education, Fine Arts, Environmental Studies and Graduate Studies; the Schulich School of Business; Atkinson College (primarily evening studies and some distance-learning opportunities); Osgoode Hall Law School. As the largest common-law school in Canada, the Osgoode Hall Law School has developed a curriculum of legal studies in both traditional and new areas of study. The Glendon Campus offers 19 liberal arts programs as well as specialized programs in translation and international studies.

A Renowned Faculty

In 1998, Maclean's magazine ranked York first among Canada's comprehensive universities for the number of classes taught by tenured faculty and for the number of faculty with PhDs. York is also within the top three educational institutions in the country for research grants for Social Sciences & Humanities, and Medical & Science programs.

Fifty-seven of the York Faculty members are fellows of the Royal Society of Canada. Michael Ondaatje, Glendon College English professor, is author of The English Patient, winner of the Governor General's Award and the Booker Prize. Physics & astronomy professor Marshall McCall is responsible for the discovery of two galaxies.

Highlights

- York is the third largest university in Canada; it offers a wide selection of graduate and undergraduate courses
- Progressive interdisciplinary programs such as Cultural Studies
- Two campuses within the metropolitan area of Toronto

University Statistics

Year Founded: 1959
Academic Options: undergraduate/graduate
Calendar Year: fall semester (Sept-Dec); winter semester (Jan-Apr); summer semester (May-Aug)

DISCIPLINES/MAJORS OFFERED

York offers more than 100 degree programs, including programs in the following areas.

Atkinson College: Administrative Studies, Accounting, Computer Science, General Science, Health Admin, HR Mgmt, Humanities, Marketing, Social Sciences

Business Administration: Accounting, Econ, Entrepreneur & Family Bus, Finance, Mgmt Sci/IS, Mktg, Org Behavior & IR, Strategic Mgmt

Education

Environmental Studies

Arts: African, Anthro, Applied Math, Canadian, Classical, Classics, Comp Sci, Coordinated Bus, Creative Writing, East Asian, Econ, Econ & Bus, English, French, Geog, German, Greek, Health & Society, History, Humanities, Individualized, Kines & Health Sci, Labour, Latin American & Caribbean, Law & Society, Lang/Lit & Ling, Mass Communications, Math, Math for Comm, Phil, Poli Sci, Psych, Public Policy & Admin, Religious, Sci/Tech/Culture/Society, Social & Political Thought, Sociology, Stats, Urban, Women's

Fine Arts: Cultural Studies, Dance, Design, Film & Video, Theatre, Visual Arts

Glendon College

Osgoode Hall Law School

Pure & Applied Science: Applied Math, Astronomy, Atmospheric Chem, Bio, Chem, Comp Sci, Earth & Atmospheric Sci, Env Sci, Geog, Kines & Health Sci, Math, Physics, Psych, Space & Communication Sci, Stats

Social Work: (Glendon Campus) Humanities, International Studies, Social Science, Translation

ADMISSIONS CRITERIA & PROCEDURES

Students must meet one of the following for admission eligibility:

• Canada: Grade 12, high school diploma and faculty-specific requirements for all provinces

except Ontario and Quebec. Ontario: Ontario Secondary School Diploma and six Ontario Academic Credits (OACs), including faculty-specific requirements. Quebec: minimum of 12 academic courses from CEGEP.

• International Baccalaureate: a minimum of 24 points with three passes at the standard level and three passes at the higher level OR two passes at the standard level and four passes at the higher level. Transfer credit may be awarded for higher level courses with grades of five or better.

• General Certificate of Education: two advanced level passes and three GCSE passes OR three advanced level passes and one GCSE pass. Transfer credit may be awarded for advanced level passes depending on the student's grades and the faculty applied to.

• United States: minimum of a B average on academic high school work and a combined SAT I score of 1100 or a composite ACT score of 24. Transfer credit of up to two full courses may be awarded for scores of 4 or 5 on the Advanced Placement examinations.

Candidates who have not studied in English at the secondary school level for at least four years must submit an acceptable score on the TOEFL (560 paper-based or 220 computer-based); MELAB (85); or IELTS (7). Applicants to the Glendon Campus can provide proof of their proficiency in English or French.

All programs begin in September (deadline is May 1). Atkinson and arts programs begin in January (deadline is November 1). Atkinson, Glendon, and science programs begin in May (deadline is March 1).

Limited enrolment programs may require a higher average and specific preparation in certain subject areas. For more information or to obtain an application, contact the Office of International Admissions. The application is also available on York's website.

Admissions at a Glance

Minimum GPA: varies by program

Minimum English Requirements:
TOEFL 560 (paper) or 220 (computer), MELAB 85 or IELTS 7.0

Application Fee: C$60 (international)

Application Deadlines: May 1 (September entry)

ACADEMIC FACILITIES

York's five libraries rank among the best in Canada, with over four million items, including microforms, maps, films, videos, archives, sound recordings, compact discs, and two million books and journals.

York provides students with access to over 900 computer terminals, an observatory with a 60cm telescope, a full sound stage/television studio and extensive laboratory facilities.

Student & Faculty Profile

Total Enrolment: 38,500

Undergraduate Enrolment: 34,400

# of Faculty: not available

Student/Faculty Ratio: 16:1

Male/Female Students: not available

First-Year Class Sizes: 25 (average)

Undergraduate Acceptance Rate: not available

Undergraduate Enrolment by Discipline: not available

SCHOLARSHIPS & FINANCIAL ASSISTANCE

Undergraduate applicants are considered at the time of admission for entrance scholarships, ranging in value from C$500 to $4,000. An application is necessary for larger awards (up to C$7,800 per year for Canadian students and up to C$10,500 per year for international students). Canadian and international students at York are also eligible for continuing student scholarships, based on their performance in York University courses. Last year, the maximum continuing scholarship was worth C$2,500.

Expenses at a Glance

Tuition (undergraduate, full-time):
- In-Province: C$3,550/year
- Out-of-Province: C$3,550/year
- International: C$10,200 (School of Business: $12,654/year)

Fees, Books, Materials: C$800/year

Accommodation:
- Private: C$800/month
- Residence: C$4,650/year
- Homestay: not available

Health Insurance: C$680 (international)

CAMPUS & LOCATION

City Population:	3,000,000
Cost of Living:	high
Climate Range:	-11° to 27°C
Campus Setting:	urban
# of Students in Residence:	2,200

York University—Canada's third largest university—comprises both the York and Glendon Campuses. The 220-hectare York Campus in Toronto's northwest section has extensive academic facilities—five libraries, computing services, visual arts studios, theatres, modern laboratories, an astronomical observatory, and all manner of research facilities. The Glendon Campus has fewer than 2,000 students. Located in mid-town Toronto, Glendon is only minutes away from a wide variety of boutiques, restaurants and pubs. The campus is a park-like setting, with an historic mansion, and superb athletic and academic facilities.

Named by Fortune Magazine as one of the world's best cities in which to live, Toronto is Canada's largest urban centre and is internationally recognized as a world-class cultural and economic centre. Toronto is also a major production centre for theatre, film and television and home to many major sports teams. A vibrant, multicultural city, Toronto has a well-deserved reputation for safety and cleanliness. Students can find theater, music and restaurants from all over the globe. Toronto is a city of neighborhoods, each with its own distinct character.

ATHLETICS & EXTRACURRICULAR ACTIVITIES

York has 29 teams that compete with other Canadian universities. Athletes of all abilities can participate in York's extensive recreational programs. York's athletic facilities are among the best in Canada and include: the Metropolitan Toronto Indoor Track & Field Center, six NHL-sized ice rinks, the National Tennis Center; swimming pool, aerobic studios, squash courts, sports injury clinic, weight room, and the York Stadium.

STUDENT SUPPORT SERVICES

York offers career services to help students to find jobs. The Centre for Academic Writing offers practical instruction in all aspects of writing. The Computer-Assisted Writing Centre gives students access to wordprocessing software at its computer facilities. Personal and academic counselling is offered through the Counselling and Development Centre. The Financial Aid Office provides information on financial aid, scholarships, awards, and a part-time on-campus job listing. York International advises international student on such issues as immigration and employment regulations, orientation, housing, financial aid and fee payments, health and travel.

Students whose first language is not English can prepare for university study or take general intensive study programs. Degree students can take degree-credit ESL courses.

University Recognition

- In 1998, Maclean's magazine ranked York first among comprehensive universities in Canada in terms of number of classes taught by tenured professors, number of faculty members with PhDs and more teaching awards than any other comprehensive university in Canada

International Students

University Enrolment: 1,700

% of University Enrolment: 3%

Countries of Origin: International students at York come from many countries, including France, England, Sweden, Mexico, Hong Kong, Taiwan, Ghana, Kenya and the United States.

Colleges

IN

Ontario

ALGONQUIN COLLEGE OF APPLIED ARTS & TECHNOLOGY OTTAWA, ONTARIO

College Mission

...to provide high quality career-oriented education and training which responds to the needs of learners, the community and society

Student Voice:

What Algonquin gave me was a platform, a broad-base of knowledge....By the time I graduated, I was completely confident saying I could do any job I was trained to do, in my field.

Michel Firlotte
Systems Analyst,
Computer Technology - Computing Science, 1994

CONTACT INFORMATION
Admissions Office
Algonquin College of Applied Arts & Technology
Woodroffe Campus,
1385 Woodroffe Avenue
Ottawa, Ontario
Canada K2G 1V8
PH 1-613-727-4723 ext. 7031 or 7038
FAX 1-613-727-7665
EMAIL intl1@algonquinc.on.ca
INTERNET http://www.algonquinc.on.ca

COLLEGE OVERVIEW

Algonquin College of Applied Arts & Technology (Algonquin), established in 1967, is the largest community college in eastern Ontario. Nearly 100 academic and career-oriented programs are offered through its 11 sectors: Computer/Telecommunications & Engineering Technology; Business; Justice/Security; Social/Community Services; Media/Design; Hospitality/Tourism; Health & Life Sciences; Transportation & Building Trades; Access; Renfrew County; and Lanark County.

Academic Programs

Algonquin strives to assist students in acquiring the skills and knowledge necessary for success in the global marketplace. With a great deal of input from the local community and its own students, the Algonquin faculty delivers innovative programs using a variety of teaching methods and approaches. Students may participate in group projects, laboratory experiments, fieldwork and case studies. Class instructors have professional experience in their field and can offer insight into the job market.

Many of the academic programs at Algonquin feature optional co-op programs which provide students with work experience and hands-on opportunities to practise skills learned in the classroom. Placements are available in fields such as business administration, computer engineering technology and automated office techniques.

Algonquin, with numerous partnerships with high-profile corporations such as Sun Microsystems and Digital, is emerging as a leader in the fields of telecommunications and computer engineering.

University Transfer Programs

Algonquin has formal transfer agreements with numerous universities in Canada and abroad including Carleton University, McMaster University, University of Ottawa, Ryerson Polytechnic University, The University of Western Ontario, Lakehead University, University of Lethbridge and The University of Western Sydney. Students in diploma programs such as nursing, business, civil engineering, electronics engineering technology, social service and early childhood education receive transfer credits towards a baccalaureate degree.

Flexibility

Algonquin understands that many students are unable to accommodate a traditional study schedule. The college offers numerous part-time and evening programs which allow students to pursue their studies while maintaining full-time careers. The Continuing Education Department offers courses to help employed students prepare for future studies by delivering programs which enable students to upgrade their academic skills at their own pace.

Highlights

- Co-op opportunities available in a variety of diploma programs
- Many diploma programs can be used as credit towards a university degree
- Unique educational opportunity in the nation's capital
- Ottawa is know as Silicon Valley North due to its many high-technology companies

College Statistics

Year Founded: 1967
Academic Options: diploma/certificate
Calendar Year: fall term (Sep-Dec); winter term (Jan-May); spring term (May-Aug)

ACADEMIC PROGRAMS

Business: Bus (Acc, IS, Insurance, Mktg, Retailing), Bus Admin (Acc, Finance, General, HR Mgmt, IS, Mktg, Materials Mgmt), Comp Programmer, Int'l Trade, Small Bus Mgmt

Computer/Telecommunications & Engineering Technologies: Comp Eng, Comp Systems Tech'n, Comp (Comp Sci), Comp Sci, Elect Eng, Elect Eng Tech'n (Digital), Electro-Mech Eng Tech'n (Robotics), Mech Eng, Precision Electronics Assembler, Arch, Civil Eng, Construction Eng Tech'n, GIS, Technical Writer

Health & Life Sciences: Chem Tech (Biochem), Dental Assistant, Dental Hygiene, Env Tech, Fire Protection Safety Tech'n, Occupational Health & Safety Tech'n, Pharmacy Assistant, Respiratory Therapy, Nursing, Practical Nursing

Justice/Security: Information Security Systems, Police Foundations Training, Security & Alarms Tech'n, Security Mgmt

Media/Design: Advertising (Creative), Animation (Television), Broadcasting (Radio, Television), Graphic Design Production, Graphics Tech'n (Printing), Horticulture & Landscaping Tech'n, Interactive Multimedia, Journalism (Print), Photography, Public Relations, Theatre Arts

Social/Community Services: Child & Youth Worker, Early Childhood Education, Social Service Worker, Applied Museum Studies, Archive Tech'n, Library & Info Tech'n, Recreation Facilities Mgmt

Access Programs: Int'l Access, ESL, Introduction to Nontraditional Occupations

Transportation & Trades: Power Eng Tech'n, Alignment & Brakes Mechanic, Auto Body, Air Conditioning & Refridgeration, Carpenter, Construction Carpentry

ADMISSIONS CRITERIA & PROCEDURES

The admission policies of Algonquin ensure that all applicants are considered in an equitable and consistent manner. The basic requirement for admission to Algonquin is an Ontario Secondary School Diploma (OSSD), or its equivalent; applicants should have successfully completed a senior-level English course. Many programs have additional requirements: all technology programs require senior mathematics. Students should contact the Admissions Office for further details.

Canadian students must submit a nonrefundable application fee of C$65 along with a completed application form to the Ontario College Application Service (OCAS) in Guelph, Ontario. Canadian applicants who have not obtained an OSSD but are 19 years of age may be considered for admission to the college.

Non-native English speakers who wish to apply for full-time diploma programs must submit a TOEFL score of 550 or higher for direct entry, along with official academic transcripts. International applicants with a TOEFL score between 500 and 550 will be automatically accepted into the International Access program. This program provides additional language training while offering a selection of credit courses to help prepare students for further studies. Completed international applications, including the nonrefundable C$250 deposit, should be directed to the International Admissions Office. Only officially translated documents will be accepted.

Admissions at a Glance

Minimum GPA: no set minimum

Minimum English Requirements: Ontario Grade 12 or equivalent, or TOEFL 550

Application Fee: C$65 (Canadian), $250 (international)

Application Deadlines: March 1

ACADEMIC FACILITIES

Algonquin takes pride in its academic facilities, offering modern classrooms and program-specific laboratories with the latest research and experimental equipment. There are designated labs for a diverse spectrum of disciplines, including a cooking lab and a turbine engine lab.

The college understands how important technology is to a modern education. There are 73 labs equipped with Pentium computers at Algonquin, several which are open 24 hours a day. All students have Internet and email access. Learning Resource Centres, located on both campuses, provide students with access to major databases, CD-ROM networks, books, audiovisual materials and reference assistance.

Student & Faculty Profile

Total Enrolment: 11,000

Full-Time Enrolment: 11,000

# of Faculty: 600

Student/Faculty Ratio: 18:1

Male/Female Students: not available

Academic Class Sizes: 25-30

Enrolment by Program Type:

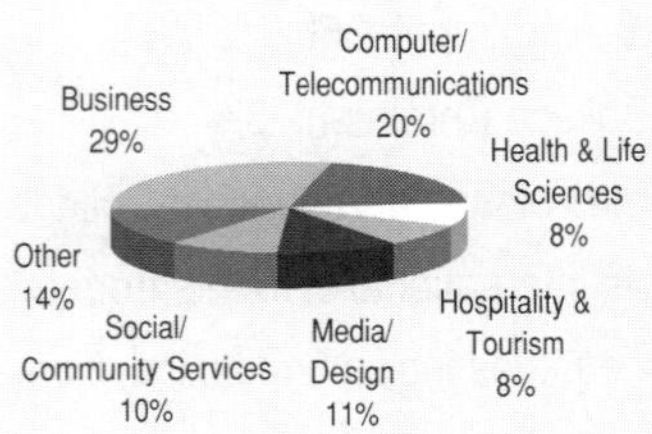

SCHOLARSHIPS & FINANCIAL ASSISTANCE

Algonquin offers financial assistance in four forms: loans, scholarships, bursaries and work-study. Both federal and provincial loan programs operate on a need basis. Financial need is also the main consideration for awarding bursaries. Several scholarships are granted on the basis of high academic performance. There are four areas that administer awards: the Financial Aid Office, the Registrar's Office, individual academic departments and the Students' Association.

Currently, international students cannot apply for financial assistance at Algonquin.

Expenses at a Glance

Tuition (full-time):

In-Province: C$1,947/year

Out-of-Province: C$1,947/year

International: C$9,895/year

Fees, Books, Materials: C$500-700/year

Accommodation:

Private: C$500-600/month

Residence: n/a

Homestay: C$600/month

Health Insurance: C$540/year

CAMPUS & LOCATION

City Population:	1,027,000
Cost of Living:	high
Climate Range:	-15° to 30°C
Campus Setting:	urban
# of Students in Residence:	n/a

There are two Algonquin campuses in the Ottawa area: the Woodroffe campus in the west and the Rideau campus in the east. Both campuses offer a wide variety of amenities and services, including food courts, student centres and housing services. Students will enjoy studying in the tranquil settings of both campuses amidst the hustle and bustle of Ottawa.

Situated in eastern Ontario, Ottawa hosts many festivals and celebrations each year. Ottawa is the capital of Canada and therefore is home to many national museums including the Museum of Civilization and the Museum of Science & Technology. Ottawa is also home to the prestigious National Art Gallery. Ottawa and its surrounding communities have a combined population of well over one million people. The city is located along the Rideau Canal, which, in the winter, becomes the world's largest natural outdoor skating rink. Ottawa also boasts a professional hockey team, which is a source of great pride within the city. Students will find Ottawa a friendly, safe city, home to many outdoor markets, biking trails and distinct neighbourhoods.

The city has a variety of rich cultural communities that reflect Canada's policy of diversity and tolerance. As a national capital, Ottawa hosts a large number of embassies from around the world.

ATHLETICS & EXTRACURRICULAR ACTIVITIES

The goal of Algonquin's Athletic Department is to enrich the college experience for all its participants through activity, fun and involvement, and to constantly develop new programs to meet the needs of students and current trends in recreation. The college competes in several sports at the varsity level and has a large intramural system. Students can join in activities such as soccer, hockey, basketball and badminton. The department also offers many instructional programs such as judo, yoga and aerobics. Algonquin's athletic facilities have recently undergone renovations and now include a double gymnasium, an aerobic/combative room, a weight-training facility, outdoor playing fields and a therapy room.

There are numerous social and cultural organizations active at Algonquin. The Algonquin College Students' Association provides a variety of services for the student body including coordinating projects and social events. The Student Centre is the hub of all student activity and is home to several student lounges, the student newspaper and the Students' Association.

College Recognition

- Member of the Association of Colleges of Applied Arts & Technology of Ontario
- Member of Association of Canadian College Schools of Business, Human Resources Professionals of Ontario, Canadian Financial Planning Institute, Insurance Institute of Canada, and Council of Second Language Programs
- Credit granted towards CGA designation

STUDENT SUPPORT SERVICES

Algonquin strives to provide students with a comprehensive support system in order to create a positive learning environment. Counselling Services can offer advice on a variety of issues including career goals, educational planning and personal issues. Students can also find assistance through the peer tutoring and support system. Other facilities include health services, a housing referral service and Placement Services.

The International Education Centre (IEC) acts as a liaison between the school and its overseas students. IEC offers assistance with admissions, academic tutorials, campus information, banking and transportation. IEC also operates the homestay program and organizes social events for international students.

International Students

College Enrolment: 350

% of College Enrolment: 3%

Countries of Origin: Algonquin College hosts international students from over 50 countries including Mexico, Korea, Colombia and Japan.

GEORGE BROWN COLLEGE TORONTO, ONTARIO

College Mission

...to provide innovative, applied education and training programs for adults seeking to enhance their employability in the short and long term....through programs supported by high-quality educators and trainers, which reflect the broad-based employment and societal needs of a large, diverse urban centre

Student Voice:

After getting a degree in fine arts at York University and working for several years in marketing...I realized that the only way to move forward with my career was to return to school and get a diploma....George Brown prepared me extremely well for the specifics of sports and events marketing.

Denise Dorfman
Sport and Event Marketing, 1998

CONTACT INFORMATION
International Centre
George Brown College
PO Box 1015, Station B
Toronto, Ontario
Canada M5T 2T9
PH 1-416-415-2115
FAX 1-416-415-2120
EMAIL info@gbrownc.on.ca (Cdn);
intlcen@gbrownc.on.ca (int'l)
INTERNET http://www.gbrownc.on.ca

COLLEGE OVERVIEW

George Brown College of Applied Arts & Technology (George Brown) is committed to providing high-quality instruction and facilities in a wide variety of fields to prepare students for the changing and expanding contemporary workplace. George Brown, the only community college in downtown Toronto, was founded in 1967 to serve the city of Toronto as part of a province-wide system of colleges. George Brown now has three campuses to serve the city of Toronto. The college offers 100 certificate and diploma programs, which have been developed in partnership with business, industry and community leaders, and provides a mixture of theoretical and applied education. The college is named after George Brown, the 19th-century Liberal Leader, Father of Confederation and founder of the Globe newspaper.

Areas of Study

George Brown offers a wide variety of programs, divided into the following areas: the Faculty of Business and Creative Arts, which includes the School of Business, the School of Art & Design, the School of Performing Arts and the School of Interdisciplinary Studies; the Faculty of Community Services & Health Sciences is divided into Community Services Programs and Health Sciences Programs; the Hospitality & Tourism Centre; and the Faculty of Technology, which includes Information Technology; in addition, a variety of apprenticeship, college preparation and distance education programs are offered to George Brown students.

In highly specialized programs that range from accounting to microelectronics manufacturing technology, George Brown seeks to provide its students with career-oriented skills directly applicable in the modern workforce.

Additional Programs

The college preparation programs offered at George Brown include the Academic Bridging programs and ESL programs. Academic Bridging programs help students address gaps in their education or qualifications, whether in mathematics, English or the sciences, or focus on general employment skills in areas like reading, writing and job search techniques. The ESL courses available at George Brown range from intermediate to advanced levels. There is also an English language program offered during the summer which is less intensive and focuses on speaking and listening and cultural experiences.

Apprenticeship programs allow students to study, train and work in a specific skilled trade by combining college courses and paid work experience. Apprenticeship courses are offered in the fields of technology, fashion and hospitality.

Highlights

- Toronto's only downtown community college
- Approximately 100 certificate and diploma programs
- Three campuses with a variety of services and facilities

College Statistics

Year Founded: 1967
Academic Options: certificate/diploma/postdiploma
Calendar Year: fall semester (Sept-Dec); spring semester (Jan-Apr); summer semester (May-Aug)

ACADEMIC PROGRAMS

Business: Accounting; Financial Planning; Health Information Management; Human Resources Management; International Trade (Postdiploma); Investment Sales Assistant; Logistics Management; Management Studies; Marketing; Office Administration (Medical); Small Business; Sport and Event Marketing (Postdiploma)

Community Services Programs: Activation Coordination/Gerontology; Child & Youth Worker; Community Worker; Early Childhood Development; Human Services Counsellor; Intervenor for Deaf-Blind Persons

School of Art & Design: Fashion Management & Design; Furniture Repair, Finishing & Design; Graphic Design; Internet Web Page Design & Multimedia Authoring (Postdiploma); Printing Technologies; Theatre

General Arts & Science: University Transfer (Diploma)

Health Sciences: Fitness & Lifestyle; Nursing

Hospitality: Baking; Chef Training; Culinary Management; Food & Beverage Management; Food & Nutrition Management; Food Preparation; Hotel Management

Engineering Techology: Architecture, Building & Construction; Electrical/Electronic (Electronics Technician CD-ROM, Power & Industrial Control), Environmental Systems (Air Conditioning & Refrigeration Technician/Technologist, Appliance Servicing Technician, Gas Technician), Information Technology (Computers), Mechanical Engineering

ADMISSIONS CRITERIA & PROCEDURES

Canadian and international students in Canada apply for most programs through the Ontario College Application Service (OCAS) (at PO Box 810, Guelph, Ontario, Canada, N1H 6M4, or online at http://www.ocas.on.ca/online/on1nfram.htm). OCAS requires a C$65 application fee.

Domestic students may apply for a few programs directly to George Brown. For further information students should contact George Brown (by phone at 1-800-265-2002 or by email at info@gbrownc.on.ca).

International students in Canada and overseas apply directly to the college for all programs; international applications for postsecondary programs do not require an application fee.

For admission to programs beginning in September, students should submit their application (together with transcript translated into English) between January 1 and March 1, after which date applications will be considered as space in the program becomes available.

Most programs require an Ontario Secondary School Diploma (OSSD) or equivalent. Postdiploma programs require a college diploma or university degree. Some programs ask for specific skills, work background or life experiences. Students over 19 years of age who apply as mature students will be asked to write a test in the required skills and/or attend an interview.

Admissions at a Glance

Minimum GPA: n/a

Minimum English Requirements: one of the following: TOEFL 550 or equivalent; English-language high school diploma; final level of George Brown ESL program; or grade 12 on English entrance exam

Application Fee: C$65 (through OCAS); no fee when applying directly to programs at George Brown

Application Deadlines: rolling admissions; March 1 for priority entry in September

ACADEMIC FACILITIES

George Brown offers students academic facilities complemented by the first-rate educational amenities available in the city of Toronto.

All students, staff and faculty have access to the resources, facilities and services available at the Learning Resource Centres on all George Brown campus. Students have access to books, periodicals, films, videos and VCRs, computers and software, audiocassettes and newspapers. Each centre offers facilities for research and study, the viewing of films and videos, academic and personal computing and some special needs services. Resource centre staff are available to help students locate the information they require during their studies, projects and assignments.

The city of Toronto offers many amenities that can be useful to study at George Brown, including Canada's best selection of libraries, museums and bookstores. The Royal Ontario Museum, Ontario Science Centre, Ontario Place and the Ontario Exhibition can supply students with valuable educational opportunities.

Student & Faculty Profile

Total Enrolment: 52,000

Full-Time Enrolment: 10,000

\# of Faculty: 650

Student/Faculty Ratio: 15:1

Male/Female Students: 50%/50%

Academic Class Sizes: 30 (average)

Enrolment by Program Type: not available

SCHOLARSHIPS & FINANCIAL ASSISTANCE

Applicants to full-time programs who are Canadian citizens or permanent residents may be eligible for financial assistance through the Ontario Student Assistance Program (OSAP). OSAP information workshops are given during the summer (from May to July) in the college's Financial Assistance Office.

George Brown College provides bursaries through the Student Assistance Fund and most departments have bursaries and awards that are available to registered students who meet specific criteria. The college also offers a limited work-study program that provides on-campus student employment.

Expenses at a Glance

Tuition (full-time):

- In-Province: C$1,473-$1,836/year
- Out-of-Province: C$1,473-$1,836/year
- International: C$9,375/year

Fees, Books, Materials: varies

Accommodation:

- Private: C$800-1,000/month
- Residence: n/a
- Homestay: C$175/week

Health Insurance: C$540/year

CAMPUS & LOCATION

City Population:	3,000,000
Cost of Living:	medium-high
Climate Range:	-11° to 27°C
Campus Setting:	urban
# of Students in Residence:	n/a

George Brown is made up of three campuses: the Casa Loma campus, the Nightingale campus and the St. James campus.

All three of George Brown's campuses are located in downtown Toronto, Ontario, Canada's financial and cultural capital. Toronto has been recognized by the United Nations as the world's most multicultural city. Different ethnic neighbourhoods operate side by side, and maintain their own cultures in the wide diversity of restaurants, festivals, community centres and shopping districts in the area, including those of Chinatown and Little Italy. The downtown is clean, lively and small enough to be travelled by foot; and with its street cars, buses, and subway system, Toronto offers one of the most easy-to-use and economical public transportation systems in North America. Metropolitan Toronto offers a world-class list of athletic, recreational and cultural amenities, all set in a safe and liveable city; popular destinations within the city are SkyDome, the CN Tower and the Harbourfront.

Toronto is located close to a number of world-class cities and natural destinations. Niagara Falls, Montreal, Ottawa and New York are within a day's driving time.

ATHLETICS & EXTRACURRICULAR ACTIVITIES

George Brown offers two campus gymnasia that host a variety of recreational programs ranging from aerobics to tai chi. Students may also participate in many intramural activities including badminton, basketball, touch football, volleyball, soccer, tennis and table tennis.

George Brown boasts an impressive array of varsity teams. As a member of the Ontario Colleges Athletic Association, its men's and women's teams, compete in sports including soccer (indoor and outdoor), basketball, badminton, volleyball and baseball.

George Brown also offers a variety of student clubs to meet the varied needs of its diverse student body. These include organizations of religious, cultural, regional and recreational interest that allow students to meet with peers in a social setting.

College Recognition

- 1998 Program Excellence from the Association of Canadian Community Colleges (ACCC) for Electronics Technician Distance Education certificate program
- George Brown students received a 1997 American Marketing Association award for outstanding fundraising activities
- George Brown Professor Karen Chandler was the 1997 winner of the Canadian Child Care Federation's highest national award—the Award for Excellence in Child Care
- Expogast '98 Culinary World Cup Champions—representing Canada

STUDENT SUPPORT SERVICES

George Brown students are well served by a variety of student services available on campus. Students at George Brown have access to career, personal and academic counselling; employment posting and career information; a peer-support program; and alumni affairs, tutoring and housing services. George Brown also hosts a variety of special student events throughout the year.

The college offers special services to aboriginal, special needs and mature students, and is committed to making its programs accessible to the widest possible range of students.

International students at George Brown can take advantage of the college's counselling and support services to make a smooth transition to life and study in Canada.

International Students

College Enrolment: 200

% of College Enrolment: 2%

Countries of Origin: International students at George Brown come from countries including Japan, Korea, China, Taiwan, Colombia, Mexico, Brazil, Spain, Europe and the Middle East.

LAMBTON COLLEGE
SARNIA, ONTARIO

College Mission

...to be a progressive,

innovative college committed

to high-quality education and

services

Student Voice:

I feel that Lambton College has given me the valuable skills that will help me the most in my career...I must say that I owe it all to the dedicated professors at Lambton College.

Yvan B. Nugent, Graduate Accounting

CONTACT INFORMATION
Information and Recruitment Services
Lambton College
1457 London Road
Sarnia, Ontario
Canada N7S 6K4
PH 1-519-542-7751
FAX 1-519-542-0991
EMAIL info@lambton.on.ca
INTERNET http://www.lambton.on.ca

COLLEGE OVERVIEW

Lambton College (Lambton), founded in 1966, aims to produce graduates fully prepared for employment success; the school prides itself on its career placement record. Lambton is located in Sarnia, a major site of chemical and chemical process industry. The college's programs relate directly to the region's economic opportunities; the college maintains close, beneficial ties with business and industry.

Many of Lambton's programs have a co-op component, integrating in-college academic terms with paid work experience. The co-op program encourages students to develop financial responsibility and to establish business contacts.

Lambton graduates are eligible for university admission. Graduates of two-year programs are eligible for first-year entry; three-year program graduates are eligible for second-year entry at most Ontario universities. Lambton has established agreements with some universities in Canada, the US and Mexico for direct credit transfers from specific college programs.

The School of Applied & General Arts

The school's programs are intended for students looking to develop the essential life skills necessary to build a rewarding and flexible career.

The School of Business & Law

Lambton is committed to ensuring that business students gain an understanding and appreciation of the various areas of business, and the socio-economic environment in which business is conducted. Graduates of Lambton's business programs develop the skills to successfully compete in the business world.

The School of Technology & Applied Sciences

Lambton offers a wide variety of programs to prepare flexible and competitive technology graduates. Students work with the latest research and experimental equipment and gain hands-on training from professionals.

Information Technology Education Centre

The world of information technology is one of rapid change and growth, and the Information Technology Education Centre delivers programs to meet the needs of IT professionals. The centre's programs provide graduates with the knowledge and skills to succeed in the ever-evolving IT environment.

Business, Industry & International Centre

The centre exists to provide flexibility in learning and quality in delivery to clients in the Sarnia/Lambton area, and the national and international markets.

Highlights

- Majority of programs offer a co-op component
- Direct credit transfers for specific programs with Canadian and international colleges and universities
- More than C$3.5 million in computer equipment available for student use

College Statistics

Year Founded: 1966

Academic Options: diploma/certificate

Calendar Year: fall term (Sept-Dec); winter term (Jan-Apr); spring term (May-Aug)

ACADEMIC PROGRAMS

School of Applied & General Arts: General Arts & Science; Graphic Design Fundamentals; Media Fundamentals; Parks/Nursery Technician; Parks/Golf Course Technician; Sports Facilities & Recreation Administration

School of Business & Law: Accounting; Business; Business Administration; Marketing; Human Resources; Pre-Business; Correctional Worker; Police Foundations/Law & Security Administration

School of Health Hospitality & Community Services: Child & Youth Worker; Culinary Management; Human Services Foundation; Nursing; Practical Nursing; Personal Support Worker; Pre-Health Sciences; Social Service Worker

School of Technology & Applied Science: Chemical & Mechanical Eng Technician; Chemical, Mechanical and Electronics (Electronics & Applications) Eng Technology; Environmental Technology; Industrial Hygiene Technology (Occupational Health Safety); Instrumentation & Control Eng Technician; Mechanical Eng Drafting Technician; Pre-Technology; Major Appliance Servicing, Motive Power Fundamentals; Welding Techniques

Information Technology Education Centre: Computer Programmer; Computer Programmer Analyst; Microcomputer Management; Office Administration

Business Industry & International Centre: Fire Science Technology

ADMISSIONS CRITERIA & PROCEDURES

Candidates may obtain applications from high schools, from the Information and Recruitment Services at Lambton or from the Ontario College Application Service (OCAS). Applications must be submitted to OCAS. All applications for admission received before March 1 are given equal consideration and are judged according to the same standards and criteria; applications received after March 1 will be accepted on a first-come, first-admitted basis.

The admissions criteria at Lambton vary by program. Applicants to some programs may be asked to submit proof of completion of specific secondary school prerequisites, to complete questionnaires, to submit portfolios or to demonstrate specific skills. Students should contact Lambton for more information.

Candidates may apply under mature student status if they are over 19 years old and do not have a secondary school diploma. Applicants who lack the minimum educational requirements will need to attend an assessment session to determine mathematical and communication skills.

International students are welcome at Lambton but must be aware that some programs are not available for non-Canadian students due to enrolment limitations. Some programs may have minimum English requirements for non-native speakers. Interested students should contact the International Office at Lambton.

Admissions at a Glance

Minimum GPA: no set minimum

Minimum English Requirements: evaluated on case-by-case basis for ESL students

Application Fee: C$65 (Canadian and international)

Application Deadlines: rolling admissions; priority deadline is March 1

ACADEMIC FACILITIES

Lambton college seeks to be academically and technologically current, preparing students for success in today's changing business environment. The college is equipped with laboratories, shops, studios, greenhouses, classrooms and a library. The college offers over C$3.5 million worth of computer equipment for student use; the computing facilities are open 24 hours per day.

SCHOLARSHIPS & FINANCIAL ASSISTANCE

The Financial Aid Office processes and approves all monetary awards, bursaries, scholarships and loans. Students in postsecondary, upgrading, certificate and skills-training programs are eligible to receive benefits from the Ontario Student Assistance Program (OSAP). The Ontario Student Opportunity Trust Fund (OSOTF) makes available financial awards to students who can demonstrate financial need. In addition students may apply for a variety of Lambton scholarships and bursaries. Financial assistance is also available for students requiring childcare services. Applications are available at the financial aid office.

The Department of Cooperative Education & Career Services is available to assist students gain financial independence through co-op placement and career search. Instruction is available in the fundamentals of the job search, and graduates are given the opportunity to be interviewed by company representatives who participate in the college's on-campus recruiting program.

Student & Faculty Profile

Total Enrolment: 12,600

Full-Time Enrolment: 2,675

# of Faculty: 260

Student/Faculty Ratio: 50:1

Male/Female Students: 50%/50% (approx)

Academic Class Sizes: not available

Enrolment by Program Type: not available

Expenses at a Glance

Tuition (full-time):
- In-Province: C$1,702/year
- Out-of-Province: C$1,702/year
- International: C$9,215/year

Fees, Books, Materials: not available

Accommodation:
- Private: C$6,000/year (approx)
- Residence: C$4,825/year
- Homestay: C$5,250/year

Health Insurance: C$540/year

CAMPUS & LOCATION

City Population:	75,000
Cost of Living:	medium
Climate Range:	-10° to 26°C
Campus Setting:	suburban
# of Students in Residence:	120

Lambton College was founded in 1966 as one of the 25 colleges of applied arts & technology in Ontario. Lambton is funded and accredited by the Ministry of Education & Training in Ontario, which is responsible for the quality and integrity of each Lambton program.

Lambton College's main campus is comprised of two buildings spread over 50 hectares of land. The main campus houses Lambton's postsecondary, continuing education and international programs, the Centre for Advanced Process Technology, the Centre for Environmental Management & Safety, the Management Centre and the Computer Centre. The Riverside campus, located in downtown Sarnia, houses some of Lambton's access programs. Lambton's third campus houses the Industrial Fire School, the only one of its kind in Canada. Lambton's on-campus coed residence offers 120 single rooms, four lounges, free laundry facilities and a meal plan.

The Sarnia area of Ontario is commonly known as Bluewaterland, and is located at the southern end of Lake Huron. Sarnia is connected to a large network of metropolitan areas within a day's drive, including Toronto, Cleveland and Detroit. The area offers the natural advantages of being situated in the Great Lakes region, with beaches, fishing, watersports and many other recreational possibilities.

ATHLETICS & EXTRACURRICULAR ACTIVITIES

The athletics department provides students with the opportunity to participate in recreational, intramural and varsity activities. Outdoor facilities include a football and soccer field, four tennis courts and a softball diamond. Indoor facilities consist of a gymnasium with a weight-training room, a cardio room and a sports injury lab. The gymnasium and outdoor facilities are available to students throughout the day on an informal basis when classes are not in session.

The college's varsity teams, the Lambton Lions, compete in the Ontario College Athletic Association (OCAA) and the Canadian Colleges Athletic Association. Varsity teams include men's basketball, cross-country running, men's and women's soccer, volleyball, touch football, rugby and badminton. The campus has erected a multi-use sports complex, which houses the Sarnia Sting Junior A hockey team and hosts a variety of events.

STUDENT SUPPORT SERVICES

Lambton provides extensive student services to its student population. The Counselling Services Office provides educational planning, career planning, goal setting and personal advice and support. The college's learning centre offers programs and activities in peer tutoring, learning support and selected computer assistance. The First Nations Students Centre supports a variety of services in an informal social atmosphere for its constituent students, including counselling and peer tutoring. The International Centre provides a wide range of assistance and information to international students on issues concerning visas, housing, travelling, college programs and related subjects.

Lambton's community-based childcare centres provide full daycare for young children. In addition, before- and after-school programs for children up to 12 years of age are available.

College Recognition

- Accredited by the Ministry of Education & Training of the government of Ontario

International Students

College Enrolment: 9

% of College Enrolment: less than one per cent

Countries of Origin: not available

Northern College of Applied Arts & Technology Timmins, Ontario

College Mission

...to provide a full range of educational and training opportunities...to provide high-quality education that is integrated, equitable, relevant and accessible...to establish a college presence throughout the north in a flexible, multi-community service network

Contact Information

Northern College of Applied Arts & Technology
PO Box 3211
Timmins, Ontario
Canada P4N 8R6
PH 1-705-235-3211
FAX 1-705-235-7279
EMAIL info@northernc.on.ca
INTERNET http://www.northernc.on.ca

Student Voice:

The most positive experience for me at Northern College is being in smaller classes which allow for more opportunity to learn and work with students and faculty on a more personal level.

Debra Shalla
Business Administration

COLLEGE OVERVIEW

Northern College of Applied Arts & Technology (NC) is one of 25 colleges in the Ontario education system and is publicly funded by the provincial government through the Ministry of Education. NC's objective is to provide students with the best possible training environment, modern facilities and highly personalized instruction.

Applied Arts Programs

NC offers 18 programs in applied arts, in fields as diverse as social work and graphic design. Students enrolled in applied arts programs benefit from field work placements during the program, which provide them with the opportunity to practise skills learned in the classroom, to gain new knowledge and to make contacts with professionals working in their field.

Applied Technology Programs

NC offers nearly 25 applied technology programs at the Kirkland Lake, Haileybury and Timmins (Porcupine) campuses. The Kirkland campus is renowned for its technology programs, including NC's unique three-year program in welding engineering technology, and programs in computer science, information systems and electrical engineering. The Haileybury campus houses the internationally recognized Haileybury School of Mines. Graduates from the mining or instrumentation programs have gone on to top positions in mining and related industries.

Business Programs

NC business programs are widely recognized by employers in northern Ontario and across the country. The accounting and marketing programs are designed to meet the needs of both local and national business corporations as they approach the 21st century.

Aboriginal Programs

The Department of Aboriginal Programs & Services strives to meet the educational and training needs of Aboriginal students at any of NC's campuses or First Nations adult education sites. NC's eight Aboriginal programs are open to both native and non-native students.

Highlights

- Offer both full- and part-time options
- Optional cooperative education programs available in selective areas of study
- Renowned for programs in welding engineering technology, mining technology and information systems

College Statistics

Year Founded: 1967

Academic Options: diploma/certificate

Calendar Year: fall semester (Sept-Dec); winter semester (Jan-Apr)

ACADEMIC PROGRAMS

Aboriginal Programs: Cree Interpreter/Translator, Entrepreneurship, First Nations Constable, General Arts & Science, General Vocational Preparation, Intro Mgmt, Journalism (Print & Broadcast), Native Child & Community Worker, Native Counsellor, Nursing, Paramedic, Teacher Ass't

Applied Arts: Child & Youth Worker, College Vocational Program, Community Gerontology, Developmental Services Worker, Drug & Alcohol Counsellor, Early Childhood Ed, Fine Arts & Crafts, General Arts & Science, Graphic Design Fundamentals (Electronic Design & Publishing), Police Foundations, Social Service Worker

Applied Technology: Architectural Technician & Technology, Civil Eng Technician & Technology (Survey Option), Comp Sci Tech, Construction Building Mgmt Technician, Electrical Eng Technician, Electrical Eng Tech, Environmental Eng Tech, Heavy Duty Equipment Mechanic, IS, Instrumentation Eng Technician, Millwright/Mechanic, Mining Eng Technician, Motor Vehicle Mechanic, Survey Eng Technician/Technology, Water Resources Eng Tech, Welding Engineering Technician & Technology, Welder-Fitter

Business: Accounting, Bus Admin, IS, Marketing, Internet Website Development, Office Admin

Department of Health Sciences: Nursing, Practical Nursing, Veterinary Technician

ADMISSIONS CRITERIA & PROCEDURES

Applications for NC can be obtained through the Office of Admissions or online from the Ontario College Online Application Services at http://www.ocas.on.ca. All NC programs require the completion of Grade 12 English (or its equivalent); computer literacy and keyboarding skills are highly recommended. Ontario residents who are 19 years of age or older and do not possess an Ontario Secondary School Diploma (OSSD) may be accepted following appropriate testing. Many programs have individual admission requirements; students should consult the NC calendar for additional information.

International applicants whose first language is not English must demonstrate proficiency in both written and spoken English by submitting minimum TOEFL scores of 500. All transcripts and documentation should be accompanied by a certified translation, if applicable.

Admissions at a Glance

Minimum GPA: no set minimum

Minimum English Requirements: TOEFL 500

Application Fee: C$40 (Canadian and international)

Application Deadlines: March 1 (fall semester)

ACADEMIC FACILITIES

NC campuses have a complete collection of books and publications dealing with business and technical matters, as well as related subjects. NC students have access to a variety of general and special interest magazines and periodicals, as well as vocational guidance pamphlets, brochures, films and other audiovisual materials.

The Porcupine campus houses many computer labs, skills shops, a nursing lab and AutoCAD labs. The campus also supports a Business Centre and a Learning Resource Centre, equipped with computers, printers and Internet access. Students enrolled at any of NC's satellite sites or studying through the Open Learning program may borrow materials from any of the Learning Resource Centres.

Student & Faculty Profile

Total Enrolment: 1,400

Full-Time Enrolment: 1,400

# of Faculty: 125

Student/Faculty Ratio: 20:1

Male/Female Students: 44%/56%

Academic Class Sizes: 20-25

Enrolment by Program Type:

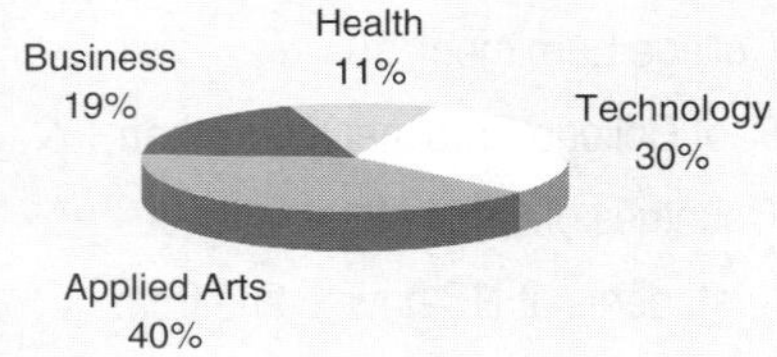

SCHOLARSHIPS & FINANCIAL ASSISTANCE

All students are eligible for NC scholarships, bursaries and awards, administered by individuals, and by public and private organizations. NC also offers entrance awards and scholarships to mature students.

Ontario resident students are eligible to receive benefits from the Ontario Student Assistance Program (OSAP). The Ontario Student Opportunity Trust Fund (OSOTF) makes available financial awards to students who can demonstrate financial need.

Further details on financial assistance can be obtained through the Student Services or Financial Aid Offices.

Expenses at a Glance

Tuition (full-time):

- In-Province: C$1,801/year
- Out-of-Province: C$1,801/year
- International: C$9,740/year

Fees, Books, Materials: C$500-1,000/year

Accommodation:

- Private: C$500/month
- Residence: C$1,300-1,500/semester
- Homestay: varies

Health Insurance: C$81/year

CAMPUS & LOCATION

City Population:	45,000 (Timmins only)
Cost of Living:	medium
Climate Range:	-20° to 28°C
Campus Setting:	rural
# of Students in Residence:	185

The largest of Northern College of Applied Arts & Technology's campuses is the Porcupine campus, located in Timmins, Ontario. The Kirkland Lake campus, which existed as the Northern Ontario Institute of Technology (NOIT) until 1969, is well-known for its technology programs and for its one-year law enforcement certificate program. Other NC campuses include Kapuskasing, Moosonee, and Haileybury, which has an international reputation for developing and leading mining education projects. Not all courses are offered at all NC campuses; students should consult the calendar for further information.

NC provides daycare facilities and on-campus housing on both the Kirkland Lake and the Porcupine campuses. Kirkland Lake has a residence hall that accommodates 34 students; the Porcupine campus has a 120-room residence hall on campus. Room and board facilities are available in all NC districts. The college maintains a housing registry through which students can seek assistance in finding reasonably priced accommodation. NC also offers a homestay program to international students.

Timmins has a population of approximately 45,000 and is located in northeastern Ontario. Timmins is one of the most mineral-rich areas in North America, with gold and base mineral (copper, zinc) making up the majority of the mining industry. Timmins is 600 kilometres outside Toronto and enjoys hot summers and snowy winters.

ATHLETICS & EXTRACURRICULAR ACTIVITIES

NC supports hockey teams at the Kirkland Lake and the Haileybury campuses. NC varsity teams include cross-country, badminton, golf and curling. The Porcupine campus houses complete athletic facilities, including a gymnasium, a weight-training room, squash and racquetball courts, and a sauna.

Activities available to NC students vary from campus to campus. All five campuses have a Student Administrative Council (SAC), composed of peer-elected students. The SACs plan various activities throughout the year for NC students, including barbecues, orientation activities, winter carnivals, fishing derbies, fund-raising projects, pub nights and concerts.

Students may join any of the numerous student clubs based on NC campuses.

STUDENT SUPPORT SERVICES

The purpose of the International Education & Training (IET) Office is to recruit international students and foster international partnerships through human resources development. The IET office provides many services to NC international students including local airport pickup, a campus orientation program, personal and academic counselling, immigration information (student visas, work permits, passports, health insurance), homestay programs, information about on- and off-campus housing, public transportation, peer tutoring and assistance with university transfers.

NC's Placement Office offers a number of services to college students, graduates and employers; these services include a register of graduates from all fields of study and for students willing to work part-time, on-campus recruiting, interviewing facilities, collection and screening of resumes, job service for local employers, and labour trend information.

Counselling and peer tutoring services are available to all students who may be experiencing academic or personal difficulties during their studies at NC.

College Recognition

- A number of NC's programs are accredited, including Drug & Alcohol Counsellor, Architectural Engineering Technology and Veterinary Technician

International Students

College Enrolment: 10

% of College Enrolment: less than 1%

Countries of Origin: International students at NC have come from countries including Malaysia, Hong Kong, Zimbabwe, Pakistan, India, Sweden and Cameroon.

PROFILES OF Universities & Colleges IN Quebec

Universities

IN

Quebec

Bishop's University Lennoxville, Quebec

University Mission

...to provide a sound and liberal education primarily at the undergraduate level, and, through excellence in teaching, scholarship and research, encourage individuals to realize their full potential in their intellectual, spiritual, social and physical dimensions

Student Voice:

Bishop's was my choice because I wanted to be a name, not a number. I have really enjoyed the friendly atmosphere, along with the personalized style of teaching that each professor provides for their students.

Richard Bailey
Business Administration

CONTACT INFORMATION
Liaison Office
Bishop's University
Lennoxville, Quebec
Canada J1M 1Z7
PH 1-800-567-2792 ext. 2681
FAX 1-819-822-9661
EMAIL liaison@ubishops.ca
INTERNET http://www.ubishops.ca

UNIVERSITY OVERVIEW

Since 1843, Bishop's has dedicated itself to providing students with a well-rounded, liberal education through 35 departments offering four undergraduate degrees and four graduate degrees. The relaxed atmosphere and small size of the university lends Bishop's a comfortable academic and social atmosphere.

Academic Programs

Bishop's has integrated its academic resources into a single faculty. This allows Bishop's to better coordinate academic affairs and provide maximum flexibility in the design of programs. Academic disciplines are represented by departments which are grouped into four divisions: Business & Economics, Humanities, Natural Sciences & Mathematics and Social Sciences; the School of Education offers additional programming within the faculty. Undergraduate programs lead to bachelor degrees in arts, science, education and business administration.

Bishop's also offers graduate programs leading to a Master of Arts in History or Education as well as two Master of Education programs.

Personalized Learning

Many of the programs offered at Bishop's can be pursued as either a minor or a major and students are encouraged to plan their own program of study with the advice of their faculty members. Bishop's strives to provide students with options and flexibility in designing their academic programs.

Bishop's approach to personalized education emphasizes personal contact between faculty and students through small classes and frequent use of seminars, laboratories and tutorials. Interdisciplinary studies are woven into every program at Bishop's and course content is frequently reviewed to ensure that it is relevant in today's modern world.

Global Perspective

Bishop's sponsors one of the largest student exchange programs in Canada. The university has study agreements with over 200 universities worldwide in countries including Australia, Belgium, England, France, Germany, Italy, Korea, Malta, Mexico, Norway, Spain, Sweden, Switzerland and the US. Students can spend a semester or an entire year cultivating a better understanding of the global environment.

Highlights

- Small, personal learning environment with emphasis on faculty to student interaction
- Many study abroad and student exchange programs available
- Liberal education enriched by research provides flexible career options

University Statistics

Year Founded: 1843
Academic Options: undergraduate/graduate
Calendar Year: fall semester (Sept-Dec); winter semester (Jan-Apr); summer session (May-Aug)

DISCIPLINES/MAJORS OFFERED

Williams School of Business and Economics: Accounting, Business & Economics, Economics, Finance, Human Resources & Business Management, International Business, Management Science & Information Systems, Marketing, Political Economy

School of Education: Secondary Teaching, Elementary Teaching

Division of Humanities: Liberal Arts, Classical Studies, Drama, English, Études français et québécoises, Fine Arts, History, Modern Languages (English Language & Composition, German, Italian, Japanese, Spanish), Music, Philosophy, Religion

Division of Natural Sciences & Mathematics: Biochemistry, Biological Sciences, Chemistry, Computer Science, Mathematics, Physics

Division of Social Sciences: Geography, Political Economy, Political Studies, Psychology, Sociology & Anthropology

Multidisciplinary Programs: Canadian Studies & Quebec Studies, Women's Studies

ADMISSIONS CRITERIA & PROCEDURES

The admissions criteria at Bishop's varies for each program. Normally, students who have completed the highest level of secondary school studies, including a college preparatory curriculum, will be considered for admission. A minimum grade average will determine a student's eligibility for admission. In general, an average of 73 per cent or higher, or equivalent, will be adequate for admission to Education, Humanities, Natural Science and Social Science programs. Students applying to the Business & Economics division should have a grade average of 75 per cent or higher, or equivalent. For further information, students should contact the Bishop's Liaison Office.

A completed application form must be accompanied by academic transcripts and a nonrefundable C$55 application fee and must be submitted to the Director of Admissions. The deadline for applications is March 1 for the fall semester and October 15 for the winter semester. Most programs begin during the fall semester, but are also open for admission in January.

In addition to the above, international students are required to submit proof of English proficiency; the English-language admission requirement can be satisfied by submitting a TOEFL score of 550, MELAB score of 85 or IELTS score of 6.5. American students are also required to submit an SAT score of 1100 or higher in order to be considered for admission. All international students are required to submit a signed statement of financial responsibility from the student's sponsor.

Admissions at a Glance

Minimum GPA: 73%

Minimum English Requirements:
TOEFL 550, MELAB 85, IELTS 6.5

Application Fee: C$55 (Canadian and international)

Application Deadlines: October 15 (winter semester); March 1 (fall semester)

ACADEMIC FACILITIES

Bishop's is committed to improving the facilities it has to offer its students. The university made more than C$25 million in renovations to the campus and academic facilities, including the classrooms and laboratories, since the beginning of the 1990's.

The John Bassett Memorial Library houses a collection of nearly 500,000 items including books, journals, microforms, video-recordings and other non-print materials. In addition, the Writing Centre offers academic writing consultations and workshops throughout the year.

The Cole Computer Centre houses the majority of the more than 160 computers on campus that are available to students. The centre also maintains a fibre-optic Novell network supporting the entire university. There are 10 other on-campus computer labs located in areas including the student residences and departmental classrooms. All Bishop's students have email and Internet access.

Student & Faculty Profile

Total Enrolment: 2,361

Undergraduate Enrolment: 2,333

# of Faculty: 148

Student/Faculty Ratio: 16:1

Male/Female Students: 49%/51%

First-Year Class Sizes: 35 (average)

Undergraduate Acceptance Rate: 80%

Undergraduate Enrolment by Discipline:

SCHOLARSHIPS & FINANCIAL ASSISTANCE

Bishop's offers three forms of financial assistance to students including merit-based awards and need-based bursaries and loans. Scholarships normally range between C$1,000 and $5,000 and can be renewed annually. Students wishing to be considered for financial awards must have their admissions applications submitted to the Admissions Office before March 1. Canadian students may also apply for both federal and provincial loans programs. Further information can be obtained by contacting the Financial Aid Office.

Assistance to international students is limited. Those students from abroad who have completed one year of studies are eligible for university scholarships.

Expenses at a Glance

Tuition (undergraduate, full-time):
In-Province: C$1,700/year
Out-of-Province: C$3,200/year
International: C$8,200-9,200/year

Fees, Books, Materials: C$1,300/year

Accommodation:
Private: C$475-550/month
Residence: C$525-590/month
Homestay: C$470/month

Health Insurance: C$520/year

CAMPUS & LOCATION

City Population:	5,000
Cost of Living:	medium
Climate Range:	-10° to 20°C
Campus Setting:	rural
# of Students in Residence:	515

Bishop's is located in the town of Lennoxville, in the heart of the Eastern Townships of southern Quebec. The 200-hectare campus rests at the junction of the St. Francis and Massawippi Rivers. The campus is designed to provide a tranquil and peaceful learning environment. Academic life is focused around the Bishop's University Quad, a series of buildings which have stood for more than 100 years. Students can take advantage of the quiet, tree-filled grounds to study or relax with friends. The campus includes a three-hectare wetland conservation area that acts as an on-campus laboratory for the biology and geography departments. The university's six residences offer both co-educational and single-sex accommodation. First-year students are encouraged to live on campus and experience the friendly, family atmosphere that the Bishop's community offers.

Lennoxville is a primarily English-speaking town within the mostly French-speaking province of Quebec; however, either language can be used in Lennoxville. Several major lakes and ski resorts in the area allow for year-round outdoor recreational opportunities. Sherbrooke, Quebec's seventh largest urban centre, is only 5 kilometres away. With the Canada-US border nearby, Vermont, New Hampshire and Maine are all within a short drive of Lennoxville.

ATHLETICS & EXTRACURRICULAR ACTIVITIES

Bishop's offers its students a diverse selection of athletic programs at the interuniversity, intramural and recreational levels. The university is a member of the Quebec Students Sports Federation and competes in numerous men's and women's sports, including basketball, football, golf, ice hockey, soccer, rugby and alpine skiing. A large intramural program offers competitive sports in men's, women's and co-educational leagues. The Recreational Instruction Program offers a wide variety of non-competitive, life-enhancing, instructional activities such as yoga, kayaking and the martial arts.

The John H. Price Sports & Recreation Centre plays a vital role in fulfilling the concept of a total education at Bishop's. The centre houses a double gymnasium, a 25-metre swimming pool with diving platforms, tennis and squash courts, gymnastics facilities and a fully-equipped weight training facility. Other notable facilities on campus include the W.B. Scott Memorial Rink and Coulter Field, a 3000-seat football stadium.

There are over 50 cultural and social student organizations meeting on campus as well as a student newspaper, radio station, theatre company and art gallery.

University Recognition

- One of the largest student exchange programs in Canada
- Ranked among top-third of undergraduate universities for 8 consecutive years by Maclean's
- 16 Rhodes Scholarship winners have studied at Bishop's, the most recent in 1998
- Desmond Tutu accepted Bishop's offer of an honorary degree over 130 other offers

STUDENT SUPPORT SERVICES

Students can take advantage of the many support services available at Bishop's throughout the year. Counselling Services assists students with personal concerns related to university life, family difficulties and other issues. The Employment Resources Centre offers educational and support services to students undertaking a career or job search. Other student services include a campus ministry, student government and health services.

International students may visit the International Student Exchange Office for advice regarding immigration concerns, academic options and Canadian culture. Foreign students who need additional English language assistance may take ESL classes through Bishop's Office of Continuing Education.

International Students

University Enrolment: 141

% of University Enrolment: 8%

Countries of Origin: International students at Bishop's represent 43 countries such as Korea, Germany, Brazil and the USA.

CONCORDIA UNIVERSITY
MONTREAL, QUEBEC

University Mission

...to combine the best of the academic world with the best of the outside world; Concordia graduates learn to adapt and be flexible, and have the openness of mind and spirit that are the best preparation for life beyond the year 2000

Student Voice:

Concordia has given me the "real world" experience that I needed to succeed in my field ....plus the encouragement to go out and practise my new skills.

Monika Conway
Bachelor of Science

CONTACT INFORMATION
Office of the Registrar
Concordia University
1455 de Maisonneuve Blvd. West
Montreal, Quebec
Canada H3G 9Z9
PH 1-514-848-2668
FAX 1-514-848-2621
EMAIL admerg@topaz.concordia.ca
INTERNET http://www.concordia.ca

UNIVERSITY OVERVIEW

Founded in 1974 through a merger between Montreal: Loyola College and Sir George Williams University, Concordia University (Concordia) is a large comprehensive university dedicated to strong academic achievement from a real-world perspective. Concordia offers an exceptional educational environment with innovative curricula and small class sizes.

Academic Programs

Concordia offers more than 150 undergraduate programs in four faculties: the Faculties of Arts & Science, Commerce & Administration, Engineering & Computer Science, and Fine Arts. Within the Faculty of Arts & Science are the Liberal Arts College, Lonergan University College, School of Community & Public Affairs, Science College and the Simon de Beauvoir Institute. These colleges allow students to take special courses and participate in special-interest seminars and extracurricular activities.

The Graduate School offers more than 80 master's, doctoral and postdiploma programs. Concordia also offers a number of distance education and professional programs.

Students in most programs can choose to participate in study abroad and student exchange programs. For example, students can spend a year in Florence or study in Peking.

Co-op Program

Concordia boasts one of the highest co-op placement rates of any university in North America (97 per cent). The co-op program offers experience in a broad range of fields including areas such as accounting, mathematics, electrical engineering and software systems. By combining outside work training with academic study in a chosen discipline, students gain practical experience, improving their employability after graduation.

The Concordia Experience

The focus at Concordia is on the students: class sizes are kept small to facilitate personalized instruction, and university facilities are designed to suit the needs of a diverse student body.

The university strives to break down the traditional, artificial barriers between higher education and the real world outside, ensuring that students receive a relevant, applicable education. Many of the faculty at Concordia have industry experience.

Highlights

- Highest co-op placement rate in Canada
- Multicultural, multilingual learning environment
- 500 companies come to Concordia every year to recruit graduates

University Statistics

Year Founded: 1974
Academic Options: undergraduate/graduate
Calendar Year: fall term (Sept-Dec); winter term (Jan-May)

DISCIPLINES/MAJORS OFFERED

Faculty of Arts & Science: Biology, Chemistry, Biochemistry, Classics, Communication Studies, Economics, Education, English, Études françaises, Exercise Science, Geography, History, Human Relations, Individual Studies Program, Journalism, Leisure Sciences, Mathematics & Statistics, Modern Languages & Linguistics, Philosophy, Physics, Political Science, Psychology, Religion, Science & Human Affairs, Sociology & Anthropology, Southern Asia Studies, TESL, Theological Studies, Urban Studies, Women's Studies

Faculty of Commerce & Administration: Accountancy, Decision Sciences & Management Information Systems, Economics, Finance, International Business, Management, Marketing

Faculty of Engineering & Computer Science: Computer Applications, Computer Systems, Information Systems, Software Engineering, Software Systems, Building Engineering, Civil Engineering, Computer Engineering, Electrical Engineering, Industrial Engineering, Mechanical Engineering

Faculty of Fine Arts: Art Education, Cinema, Creative Art Therapies, Contemporary Dance, Design Art, Digital Image/Sound & the Fine Arts, Interdisciplinary Studies, Music, Studio Arts (Ceramics, Fibres, Painting & Drawing, Photography, Print Media, Sculpture), Theatre, Women & the Fine Arts

ADMISSIONS CRITERIA & PROCEDURES

The university accepts those candidates possessing the strongest qualifications and potential. Applicants who have achieved university admissions eligibility in their province, state or country are considered provided they have completed a minimum of 12 years of schooling. Completed applications must be accompanied by a C$40 application fee. All applications should be directed to the Office of the Registrar. Most programs begin in the fall semester. The deadline for applications for the fall semester is July 1.

Requirements for specific programs may include portfolios, interviews and a letter of intent. In some cases, where demand is strong, limited resources may require restricted admissions. Students are encouraged to apply early.

Canadian students wishing to enrol at Concordia must have completed their senior year of secondary education with a minimum overall average of 65 per cent in appropriate subjects.

International students whose first language is not English must provide documentation of proficiency. Concordia accepts a TOEFL score of 550, a MELAB score of 85 or an IELTS score of 6.5. Successful completion of the university's Advanced II level of the Intensive English Language Program also satisfies this requirement.

Students may apply electronically via the World Wide Web at http://www.concordia.ca/admissions.

Admissions at a Glance

Minimum GPA: n/a

Minimum English Requirements:
TOEFL 550, MELAB 85, IELTS 6.5

Application Fee: C$40 (Canadian and international)

Application Deadlines: March 1 (fall term); November 1 (winter term)

ACADEMIC FACILITIES

The Georges P. Vanier Library and Webster Library hold a combined total of over two million items including government publications, CD-ROMs, online databases and periodicals. The Instructional & Information Technology Services (IIT) department manages a number of computer labs, containing over 300 Macintosh and IBM-compatible computers. IIT also has a complete array of multimedia facilities: media labs, sound studios and a fully equipped television studio.

Learning Support Services helps students improve their academic skills and learning potential. The office provides tutorials and workshops in a broad range of subject areas including writing composition, mathematics and science.

Student & Faculty Profile

Total Enrolment: 25,984

Undergraduate Enrolment: 24,353

# of Faculty: 1,680

Student/Faculty Ratio: 16:1

Male/Female Students: 48%/52%

First-Year Class Sizes: 41 (average)

Undergraduate Acceptance Rate: 71%

Undergraduate Enrolment by Discipline:

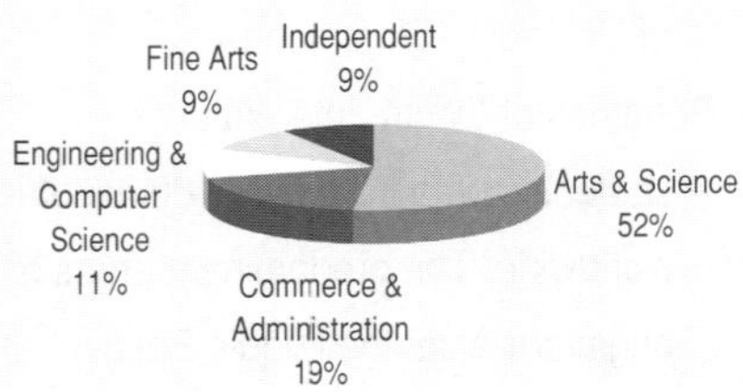

SCHOLARSHIPS & FINANCIAL ASSISTANCE

The Financial Aid Office handles all requests for loans, as well as awarding scholarships. Concordia offers a number of tuition scholarships to Canadian students entering their first year of studies. These scholarships are awarded on the basis of high academic achievement. Provincial government assistance is available in the form of loans and bursaries and is determined by financial need. Canadian scholarships, bursaries and loans are generally not available to international students.

Expenses at a Glance

Tuition (undergraduate, full-time):
In-Province: C$1,668/year
Out-of-Province: C$3,170/year
International: C$9,170-10,000/year

Fees, Books, Materials: C$1,325-1,930/year

Accommodation:
Private: C$625-650/month
Residence: C$365-400/month
Homestay: n/a

Health Insurance: C$475/year

CAMPUS & LOCATION

City Population:	3,328,300
Cost of Living:	high
Climate Range:	-15° to 27°C
Campus Setting:	urban/suburban
# of Students in Residence:	144

Concordia has two campuses; the Sir George Williams campus is located in downtown Montreal and the Loyola campus is located in the residential west-end of the city. The two campuses, 7 kilometres apart, are connected by a free shuttlebus service.

The Sir George Williams campus comprises a group of owned and rented buildings surrounding the Henry F. Hall Building, which features 15 floors of classrooms, auditoriums and laboratories. The campus is also home to the new C$65 million J.W. McConnell Building, which houses the R. Howard Library.

The Loyola campus is located on a 20-hectare tree-filled site with notable facilities, including Montreal's newest Concert Hall.

Montreal is the largest city in the province of Quebec and is one of Canada's premier commercial, industrial and financial centres. Situated on an island where the St. Lawrence and Ottawa Rivers meet, Montreal is one of the world's largest French-speaking cities. As one of North America's oldest cities, its historical origins are preserved and displayed in the architecture of Old Montreal. The Laurentian Mountains and the rolling countryside of the Eastern Townships are nearby and offer a number of year-round outdoor recreational activities.

Montreal is a bustling, vibrant city that revels in the arts, featuring world-class jazz and comedy festivals as well as a major symphony and ballet company. The city hosts many major spectator sporting events including the Montreal Grand Prix.

ATHLETICS & EXTRACURRICULAR ACTIVITIES

Concordia has a proud tradition in collegiate athletics. The university believes that athletics are an integral part of student life, whether students are participants, organizers or fans. There are three recreational facilities offering programs and activities at every level. Recreational activities include kung fu, floor hockey, soccer, modern dance, basketball and rugby.

There are over 125 student organizations that meet on campus. Students have the opportunity to interact with peers who have similar interests in political, social and cultural arenas. Concordia has a student-run newspaper and TV and radio stations.

University Recognition

- Member of CUCC
- Member of the Conference of Rectors & Principles of Universities of Quebec
- Faculty of Commerce & Administration Accredited by AACSB - The International Association for Management Education

STUDENT SUPPORT SERVICES

Concordia is responsive to the needs of its students, providing a variety of services such as personal counselling and academic advising. Every student meets with an academic counsellor throughout their studies. Other important resources include a Career & Placement Service Office, Healthcare Office and Peer Helper Centre.

Orientation programs for both Canadian and international students are designed to make the transition to university life easier.

The International Students Office is the liaison between international students and the university, offering advice on immigration issues, housing, academia and cultural adaptation.

International Students

University Enrolment: 1,104

% of University Enrolment: 4%

Countries of Origin: International students come from over 160 countries worldwide. The predominant areas of origin are Asia, the Middle East, Eastern Europe and the US.

McGill University Montreal, Quebec

University Mission

...to provide advanced learning through teaching, scholarship and service to society by offering to outstanding undergraduate and graduate students the best education available

Student Voice:

...I learned that a McGill education was more than an opportunity to develop linguistics, critical, and analytic skills, but an invitation to explore the rich diversity of human behaviour and creative expression.

Sara Anderson
BA 1996, MA 1997
Bethesda, Maryland, USA

CONTACT INFORMATION
Admissions & Registrar's Office
McGill University
847 Sherbrooke Street West
Montreal, Quebec
Canada H3A 3N6
PH 1-514-398-3910
FAX 1-514-398-4193
EMAIL admissions@aro.lan.mcgill.ca
INTERNET http://www.mcgill.ca

UNIVERSITY OVERVIEW

McGill University (McGill) is one of Canada's largest universities with almost 30,000 students, 3,000 full-time faculty and 44 affiliated research institutes.

Located in the primarily French-speaking city of Montreal, Quebec, McGill's language of instruction is English; however, McGill is unique in that students may submit all coursework, including term papers and examinations, in either English or French.

Academic Programs

McGill's 12 faculties offer undergraduate and graduate programs in some 300 disciplines. Most undergraduate degrees require a minimum of four years of full-time study.

Students pursuing graduate-level studies may earn a master's degree or PhD in almost all of the disciplines at McGill.

Highlights

- Internship, co-op, work study and exchange programs available
- Part- and full-time possibilities
- Continuing education and professional development courses are available

University Statistics

Year Founded: 1821
Academic Options: undergraduate/graduate
Calendar Year: fall semester (Sept-Dec); spring semester (Jan-Apr)

Co-op/Internship & Exchange Programs

Cooperative education (co-op) and internship programs at McGill are organized and administered through each faculty. Co-op and internship experiences provide students with the competitive advantage of having work experience related to their field of study prior to graduation.

The engineering and science faculties have created the Internship Year for Engineering & Science (IYES); over 30 companies participate in IYES by offering salaried placements that last eight to 16 months. This program allows students to gain valuable, professional work experience concurrently with their undergraduate studies.

McGill offers international exchange agreements with 500 schools around the world. Participating students study over one or two semesters overseas and pay regular McGill tuition rates. Qualified students should have completed one year of study with a minimum GPA of 3.0.

Continuing Education Programs

McGill's Centre for Continuing Education (CCE) aims to meet the educational needs and aspirations of the adult segment of society. The centre provides ongoing educational opportunities for career and personal advancement. The CCE offers programs in two areas: Career Development and General Interest. The programs available include career & management studies, accounting, languages & translation, professional development for teachers, general studies, learning in retirement and development programs in cooperation with professional associations.

DISCIPLINES/MAJORS OFFERED

McGill offers some 300 degree programs, including programs in the following areas:

Agricultural & Environmental Sciences
Architecture
Arts
Centre for Continuing Education
Communication Sciences & Disorders
Dentistry
Dietetics & Human Nutrition
Education
Engineering
Graduate Studies & Research
Law
Library & Information Studies
Management
McGill School of Environment
Medicine
Music
Nursing
Physical & Occupational Therapy
Religious Studies
Science
Social Work
Urban Planning

ADMISSIONS CRITERIA & PROCEDURES

Admission to McGill is highly competitive, and students who present the minimum requirements are not necessarily guaranteed acceptance to McGill. All applicants must complete and submit an application for admission form to the Admissions & Registrar's Office (ARO) accompanied by the C$60 nonrefundable application fee.

Each program has an extensive list of individual admission requirements in addition to the general qualifications; students should contact the ARO for specific program admission information. All applicants must provide evidence of secondary school completion and should submit an official secondary school transcript, complete with grades and classes taken.

Applicants following a US high school curriculum are advised to write the SAT I and three appropriate SAT IIs. A-level applicants should complete three papers with grades of at least C to support their application. Applicants whose first language is not English are required to submit evidence of English language proficiency; a TOEFL score of 550, a MELAB score of 85, an IELTS score of 6.5 or completion of a McGill Certificate of Proficiency in English are acceptable minimum admission requirements.

Admissions at a Glance

Minimum GPA: varies

Minimum English Requirements:
- TOEFL 550, IELTS 6.5, MELAB 85 or a McGill Certificate of Proficiency in English

Application Fee: C$60 (Canadian and international)

Application Deadlines: in-province: Mar 1 (Sept sem), Nov 1 (Jan sem); out-of-province: Feb 1 (Sept sem), Sept 1 (Jan sem); int'l: Jan 15 (Sept sem), Sept 1 (Jan sem)

ACADEMIC FACILITIES

McGill's 16-library network is one of the largest in Canada and holds more than five million books and journals. Students can access the online library catalogues and indices from library workstations or from departmental or personal computers.

Over 31 computer laboratories are available for student use in various departments and faculties including management, arts, engineering, education, medicine, music and law. More than 100 library terminals provide Internet access; student residence rooms also provide either standard or high-speed Internet access.

Three of the 13 Canadian Networks of Centres of Excellence are located at McGill. McGill houses 44 research centres and affiliated institutes, and its researchers work with colleagues in 26 interuniversity research centres.

The university is affiliated with a number of museums and hospitals in and around Montreal.

Student & Faculty Profile

Total Enrolment: 29,729

Undergraduate Enrolment: 23,802

# of Faculty: 2,300 (full-time)

Student/Faculty Ratio: 12:1 (average)

Male/Female Students: 46%/54%

First-Year Class Sizes: 25-250

Undergraduate Acceptance Rate: 50%

Undergraduate Enrolment by Discipline:

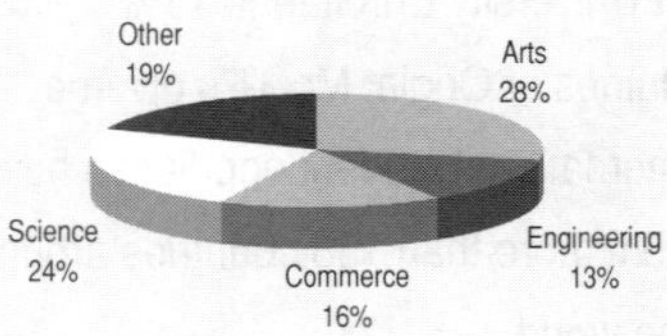

SCHOLARSHIPS & FINANCIAL ASSISTANCE

McGill offers an extensive range of entrance scholarships to students with outstanding academic records and proven leadership abilities. Awards range in value from C$2,000 to $15,000 and are renewable; several include travel grants based on the distance a student must travel to arrive in Montreal. Awards can be used to subsidize the cost of tuition, student fees, books and residential housing on campus.

Expenses at a Glance

Tuition (undergraduate, full-time):
- In-Province: C$1,670/year
- Out-of-Province: C$3,170/year
- International: C$8,300-12,000/year

Fees, Books, Materials: C$2,120-2,450/year

Accommodation:
- Private: C$725/month
- Residence: C$6,000/year
- Homestay: n/a

Health Insurance: included in fees

CAMPUS & LOCATION

City Population:	3,000,000
Cost of Living:	low
Climate Range:	-15° to 26°C
Campus Setting:	urban
# of Students in Residence:	1,600

McGill University was founded in 1821 in Montreal, Quebec on an 18-hectare estate bequeathed by James McGill to provide a facility for the education of Quebec's English-descended population. In 1906 the MacDonald campus was added at the western tip of the island of Montreal. Today, McGill's main campus includes 70 buildings on 32 hectares at the foot of the Mount Royal Park in downtown Montreal. The MacDonald campus is set on 640 hectares of wooded land on the edge of Lake St. Louis.

McGill has six undergraduate residence halls with fully furnished rooms. The McConnell, Gardner and Molson halls overlook the campus and are home to about 220 students each; all of these halls have coeducational and single-sex floors. Douglas and Solin halls are both coeducational; Douglas is arranged by suites with single rooms and Solin offers apartment-style housing. Royal Victoria College is an all-female complex housing 262 students.

Montreal is the largest city of Quebec and home to over three million people representing both French- and English-speaking communities; although it is officially a French-speaking city, Montreal is functionally bilingual (French and English). Montreal combines all of the conveniences of a large cosmopolitan city with the safety and affordable living of a small town.

ATHLETICS & EXTRACURRICULAR ACTIVITIES

McGill ranks fourth among Canadian universities in the number of intercollegiate sports organizations on campus; McGill offers 15 varsity teams and 17 sports clubs. McGill also offers more than 700 intramural teams to students looking for a less competitive atmosphere. McGill athletic facilities include a new fitness room (opened in 1997), the Sir Arthur Curries Memorial Gymnasium, the McGill Fieldhouse (featuring a six-lane, 200-metre indoor running track), Molson Stadium, McConnell Winter Arena, Memorial Pool (with a 25-metre, eight-lane racing pool), the Seagram Sport Science Centre and the McGill Sport Medicine Clinic.

McGill supports more than 100 student organizations, activities, clubs and services that are organized and maintained by students.

STUDENT SUPPORT SERVICES

The Orientation Centre at McGill is staffed by experienced returning students. It is open from mid-August to the beginning of September to serve new students who may need advice, information or assistance.

At the beginning of each year, first-year students are paired with a coordinator who can address any questions or concerns new students may have. These coordinators can provide information regarding course selection, counselling, tutoring services and support to students in need of academic assistance.

Other student resources available on campus include career placement, counselling, and international student and health services. Chaplaincy, writing tutorial clinics, crisis hotlines, a sexual assault centre, a daycare, several ombudspersons, a student financial aid office and an intensive English and French language centre are also available to all McGill students.

University Recognition

- Among the smallest average undergraduate class sizes at a research-intensive university according to Maclean's magazine (1998)

International Students

University Enrolment: 3,953

% of University Enrolment: 13%

Countries of Origin: McGill's diverse international student population hails from more than 138 countries around the world.

PROFILES OF Universities & Colleges IN The Atlantic Provinces

Universities

IN

The Atlantic Provinces

DALHOUSIE UNIVERSITY
HALIFAX, NOVA SCOTIA

University Mission

...to provide a thoroughly challenging, highly relevant educational experience for students who are ready to assume the responsibilities and rewards of leadership

Student Voice:

Academically, Dalhousie is an Ivy League calibre school without the Ivy League price tag, giving us access to some of the best academics in the world

Meghan Brown
Bachelor of Science
Marine Biology

CONTACT INFORMATION
Office of the Registrar
Dalhousie University
Halifax, Nova Scotia
Canada B3H 4H6
PH 1-902-494-2450
FAX 1-902-494-1630
EMAIL registrar@dal.ca
INTERNET http://www.dal.ca

UNIVERSITY OVERVIEW

Dalhousie University was founded in 1818 by the Earl of Dalhousie with the help of booty captured during the War of 1812. Dalhousie has been providing quality university education almost fifty years longer than Canada has been a country, and today is the largest university in Nova Scotia and one of Canada's top research and teaching universities. Dalhousie offers a comprehensive range of more than 3,600 classes in 127 undergraduate, graduate and professional degree programs.

Academic Programs

Dalhousie offers undergraduate degree programs leading to Bachelor of Science, Engineering, Commerce and Arts degrees. Several majors leading to the Bachelor of Science and the Bachelor of Arts degrees can be completed in three years, but most undergraduate degrees require a minimum of four years of study. At the graduate level, Dalhousie offers programs of study leading to over 20 doctoral and masters degrees.

Co-op Program Options

Dalhousie offers a cooperative education program in several departments to allow students to combine academic study with career-related work experience. Co-op programs are currently available in architecture, biochemistry, chemistry, commerce, computer science, earth sciences, economics, engineering, marine biology, mathematics, physics and statistics.

Study/Work Abroad

Dalhousie has more than 50 permanent student exchange programs with countries such as Germany, Sweden, Mexico, and Russia. The Lester Pearson International (LPI) centre is a Dalhousie-based institute that provides information on study and work abroad opportunities and provides financial support for study, work and practicum placements overseas.

DalTech

Dalhousie's recent amalgamation with the Technical University of Nova Scotia (TUNS) has greatly improved the university's ability to explore new applied technologies. TUNS was renamed DalTech and has become a college within the Dalhousie system. DalTech has added the Faculties of Architecture, Engineering and Computer Science to the university's offerings of courses.

Alumni Success

Dalhousie is renowned for the success of its more than 70,000 alumni. They include two Canadian Prime Ministers and 71 Rhodes Scholars (including eight in the last 11 years).

Highlights

- Extensive co-op programs available in many departments
- Advanced technical education and research opportunities through DalTech
- Study & work abroad programs and support

University Statistics

Year Founded: 1818

Academic Options: undergraduate/graduate

Calendar Year: first term (Sept-Dec); second term (Jan-Apr)

DISCIPLINES/MAJORS OFFERED

Faculty of Architecture: Environmental Design Studies

Faculty of Arts & Social Sciences: Canadian Studies, Classics, Comparative Religion, Contemporary Studies & Linguistics, Costume Studies, English, French, German, History, International Development Studies, Music, Philosophy, Political Science, Russian Studies, Sociology & Social Anthropology, Spanish, Theatre, Women's Studies

Faculty of Computer Science: Computer Science

Faculty of Dentistry

Faculty of Engineering: Biological, Chemical, Civil, Electrical & Computer, Industrial, Mechanical, Metallurgical, Mining

Faculty of Graduate Studies

Faculty of the Health Professions: Health Education, Kinesiology, Nursing, Occupational Therapy, Pharmacy, Physiotherapy, Recreation, Social Work

Faculty of Law

Faculty of Management: Accounting, Economics, Finance, International Business, Management, Management Info Systems, Marketing, Public-Sector Management

Faculty of Medicine

Faculty of Science: Biochemistry, Biology, Chemistry, Earth Science, Economics, Marine Biology, Mathematics, Microbiology & Immunology, Neuroscience, Physics, Psychology, Statistics

ADMISSIONS CRITERIA & PROCEDURES

Applications for admission can be obtained from the Registrar's Office or from Dalhousie's web site. Applicants must submit a completed application form, a C$35 application fee and all academic transcripts. American applicants must also submit official SAT scores. Applicants whose first language is not English must submit a TOEFL 580, MELAB 90 or IELTS 7.0; students whose TOEFL score is between 550 and 580 and who meet all the other admission requirements will be admitted to the university conditional on completion of the International Language Institute's (ILI) university preparatory program.

Canadian and American applicants must apply by April 1; international applications must be submitted by June 1. Several programs have separate application deadlines; potential students should contact Dalhousie for further information. Applicants should be aware that the following undergraduate programs require students to have at least one year, or more, of university credit prior to entry: environmental design studies, occupational therapy, pharmacy, physiotherapy and social work.

Canadian applicants except those from Quebec and Ontario must have a minimum of five grade 12 university preparatory classes with an overall minimum average of 70 per cent. Applicants from Quebec must have first year CEGEP with a minimum 70 per cent average with no individual academic below 65 per cent. Applicants from Ontario must have five OAC or grade 13 credits with a minimum 70 per cent average. American applicants must have a strong B average and an SAT 1,100.

Admissions at a Glance

Minimum GPA: 70%

Minimum English Requirements: TOEFL 580, MELAB 90, IELTS 7.0

Application Fee: C$35-50 (Canadian and international)

Application Deadlines: June 1 (Canadian and American applicants); April 1 (international applicants)

ACADEMIC FACILITIES

The Dalhousie library system has a combined collection of over 1.8 million volumes, 500,000 microform items, 100,000 maps and subscriptions to over 10,000 periodicals. The library system includes the Killam Memorial Library for the Humanities, Social Science and the Sciences; the Sir James Dunn Law Library; the Kellogg Health Sciences Library; and the DalTech Library. Dalhousie is also a member of Novanet, a cooperative borrowing network involving eight other college and university libraries in the province.

University Computing & Information Services (UCIS) maintains seven mainframe systems as well as over 35 micro computer labs on the Dalhousie campus, which offer support for several computing platforms including UNIX, PC and Macintosh systems.

Equipment and facilities for on-campus research include several electron microscopes, a nuclear reactor, an aquatron, an arts centre and several language laboratories.

Student & Faculty Profile

Total Enrolment: 13,423

Undergraduate Enrolment: 9,891

# of Faculty: 1,033

Student/Faculty Ratio: 13:1

Male/Female Students: 46%/54%

First-Year Class Sizes: 30-800

Undergraduate Acceptance Rate: 70%

Undergraduate Enrolment by Discipline:

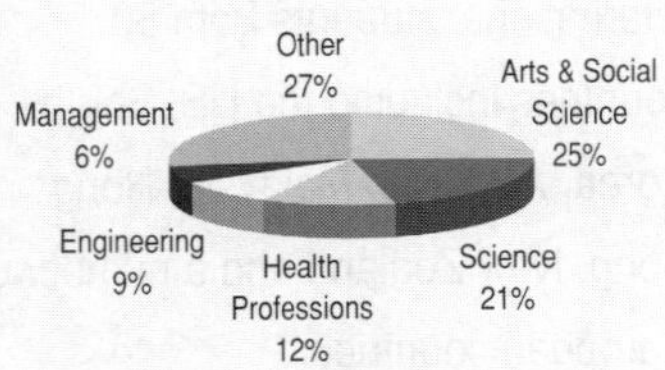

SCHOLARSHIPS & FINANCIAL ASSISTANCE

Students who apply to Dalhousie directly from high school before March 15 are automatically considered for scholarships. Scholarships are based on academic merit and are between C$500 and $6,000.

Students who are already enrolled at Dalhousie can apply to the Registrar's Office for a bursary. Bursaries are usually between C$500 and $1,500 and although they are distributed based on financial need, recipients are usually required to be in satisfactory academic standing.

Expenses at a Glance

Tuition (undergraduate, full-time):
- In-Province: C$3,850/year*
- Out-of-Province: C$3,850/year*
- International: C$6,550/year*

Fees, Books, Materials: C$800/year*

Accommodation:
- Private: C$400-700/month*
- Residence: C$4,900/year*
- Homestay: n/a

Health Insurance: C$355/year*

CAMPUS & LOCATION

City Population:	350,000
Cost of Living:	medium
Climate Range:	-10° to 25°C
Campus Setting:	urban
# of Students in Residence:	1,229

Dalhousie is located in the port city of Halifax, Nova Scotia, the commercial, technological and educational centre of Atlantic Canada. Halifax's population of 350,000 means that it can combine the services of a large city with the low crime rate and relaxed pace of life of a smaller community. Halifax offers a temperate climate with warm summers and crisp winters; students should come prepared with appropriate clothing for all four seasons. Outdoor activities such as hiking, sailing and camping are available year-round.

Residence halls provide on-campus housing for approximately 1,200 students in furnished single and double rooms. All students who live in the residence halls are required to participate in a meal plan; the combined cost is approximately C$4,900 for the academic year. The university also owns a limited number of apartment-style housing units for returning students and students with families. The university's location in a residential area of Halifax ensures that there are a variety of conveniently located houses and apartments available for rent; the Off-Campus Housing Office maintains a listing of affordable and nearby rental accommodations.

ATHLETICS & EXTRACURRICULAR ACTIVITIES

The Dalhousie varsity athletics program is one of the best in Canada, and intercollegiate competition honours are commonplace in the university's recent history. The university sponsors 13 varsity teams in such sports as soccer, basketball, volleyball, swimming, track & field and ice hockey. More than 50 intramural and club sport programs are also available for recreational competition.

The Dalplex centre serves as the focus for on-campus recreation. Dalplex houses an Olympic-sized swimming pool, weight rooms, a golf green, a climbing wall and numerous athletic courts. Dalplex also offers the Fun Zone, a play area for children with a babysitting and daycare service. All full-time students have automatic access to all the Dalhousie recreation facilities.

The chaplaincy at Dalhousie provides facilities for five chaplains representing the Anglican, Baptist, Catholic, Lutheran, and Latter Day Saints traditions, and contact ministers for the campus are designated by the Jewish, Presbyterian, and Orthodox traditions. Chaplains are available through appointments and in the case of emergencies.

University Recognition

- Dalhousie is regularly ranked among the top 10 Canadian universities by Maclean's magazine
- Dalhousie alumni include two Canadian prime ministers and 71 Rhodes Scholars

STUDENT SUPPORT SERVICES

Academic advisers are available to answer questions about any general academic concerns, and students can seek their assistance with issues such as conflicts with faculty, improvement of study skills or difficulties with academic programs.

The Student Employment Centre (SEC) provides students with listings of permanent, part-time and summer employment opportunities. SEC also provides assistance with resume preparation, interview techniques and study- or work-abroad programs.

The International Student Centre (ISC) is concerned with ensuring that the educational experience of international students at Dalhousie is an enjoyable one. ISC provides information and counselling in all areas of concern to international students.

International Students

University Enrolment: 940

% of University Enrolment: 7%

Countries of Origin: Dalhousie attracts international students from 80 countries including the US, South Korea, Australia, Malaysia, Hong Kong, New Zealand and a number of European countries.

MEMORIAL UNIVERSITY OF NEWFOUNDLAND ST. JOHN'S, NEWFOUNDLAND

University Mission

...to remain committed to excellence in teaching, research and scholarship, and service to the general public....to recognize a special obligation to educate the citizens of Newfoundland and Labrador, to undertake research in the challenges this province faces and to share its expertise with the community

Student Voice:

MUN has some of the best facilities and services I've seen. There is help for literally every type of problem you might encounter as a student.

Nadine Hunt
Fourth Year, Business Student

CONTACT INFORMATION
Office of Student Recruitment & Promotion
Memorial University of Newfoundland
St. John's, Newfoundland
Canada A1C 5S7
PH 1-709-737-8896/8640
FAX 1-709-737-8611
EMAIL sturecru@morgan.ucs.mun.ca
INTERNET http://www.mun.ca

UNIVERSITY OVERVIEW

Memorial University of Newfoundland (MUN) was established in 1925 as a tribute to the Newfoundland soldiers who died in World War I. Today, MUN is one of Canada's outstanding academic and research institutions. MUN is dedicated to maintaining small first-year classes, maintaining the best teacher-to-student ratio in the country.

The university offers courses on four campuses: two in Newfoundland, one on the French island of St - Pierre and another in Harlow, England.

Academic Programs

MUN offers a full range of programs in undergraduate and graduate degrees, including diploma, degree and advanced diploma programs at one of the world's foremost centres for ocean studies, the Fisheries & Marine Institute of MUN.

At the undergraduate level, students can earn bachelor's degrees in arts, business administration, commerce, education, engineering, fine arts, maritime studies, music, nursing, science, physical education, recreation, social work and technology. Some programs provide co-op opportunities for students who wish to combine classroom learning with practical experience.

Marine Institute

MUN's island location is a prime setting to offer programs covering all aspects of fisheries and marine technology. Programs range from Canada's only Bachelor of Maritime Studies to specialized diplomas and training.

In addition to providing top-quality education, the Marine Institute conducts research in areas such as seafood harvesting and processing, marine safety and navigation, marine communications and fisheries innovation.

The institute attracts experts and students nationwide and internationally. One of its mandates is to foster economic development in the marine sectors of the Newfoundland economy, enabling Newfoundlanders to continue working in the marine industry.

Sir Wilfred Grenfell College

The west coast city of Corner Brook is home to MUN's Sir Wilfred Grenfell College (Grenfell), which offers degree programs in a variety of disciplines, including two programs in fine arts. Grenfell also offers programs in environmental studies and environmental science; in addition, a forestry program was recently introduced, which has its home in the new Forest Centre.

ESL

MUN offers a 12-week intensive English program that develops academic language skills for students preparing to enrol in full-time university studies. At the end of the program students may write the TOEFL, the results of which may be used when applying for admission to the university.

Highlights

- MUN is the only university in Canada to offer a Bachelor of Maritime Studies
- MUN's programs can be achieved through part-time study
- The Marine Institute, one of the world's best centres for ocean studies, is the primary location for MUN's various marine programs

University Statistics

Year Founded: 1925
Academic Options: undergraduate/graduate
Calendar Year: fall semester (Sept-Dec); winter semester (Jan-May); spring semester (May-Aug)

DISCIPLINES/MAJORS OFFERED

Faculty of Arts: Anthro, Cdn Studies, Classics, Comp Sci, Drama & Music, Econ, English, Fine Arts, Folklore, French, Geog, German, History, Law & Society, Linguistics, Math & Stats, Medieval Studies, Phil, Poli Sci, Psych, Religious Studies, Russian, Sociology, Sociology/Anthropology, Spanish, Theatre, Visual Arts

Faculty of Business Administration: Accounting, Mktg, HR & Labour Relations, Fin, Small Bus/Entrepreneurship, IS, Mgmt Sci

Faculty of Education: Prim, Elem, Intermediate–Secondary, Native & Northern, Music, Special, Vocational

Faculty of Engineering: Civil, Elec, Mech, Ocean & Naval Arch

Faculty of Medicine

Faculty of Science: Behavioural Neurosci, Biochem, Bio, Chem, Comp Sci, Dietetics, Earth Sci, Environmental Sci, Geog, Math & Stats, Pharmacy, Physics and Physical Oceanography, Psych

Marine Institute: Maritime Studies (Marine Eng Tech, Nautical Sci Tech)

School of Continuing Education

School of Graduate Studies

School of Music: General Music Studies, Music History & Lit, Performance, Theory & Composition

School of Nursing

School of Pharmacy: Pharmacy

School of Physical Education: Recreation, Physical Ed

School of Social Work: Social Work

ADMISSIONS CRITERIA & PROCEDURES

All applicants must complete and submit an application form with a nonrefundable application processing fee. The fee is C$40 for first-year Canadian undergraduate students and previous MUN students, and C$80 for international and transfer applicants.

Newfoundland and Labrador applicants must have graduated from a recognized high school and completed one credit in English language 3101, two in thematic literature or literary heritage and two in mathematics and science, with an overall minimum average of 70 per cent.

Applicants from other parts of Canada must have a Grade 12 diploma and have satisfactorily completed a university preparatory program. The university may recognize certain Grade 13/OAC subjects for credit that are equivalent to MUN courses.

Transfer students must submit their high school diploma and official transcripts from all universities or colleges previously attended.

International undergraduate applicants must meet the English language requirement by submitting a minimum language test score of TOEFL 550 or IELTS 6. All academic documents must be submitted to the admissions office, with a notarized English translation if applicable. International applicants may be required to submit a statement outlining sufficient financial resources to cover the cost of an education at MUN.

All students may be required to submit medical proof of their physical fitness.

Admissions at a Glance

Minimum GPA: 70%

Minimum English Requirements:
TOEFL 550 or IELTS 6.0

Application Fee: C$40 (first-year undergraduate or previously attended MUN), $80 (int'l, transfer)

Application Deadlines: March 1 (fall semester); October 1 (winter semester); February 1 (spring semester)

ACADEMIC FACILITIES

The Queen Elizabeth II Library houses 1.2 million books and vast resource materials, including a comprehensive map library and modern print equipment for students with visual disabilities. MUN's on-campus computer network is highly advanced, and provides hundreds of computer terminals for student use throughout the campus.

The science department operates research and educational centres, including MUN's Centre for Earth Resources Research, Ocean Sciences Centre, Botanical Garden and the Laboratory for Genetics, Evolution & Molecular Systematics. These centres are available to undergraduate students who want to work with specialists to broaden their academic experience.

Student & Faculty Profile

Total Enrolment: 15,852

Undergraduate Enrolment: 14,366

# of Faculty: 1,474

Student/Faculty Ratio: 10:1

Male/Female Students: 42%/58%

First-Year Class Sizes: 50 (average)

Undergraduate Acceptance Rate: varies with each program

Undergraduate Enrolment by Discipline:

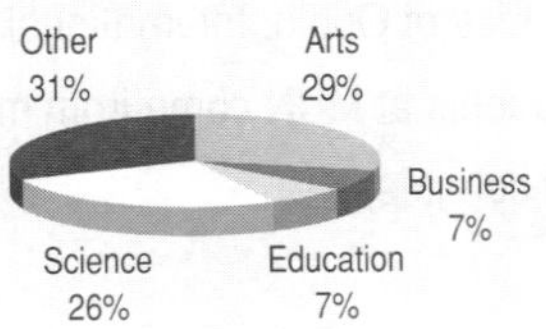

SCHOLARSHIPS & FINANCIAL ASSISTANCE

Students in need of financial aid may apply for MUN's various scholarships, bursaries and awards.

Students with exceptional academic standing may be awarded up to C$25,000 through an Alumni Association scholarship. Scholarship information may be obtained through the Student Aid Division.

Students may also work part-time in a faculty or school through the university-funded, award-winning Memorial Undergraduate Career Experience Program.

Expenses at a Glance

Tuition (undergraduate, full-time):
In-Province: C$3,300/year
Out-of-Province: C$3,300/year
International: C$6,600/year

Fees, Books, Materials: C$500/year

Accommodation:
Private: C$400-700/month
Residence: C$875-1,950/semester
Homestay: n/a

Health Insurance: C$81/year (Canadian); $468/year (international)

CAMPUS & LOCATION

City Population:	175,000
Cost of Living:	medium
Climate Range:	-10° to 24°C
Campus Setting:	urban
# of Students in Residence:	1,500

Memorial University of Newfoundland's main campus is settled on 88 hectares of scenic grounds in St. John's, one of North America's oldest cities and the capital of Newfoundland and Labrador.

Situated on Canada's eastern coast, MUN's St. John's campus offers two housing options: Paton College, a dormitory-style residence that includes a meal plan and a quiet floor; and Burton's Pond, a self-contained apartment for senior students and families located minutes from classes. Students wishing to live off campus may find assistance through the housing office, which keeps a comprehensive list of local accommodation.

The province offers extensive opportunities for both recreational and cultural activities, tracing its roots as far back as the 16th century when the first settlers arrived. This historical background, coupled with the province's unique physical environment, makes it an ideal place to study disciplines such as anthropology, biology and earth sciences. The region's close proximity to the Atlantic Ocean and wild terrain offer a wide variety of recreational activities such as hiking, fishing and sailing.

ATHLETICS & EXTRACURRICULAR ACTIVITIES

Athletes can compete on any of the university's varsity sports teams, many of which have earned a distinguished reputation at the Atlantic University Athletic Association (AUAA) competition in past years. In addition, students can participate in the university's extensive intramural sports programs or any of the other recreational activities offered, such as swimming, aerobics and martial arts.

Athletics facilities include the Strength & Conditioning Centre, which provides cardiovascular exercise and weight-lifting equipment, and the Aquarena, which houses an Olympic-size swimming pool. Plans are underway to build the Memorial University Sports Centre, which will be the largest sports centre in Atlantic Canada.

There are dozens of clubs and societies for students to join, as well as a Student Volunteer Bureau, which provides a variety of volunteer programs, both on and off campus. Students interested in photography, journalism or radio broadcasting can join the student-run newspaper or the student radio station.

University Recognition

- MUN operates an award-winning undergraduate Career Experience Program
- Science graduates have a strong record of employment with government laboratories and industry
- MUN's Faculty of Business Administration was the first Canadian university to establish a commerce co-op curriculum

STUDENT SUPPORT SERVICES

An airport pickup service is available to international students provided they notify the International Student Adviser at least two weeks in advance. A reception service is offered in August and September by the Canadian Bureau of International Education (CBIE), with representatives available daily at various airport locations to help if students encounter any problems. The International Student Centre is responsible for helping new students become familiar with the campus and its services, as well as for providing guidance to students regarding all aspects of their stay in Newfoundland.

Students who need personal advising can receive assistance through MUN's counselling centre. The Learning Enhancement Centre provides courses and activities to help students enhance their ability to learn through various techniques and concepts.

International Students

University Enrolment: 359

% of University Enrolment: 2%

Countries of Origin: International students at MUN come from more than 60 countries.

SAINT MARY'S UNIVERSITY
HALIFAX, NOVA SCOTIA

University Mission

...to achieve excellence in teaching and research; outreach to regional, national and international communities; service to students; public accessibility; and fiscal responsibility

Student Voice:

Over the past two years at Saint Mary's I have had the opportunity to excel in both my academic and athletic pursuits. As an international student, I find Saint Mary's to be a wonderful environment in which I can grow as an individual.

Amanda Wanigatunga, Sri Lanka

CONTACT INFORMATION

Admissions
Saint Mary's University
Halifax, Nova Scotia
Canada B3H 3C3
PH 1-902-420-5415
FAX 1-902-496-8100 (Cdn);
1-902-496-8160 (int'l)
EMAIL admissions@stmarys.ca (Cdn);
admit.international@stmarys.ca (int'l)
INTERNET http://www.stmarys.ca

UNIVERSITY OVERVIEW

Saint Mary's University (Saint Mary's) was founded in 1802 and maintains a reputation as a progressive academic institution dedicated to excellence in teaching and research. Saint Mary's boasts the largest Faculty of Arts in Atlantic Canada, a research-intensive Faculty of Science, and the Frank H. Sobey Faculty of Commerce, the leading business school in Atlantic Canada. The university also offers a number of interdisciplinary and preprofessional programs.

The Saint Mary's campus has a strong international presence, and the university has established exchange programs with schools in Bermuda, China, France, Great Britain, Japan, Mexico, Norway, Quebec and the US.

The Frank H. Sobey Faculty of Commerce

The Frank H. Sobey Faculty of Commerce offers undergraduate and graduate programs in all areas of business, as well as the only Executive Master of Business Administration (EMBA) degree in Atlantic Canada. It is also the only faculty in the region to offer a combined degree in computing science & business administration. The opening of the new Sobey Building marks the beginning of a new era at the university. The facility rivals the best instructional and learning facilities in North America. Saint Mary's will introduce a PhD in management in 1999, making Saint Mary's the only university in Atlantic Canada to offer all levels of business education.

Co-op Programs

The cooperative education option provides undergraduate students with the opportunity to gain practical work experience in an area related to their chosen field, as well as a chance to test the theoretical knowledge gained in the classroom. Co-op work terms encourage personal growth and allow students to evaluate their chosen professions and to make educated career decisions.

Co-op programs are currently offered in the following fields of study: biology, chemistry, computing science & business administration, environmental studies, geology, and small business & entrepreneurship.

Graduate Studies and ESL

Saint Mary's is primarily an undergraduate degree-granting institution; however, it does offer a number of graduate degrees in specialized areas of study. Master's degrees are offered in the following areas: astronomy, Atlantic Canada studies, business administration, criminology, history, international development studies, philosophy and women's studies.

The university offers year-round language, culture and orientation programs for students whose native language is not English.

Highlights

- Founded in 1802, Saint Mary's is one of Canada's oldest universities
- Saint Mary's TESL centre offers English instruction and orientation
- Co-op option available for many programs

University Statistics

Year Founded: 1802
Academic Options: undergraduate/graduate
Calendar Year: Sept-Dec (fall term); Jan-Apr (spring term); May-Aug and Jul-Aug (summer term)

DISCIPLINES/MAJORS OFFERED

Faculty of Arts: Anthropology, Classics, Criminology, Economics, English, Geography, History, Irish Studies, Linguistics, Mathematics, Modern Languages, Philosophy, Political Science, Psychology, Religious Studies and Sociology

Faculty of Commerce & Business Administration: Accounting, Computing & Information Systems, Computing Science & Business Administration, Economics, Finance, General Business Studies, Global Business Management, Human Resource Management & Industrial Relations, Management, Marketing, Small Business & Entrepreneurship

Faculty of Science: Astrophysics, Biology, Chemistry, Computing Science & Business Administration, Computing Science, Engineering, Environmental Studies, Geology, Geology/Commerce, Geology/Geography, Mathematics, Physics, Psychology

Interdisciplinary Studies: Asian Studies, Atlantic Canada Studies, International Development Studies, Women's Studies

Minors and Certificates: Certificate in German Language & Culture, Certificate in Spanish Language & Hispanic Culture, Certificate of Chinese Studies, Certificate of Japanese Studies, Film Studies, Image Studies

Preprofessional Programs: Pre-architecture, Predentistry, Prelaw, Premedicine, Pre-optometry, Pretheology, Pre-veterinary Medicine, Pre-occupational Therapy

ADMISSIONS CRITERIA & PROCEDURES

Candidates for admission must submit completed application forms along with transcripts of high school grades and official copies of university transcripts forwarded directly from the institution attended. An application fee of C$35 must accompany the application package, as well as a C$15 residence application fee for students who wish to live on campus.

Canadian students should have maintained a 65 per cent average in their studies. International students must also have the equivalent of the Nova Scotia high school diploma, or the British or Caribbean General Certificate of Education with passes in at least five subjects, plus two subjects which must be at the advanced level. Students whose first language is not English, and who have not attended an English language secondary school, are required to have English proficiency text scores sent directly from the testing centre. The standard for admission to the university is TOEFL 550 or equivalent.

Admissions at a Glance

Minimum GPA: 65%

Minimum English Requirements:

TOEFL 550 or equivalent

Application Fee: C$35 (Canadian & international)

Application Deadlines: Canadian: July 1 (fall term), Nov 1 (spring term); international: Apr 1 (fall term, Aug 1 (spring term)

ACADEMIC FACILITIES

Saint Mary's recently opened the Sobey Building—a new facility that is one of the best instructional and learning facilities in North America. The computer lab capacity at the university has more than doubled; there is close to C$1 million invested in new computers; classrooms are wired for voice, video and data projectors; rooms are hooked into a sophisticated media delivery system that allows for videoconferencing; and there are Internet connections in every room and meeting space.

In addition to the new Sobey Building, Saint Mary's has over 883,000 holdings in its Patrick Power Library. The library belongs to a consortium of Nova Scotia libraries, enabling students to borrow from province-wide libraries with a combined collection of two million volumes.

The Atlantic Centre has responded to the needs of students with disabilities since the 1960s by providing a wide range of services. Saint Mary's is the first university in North America to offer speech recognition software for students, allowing students with disabilities greater access to the content of university lectures.

Student & Faculty Profile

Total Enrolment: 7,200

Undergraduate Enrolment: 6,800

# of Faculty: 421

Student/Faculty Ratio: 17:1

Male/Female Students: 50%/50%

First-Year Class Sizes: 48 (average)

Undergraduate Acceptance Rate: 75%

Undergraduate Enrolment by Discipline:

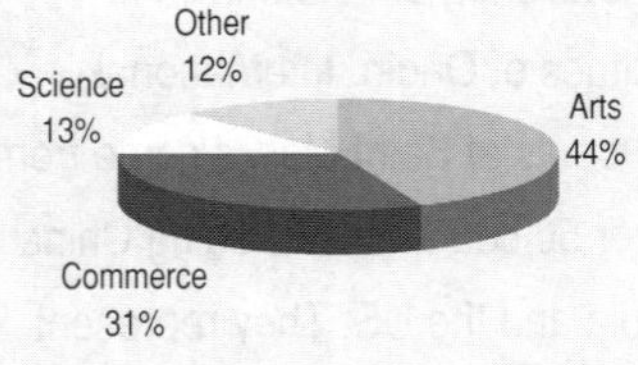

SCHOLARSHIPS & FINANCIAL ASSISTANCE

Scholarships and bursaries totalling C$1.5 million are available each year to students at Saint Mary's. The scholarships and bursaries administered by Saint Mary's are divided into three categories: entrance scholarships administered by the Admissions Office in cooperation with the Senate Scholarship Committee; achievement scholarships; and named scholarships and bursaries administered by the Financial Aid Office in cooperation with the Senate Scholarship Committee.

Canadian students requiring financial assistance to help meet their educational expenses should apply for Canada Student Loans. Application is made in the student's home province.

Expenses at a Glance

Tuition (undergraduate, full-time):

In-Province: C$3,820/year

Out-of-Province: C$3,820/year

International: C$7,130/year

Fees, Books, Materials: C$650/year

Accommodation:

Private: C$400-600/month

Residence: C$4,450-5,350/year

Homestay: n/a

Health Insurance: C$264/year

CAMPUS & LOCATION

The main campus of Saint Mary's University is located on a 12-hectare plot, with many satellite campuses, including a campus in the World Trade & Convention Centre in downtown Halifax. Saint Mary's boasts residence facilities for single or married students, as well as complete student services and the best athletic facilities in Atlantic Canada.

Saint Mary's is a 15-minute walk from downtown Halifax, which offers shopping areas, banks, restaurants and cinemas. The university is surrounded by stately trees in the beautiful South End of the port city.

Founded in 1749, Halifax is a vibrant, cosmopolitan, coastal city with the second largest natural harbour in the world and a rich and varied history. It is home to the famous Citadel Hill and Point Pleasant Park. Halifax is the centre for business, education and research in Atlantic Canada, and offers all the excitement of a big city with a small town atmosphere. Colourful autumns, warm springs and temperate winters make the city enjoyable year-round.

City Population:	342,000 (Halifax Regional Municipality)
Cost of Living:	medium
Climate Range:	-6° to 23°C
Campus Setting:	urban
# of Students in Residence:	1,100

ATHLETICS & EXTRACURRICULAR ACTIVITIES

Saint Mary's prides itself on its student athletes, renowned for their excellence on the field, rink and court. Known as the Huskies, the varsity athletic teams compete in men's soccer, football, ice hockey, track & field and basketball; and in women's ice hockey, field hockey, basketball, soccer, track & field and volleyball.

For students wishing to participate in recreational leagues, Saint Mary's has an extensive intramural sports program. The program offers men's, women's and coed leagues in ice hockey, volleyball, basketball, broomball, softball and soccer. Club sports on campus include rugby, men's baseball, women' baseball, men's volleyball, women's hockey, badminton, self-defense and cross-country running. Professional instruction is also available in aerobics, tennis, squash, racquetball, fencing, dance, martial arts, skating, swimming and weight-training.

All full-time students are automatically members of the university's well-equipped sports, fitness and recreational facility, the Tower. The Tower has four squash and two racquetball courts, a field house, an aerobics room, a weight room, a sauna, a steam room, a hot tub, a pro shop and a Sports Medicine clinic. As well, there is an all-weather track & field facility, the only multipurpose artificial turf in Atlantic Canada, and three tennis courts.

University Recognition

- Maclean's magazine has ranked Saint Mary's in the top five, in the categories of Highest Quality, Leaders of Tomorrow, Best Overall and Most Innovative
- Students and faculty consistently ranked high for qualifications and for success in academic competitions

STUDENT SUPPORT SERVICES

International students have many opportunities to involve themselves in multicultural and Canadian cultural events. In the second semester of the school year, Saint Mary's hosts many international nights, showcasing various cultures, including African, Caribbean, Arab, Indian, Chinese and Southeast Asian.

The International Student Adviser provides support, assistance and advice to international students at Saint Mary's. Information and assistance is provided to students on immigration, job opportunities on campus, health insurance and benefits, cost of living, scholarships & bursaries, and other issues. The newsletter Vistas provides information on matters concerning international students.

The International Centre was created to serve as a resource to the University and the community and as a service for international students.

International Students

University Enrolment: 800

% of University Enrolment: 11%

Countries of Origin: International students at Saint Mary's come from over 50 countries, including China, India and the US. They represent every continent of the world.

St. Francis Xavier University Antigonish, Nova Scotia

University Mission

...to educate global leaders by providing a quality, innovative learning experience in a caring environment

Student Voice:

StFX has provided me with the perfect setting for true learning. In the classroom I have been challenged and met those challenges with the help of all those around me—friends, faculty and staff.

Tim McIntyre
1998 President of the StFX Students' Union

Contact Information
Admissions Office
St. Francis Xavier University
PO Box 5000
Antigonish, Nova Scotia
Canada B2G 2W5
PH 1-902-867-2219
FAX 1-902-867-2329
EMAIL admit@stfx.ca
INTERNET http://www.stfx.ca

UNIVERSITY OVERVIEW

St. Francis Xavier University (StFX) was founded in 1853 to educate the relatively large, but widely dispersed Catholic population in the province of Nova Scotia. In the almost 150 years since its founding, StFX has continually grown to meet the demands of a changing world and now offers more than 30 programs at the undergraduate and graduate levels through its Faculties of Arts and Sciences. The university offers several unique programs in both faculties, including Celtic studies, aquatic resources and jazz studies.

Personalized Education

StFX is committed to maintaining an intimate learning environment that offers comfortable class sizes, easy accessibility to professors and open and continuous dialogue between students and professors. The university strives to develop mature, intelligent individuals who can contribute to society locally, nationally and internationally. The unique WebFX program combines the latest technology with innovative teaching techniques and positions StFX as a leader in the world-connected learning community of the twenty-first century. A wide variety of teaching methods are used at StFX, including small seminars, group projects and simulations. Students graduate from StFX knowing that they have developed the communication and critical-thinking skills necessary to succeed in the modern world.

Global Perspective

Students will find that StFX is an active participant in the new global environment, offering many programs and courses with an international focus.

The Coady International Institute, on the StFX campus, is a world-renowned centre for excellence in education and training for community-based development. The institute provides a forum for the global exchange of information and makes StFX a diverse and exciting place to learn.

In addition, StFX has exchange agreements with 18 colleges universities in the US, as well as with institutions in Mexico, France and England. These agreements allow students the opportunity to spend a semester abroad learning about the global environment firsthand.

Practical Experience

StFX understands how important practical experience is to success in the modern working world. Several programs at StFX have optional co-op programs or incorporate real-world experience through fieldwork, internships, case studies and service learning projects.

Highlights

- Small, intimate learning environment in one of Canada's oldest Catholic universities
- Thirty areas of study to choose from
- International student exchange opportunities available
- Several programs have co-op option

University Statistics

Year Founded: 1853

Academic Options: undergraduate/graduate

Calendar Year: fall term (Sept-Dec); spring term (Jan-Apr)

DISCIPLINES/MAJORS OFFERED

Faculty of Arts: Accounting; Aquatic Resources; Business Administration; Catholic Studies; Celtic Studies; Economics; Education; English; French; History; Human Kinetics; Information Systems; Management (Marketing, Human Resources, Finance); Mathematics, Statistics & Computer Science; Modern Languages; Music; Philosophy; Political Science; Psychology; Religious Studies; Sociology/Anthropology; Women's Studies

Faculty of Science: Aquatic Resources; Biology; Chemistry; Engineering; Geology; Human Kinetics; Human Nutrition; Mathematics, Statistics & Computer Science; Nursing; Physics

ADMISSIONS CRITERIA & PROCEDURES

Students can obtain an application package by contacting the Admissions Office at StFX. Applicants should be aware that admission requirements vary from program to program; potential students should check with the Admissions Office for specific requirements. Normally, students who have completed an appropriate secondary school curriculum with an average of 65 per cent or higher will be considered for admission. Programs with limited enrolment may require a higher average.

International students must hold a GCE, or its equivalent, and have no senior mark below a C standing to be considered for admission to StFX. Those students who are not native speakers of English must also submit a TOEFL score of 550 or higher. International students are required to have adequate medical coverage before registering at StFX; private health insurance plans are available.

A completed application package must include an application form accompanied by official academic transcripts, all other pertinent information and a nonrefundable C$30 application fee. Completed applications should be addressed to the Admissions Officer at StFX. Canadian students must submit completed applications by June 1; the deadline for international applications in April 1. Canadian students applying directly from secondary school wishing to be considered for scholarships must submit their applications by March 1.

Admissions at a Glance

Minimum GPA: 65%

Minimum English Requirements:
TOEFL 550 with TWE 4.0

Application Fee: C$30 (Canadian and international)

Application Deadlines: June 1 (Canadian); April 1 (international)

ACADEMIC FACILITIES

StFX strives to provide students with the highest quality of learning environment possible. Every classroom is equipped with modern technologies designed to facilitate learning. A full range of traditional and multimedia learning aids will maximize every classroom experience. All residence rooms are wired for computer access, telephone and cable television. Each student automatically has access to the system for no additional cost and is given a telephone voice mailbox account.

The Angus L. Macdonald Library, built in 1965, has doubled in size in the last 20 years. The library has an extensive collection and is a member of Novanet, a network of databases combining the resources of nine universities in Nova Scotia. Xavier Hall, a historic site built in the 1880's, is now home to new computer lab. Every student has a WebFX account that provides access to the university's comprehensive computer network and to the Internet. StFX's numerous computer labs provide students with almost unlimited access to the university's computer resources.

Student & Faculty Profile

Total Enrolment: 3,554

Undergraduate Enrolment: 3,210

# of Faculty: 250

Student/Faculty Ratio: 17:1

Male/Female Students: 45%/55%

First-Year Class Sizes: 26-50

Undergraduate Acceptance Rate: 88%

Undergraduate Enrolment by Discipline:

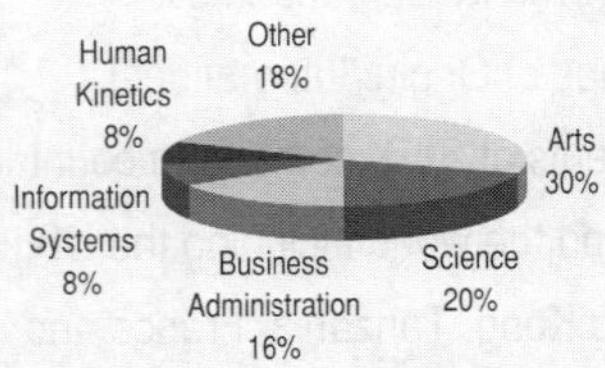

SCHOLARSHIPS & FINANCIAL ASSISTANCE

Students attending StFX have several forms of financial assistance available to them. StFX offers numerous entrance scholarships to Canadian students with high academic standing and demonstrated leadership abilities. These scholarships have a maximum value of C$20,000 to help cover the costs for four years of study. All students are eligible for In-Course and Christmas Scholarships after completion of one semester at StFX. The university also offers a number of need-based bursaries ranging in value of C$100 to $400. Canadian students may also be eligible for federal or provincial loan programs. Applications for bursaries and loan information can be obtained through StFX's Financial Aid Office.

Expenses at a Glance

Tuition (undergraduate, full-time):
In-Province: C$3,956/year
Out-of-Province: C$3,956/year
International: C$6,956/year

Fees, Books, Materials: up to C$1,000/year

Accommodation:
Private: C$550-700/month
Residence: C$600/month
Homestay: may be arranged

Health Insurance: C$650/year

CAMPUS & LOCATION

City Population:	6,000
Cost of Living:	low
Climate Range:	-10° to 25°C
Campus Setting:	rural
# of Students in Residence:	1,400

St. Francis Xavier University's campus is a nostalgic blend of historic and modern buildings in a tranquil, tree-filled setting. With 30 buildings and several playing fields resting on 40 hectares, StFX provides students with a complete learning environment. A building program was implemented in the 1960's to complement the traditional architecture on campus and since that time other projects have included a student union complex and an academic centre.

StFX is one of the main employers of the town of Antigonish, along with the hospital and local resource-based industry. Antigonish is a small town of 6,000 residents that provides a safe, friendly atmosphere for students with many quaint shops and intimate cafes. The local residents are friendly and responsive and the community is very involved in many activities on campus including cultural and spectator sporting events. In addition, there are numerous outdoor recreational opportunities including beaches for swimming, hiking and mountain biking trails and golf courses. Antigonish, located on the Gulf of St. Lawrence in Nova Scotia, derives it name from the Mi'kmaq First Nation's language, and means "where branches are torn off" (by bears looking for beech nuts).

ATHLETICS & EXTRACURRICULAR ACTIVITIES

Students are able to enjoy a rich and diverse social life while studying at StFX. The university has a strong tradition in athletics at the recreational, intramural and varsity level. StFX is a member of the Atlantic Universities Athletic Association and competes in such sports as women's and men's rugby, hockey, basketball and soccer, and men's football. Intramural programs encourage students to stay active and help StFX offer a well-rounded learning environment. There are a number of non-credit instructional programs in a wide variety of areas including aerobics and swimming. Athletic facilities available on campus include multi-purpose gymnasia, a swimming pool, racquet courts, weight rooms and a hockey rink.

StFX boasts a myriad of student clubs and societies, many of which are culturally oriented. A student-run newspaper and radio station keep students informed of current events on campus and beyond. Bauer Theatre is home to StFX's amateur theatre group, Theatre Antigonish. The Department of Music produces several concerts and recitals at the University Auditorium, and the Antigonish Performing Arts Series brings many world-renowned performers to the StFX campus.

University Recognition

- StFX is a member of the Association of Universities & Colleges of Canada (AUCC)
- Association of Atlantic Universities
- Association of Commonwealth Universities
- International Association of Universities

STUDENT SUPPORT SERVICES

StFX strives to provide all the resources and services students may need in making the transition to university life. The Chaplaincy is one of the central elements in StFX's student support services and provides spiritual support and guidance. Students also have the opportunity to meet with professionally trained counsellors throughout the year. Counsellors at StFX are able to address both academic and personal concerns, and provide support services including off-campus referrals. Faculty members are also available to provide academic assistance. The Health Centre provides students with comprehensive care during their time at StFX.

An international student advisor can offer assistance concerning immigration and cultural issues for students from abroad.

International Students

University Enrolment: 110

% of University Enrolment: 3%

Countries of Origin: International students at StFX come from countries around the world including the US, Hong Kong, Tanzania, France and India.

UNB UNIVERSITY OF NEW BRUNSWICK FREDERICTON, NEW BRUNSWICK

University Mission

...to be known for its excellence in teaching by providing students with the highest possible quality instruction, library and laboratory resources...and an environment conducive to the development of the whole person

Student Voice:

Friendly peers, supportive faculty members and small classes have created a family-like environment that has assisted me academically and athletically.

Chris Zanutto

CONTACT INFORMATION
Registrar's Office
University of New Brunswick
Fredericton Campus
PO Box 4400
Fredericton, New Brunswick
Canada E3B 5A3
PH 1-506-453-4865
FAX 1-506-453-5016
EMAIL UNBFACTS@unb.ca
INTERNET http://www.unb.ca

UNIVERSITY OVERVIEW

Established in 1785 as an academy and once known as the College of New Brunswick, the University of New Brunswick (UNB) provides undergraduate and graduate degree programs on campuses in both Fredericton and Saint John. UNB has a proud history as a leader in Canadian education; Canada's first engineering courses were offered by UNB in 1854. Today, students can choose from over 75 innovative programs in 10 faculties.

UNB's degree programs are integrative and progressive, allowing students to combine programs and majors into highly individualized curricula. The Faculty of Science exemplifies this approach, allowing students to choose from 11 interdepartmental programs involving specialization in two subject areas.

Undergraduate, Graduate and Special Programs

UNB offers programs leading to bachelor's degrees in arts, business administration, computer science, education, kinesiology, medical laboratory science, nursing, office management, recreation & leisure studies and science. A co-op education option is available in many of UNB's degree programs.

In addition to the undergraduate degree programs, UNB offers a variety of graduate degrees at both the PhD and master's levels. UNB also offers certificates and special programs in subjects ranging from critical care nursing to hydrographic surveying, as well as a number of programs in cooperation with the government, business and industry.

The Leonardo Degree

Following the example of the Renaissance master Leonardo da Vinci, UNB offers students a chance to study both arts and science at the undergraduate level. By studying arts and sciences for four years, students can earn a Bachelor of Arts and Science degree (BASc). Students can also continue studying for another year and earn both a BA and a BSc degree, with a major in each degree.

Research at UNB

UNB is a major centre of research for the Atlantic provinces, hosting the Biomedical Engineering Centre, the Centre for Conflict Studies, the Centre for Nuclear Energy and the Centre for Research in Engineering & Applied Science.

Non-Degree Options

UNB's English Language Program offers total immersion in English, and is a popular program internationally. UNB also offers exchange programs with universities in Sweden, Germany, France and the US. The faculty offers students a one-year international placement opportunity at the European Business Management School at the University of Swansea in Wales.

Highlights

- Over 75 academic programs in 10 faculties
- Co-op education opportunities are available in many degree programs
- Leonardo Degree allows student to earn BA and BSc degrees concurrently

University Statistics

Year Founded: 1785
Academic Options: undergraduate/graduate
Calendar Year: fall semester (Sept-Dec); winter semester (Jan- Apr)

DISCIPLINES/MAJORS OFFERED

Faculty of Administration: Accounting, Finance, Industrial Relations/Human Resources Management, International Business, Operations Management, Marketing

Faculty of Arts: Anthropology, Classics & Ancient History, Economics, English, French, German & Russian, History, Philosophy, Political Science, Psychology, Sociology, Spanish

Faculty of Computer Science: Hardware Systems, Information Systems, Multimedia Systems, Numerical & Statistical Computation, Software Systems, Theory of Computing

Faculty of Education: Education

Faculty of Engineering: Chemical, Civil, Computer, Electrical, Geological, Mechanical, Surveying

Faculty of Forestry/Environment: Forestry, Forestry Engineering

Faculty of Kinesiology: Kinesiology (BA, BSc), Recreation & Leisure Studies

Faculty of Law

Faculty of Nursing: Nursing

Faculty of Science: Applied Chemistry, Applied Physics, Biology, Co-op Biology, Chemistry, Co-op Chemistry, Environmental Geochemistry, Geology, Mathematics, Physics

ADMISSIONS CRITERIA & PROCEDURES

Students can apply via the UNB internet site or submit application forms by mail. Students should submit official copies of their high school transcripts, and any post-secondary transcripts, with their application in order to avoid any delay in the admissions consideration. UNB allows students to apply throughout the year; however, students applying for the fall term are given priority if they have submitted their application form and transcripts by March 30. The deadline for scholarship applications is February 15; students are not required to submit a scholarship application to be considered for the UNB Scholarship Guarantee program.

Admission requirements at UNB vary according to a student's country of origin and their intended program of study. Students whose first language is not English are normally required to present a TOEFL score of 550 or higher, an IELTS score of 6.5 or higher, or equivalent.

International students may be accepted into UNB's co-op programs.

Admissions at a Glance

Minimum GPA: varies

Minimum English Requirements:
TOEFL 550 (paper-based), 213 (computer-based) or higher; MELAB 85 or higher; IELTS 6.5 or higher

Application Fee: C$25 (Canadian and international)

Application Deadlines: rolling applications; February 15 (scholarship deadline); March 30 (priority deadline)

ACADEMIC FACILITIES

Upon enrolment, all UNB students are assigned a computer access code enabling them to log onto the university's computer systems. Computer resources available on the UNB system include email, electronic networking for professors and students, Internet access, and UNB's online course registration, course time table and grade information services. UNB offers its students over 700 computer terminals and 30 networked labs, and many courses are available over the internet. Students can also connect their own computers to Resnet, the residence network.

Student & Faculty Profile

Total Enrolment: 9180

Undergraduate Enrolment: 8,100

# of Faculty: 600

Student/Faculty Ratio: 15:1

Male/Female Students: 50%/50%

First-Year Class Sizes: 65 (average)

Undergraduate Acceptance Rate: 80%

Undergraduate Enrolment by Discipline:

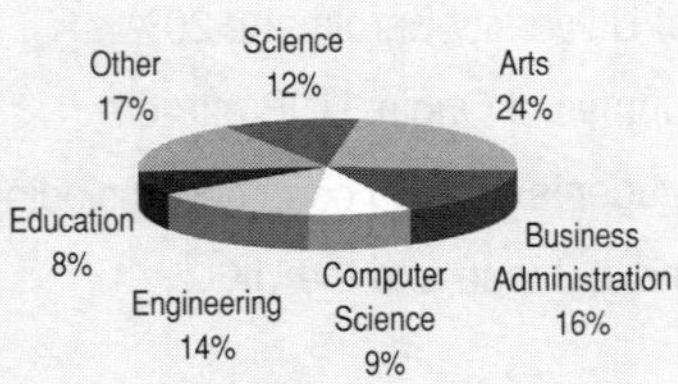

SCHOLARSHIPS & FINANCIAL ASSISTANCE

The UNB Scholarship Guarantee program provides scholarships to new first-year students. Students with an entering average of 90 per cent or higher (as determined by the Registrar's Office) receive C$1,000; students with averages between 85-89% receive C$500.

Government student loans and bursaries are available to students requiring financial assistance. UNB offers a significant number of scholarships, over and above the entrance scholarships. New students should complete the Scholarship Ap plication form, which accompanies the application package. Entering students are typically notified in May if they have received a scholarship.

Expenses at a Glance

Tuition (undergraduate, full-time):
In-Province: C$3,290/year*
Out-of-Province: C$3,290/year*
International: C$5,590/year*

Fees, Books, Materials: C$800/year*

Accommodation:
Private: C$500-$600/month*
Residence: C$4,450-4590/year*
Homestay: n/a

Health Insurance: C$275/year*

CAMPUS & LOCATION

City Population:	65,000 (Fredericton)
Cost of Living:	medium
Climate Range:	-30° to 30°C
Campus Setting:	urban
# of Students in Residence:	1,500

UNB is situated on campuses in Fredericton and Saint John, the governmental and commercial capitals of New Brunswick respectively. These two campuses allow students flexibility in their place and field of study, as well as the advantage of having the facilities of two full campuses within driving distance. Admissions, academic standards, degree programs and financial aid are fully coordinated between both campuses. Fredericton's campus is larger and offers a larger course selection, while the Saint John campus offers a more intimate learning atmosphere. In a few areas, subjects started in Saint John are completed in Fredericton.

Both Fredericton and Saint John are situated on the Saint John River. Overlooking the historic provincial capital of New Brunswick, the Fredericton campus offers a peaceful, natural haven for study with several parks within walking distance of the campus. A professional theatre company, a major art gallery, a lively farmers market and many historic sites are among the city's attractions. Saint John offers UNB students a more urban centre for learning with the amenities to match; Saint John is the largest centre for business and industry in the area. Both cities offer exciting nearby travel destinations with picturesque drives, beaches, skiing and recreational fishing in the immediate area.

New Brunswick is an ideal location for students wishing to explore the east coast of Canada and the United States. Historic and scenic sites like the Annapolis Valley and the Cabot Trail are close-by holiday destinations.

ATHLETICS & EXTRACURRICULAR ACTIVITIES

Campus Recreation and the UNB Varsity Reds Athletics program provide students with a wide variety of opportunities to participate in recreational and varsity athletics at UNB. Campus Recreation offers a number of fitness and intramural sports programs using the university's pool, gymnasia, climbing wall, sports fields, hockey rinks and the various recreational facilities available in Fredericton. The Varsity Reds Athletics men's and women's teams compete regionally and nationally.

Clubs and organizations available on campus span almost every possible interest from political science to scuba diving. The cultural facilities available to UNB students include an art centre that hosts several exhibits each year and a music centre that offers regular concerts and music programs.

STUDENT SUPPORT SERVICES

UNB strives to be accessible to all. Support services are provided under the direction of the Dean of Student Affairs & Services. Key services include academic and personal counseling services, services for students with disabilities, an international student advisor and health services. The International Student Advisor's Office provides assistance with the homestay program, international student societies and cultural events, campus orientation and counselling.

International students are welcomed at UNB through the many international societies sponsored by the International Student Advisor's Office. These organizations encourage all students to participate; the success of these organizations is evident in the many international festivals and events hosted and supported by the campus community.

University Recognition

- Faculty members have received national and international distinctions in teaching and research

International Students

University Enrolment: 400

% of University Enrolment: 20%

Countries of Origin: UNB attracts students from 55 countries, including India, Japan and the UK.

UNIVERSITY OF PRINCE EDWARD ISLAND CHARLOTTETOWN, PRINCE EDWARD ISLAND

University Mission

...to encourage and assist people to acquire the skills, knowledge and understanding necessary for critical and creative thinking

Student Voice:

I've seen into the heart of the campus and I like what I've seen. I've found that UPEI students, like Prince Edward Islanders, are intensely passionate when it comes to something they believe in. I am very proud to be a graduate of the University of Prince Edward Island.

Timothy Willis
Class of 1998 Valedictorian

CONTACT INFORMATION
University of Prince Edward Island
550 University Avenue
Charlottetown, Prince Edward Island
Canada C1A 4P3
PH 1-902-566-0674 or
1-800-606-UPEI (toll-free)
FAX 1-902-628-4319
EMAIL liaison@upei.ca
INTERNET http://www.upei.ca

UNIVERSITY OVERVIEW

The University of Prince Edward Island (UPEI) is a small, primarily undergraduate university serving the academic postsecondary needs of Prince Edward Island and beyond. UPEI is a public, non-denominational university with a 150 year heritage that extends back to predecessor institutions that have included the Central Academy, Prince of Wales College, Saint Andrew's College and Saint Dunstan's University. As the province's only university, it serves an important role in the cultural, economic and social fabric of the island.

Choices at UPEI

The university offers bachelor's degrees in arts, science, nursing, business administration, education and music. Honours programs are available within several undergraduate degree programs and offer advanced students a more challenging academic environment. Students may also continue their studies at UPEI at the graduate level.

UPEI offers students the chance to complete their preprofessional years of education in the fields of agriculture, architecture, dentistry, law, medicine, occupational therapy, physiotherapy, social work and veterinary medicine. Students studying veterinary medicine may continue their studies at UPEI's Atlantic Veterinary College, which offers DVM, MSc and PhD programs.

A Teaching-Based University

Although the university has an active research community and hosts several research institutes, UPEI is committed to providing its students with an educational experience characterized by its excellence in teaching. This commitment to teaching is best reflected in the university's very low student-to-teacher ratio of 12 to 1 and the intimate learning environment cultivated in the small classes typical of UPEI's programs. UPEI ensures that all students have access to their teachers.

Other Points of Interest

The L.M. Montgomery Institute at UPEI, affiliated with the Faculty of Arts, has been established to celebrate and research the work, life, home and influence of Lucy Maud Montgomery, the Prince Edward Island based writer of the famous Anne of Green Gables novels. The L.M. Montgomery Institute also operates an ESL school during the summer that offers both English language training and an introduction to Canadian culture.

The Information Technology in Education Centre (ITEC) is located in the Robertson Library and offers students modern telelearning classrooms that facilitate computer and technology training and education; a wide variety of information resources and noncredit courses are also available. The centre also hosts several alternative-learning workshops.

Highlights

- Very low student-to-faculty ratio and small class sizes ensure a personalized education
- Computer network access in all residence rooms
- Comfortable and affordable setting with well-equipped facilities

University Statistics

Year Founded: 1969

Academic Options: certificate/diploma/undergraduate/graduate

Calendar Year: semester 1 (Sept-Dec); semester 2 (Jan-Apr)

DISCIPLINES/MAJORS OFFERED

Faculty of Arts: Anthropology, Canadian Studies, Economics, English, French, German, History, Music (BA, BMus), Political Studies, Psychology, Religious Studies, Sociology, Sociology/Anthropology, Spanish

School of Business Administration: Business Administration (internship option), Business in Tourism & Hospitality

Faculty of Education

School of Nursing

Faculty of Science: Biology, Chemistry, Computer Science, Family & Nutritional Sciences, Mathematics, Mathematics with Engineering, Physics, Psychology

Faculty of Veterinary Medicine

Preprofessional Programs: Agriculture, Architecture, Dentistry, Law, Medicine, Occupational Therapy, Physiotherapy, Social Work, Veterinary Medicine

Diploma Programs: Adult Education, Engineering (3 years), Inclusive Education, Public Administration, School Librarianship

ADMISSIONS CRITERIA & PROCEDURES

Requirements for admission to UPEI are successful completion of a Canadian senior secondary program in an acceptable university preparatory curriculum, or equivalent; an overall average of 65 per cent (75 per cent for Quebec Secondary V students) is required in the following subjects:

- for BA, BBA programs: English, math and three acceptable academic electives
- for BSc programs: English, math, two sciences (if grade 12 chemistry is not selected, successful completion of grade 11 chemistry is required) and one acceptable academic elective

The prerequisite requirements may vary by program and there are special requirements for nursing, education and veterinary medicine programs; students should contact their intended faculty for further information.

American students are evaluated by secondary school marks and class standing.

Other international students must meet standards equivalent to those required of Canadian students. Students whose first language is not English are required to submit a TOEFL score or its equivalent; a minimum TOEFL score of 550 is acceptable for most programs.

UPEI encourages prospective students who are interested in the university to visit the campus. The UPEI staff will provide a tour of the campus and its facilities and introduce prospective students to current students and faculty members. Prospective students can spend a night in student residence, taste the food and attend a few classes.

Health insurance through UPEI is mandatory; however, students will be refunded if already covered.

Admissions at a Glance

Minimum GPA: 65%; 75% for Quebec Secondary V

Minimum English Requirements: TOEFL 550 or equivalent

Application Fee: C$35 (Cdn & int'l)

Application Deadlines: August 17 (semester 1); December 4 (semester 2); may vary by program

ACADEMIC FACILITIES

Among the facilities available to UPEI students are the Robertson Library, the KC Irving Chemistry Centre, the newly renovated Cass Science Hall, the Information Technology in Education Centre and the Atlantic Veterinary College and Teaching Hospital.

The Robertson Library, is open 84 hours per week to allow students access to its more than 300,000 books, 1,500 current periodicals, 75,000 bound periodicals and journals, and its extensive collection of audiovisual materials, which includes more than 133,000 microforms, films, cassettes, videos and slides. A number of online databases are available to UPEI students over the Campus-Wide-Information-System and several specialized CD-ROM based databases are available on campus.

The Faculty of Science offers students advanced lab and research facilities with modern research tools and equipment.

Student & Faculty Profile

Total Enrolment: 2,439 (full-time)

Undergraduate Enrolment: 2,400

# of Faculty: 200

Student/Faculty Ratio: 12:1

Male/Female Students: 38%/62%

First-Year Class Sizes: 22

Undergraduate Acceptance Rate: 60%

Undergraduate Enrolment by Discipline:

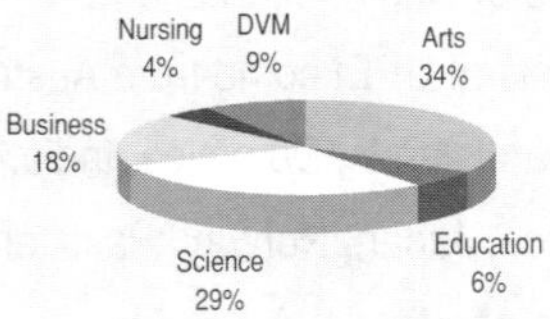

SCHOLARSHIPS & FINANCIAL ASSISTANCE

UPEI offers financial aid to eligible students through approximately 150 scholarships ranging from C$1,000 to $3,500 in value. In addition to its scholarships, UPEI offers bursaries of up to C$500 in value, which are distributed based on academic performance or financial need. UPEI also works in conjunction with the Canada Student Loan Program to ensure that its academic programs are accessible to all students.

Students may also seek part-time employment at UPEI as a means of financing their education; UPEI employs upwards of 400 students per year. There are also many part-time employment opportunities in the surrounding area.

Expenses at a Glance

Tuition (undergraduate, full-time):

- In-Province: C$3,310/year
- Out-of-Province: C$3,310/year
- International: C$6,710/year

Fees, Books, Materials: C$1,500/semester (varies by program)

Accommodation:

- Private: C$450-550/month
- Residence: C$2,421-2,882/semester
- Homestay: n/a

Health Insurance: C$138-276/yr (Cdn), $633-1,687 (int'l)

CAMPUS & LOCATION

City Population:	31,400
Cost of Living:	medium
Climate Range:	-20° to 28°C
Campus Setting:	urban
# of Students in Residence:	375

UPEI's campus rests on 50 hectares of land in the city of Charlottetown, the capital of Prince Edward Island. The campus is home to both century-old buildings and modern facilities. Recent additions to the campus include the K.C. Irving Chemistry Centre, the Wanda Wyatt Dining Hall and the Young Canada Games Sports Centre, which is equipped with weight & cardio training rooms, an indoor track, a triple gymnasium, an aerobics area and squash & racquetball courts. Among the technological features of the campus are network connections in all of the residence rooms that allow students to access the Campus-Wide-Information-System as well as the Internet.

Prince Edward Island is an attractive province with much to offer in natural recreational opportunities and cultural events. The island offers UPEI students sight-seeing, skiing, fishing, windsurfing, sea kayaking, golfing and snowboarding opportunities and much more. Students will enjoy the kilometres of sandy beaches, and the comfortable and relaxed pace of life on the island. Prince Edward Island was made famous through Anne of Green Gables and other works by Lucy Maud Montgomery. The novels inspire thousands of people to visit the island every year. Prince Edward Island is now linked to the mainland of Canada by the Confederation Bridge, one of the country's most ambitious civic works of the decade and a symbol of Prince Edward Island's important role in the history of the nation. UPEI is only 300 kilometres from Fredericton, New Brunswick and Halifax, Nova Scotia.

ATHLETICS & EXTRACURRICULAR ACTIVITIES

All full-time students are members of the UPEI Student Union which operates a newspaper and organizes many social functions at the Student Union Building. The student body at UPEI coordinates many cultural, religious, political and community organizations, including a theatre society, debating team, jazz band, a student newspaper and chorus. International students will appreciate the International Students Association, which arranges cultural and social functions and field trips, and allows international students to meet each other, share experiences and experience more of their host country.

The Young Canada Games Sports Centre offers popular fitness classes, recreation programs, sports equipment and intramural leagues. UPEI's Panthers athletics teams compete in varsity sports within both the AUAA and CIAU leagues. Women's teams include soccer, field hockey, basketball and volleyball; men's teams compete in soccer, basketball and hockey.

An extensive intramural program is available to both men and women, and includes rugby, hockey, squash, broomball, touch football, softball, basketball, volleyball, badminton and golf, among others.

University Recognition

- Member of the AUCC, the International Association of Universities and the Association of Atlantic Universities
- Ranked high in the Maritime Provinces Higher Education Commission Survey of Class of 1996 graduates for class size, access to faculty, quality of teaching, employment of graduates and graduate satisfaction with the investment of time and money in obtaining a degree

STUDENT SUPPORT SERVICES

UPEI offers advising services to all first-year students. During a student's time at UPEI student counsellors and career advisers are always available to lend assistance regarding personal, academic or career concerns or planning. There is also a peer tutoring service for students needing advice on academic issues.

The Student Development Office is able to handle international students' concerns and offers orientation and information regarding immigration, cultural and academic matters.

For students with children, UPEI has a daycare centre. Other services offered include chaplaincy services, mature and part-time student services, and a health centre.

International Students

University Enrolment: 81 (full-time)

% of University Enrolment: 3%

Countries of Origin: International students at UPEI come from Australia, Cayman Islands, Dominica, India, Jamaica, Japan, Norway, Pakistan, Russia and the USA.

Colleges

IN

The Atlantic Provinces

College of the North Atlantic Newfoundland & Labrador

College Mission

to develop and operate all facets of nonuniversity, postsecondary, vocational and continuing education programs in the province of Newfoundland and Labrador

Student Voice:

I chose the College because it was a recognized college…the class sizes were smaller, and you got to know your peers and your instructors.

Laura Lee Hayes

CONTACT INFORMATION
College of the North Atlantic
PO Box 5400
432 Massachusetts Drive
Stephenville, Newfoundland & Labrador
Canada A2N 2Z6
PH 1-888-982-2268 (toll free) or 1-709-758-7282
FAX 1-709-758-7302
EMAIL info@northatlantic.nf.ca
INTERNET http://www.northatlantic.nf.ca

COLLEGE OVERVIEW

The College of the North Atlantic, officially amalgamated in 1997, is Newfoundland and Labrador's public college. It is one of the largest postsecondary educational and skills training centres in Atlantic Canada, offering over 70 full-time programs and more than 300 part-time courses. The college operates 18 campuses throughout the province, many of which have long histories in providing postsecondary education and training.

The college produces about 3,000 graduates a year from career-oriented certificate and diploma programs that range in length from one to three years. A range of programs are offered in the areas of applied arts, business, health sciences, industrial education/trades, natural resources, information technology and ESL.

Cooperative Education

The college offers cooperative education through a partnership with industry and business. Co-op placements are 15-week semesters that enable students to integrate academics with paid, full-time employment. Every year, approximately 300 College of the North Atlantic students complete work terms. A limited number of co-op placements may be available to international students, giving them exposure to a Canadian work environment. Some of the courses have mandatory co-op elements.

University Transfer

The College of the North Atlantic has formal agreements in place with several universities in Canada and the United States. These agreements permit a relatively seamless transfer from college diploma to university degree program. Currently there are agreements in place for graduates of engineering technology, community studies, health sciences and visual arts. Graduates of business administration and office administration programs can receive advanced standing.

English as a Second Language

The English as a Second Language (ESL) program at North Atlantic includes full-time courses from beginner to advanced levels, as well as short immersion programs incorporating travel and extracurricular activities, TOEFL preparation and English for specific purposes. All ESL admissions are conducted through the college's Prince Philip Drive Campus, located in St. John's.

Highlights

- 18 campuses throughout the province of Newfoundland and Labrador
- Large selection of programs ranging from one to three years in duration
- Cooperative education program offered for some programs

College Statistics

Year Founded: 1997 (amalgamation of five public colleges)

Academic Options: certificate/diploma

Calendar Year: fall term (Sep-Dec); winter term (Jan-Apr); intersession (May-Jun); summer term (May-Aug)

ACADEMIC PROGRAMS

Academic/Access Programs: Adult Basic Education (ABE), College University Prep Program (CUPP)

Applied Arts: 2-Yr Diploma: Community Rec Leadership, Community Studies, Digital Animation, Early Childhood Educ, Food Service & Nutr Mgmt, Graphic Arts, Journalism, Multimedia Comm, Multimedia Prod, Music Industry & Perf, Sound Tech, Textile Studies, Travel Counsellor, Visual Arts

Business Studies: 3-Yr Diploma: Bus Mgmt; 2-Yr Diploma: Bus Admin, Office Admin; Adv Diploma: Continuous Quality Improvement Specialist

Health Sciences: 3-Yr Diploma: Med Lab Sci, Med Radiography, Resp Therapy; 1-Yr Cert: Diagnostic Ultrasonography, Occupat'l Therapists Ass'ts, Physiotherapists Ass'ts

Industrial Education/Trades: The college offers almost 30 apprenticeship programs.

Natural Resources: 3-Yr Diploma: Env Tech; 2-Yr Diploma: Adventure Tourism, Fish & Wildlife Tech'n, Forest Res Tech'n, Mineral Tech'n, Natural Res Techn'n

Engineering Technology: 3-Yr Diploma: Aircraft Maintenance Eng, Arch Eng, Auto Tech, Civil Eng Tech, Elec Eng, Electronics Eng, Geomatics Eng, Industrial Eng, Mech Eng, Petroleum Eng, Pulp & Paper Eng Tech; 2-Yr Diploma: Auto Tech'n, Civil Eng Tech'n, Mining Eng Tech'n, Welding Eng Tech'n; 1-Yr Postdiploma: Safety Eng

Information Technology: 3-Yr Diploma: Comp Interface Design & Prog, Prog Analyst (Bus), Prog Analyst (Networking); 2-Yr Diploma: Microcomp Support Specialist, Microcomp Support Tech'n, Prog Analyst (Business) Grad Enhancement, Prog Analyst (Networking or Scientific); co-op programs

ADMISSIONS CRITERIA & PROCEDURES

All Canadian applicants must have achieved high school graduation or its equivalent, or meet the college's mature student policy.

International students applying to study at the College of the North Atlantic must provide proof of their academic standing equivalent to the Newfoundland and Labrador high school diploma. Applicants who completed their secondary studies in an educational system modelled after the British system should present their General Certificate in Secondary Education.

Both Canadian and international students may be required to have completed specific program prerequisite courses prior to entering certain programs. Mathematics, English, physics, chemistry and biology are examples of courses frequently required for entry to academic programs. Both Canadian and international students may receive advanced standing for up to 75 per cent of the content of their program of study. Transcripts are assessed on an individual basis.

For international students who are not native speakers of English and who are seeking direct admission to a program, a TOEFL score of 550, or its equivalent, is required. Applicants to the college's ESL program are not required to submit TOEFL scores.

Students must pay an C$85 confirmation fee upon acceptance.

Admissions at a Glance

Minimum GPA: 2.0

Minimum English Requirements: 550 (direct admission)

Application Fee: C$30 (Canadian and international)

Application Deadlines: first-come, first-served basis

ACADEMIC FACILITIES

Serving the province through 18 campuses, the college has a wide variety of facilities and a large range of equipment available for student use. Along with resource and academic libraries, the college operates a Manufacturing Technology Centre, two Early Childhood Education Day Care training centres, an Engineering Technology Training Centre, a Canadian Welding Test Centre, a college-based General Motors training centre, and several other advanced facilities. The college is also the site of the only full-size drilling rig used for training purposes in Atlantic Canada, as well as the only Series 5 Full Size Well Control Simulator by Digitran.

Student & Faculty Profile

Total Enrolment: 12,000

Full-Time Enrolment: 6,500

# of Faculty: 1,100

Student/Faculty Ratio: 10:1

Male/Female Students: 57%/43%

Academic Class Sizes: varies

Enrolment by Program Type:

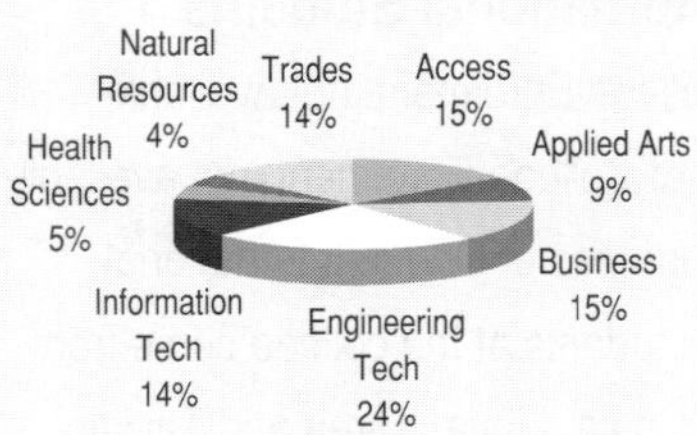

SCHOLARSHIPS & FINANCIAL ASSISTANCE

The college offers opportunities to students in many programs to compete for a variety of scholarships, bursaries, prizes and awards. Deadlines for receipt of application for bursaries and awards can be obtained through the registrar's office; although the most common deadline is October 15, students are advised to enquire well ahead of time to ensure that they do not miss deadlines for awards for which they may be eligible. To be eligible for an award, students must be registered as full-time students. Award applicants should have a GPA of at least 2.5 to be competitive.

Students should contact the Student Aid Office for assistance with financial support, including Canada Student Loans. Generally, only Canadian students are eligible for government-funded loans and scholarships.

Expenses at a Glance

Tuition (full-time):

- In-Province: C$726/semester
- Out-of-Province: C$726/semester
- International: C$3,300/semester

Fees, Books, Materials: varies

Accommodation:

- Private: C$85-100/week
- Residence: C$25-130/week
- Homestay: C$85-100/week

Health Insurance: C$500-600/year

CAMPUS & LOCATION

City Population:	172,000 (St. John's)
Cost of Living:	low
Climate Range:	-7° to 25°C
Campus Setting:	varies
# of Students in Residence:	313 (capacity)

The College of the North Atlantic offers programs and services through its 18 campus locations: Labrador City-Wabush, Happy Valley-Goose Bay, Port aux Basques, Stephenville, Corner Brook, St. Anthony, Baie Verte, Grand Falls-Windsor, Gander, Bonavista, Clarenville, Burin, Placentia, Carbonear, Seal Cove, and three campuses in St. John's at Prince Philip Drive, Ridge Road and Topsail Road.

St. John's, which is located on the southeast part of the island, is the historic commercial centre and capital of the province. It is also the province's largest city, with a population of 172,000. Students have access to a full range of resources, services and activities in the area. The other 14 campuses are dispersed throughout the province.

Recreation enthusiasts love Newfoundland and Labrador as it is a haven of activity. With its warm summers and moderate winters, outdoor activities are plentiful: golfing, downhill skiing, fishing, whale and bird watching, sports and entertainment events, hiking, or simply observing the majestic icebergs surrounding the shores in late spring or the amazing beauty of the autumnal colours. For students who prefer the indoors, the urban centres offer theatre companies, the symphony, modern and classical dance, art galleries, music festivals and an exciting nightlife.

Students travelling to the province have the option of arriving by ferry or plane. The province is served by two international airports—St. John's and Gander. St. John's has regular flights from Heathrow, London, England, making it very accessible for international students. Regional airlines also serve the province through airports located at Happy Valley-Goose Bay, Gander, Deer Lake, St. Anthony, Stephenville and Wabush.

ATHLETICS & EXTRACURRICULAR ACTIVITIES

The college's Student Activities Council organizes various activities for students throughout the year in sports, recreation, cultural and social events. Students are encouraged to participate in a variety of extracurricular activities in order to ensure that they receive a well-rounded education.

College Recognition

- Member of the Association of Canadian Community Colleges, the Canadian Bureau of International Education and World University Services Canada
- Programs are recognized by the province of Newfoundland and Labrador and by the Government of Canada
- Many of the college's programs are recognized by agencies that set national standards for accreditation (e.g., Canadian Technologist Accreditation Board)

STUDENT SUPPORT SERVICES

The college's Student Services offices provide a wide range of services. Academic and career counselling are provided by professional guidance counsellors, and student tutoring is available from the faculty. The staff are also experienced in providing support to international students. The services provided include reception upon arrival, an orientation, assistance with immigration, liaison services, general advising and counselling, language testing and aptitude testing.

In addition to coordinating the on-campus housing provided on the Burin, Happy Valley-Goose Bay and Stephenville campuses, the Student Services offices maintain a current listing of apartments and other housing options available near each campus and are available to help students find local accommodation.

International students are encouraged to take part in the college's homestay program, in order to support the development of their English language skills and to learn more about Canadian culture and lifestyles.

International Students

College Enrolment: not available

% of College Enrolment: not available

Countries of Origin: International students at the college come from China, Libya, Korea and Taiwan.

NEW BRUNSWICK COMMUNITY COLLEGE
NEW BRUNSWICK

NBCC

College Mission

...to promote personal development and self-sufficiency among New Brunswickers by offering high-quality training programs

Student Voice:

The level of training we've received at the NBCC has been outstanding! For those of us who gained co-op work experience and participated in important projects, these are experiences which will help us in the future.

Sherry Secord
Industrial Control Technology
NBCC Saint John

CONTACT INFORMATION

Admissions Services
New Brunswick Community College
6 Arran Street
Campbellton, New Brunswick
Canada E3N 1K4
PH 1-800-376-5353
FAX 1-506-789-2430
EMAIL sac02@nbnet.nb.ca
INTERNET http://www.nbcc.nb.ca

COLLEGE OVERVIEW

The New Brunswick Community College (NBCC) is a network of ten colleges, four of which offer programs primarily in French and six that offer programs primarily in English. Under the responsibility of the New Brunswick Department of Education, its mission is to promote personal development and self-sufficiency among New Brunswickers by offering high-quality training programs. As well, through creation and support of opportunities for self-sufficiency through life-long learning, the Department of Education supports a productive work environment.

The network's vision is to provide education and training opportunities at the appropriate time and place. All education and training must be based on a clear statement of the results that learners may expect and the skills they will acquire. Technical and vocational training are delivered by the community college as well as the latest, most effective distance-education training methods. The NBCC network is working to achieve ISO 9001 certification network-wide by the spring of 1999.

University Transfer Programs

The NBCC network has developed 20 university transfer programs with the following universities: Lakehead University, Thunder Bay, Ontario; University College of Cape Breton, Sydney, Nova Scotia; and St. Thomas University and the University of New Brunswick, Fredericton, New Brunswick.

Customized Training

The NBCC network designs and delivers customized training programs for specific companies or organizations. This includes identifying training needs, conducting research and development, and ensuring the availability of required resources.

Co-op Programs, Apprenticeship and Certification

A number of the programs offered by the NBCC network are cooperative education programs, integrating academic studies and paid work experience with co-operative employers. This approach gives students the opportunity to put into practice the theory they have learned while gaining valuable work experience. Apprenticeship and certification programs also rely on a combination of classroom theory and practical experience to develop the skills required to practise a trade as a journeyperson.

Centres of Excellence

The network has developed a number of Centres of Excellence in various areas of specialization that meet international standards. All staff are required to be highly qualified in their field, to remain abreast of the latest technology, to create networks and partnerships with the public and private sectors, and to adapt and transfer their skills to a wide range of situations.

Highlights

- Customized training
- Full and part-time study programs
- Co-op programs and distance learning
- Campuses throughout the province
- Apprenticeship and certification programs

College Statistics

Year Founded: 1972 (network)
Academic Options: diploma/certificate
Calendar Year: semesters (English): fall (Sept-Dec), winter (Jan-Jun), summer (Jul-Aug); trimesters (French): fall (Sept-Dec), winter (Jan-Mar), spring (Apr-Jun)

ACADEMIC PROGRAMS

University Transfer

Training Programs: Academic (Academic Studies, Second Language); Agrifood (Biotech, Food Processing Tech, Landscape); Applied Arts (Clay, Fabric Surface Design, Fashion, Graphic Design, Industrial Sewing, Native Art Studies, Textiles); Bus (Automotive Mktg & Bus Studies, Bus Tech [acc, admin, call centre admin, investment mgmt, mktg co-op, transport, elect comm]); Comm Arts (Graphic Arts, Journalism, Photography, Radio Broadcasting, Video & TV Prod]); Construction (Civil Eng Tech, Elect Tech'n, Ind Control Tech Co-op); Elect (Elect Eng Tech [avionics, comm, data systems, industrial], Elect Tech'n, Ind Control Tech Co-op); Env (Chem Tech, Env Tech); Health & Community Services (Child Care, Human Services, Med Lab Tech, Nuclear Med Tech, Nursing Asst, Pharmacy Asst, Respiratory Therapy); Heating, Ventilation, Air Conditioning & Refrigeration; Hospitality & Tourism (Cook, Facility & Accommodation, Travel & Tourism); InfoTech (Comp Hardware & Prog [elect eng tech, comp systems tech'n, elect tech, bus tech, network design & admin], Learning Tech [animation & graphics tech, elect game design tech, educ tech, knowledge eng tech, multimedia learning tech, virtual reality tech]); Marine (Aquaculture Tech, Diesel Mech, Eng, Navigation); Mech (Industrial [industrial mech, mech eng tech, mech tech'n, power eng tech], Motorized Equipment [aircraft maintenance, automotive service tech, heavy equipment repair, truck & transport service tech'n]); Metals (CNC Manufacturing Tech'n, Fabrication, Machinist, Welding [MIG, tech'n]); Protective Services (Correctional Techniques, Criminal Justice, Industrial & Retail Security, Youth Care Worker); Wood & Related Materials (Wood Processing Techniques, Woodworking Tech)

ADMISSIONS CRITERIA & PROCEDURES

To be considered for a chosen program, applicants must have obtained or be working towards a high school diploma or the equivalent and have successfully completed or be in the process of completing the course prerequisites for the program. Applicants without the prerequisites may enrol in academic studies courses that are available through NBCC.

Admissions requirements other than the completion of a secondary school diploma or equivalent may apply to some programs. Applicants may be required to: submit a satisfactory medical and immunization report; submit proof that the applicant will turn 18 during the first year of registration (for the Academic Studies Program); participate in information, orientation, interview or testing sessions; successfully complete, at the required level, a second language proficiency test, written and/or spoken, administered by the NBCC (generally, applicants must submit a TOEFL score of 550 with a minimum score of 50 in each area or a MELAB score of 85 with no section score lower than 80).

The College Admissions Service (CAS) begins processing applications for the next academic year on November 1. Fifty per cent of seats for all NBCC programs for the following year are allocated on a continuous acceptance basis until March 1. After March 1, all remaining seats in a given program are allocated until the program is full. The final deadline for admission to all NBCC programs is up to three weeks after the beginning of a particular program.

Admissions at a Glance

Minimum GPA: n/a

Minimum English Requirements: TOEFL 550, MELAB 85, or equivalent

Application Fee: C$15 (Canadian, per program choice), $100 (international)

Application Deadlines: March 1 for priority admission; three weeks prior to course for final deadline

ACADEMIC FACILITIES

TeleEducation NB has made New Brunswick a world leader in distance training and learning technology. This branch of the Department of Education is dedicated to the development of distance-training programs, employing the best delivery techniques and improving teaching methods of distance delivery. TeleEducation NB relies on telecommunication technologies such as audioconferencing, audiographics teleconferencing, videoconferencing and the Internet as the means of communication between learners and instructors. Visitors may access TeleEducation NB on the Internet at http://teleeducation.nb.ca.

TeleCampus is New Brunswick's virtual forum for online teaching and learning. It features courses and programs that can lead to formal degrees, diplomas and certificates. In addition, it provides professional development activities and other learning experiences. Services offered online include course registration; learning and evaluation; payment of tuition fees; courseware promotion and sales; professional assistance and development; Programme Development Fund. Students can access TeleCampus on the Internet at http://telecampus.com/.

The NBCC Network also has an intranet site which provides information on all ten colleges, a curriculum repository, administrative documents, ISO 9001 policies, NBCC Network policies and procedures, a site map and other information.

Student & Faculty Profile

Total Enrolment: 21,458

Full-Time Enrolment: 6,958

# of Faculty: 1,080

Student/Faculty Ratio: 8:1 (full-time)

Male/Female Students: 54%/46%

Academic Class Sizes: varies

Enrolment by Program Type:

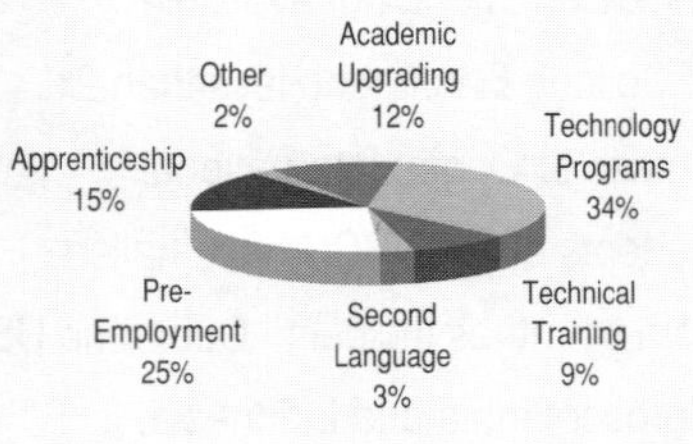

SCHOLARSHIPS & FINANCIAL ASSISTANCE

The Student Services Branch of the Department of Education provides financial assistance to New Brunswick postsecondary students through a combination of federal loans, provincial loans and bursaries. Other forms of financial assistance provided include grants, part-time funding, Canada Study Grants and the Women's Doctoral Scholarship Program. For more information visit the New Brunswick Student Aid website at http://www.gov.nb.ca/ael/stasse.htm.

Expenses at a Glance

Tuition (full-time):

- In-Province: C$2,000/year*
- Out-of-Province: C$2,000/year*
- International: C$5,000/year*

Fees, Books, Materials: C$500/year (approx)

Accommodation:

- Private: C$400-$800/month
- Residence: n/a
- Homestay: C$700/month

Health Insurance: C$50/month (approx)

CAMPUS & LOCATION

City Population:	various
Cost of Living:	medium
Climate Range:	-20° to 28°C
Campus Setting:	suburban/urban
# of Students in Residence:	n/a

The New Brunswick College of Craft and Design is located in the heart of Fredericton, and is the only postsecondary institute in the province offering a major selection of creative disciplines for the concentrated study of visual arts, design and crafts. NBCC Moncton offers over 33 regular full-time training programs, including one-year employment programs, two-year technology programs, apprenticeship training and literacy training; NBCC Moncton is the lead college in the following specialties: civil engineering technologies, electronic engineering technologies, business technology, automotive, metals and teleservice. Established in 1919 as Woodstock College, NBCC's Woodstock is the oldest vocational school of its kind in Canada and offers a number of programs unique to the network in the areas of communication arts, such as photography, journalism, TV and video production, and radio broadcasting. NBCC St. Andrews presently offers 12 full-time regular programs of one or two years duration, as well as part-time and contract training programs; it is a Centre of Excellence for training programs in heating, ventilation, air conditioning & refrigeration, hospitality & tourism, and fisheries/marine. Established in 1963, NBCC Saint John offers 25 full-time programs and has lead-in programs in electronics engineering technology, electronics technician, industrial control technology, business technology, human services, mechanical engineering, mechanical technician, medical laboratory technology and respiratory therapy. NBCC Miramichi is a modern, high-technology education institution in the central region of the province; it offers seven unique areas of specialization: animation & graphics technology, environmental technology, firefighting, heavy equipment repair, learning technologies, natural resources and protective services. The Collèges communautaires du Nouveau-Brunswick (CCNB) offer instruction primarily in French and comprises four colleges. CCNB Bathurst offers 26 full-time, part-time and contract programs enhanced by its Centre of Excellence in Information Technology (French), located in Bathurst. The primarily French-language CCNB Campbellton offers programs in health & community services and secretarial & information technology; it hosts the Centre of Excellence in Woodworking, which offers top-quality training. The French-language CCNB Dieppe offers more than 20 regular programs to nearly 650 full-time students and an array of part-time training programs to another 3,000 students; CCNB Dieppe has two other centres of learning: one in Lakeburn and the other in Richibucto. The primarily French-language CCNB Edmundston delivers postsecondary programs in the areas of agriculture, biotechnology, accommodations & hospitality, restaurant services, tourism, secretarial techniques and telecommunications; CCNB Edmundston has two centres of excellence: the Centre of Excellence of Atlantic Tourism and the Center of Excellence in Agricultural Sciences & Biotechnology.

ATHLETICS & EXTRACURRICULAR ACTIVITIES

A wide variety of facilities, activities and social organizations are available throughout the NBCC campuses. Each college offers a number of unique opportunities for exercise, relaxation and personal development. In addition, the diversity among the campuses in NBCC ensures that outdoor recreation opportunities abound for students.

College Recognition

- New Brunswick Department of Education
- Member of Association of Community Colleges of Canada (ACCC)

STUDENT SUPPORT SERVICES

Student Services at NBCC are designed to help the student through all phases of their college program. At the entry stage, appropriate information is provided to help with program selection, accommodations and financial assistance. During the course of study, professional personnel provide support services to help with successful program completion. Competent professional staff are also available to help with the transition from a program of study to the workplace or to further training.

International Students

College Enrolment: not available

% of College Enrolment: less than 2%

Countries of Origin: International students at the NBCC have hailed from countries including Cuba, the US, Morocco, India and Indonesia.

PROFILES OF Universities & Colleges IN The Northwest Territories

Colleges

IN

The Northwest Territories

AURORA COLLEGE FORT SMITH, NORTHWEST TERRITORIES

College Mission

...to support the development of the western Northwest Territories by providing quality education for careers and a focal point for research & technology development

Student Voice:

I enjoyed the closeness, with fellow students and the community, provided by a small college. Having a northern cultural perspective on my studies has helped me to better understand the socio-economic climate of the Northwest Territories, something that continues to interest me today.

Janet Lepine
Graduate of the Social Work Diploma Program

CONTACT INFORMATION
Aurora College
Box 1290
Fort Smith, Northwest Territories
Canada X0E 0P0
PH 1-867-872-7000
FAX 1-867-872-5143
EMAIL timg@auroracollege.com
INTERNET
http://www.auroranet.nt.ca/aurora

COLLEGE OVERVIEW

Aurora College (Aurora) began in 1968 as a single training course and has grown to meet the expanding needs of the peoples of northern Canada. Today, Aurora operates a college system that delivers postsecondary programs at three campuses and 14 community learning centres. The head office and administrative centre for the Aurora system is located on the Thebacha campus in Fort Smith, Northwest Territories. The Aurora system also includes the Aurora Research Institute, which offers two research centres that provide additional facilities and a wide variety of resources. The head office for the Aurora Research Institute is located in Inuvik.

Programs Offered

The courses and programs at Aurora are developed with input from the community, and respond to the needs of the area and the local economy. The college offers a range of university transfer and diploma programs, as well as trades & technology, and certificate programs. The goal of all Aurora programs is to bring the best of postsecondary education to the western Arctic region.

University transfer and diploma programs provide a starting point for further education and lay the foundation for a professional career. Diploma programs include northern nursing, management studies, natural resources technology, recreation leaders, social work and teacher education.

Trades & technology programs are intended to develop practical career-oriented skills and include carpentry, heavy duty mechanics, heavy equipment operator, a mine trades access program, observer/communicator, pretechnology and welding programs.

One-year certificate programs in office administration, management studies and northern community alcohol & drug counselling are also available at Aurora.

Partnerships

Aurora has established partnerships with several other colleges and universities in Canada in order to give students access to a wide range of educational opportunities. Without leaving the north, Aurora students can gain undergraduate degrees through supported distance education programs. Transfer agreements also allow students to continue their education at partner institutions that include University of Alberta, University of Saskatchewan, University of Northern British Columbia and the Northern Alberta Institute of Technology.

Highlights

- A variety of programs and courses at three main campuses and 13 community locations
- Aurora operates the Aurora Research Institute, a group of research and scientific centres
- Aurora has partnerships with about a dozen universities and colleges for transfer credit

College Statistics

Year Founded: 1968
Academic Options: certificate/diploma
Calendar Year: not available

ACADEMIC PROGRAMS

University Transfer: Arts & Sciences

Two-year Diplomas: Management Studies, Natural Resources Technology, Northern Nursing, Recreation Leaders, Social Work, Teacher Education

Trades & Technology: Carpentry, Electronic Engineering, Heavy Duty Mechanics, Heavy Equipment Operator, Mine Trades Access Program, Observer/Communicator, Pretechnology, Welding

One-year Certificate: Management Studies, Northern Community Alcohol & Drug Counsellor, Office Administration

ADMISSIONS CRITERIA & PROCEDURES

Aurora applicants must complete an Aurora College application form and submit it, along with supporting documents, to the nearest campus or community learning centre. Application forms may be obtained from the registrar's office at any campus, or from any community learning centre or high school in the Northwest Territories; during the summer, application forms can be obtained from the local community employment officer. Official secondary school transcripts, and postsecondary transcripts where applicable, must accompany the application. Letters of reference, a security check and a personal statement may be required by certain programs. If required, this information must accompany the application for admission. There is a C$15 application fee.

Admission requirements vary by program. Admission requirements typically include grade 12, or equivalent, and may include specific additional requirements such as a class 5 driver's license. Potential students should contact the college for program-specific admission guidelines.

Students without the prerequisite requirements for direct entry may be eligible for entry as a mature student. A mature student must be 20 years of age or older and have been out of school for at least one year. Mature students must complete the Aurora College Placement Package.

Admissions at a Glance

Minimum GPA: varies by program

Minimum English Requirements: varies by program; students may be tested by Aurora

Application Fee: C$15 (Canadian)

Application Deadlines: varies by campus

ACADEMIC FACILITIES

The Thebacha Campus Library is designed to support for students and staff throughout the Aurora system. The library currently has a collection of approximately 11,000 circulating books, 4,000 reference books and a large assortment of periodicals, scholarly journals and microform materials. While Thebacha Campus houses the main library, the other campuses maintain reference and program-specific collections and arrange for the use of governmental and community libraries for Aurora students. The Aurora Research Institute maintains a substantial reference library at its Head Office in Inuvik. Email accounts and Internet connections are available at most Aurora locations. Yellowknife Campus has a new library located in its new campus building.

SCHOLARSHIPS & FINANCIAL ASSISTANCE

A broad range of scholarships, bursaries and awards are available to Aurora students. For information students should contact the Student Services Department at any campus, the Adult Educator at any community learning centre, the Greater Northwest Territories Department of Education, Culture & Employment or the research centres of the Aurora Research Institute.

Applications for financial support must be received by June 15 for programs commencing in the fall and October 15 for programs commencing in January. An acceptance letter from the college is not necessary when applying for financial assistance.

Students may be eligible for financial assistance through Human Resources Development Canada, the Student Financial Assistance Program of NWT or the training services section of the Department of Education, Culture & Employment, Northwest Territories.

Student & Faculty Profile

Total Enrolment: 1,900

Full-Time Enrolment: 850

# of Faculty: 106

Student/Faculty Ratio: 8:1

Male/Female Students: 50%/50%

Academic Class Sizes: 10

Enrolment by Program Type: not available

Expenses at a Glance

Tuition (full-time):
- In-Province: C$1,300/year
- Out-of-Province: C$1,300/year
- International: C$1,300/year

Fees, Books, Materials: varies by program

Accommodation:
- Private: varies by campus
- Residence: C$235-350/month (excluding food costs)
- Homestay: n/a

Health Insurance: free for Canadian students

CAMPUS & LOCATION

Aurora College delivers programs from campuses in Fort Smith, Inuvik and Yellowknife, and from community locations throughout the western Northwest Territories.

The Thebacha Campus, located in a beautiful new building in Fort Smith, serves communities throughout the South Slave and Deh Cho regions. The Thebacha campus is the largest of the three regional campuses.

The Yellowknife Campus is located in the city of Yellowknife, the largest city in the Northwest Territories. Yellowknife is the political and economic capital of the region, and provides all the amenities of a small city.

Inuvik is home to the Aurora Campus and the head office of the Aurora Research Institute; the Aurora Campus is the most northern postsecondary institution in North America.

Aurora provides a limited number of places in residence accommodation for both single students and those with families. Full-time students registered in long-term programs are given priority for residence placements.

City Population:	varies by campus
Cost of Living:	medium (Fort Smith), high (Inuvik, Yellowknife)
Climate Range:	-20° to 25°C
Campus Setting:	suburban, rural
# of Students in Residence:	183

ATHLETICS & EXTRACURRICULAR ACTIVITIES

Aurora's athletic activities range from intramural sports including basketball, volleyball, soccer, badminton and hockey, to recreational programs designed to make campus life more enjoyable.

The Thebacha Campus has a wide range of athletic and leisure equipment on hand for student use. In addition to providing recreational facilities and equipment on campus, Aurora allows students to borrow equipment. The Aurora Campus in Inuvik has the largest gymnasium in the Northwest Territories, including a well-equipped weight and fitness equipment room. Students at the Yellowknife Campus have access to the extensive facilities offered within the city.

College Recognition

- Government mandated institution under the Arctic College Act

STUDENT SUPPORT SERVICES

A Student Association has been established at each Aurora College campus. The associations are responsible for organizing social activities and performing administrative duties on campus; they also operate a stationary supply store, a lounge and a canteen.

Counselling services are provided at each campus to assist students in reaching their full potential. Counsellors help students develop sound decision-making skills and implement realistic courses of action. Some of the services provided by the Student Services Department include organizing an orientation to college life and academic, vocational and personal counselling.

International Students

College Enrolment: n/a

% of College Enrolment: n/a

Countries of Origin: n/a

AUCC Member List

The following list of institutions appears courtesy of the Association of Universities and Colleges in Canada (AUCC). The information provided is the most recent available; however, in some cases its accuracy cannot be verified. Please contact the institution directly for further information.
An asterisk (*) indicates that the institute offers instruction in French.

Acadia University
PO Box 1269
Wolfville, Nova Scotia B0P 1X0 Canada
phone: 1-902-542-2201
fax: 1-902-585-1072
internet: http://www.acadiau.ca

Athabasca University
1 University Drive
Athabasca, Alberta T9S 3A3 Canada
phone: 1-403-675-6168
fax: 1-403-675-6145
internet: http://www.athabascau.ca

Augustana University College
4901 - 46 Avenue
Camrose, Alberta T4V 2R3 Canada
phone: 1-403-679-1100
fax: 1-403-679-1129
internet: http://www.augustana.ab.ca

Bishop's University
PO Box 5000, Station Lennoxville
Sherbrooke, Quebec J1M 1Z7 Canada
phone: 1-819-822-9600
fax: 1-819-822-9661
internet: http://www.ubishops.ca

Brandon University
270 - 18th Street
Brandon, Manitoba R7A 6A9 Canada
phone: 1-204-728-9520
fax: 1-204-726-4573
internet: http://www.brandonu.ca

Brescia College
1285 Western Road
London, Ontario N6G 1H2 Canada
phone: 1-519-432-8353
fax: 1-519-679-6489
internet: http://www.uwo.ca/brescia

British Columbia Open University
4355 Mathissi Place
Burnaby, British Columbia V5G 4S8 Canada
phone: 1-604-431-3000
fax: 1-604-431-3333
internet: http://www.ola.bc.ca

Brock University
500 Glenridge Avenue
St Catharines, Ontario L2S 3A1 Canada
phone: 1-905-688-5550
fax: 1-905-688-2789
internet: http://www.brocku.ca

Campion College
3737 Wascana Parkway, Suite 100
Regina, Saskatchewan S4S 0A2 Canada
phone: 1-306-586-4242
fax: 1-306-359-1200
internet: http://www.uregina.ca/campion

Carleton University
1125 Colonel By Drive
Ottawa, Ontario K1S 5B6 Canada
phone: 1-613-520-7400
fax: -
internet: http://www.carleton.ca

Collège dominicain de philosophie et de théologie*
96, avenue Empress
Ottawa, Ontario K1R 7G3 Canada
phone : 1-613-233-5696
fax: 1-613-233-6064
internet: http://www.op.org/Canada/college.htm

College of Alberta
7128 Ada Boulevard NW
Edmonton, Alberta T5B 4E4 Canada
phone: 1-403-479-8481
fax: 1-403-474-1933
internet: http://www.concordia.edmonton.ab.ca

Collège universitaire de Saint-Boniface *
200, avenue de la Cathédrale
Saint-Boniface, Manitoba R2H 0H7 Canada
phone: 1-204-233-0210
fax: 1-204-237-3240
internet: http://www.ustboniface.mb.ca

Concordia University
1455 de Maisonneuve Boulevard W
Montreal, Quebec H3G 1M8 Canada
phone: 1-514-848-2424
fax: 1-514-848-3494
internet: http://www.concordia.ca

Dalhousie University
1236 Henry Street
Halifax, Nova Scotia B3H 3J5 Canada
phone: 1-902-494-2211
fax: 1-902-494-2319
internet: http://www.dal.ca

École de technologie supérieure *
1100, rue Notre-Dame Ouest
Montréal, Quebec H3C 1K3 Canada
phone: 1-514-396-8800
fax: 1-514-396-8950
internet: http://www.etsmtl.ca

École des Hautes Études Commerciales *
3000, chemin de la Côte-Sainte-Catherine
Montreal, Quebec H3T 2A7 Canada
phone: 1-514-340-6000
fax: 1-514-340-6411
internet: http://www.hec.ca

École nationale d'administration publique *
945, rue Wolfe
Sainte-Foy, Quebec GIV 3J9 Canada
phone: 1-418-657-2485
fax: 1-418-657-2620
internet: http://www.enap.uquebec.ca

École Polytechnique de Montréal *
CP 6079, Succursale Centre Ville
Montreal, Quebec H3C 3A7 Canada
phone: 1-514-340-4711
fax: -
internet: http://www.polymtl.ca

Huron College
1349 Western Road
London, Ontario N6G 1H3 Canada
phone: 1-519-438-7224
fax: 1-519-438-3938
internet: http://www.uwo.ca/huron

Institut national de la recherche scientifique *
CP 7500, Succursale Sainte-Foy
Québec, Quebec G1V 4C7 Canada
phone: 1-418-654-2500
fax: 1-418-654-2525
internet: http://www.inrs-urb.uquebec.ca

King's College
266 Epworth Avenue
London, Ontario N6A 2M3 Canada
phone: 1-519-433-3491
fax: 1-519-433-6773
internet: http://www.uwo.ca/kings

King's University College
9125 - 50 Street NW
Edmonton, Alberta T6B 2H3 Canada
phone: 1-403-465-3500
fax: 1-403-465-3534
internet: http://www.kingsu.ab.ca

Lakehead University
955 Oliver Road
Thunder Bay, Ontario P7B 5E1 Canada
phone: 1-807-343-8110
fax: 1-807-343-8023
internet: http://www.lakeheadu.ca

Laurentian University of Sudbury
935 Ramsey Lake Road
Sudbury, Ontario P3E 2C6 Canada
phone: 1-705-675-1151
fax: -
internet: http://www.laurentian.ca

Luther College
3737 Wascana Parkway, Suite 100
Regina, Saskatchewan S4S 0A2 Canada
phone: 1-306-585-5333
fax: 1-306-585-5267
internet: http://www.saskweb.com/luthercollege

McGill University
845 Sherbrooke Street W
Montreal, Quebec H3A 2T5 Canada
phone: 1-514-398-4455
fax: 1-514-398-3594
internet: http://www.mcgill.ca

McMaster University
1280 Main Street W, Suite 20
Hamilton, Ontario L8S 4L8 Canada
phone: 1-905-525-9140
fax: -
internet: http://www.mcmaster.ca

Memorial University of Newfoundland
PO Box 4200, Station C
St. John's, New Foundland A1C 5S7 Canada
phone: 1-709-737-8000
fax: -
internet: http://www.mun.ca

Mount Allison University
65 York Street
Sackville, New Brunswick E4L 1E4 Canada
phone: 1-506-364-2269
fax: 1-506-364-2216
internet: http://www.mta.ca

AUCC Member List

The following list of institutions appears courtesy of the Association of Universities and Colleges in Canada (AUCC). The information provided is the most recent available; however, in some cases its accuracy cannot be verified. Please contact the institution directly for further information.
An asterisk (*) indicates that the institute offers instruction in French.

Mount Saint Vincent University
166 Bedford Highway, Suite 1
Halifax, Nova Scotia B3M 2J6 Canada
phone: 1-902-457-6788
fax: 1-902-445-3960
internet: http://www.msvu.ca

Nipissing University
Box 5002, Station Main
North Bay, Ontario P1B 8L7 Canada
phone: 1-705-474-3450
fax: 1-705-474-1947
internet: http://www.unipissing.ca

Nova Scotia Agricultural College
PO Box 550, Station Main
Truro, Nova Scotia B2N 5E3 Canada
phone: 1-902-893-6600
fax: -
internet: http://www.nsac.ns.ca

Nova Scotia College of Art and Design
5163 Duke Street
Halifax, Nova Scotia B3J 3J6 Canada
phone: 1-902-422-7381
fax: 1-902-425-2420
internet: http://www.nscad.ns.ca

Okanagan University College
3333 College Way
Kelowna, British Columbia V1V 1V7 Canada
phone: 1-250-762-5445
fax: -
internet: http://www.ouc.bc.ca

Queen's University at Kingston
99 University Avenue
Kingston, Ontario K7L 3N6 Canada
phone: 1-613-545-2000
fax: 1-613-545-6300
internet: http://www.queensu.ca

Redeemer College
777 Garner Road E
Ancaster, Ontario L9K 1J4 Canada
phone: 1-905-648-2131
fax: 1-905-648-2134
internet: http://www.redeemer.on.ca

Royal Military College of Canada
PO Box 17000, Station Forces
Kingston, Ontario K7K 7B4 Canada
phone: 1-613-541-6000
fax: 1-613-542-3565
internet: http://www.rmc.ca

Ryerson Polytechnic University
350 Victoria Street
Toronto, Ontario M5B 2K3 Canada
phone: 1-416-979-5000
fax: -
internet: http://www.ryerson.ca

St. Francis Xavier University
PO Box 5000, Station Main
Antigonish, Nova Scotia B2G 2W5 Canada
phone: 1-902-863-3300
fax: -
internet: http://www.stfx.ca

St. Jerome's University
81 Waterloo University Campus
Waterloo, Ontario N2L 3G3 Canada
phone: 1-519-884-8110
fax: 1-519-884-5759
internet: http://www.usjc.uwaterloo.ca

Saint Mary's University
923 Robie Street
Halifax, Nova Scotia B3H 3C3 Canada
phone: 1-902-420-5400
fax: 1-902-420-5566
internet: http://www.stmarys.ca

Saint Paul University
223 Main Street
Ottawa, Ontario K1S 1C4 Canada
phone: 1-613-236-1393
fax: 1-613-782-3005
internet: http://www.ustpaul.ca

St. Thomas University
PO Box 4569, Station A
Fredericton, New Brunswick E3B 5G3 Canada
phone: 1-506-452-7700
fax: 1-506-450-9615
internet: http://www.stthomasu.ca

Saskatchewan Indian Federated College
3737 Wascana Parkway, Suite 100
Regina, Saskatchewan S4S 0A2 Canada
phone: 1-306-779-6000
fax: 1-306-584-0955
internet: http://www.sifc.edu

Simon Fraser University
8888 University Drive
Burnaby, British Columbia V5A 1S6 Canada
phone: 1-604-291-3111
fax: -
internet: http://www.sfu.ca

Télé-université *
CP 10700, Succursale Sainte-Foy
Québec, Quebec G1V 4V9 Canada
phone: 1-418-657-2262
fax: 1-418-657-2094
internet: http://www.teluq.uquebec.ca

Trent University
PO Box 4800, Station Main
Peterborough, Ontario K9J 7B8 Canada
phone: 1-705-748-1011
fax: 1-705-748-1246
internet: http://www.trentu.ca

Trinity Western University
7600 Glover Road
Langley, British Columbia V2Y 1Y1 Canada
phone: 1-604-888-7511
fax: 1-604-888-5336
internet: http://www.twu.ca

Université de Moncton *
165, rue Massey
Moncton, New Brunswick E1A 3E9 Canada
phone: 1-506-858-4000
fax: 1-506-858-4379
internet: http://www.umoncton.ca

Université de Montréal *
CP 6128, Succursale Centre Ville
Montreal, Quebec H3C 3J7 Canada
phone: 1-514-343-6111
fax: 1-514-343-2098
internet: http://www.umontreal.ca

Université de Sherbrooke *
2500 boulevard de l'Université
Sherbrooke, Quebec J1K 2R1 Canada
phone: 1-819-821-7000
fax: -
internet: http://www.usherb.ca

Université du Québec *
2875 boulevard Laurier, bureau 100
Sainte-Foy, Quebec G1V 2M3 Canada
phone: 1-418-657-3551
fax: 1-418-657-2132
internet: http://www.uquebec.ca

Université du Québec à Chicoutimi *
555 boulevard de l'Université E
Chicoutimi, Quebec G7H 2B1 Canada
phone: 1-418-545-5011
fax: 1-418-545-5012
internet: http://www.uqac.uquebec.ca

Université du Québec à Hull *
CP 1250, Succursale B
Hull, Quebec J8X 3X7 Canada
phone: 1-819-595-3900
fax:-
internet: http://www.uqah.uquebec.ca

Université du Québec à Montréal *
CP 8888, Succursale Centre Ville
Montreal, Quebec H3C 3P8 Canada
phone: 1-514-987-3000
fax: 1-514-987-3095
internet: http://www.uqam.ca

Université du Québec à Rimouski *
CP 3300, Succursale Bureau-chef
Rimouski, Quebec G5L 3A1 Canada
phone: 1-418-723-1986
fax: 1-418-724-1525
internet: http://www.uqar.uquebec.ca

Université du Québec à Trois-Rivières *
CP 500, Succursale Bureau-chef
Trois-Rivières, Quebec G9A 5H7 Canada
phone: 1-819-376-5011
fax: 1-819-376-5012
internet: http://www.uqtr.uquebec.ca

Université du Québec en Abitibi-Témiscamingue *
445 boulevard de l'Université
Rouyn-Noranda, Quebec J9X 5E4 Canada
phone: 1-819-762-0971
fax: 1-819-797-4727
internet: http://www.uqat.uquebec.ca

Université Laval *
CP 2208, Succursale Terminus
Quebec, Quebec G1K 7P4 Canada
phone: 1-418-656-2131
fax: 1-418-656-2809
internet: http://www.ulaval.ca

AUCC Member List

The following list of institutions appears courtesy of the Association of Universities and Colleges in Canada (AUCC). The information provided is the most recent available; however, in some cases its accuracy cannot be verified. Please contact the institution directly for further information.
An asterisk (*) indicates that the institute offers instruction in French.

Université Sainte-Anne *
Pointe-de-l'Église, Nouvelle Écosse B0W 1M0 Canada
phone: 1-902-769-2114
fax: 1-902-769-2930
internet: http://www.ustanne.ednet.ns.ca

University of Alberta
1A University Campus NW
Edmonton, Alberta T6G 2E1 Canada
phone: 1-403-492-3111
fax: -
internet: http://www.ualberta.ca

University of British Columbia
2075 Wesbrook Mall
Vancouver, British Columbia V6T 1Z1 Canada
phone: 1-604-822-2211
fax: -
internet: http://www.ubc.ca

University of Calgary
2500 University Drive NW
Calgary, Alberta T2N 1N4 Canada
phone: 1-403-220-5110
fax: 1-403-282-7298
internet: http://www.ucalgary.ca

University College of Cape Breton
PO Box 5300, Station A
Sydney, Nova Scotia B1P 6L2 Canada
phone: 1-902-539-5300
fax: 1-902-562-0119
internet: http://www.uccb.ns.ca

University College of the Cariboo
PO Box 3010, Station Terminal
Kamloops, British Columbia V2C 5N3 Canada
phone: 1-250-828-5000
fax: 1-250-828-5086
internet: http://www.cariboo.bc.ca

University College of the Fraser Valley
33844 King Road
Abbotsford, British Columbia V2S 7M9 Canada
phone: 1-604-853-7441
fax: 1-604-853-9990
internet: http://www.ucfv.bc.ca

University of Guelph
50 Stone Road E, Suite 158
Guelph, Ontario N1G 2W1 Canada
phone: 1-519-824-4120
fax: -
internet: http://www.uoguelph.ca

University of King's College
6350 Coburg Road
Halifax, Nova Scotia B3H 2A1 Canada
phone: 1-902-422-1271
fax: 1-902-423-3357
internet: http://www.ukings.ns.ca

University of Lethbridge
4401 University Drive W
Lethbridge, Alberta T1K 3M4 Canada
phone: 1-403-329-2201
fax: 1-403-329-2097
internet: http://www.uleth.ca

University of Manitoba
66 Chancellors Circle
Winnipeg, Manitoba R3T 2N2 Canada
phone: 1-204-474-8880
fax: 1-204-474-7536
internet: http://www.umanitoba.ca

University of New Brunswick
PO Box 4400, Station A
Fredericton, New Brunswick E3B 5A3 Canada
phone: 1-506-453-4666
fax: 1-506-453-4599
internet: http://www.unb.ca

University of Northern British Columbia
3333 University Way
Prince George, British Columbia V2N 4Z9 Canada
phone: 1-250-960-5555
fax: 1-250-960-5791
internet: http://www.unbc.edu

University of Ottawa
PO Box 450, Station A
Ottawa, Ontario K1N 6N5
phone: 1-613-562-5800
fax: -
internet: http://www.uottawa.ca

University of Prince Edward Island
550 University Avenue
Charlottetown, Prince Edward Island C1A 4P3 Canada
phone: 1-902-566-0439
fax: 1-902-566-0420
internet: http://www.upei.ca

University of Regina
3737 Wascana Parkway, Suite 100
Regina, Saskatchewan S4S 0A2 Canada
phone: 1-306-585-4111
fax: -
internet: http://www.uregina.ca

University of Saskatchewan
105 Administration Place
Saskatoon, Saskatchewan S7N 5A2 Canada
phone: 1-306-966-4343
fax: 1-306-966-8670
internet: http://www.usask.ca

University of St. Michael's College
81 Saint Mary Street
Toronto, Ontario M5S 1J4 Canada
phone: 1-416-926-1300
fax: 1-416-926-7276
internet: http://www.utoronto.ca/stmikes

University of Sudbury
935 Ramsey Lake Road
Sudbury, Ontario P3E 2C6 Canada
phone: 1-705-673-5661
fax: 1-705-673-4912
internet: http://www.ulaurentian.ca/www/uofs

University of Toronto
27 King's College Circle
Toronto, Ontario M5S 1A1 Canada
phone: 1-416-978-2011
fax: 1-416-978-8182
internet: http://www.utoronto.ca

University of Trinity College
6 Hoskin Avenue
Toronto, Ontario M5S 1H8 Canada
phone: 1-416-978-2522
fax: 1-416-978-2797
internet: http://www.trinity.utoronto.ca

University of Victoria
PO Box 1700
Victoria, British Columbia V8W 2Y2 Canada
phone: 1-250-721-7211
fax: 1-250-721-7212
internet: http://www.uvic.ca

University of Waterloo
200 University Avenue W
Waterloo, Ontario N2L 3G1 Canada
phone: 1-519-885-1211
fax: 1-519-888-4521
internet: http://www.uwaterloo.ca

University of Western Ontario
1151 Richmond Street
London, Ontario N6A 3K7 Canada
phone: 1-519-679-2111
fax: -
internet: http://www.uwo.ca

University of Windsor
401 Sunset Avenue
Windsor, Ontario N9B 3P4 Canada
phone: 1-519-253-4232
fax: 1-519-973-7050
internet: http://www.uwindsor.ca

University of Winnipeg
515 Portage Avenue
Winnipeg, Manitoba R3B 2E9 Canada
phone: 1-204-786-7811
fax: -
internet: http://www.uwinnipeg.ca

Victoria University
73 Queen's Park Crescent E
Toronto, Ontario M5S 1K7 Canada
phone: 1-416-585-4524
fax: 1-416-585-4584
internet: http://www.vicu.utoronto.ca

Wilfrid Laurier University
75 University Avenue W
Waterloo, Ontario N2L 3C5 Canada
phone: 1-519-884-1970
fax: -
internet: http://www.wlu.ca

York University
4700 Keele Street
North York, Ontario M3J 1P3 Canada
phone: 1-416-736-2100
fax: 1-416-736-5700
internet: http://www.yorku.ca

ACCC Member List

The following list of institutions appears courtesy of the Association of Canadian Community Colleges (ACCC). The information provided is the most recent available; however, in some cases its accuracy cannot be verified. Please contact the institution directly for further information.
An asterisk (*) indicates that the institute offers instruction in French.

Alberta College
10050 Macdonald Drive
Edmonton, Alberta T5J 2B7 Canada
phone: 1-403-428-1851
fax: 1-403-424-6371
internet: http://www.abcollege.ab.ca

Alberta Vocational College
10215 - 108th Street
Edmonton, Alberta T5J 1L6 Canada
phone: 1-403-427-2823
fax: -
internet: http://www.avc.edmonton.ab.ca

Algonquin College of Applied Arts & Technology
1385 Woodroffe Avenue
Nepean, Ontario K2G 1V8 Canada
phone: 1-613-727-4723
fax: 1-613-727-7684
internet: http://www.algonquinc.on.ca

Assiniboine Community College
1430 Victoria Avenue East, PO Box 935
Brandon, Manitoba R7A 5Z9 Canada
phone: 1-204-726-6742
fax: 1-204-726-7012
internet: http://www.assiniboinec.mb.ca

Aurora College
199 McDougal Road, PO Box 1290
Fort Smith, Northwest Territories X0E 0P0 Canada
phone: 1-867-872-7000
fax: 1- 867-872-4730
internet: http://www.auroranet.nt.ca/aurora

Bow Valley College
332 - 6th Avenue SE
Calgary, Alberta T2G 4S6 Canada
phone: 1-403-297-4040
fax: -
internet: http://www.bowvalleyc.ab.ca

British Columbia Institute of Technology
3700 Willingdon Avenue
Burnaby, British Columbia V5G 3H2 Canada
phone: 1- 604-432-8419
fax: -
internet: http://www.bcit.bc.ca

Cambrian College
1400 Barrydowne Road, Station A
Sudbury, Ontario P3A 3V8 Canada
phone: 1-705-566-8101
fax: 1-705-524-7329
internet: http://www.cambrianc.on.ca

Camosun College
3100 Foul Bay Road
Victoria, British Columbia V8P 5J2 Canada
phone: 1-250-370-3841
fax: -
internet: http://www.camosun.bc.ca

Canadore College of Applied Arts & Technology
100 College Drive, PO Box 5001
North Bay, Ontario P1B 8K9 Canada
phone: 1-705-474-7600
fax: 1-705-474-2384
internet: http://www.canadorec.on.ca

Capilano College
2055 Purcell Way
North Vancouver, British Columbia V7J 3H5 Canada
phone: 1-604-986-1911
fax: 1-604-984-4985
internet: http://www.capcollege.bc.ca

Carlton Trail Regional College
623 Seventh Street, PO Box 720
Humboldt, Saskatchewan S0K 2A0 Canada
phone: 1-306-682-2623
fax: 1-306-682-3101
internet: http://www.sasked.gov.sk.ca/reg_col/carlton_trail/carlton.html

Cégep André-Laurendeau *
1111, rue Lapierre
Lasalle, Quebec H8N 2J4 Canada
phone: 1- 514-364-3320
fax: 1-514-364-7130
internet: http://www.claurendeau.qc.ca

Cégep Beauce-Appalaches *
1055 - 116e rue est
Ville de Saint-Georges, Quebec G5Y 3G1 Canada
phone: 1-418-228-8896
fax: 1-418-228-0562
internet: http://www.cegepbceapp.qc.ca

Cégep Bois-de-Boulogne *
10555, avenue de Bois de Boulogne
Montreal Quebec H4N 1L4 Canada
phone: 1-514-332-3000
fax: 1-514-332-5857
internet: http://www.collegebdeb.qc.ca

Cégep D'Alma *
675, boulevard Auger ouest
Alma, Quebec G8B 2B7 Canada
phone: 1-418-668-2387
fax: 1-418-668-3806
internet: http://www.calma.qc.ca

Cégep de Chicoutimi *
534, rue Jacques-Cartier est
Chicoutimi, Quebec G7H 1Z6 Canada
phone: 1-418-549-9520
fax: 1-418-549-1315
internet: http://www.cegep-chicoutimi.qc.ca

Cégep de Drummondville *
960, rue Saint-Georges
Drummondville, Quebec J2C 6A2 Canada
phone: 1-819-478-4671
fax: 1-819-474-6859
internet: http://www.cdrummond.qc.ca

Cégep de Jonquière *
2505, rue Saint-Hubert
Jonquière, Quebec G7X 7W2 Canada
phone: 1-418-547-2191
fax: 1-418-547-9031
internet: http://college.cjonquiere.qc.ca

Cégep de l'Abitibi-Témiscamingue *
425, boulevard du Collège, CP 1500
Rouyn-Noranda, Quebec J9X 5E5 Canada
phone: 1-819-762-0931
fax: 1-819-762-3815
internet: http://cegepat.qc.ca

Cégep de la Gaspésie et des Iles *
96, rue Jacques Cartier
Gaspé, Quebec G0C 1R0 Canada
phone: 1-418-368-2201
fax: 1-418-368-7003
internet: http://www.cgaspesie.qc.ca

Cégep de Rivière-Du-Loup *
80, rue Frontenac
Rivière-Du-Loup, Quebec G5R 1R1 Canada
phone: 1-418-862-6903
fax: 1-418-862-4959
internet: http://www.cegep-rdl.qc.ca

Cégep de Sainte-Foy *
2410, chemin Sainte-Foy
Sainte-Foy, Quebec G1V 1T3 Canada
phone: 1-418-659-6600
fax: 1-418-659-4563
internet: http://www.cegep-ste-foy.qc.ca

Cégep de Saint-Laurent *
625, avenue Sainte-Croix
Saint-Laurent, Quebec H4L 3X7 Canada
phone: 1-514-747-6521
fax: 1-514-748-1249
internet: http://www.cegep-st-laurent.qc.ca

Cégep de Sorel-Tracy *
3000, boulevard de la Mairie
Tracy, Quebec J3R 5B9 Canada
phone: 1-514-742-6651
fax: 1-514-742-1136
internet: http:www.cegep-sorel-tracy.qc.ca

Cégep de Trois-Rivières *
3500, rue de Courval
Trois-Rivières, Quebec G9A 5E6 Canada
phone: 1-819-376-1721
fax: 1-819-693-8023
internet: http://www.cegeptr.qc.ca

Cégep Heritage Collège *
325, boulevard Cité des Jeunes
Hull, Quebec J8Y 6T3 Canada
phone: 1-819-778-2270
fax: 1-819-778-7364
internet: http://www.cegep-heritage.qc.ca

Cégep Joliette-de-Lanaudière *
20, rue Saint-Charles sud
Joliette, Quebec J6E 4T1 Canada
phone: 1-450-759-1661
fax: 1-450-759-4468
internet: http://www.collanaud.qc.ca

Centennial College of Applied Arts & Technology
41 Progress Court, PO Box 631, Station A
Scarborough, Ontario M1K 5E9 Canada
phone: 1-416-289-5312
fax: -
internet: http://www.cencol.on.ca

Centre for Nursing Studies
250 Waterford Bridge Road
Saint John's, Newfoundland A1E 1E3 Canada
phone: 1-709-737-3817
fax: 1-709-737-3836
internet: -

ACCC Member List

The following list of institutions appears courtesy of the Association of Canadian Community Colleges (ACCC). The information provided is the most recent available; however, in some cases its accuracy cannot be verified. Please contact the institution directly for further information.
An asterisk (*) indicates that the institute offers instruction in French.

Champlain Regional College
1301, boulevard Portland, CP 5000
Sherbrooke, Quebec J1H 5N1 Canada
phone: 1- 819-564-3666
fax: 1- 819-564-5171
internet: http://www.champlaincollege.qc.ca

La Cité Collégiale *
801, Promenade de l'aviation
Ottawa, Ontario K1K 4R3 Canada
phone: 1-613-742-2483
fax: 1-613-742-2481
internet: http://www.lacitec.on.ca

Collège Boréal *
21, boulevard LaSalle
Sudbury, Ontario P3A 6B1 Canada
phone: 1-705-560-6673
fax: 1-705-560-1511
internet: http://www.borealc.on.ca

Collège de l'Acadie *
Centre Administratif
CP #8
La Butte, Nouvelle Écosse B0W 2L0 Canada
phone: 1-902-424-2630
fax: 1-902-424-3607
internet: http://www.ccfne.ns.ca

Collège de la Région de l'Amiante *
671, boulevard Smith-Sud
Thetford Mines, Quebec G6G 1N1 Canada
phone: 1-418-338-8591
fax: 1-418-338-3498
internet: -

Collège de l'Outaouais *
333, boulevard Cité des Jeunes
CP 5220, Succursale A
Hull, Quebec J8Y 6M5 Canada
phone: 1-819-770-4012
fax: 1-819-770-8167
internet: http://www.coll-outao.qc.ca

Collège de Limoilou *
1300, 8e avenue, CP 1400, Terminus Quebec
Quebec, Quebec G1K 7H3 Canada
phone: 1-418-647-6600
fax: 1-418-647-6798
internet: http://www.climoilou.qc.ca

Collège de Lionel-Groulx *
100, rue Duquet
Sainte-Thérèse, Quebec J7E 3G6 Canada
phone: 1-450-430-3120
fax: 1-450-430-7883
internet: http://www.clionelgroulx.qc.ca

Collège de Maisonneuve *
3800, rue Sherbrooke est
Montreal Quebec H1X 2A2 Canada
phone: 1-514-254-7131
fax: 1-514-253-7637
internet: http://www.cmaisonneuve.qc.ca

Collège de Rosemont *
6400-16e Avenue
Montreal, Quebec H1X 2S9 Canada
phone: 1-514-376-6310
fax: -
internet: http://www.crosemont.qc.ca

Collège de Saint-Hyacinthe *
3000, rue Boullé
Saint-Hyacinthe, Quebec J2S 1H9 Canada
phone: 1-450-773-6800
fax: 1-450-773-9971
internet: http://www.cegepsth.qc.ca

Collège de Saint-Jérôme *
455, rue Fournier
Saint-Jérôme, Quebec J7Z 4V2 Canada
phone: 1-450-436-1580
fax: 1-450-436-1756
internet: http://www.cegep-st-jerome.qc.ca

Collège de technologie agricole et alimentaire d'Alfred *
31, rue Saint-Paul, CP 580
Alfred, Ontario K0B 1A0 Canada
phone: 1-613-679-2218
fax: 1-613-679-2415
internet: http://www.alfredc.uoguelph.ca

Collège des Grands Lacs *
56, rue Wellesley ouest, 16ieme étage
Toronto, Ontario M7A 2B7 Canada
phone: 1-416-599-5090
fax: 1-416-599-5026
internet: http://www.grandslacs.on.ca

Collège Edouard-Montpetit *
Siège Social
945, Chemin de Chambly
Longueuil, Quebec J4H 3M6 Canada
phone: 1-450-679-2630
fax: 1-450-679-5570
internet: http://www.collegeem.qc.ca

Collège François-Xavier Garneau *
1660, boulevard de l'Entente
Quebec, Quebec G1S 4S3 Canada
phone: 1-418-688-8310
fax: 1-418-681-9384
internet: http://www.cegep-fxg.qc.ca

Collège Laflèche *
1687, boulevard du Carmel
Trois-Rivières, Quebec G8Z 3R8 Canada
phone: 1-819-375-7346
fax: 1-819-375-7347
internet: http://www.clafleche.qc.ca

Collège LaSalle *
2000, rue Sainte-Catherine ouest
Montreal Quebec H3H 2T2 Canada
phone: 1-514-939-2006
fax: 1-514-939-2015
internet: http://www.clasalle.qc.ca

Collège Saint-Jean-Sur-Richelieu *
30, boulevard du Séminaire, CP 1018
Saint-Jean-Sur-Richelieu, Quebec J3B 7B1 Canada
phone: 1-450-347-5301
fax: 1-450-347-9350
internet: http://www.cstjean.qc.ca

College of New Caledonia
3330 - 22nd Avenue
Prince George, British Columbia V2N 1P8 Canada
phone: 1-250-562-2131
fax: 1-250561-5861
internet: http://www.cnc.bc.ca

College of the North Atlantic
Provincial Headquarters
432 Massachusetts Drive, PO Box 5400
Stephenville, Newfoundland A2N 2Z6 Canada
phone: 1-709-758-7037
fax: -
internet: http://www.northatlantic.nf.ca

College of the Rockies
2700 College Way, PO Box 8500
Cranbrook, British Columbia V1C 5L7 Canada
phone: 1-250-489-8202
fax: 1-250-489-8253
internet: http://www.cotr.bc.ca

Collège universitaire de Saint-Boniface *
Ecole technique et professionnelle
200 avenue de la Cathédrale
Saint-Boniface, Manitoba R2H 0H7 Canada
phone: 1-204-233-0210
fax: 1-204-237-3240
internet: http://www.ustboniface.mb.ca

Columbia College
500 - 555 Seymour Street
Vancouver, British Columbia V6B 6J9 Canada
phone: 1-604-683-8360
fax: 1-604-682-7191
internet: http://www.columbia-college.com

Conestoga College of Applied Arts & Technology
299 Doon Valley Drive
Kitchener, Ontario N2G 4M4 Canada
phone: 1-519-748-5220
fax: 1-519-895-1097
internet: http://www.conestogac.on.ca

Confederation College of Applied Arts & Technology
1450 Nakina Drive, PO Box 398
Thunder Bay, Ontario P7C 4W1 Canada
phone: 1-807-475-6110
fax: -
internet: http://www.confederationc.on.ca

Cumberland Regional College
501 – 6th Street East, PO Box 2225
Nipawin, Saskatchewan S0E 1E0 Canada
phone: 1-306-862-9833
fax: 1-306-862-4940
internet: http://www.nlnet.melfort.sk.ca/crc/offices.html

Cypress Hills Regional College
129 - 2nd Avenue North East
Swift Current, Saskatchewan S9H 2C6 Canada
phone: 1-306-773-1531
fax: 1-306-773-2384
internet: http://www.sasked.gov.sk.ca/reg_col/cypress_hills/chrchome.html

Douglas College
700 Royal Avenue, PO Box 2503
New Westminster, British Columbia V3L 5B2 Canada
phone: 1-604-527-5400
fax: 1-604-527-5095
internet: http://www.douglas.bc.ca

Durham College of Applied Arts & Technology
2000 Simcoe Street North, PO Box 385
Oshawa, Ontario L1H 7L7 Canada
phone: 1-905-721-2000
fax: 1-905-721-3201
internet: http://www.durhamc.on.ca

ACCC Member List

The following list of institutions appears courtesy of the Association of Canadian Community Colleges (ACCC). The information provided is the most recent available; however, in some cases its accuracy cannot be verified. Please contact the institution directly for further information.
An asterisk (*) indicates that the institute offers instruction in French.

École des pêches du Nouveau-Brunswick *
Edifice Leonce Chenard
9, boulevard Saint-Pierre est
Caraquet, Nouveau-Brunswick E1W 1B6 Canada
phone: 1-506-726-2500
fax: -
internet: http://www.gov.nb.ca/dfa/ecole.htm

Fairview College
11235 - 99th Avenue, Box 3000
Fairview, Alberta T0H 1L0 Canada
phone: 1-403-835-6600
fax: 1-403-835-6698
internet: http://www.fairviewc.ab.ca

Fanshawe College of Applied Arts & Technology
1460 Oxford Street East, PO Box 4005
London, Ontario N5W 5H1 Canada
phone: 1-519-452-4100
fax: 1-519-452-3570
internet: http://www.fanshawec.on.ca

Fisheries & Marine Institute of Technology, The
PO Box 4920
Saint John's, Newfoundland A1C 5R3 Canada
phone: 1-709-778-0200
fax: 1-709- 778-0346
internet: http://www.ifmt.nf.ca

George Brown College of Applied Arts & Technology
500 MacPherson Avenue
PO Box 1015, Station B
Toronto, Ontario M5T 2T9 Canada
phone: 1-416-415-2000
fax: -
internet: http://www.gbrownc.on.ca

Georgian College of Applied Arts & Technology
One Georgian Drive
Barrie, Ontario L4M 3X9 Canada
phone: 1-705-728-1968
fax: 1-705-722-5123
internet: http://www.georcoll.on.ca

Grande Prairie Regional College
10726 - 106 Avenue
Grande Prairie, Alberta T8V 4C4 Canada
phone: 1-403-539-2911
fax: 1-403-539-2888
internet: http://www.gprc.ab.ca

Grant MacEwan Community College
10700 - 104th Avenue, PO Box 1796
Edmonton, Alberta T5J 2P2 Canada
phone: 1-403-497-5040
fax: 1-403-497-5405
internet: http://www.gmcc.ab.ca

Holland College
140 Weymouth Street
Charlottetown, Prince Edward Island C1A 4Z1 Canada
phone: 1-902-629-4217
fax: 1-902-629-4239
internet: http://www.hollandc.pe.ca

Humber College of Applied Arts & Technology
205 Humber College Boulevard, PO Box 1900
Etobicoke, Ontario M9W 5L7 Canada
phone: 1-416-675-3111
fax: 1-416-675-2427
internet: http://www.humberc.on.ca

Institut de technologie agro-alimentaire de La Pocatière *
401, rue Poiré
La Pocatière, Quebec G0R 1Z0 Canada
phone: 1-418-856-1110
fax: 1-418-856-1719
internet: -

Institut de technologie agro-alimentaire de Saint-Hyacinthe *
3230, rue Sicotte, CP 70
Saint-Hyacinthe, Quebec J2S 2M2 Canada
phone: 1-450-778-6504
fax: 1-450-778-6536
internet: -

Institut Téccart Inc. *
3155, rue Hochelaga
Montreal Quebec H1W 1G4 Canada
phone: 1-514-526-2501
fax: 1-514-526-9192
internet: http://www.teccart.qc.ca

John Abbott Collège
21275 Lakeshore Road, Box 2000
Sainte-Anne-De-Bellevue, Quebec H9X 3L9 Canada
phone: 1-514-457-6610
fax: 1-514-457-4730
internet: http://www.johnabbott.qc.ca

Justice Institute of British Columbia
715 McBride Boulevard
New Westminster, British Columbia V3L 5T4 Canada
phone: 1-604-525-5422
fax: 1-604-528-5518
internet: http://www.jibc.bc.ca

Keewatin Community College
436 - 7th Street, PO Box 3000
The Pas, Manitoba R9A 1M7 Canada
phone: 1-204-623-3416
fax: 1-204-623-7316
internet: http://www.keewatincc.mb.ca

Kemptville College of Agricultural Technology
PO Box 2003
Kemptville, Ontario K0G 1J0 Canada
phone: 1-613-258-8336
fax: 1-613-258-8477
internet: http://www.kemptvillec.uoguelph.ca

Keyano College
8115 Franklin Avenue
Fort McMurray, Alberta T9H 2H7 Canada
phone: 1-800-251-1408
fax: 1-403-791-1555
internet: http://www.keyanoc.ab.ca

Kwantlen University College
12666 - 72nd Avenue, PO Box 9030
Surrey, British Columbia V3W 2M8 Canada
phone: 1-604-599-2100
fax: 1-604-599-2068
internet: http://www.kwantlen.bc.ca

Lakeland College
5707 - 47th Avenue West
Vermilion, Alberta T9X 1K5 Canada
phone: 1-403-853-8420
fax: 1-403-853-7355
internet: http://www.lakelandc.ab.ca

Langara College
100 West 49th Avenue
Vancouver, British Columbia V5Y 2Z6 Canada
phone: 1-604-323-5511
fax: 1-604-323-5555
internet: http://www.langara.bc.ca

Lambton College of Applied Arts & Technology
1457 London Road, PO Box 969
Sarnia, Ontario N7T 7K4 Canada
phone: 1-519-542-7751
fax: 1-519-542-6667
internet: http://www.lambton.on.ca

Lethbridge Community College
3000 College Drive South
Lethbridge, Alberta T1K 1L6 Canada
phone: 1-403-320-3200
fax: 1-403-320-1461
internet: http://www.lethbridgec.ab.ca

Loyalist College of Applied Arts & Technology
Wallbridge-Loyalist Road, PO Box 4200
Belleville, Ontario K8N 5B9 Canada
phone: 1-613-969-1913
fax: 1-613-962-1376
http://www.loyalistc.on.ca

Malaspina University - College
900 Fifth Street
Nanaimo, British Columbia V9R 5S5 Canada
phone: 1-250-755-8710
fax: 1-250-755-8725
internet: http://www.mala.bc.ca

Marianopolis College
3880 Côte des Neiges
Montreal, Quebec H3H 1W1 Canada
phone: 1-514-931-8792
fax: 1-514-931-6786
internet: http://www.ccaa.ca/marianopolis.htm

Medicine Hat College
299 College Drive SE
Medicine Hat, Alberta T1A 3Y6 Canada
phone: 1-403-529-3819
fax: 1-403-504-3517
internet: http://www.mhc.ab.ca

Michener Institute for Applied Health Sciences
222 St. Patrick Street
Toronto, Ontario M5T 1V4 Canada
phone: 1-416-596-3101
fax: 1-416-596-3180
internet: http://www.michener.on.ca

Mohawk College of Applied Arts & Technology
Fennell Avenue and West 5th, PO Box 2034
Hamilton, Ontario L8N 3T2 Canada
phone: 1-905-575-1212
fax: 1-905-575-2330
internet: http://www.mohawkc.on.ca

Mount Royal College
4825 Richard Road S.W.
Calgary, Alberta T3E 6K6 Canada
phone: 1-403-240-6111
fax: 1-403-240-6698
internet: http://www.mtroyal.ab.ca

ACCC Member List

The following list of institutions appears courtesy of the Association of Canadian Community Colleges (ACCC). The information provided is the most recent available; however, in some cases its accuracy cannot be verified. Please contact the institution directly for further information.
An asterisk (*) indicates that the institute offers instruction in French.

New Brunswick Community Colleges
Department of Advanced Education & Training
470 York Street, PO Box 6000
Fredericton, New Brunswick E3B 5H1 Canada
phone: 1-506-453-2597
fax: 1-506-453-3806
internet: http://www.gov.nb.ca/ael/nbcc

Niagara College of Applied Arts & Technology
300 Woodlawn Road, PO Box 1005
Welland, Ontario L3B 5S2 Canada
phone: 1-905-735-2211
fax: 1-905-788-9451
internet: http://www.niagarac.on.ca

Nicola Valley Institute of Technology
2196 Quilchena Avenue, PO Box 399
Merritt, British Columbia V1K 1B8 Canada
phone: 1-250-378-3300
fax: 1-250-378-3332
internet: http://www.nvit.bc.ca

North Island College
2300 Ryan Road
Courtenay, British Columbia V9N 8N6
phone: 1-250-334-5270
fax: 1-250-334-5269
internet: http://www.nic.bc.ca

North West Regional College
1381 - 101st Street
North Battleford, Saskatchewan S9A 0Z9 Canada
phone: 1-306-937-5100
fax: 1-306-445-1575
internet: http://www.nwrc.sk.ca

Northern Alberta Institute of Technology
11762 - 106th Street
Edmonton, Alberta T5G 2R1 Canada
phone: 1-403-471-7400
fax: 1-403-471-8583
internet: http://www.nait.ab.ca

Northern College of Applied Arts & Technology
Highway 101 East, PO Box 3211
Timmins, Ontario P4N 8R6 Canada
phone: 1-705-235-3211
fax: 1-705-235-7279
internet: http://www.northernc.on.ca

Northern Lights College
11401 - 8th Street
Dawson Creek, British Columbia V1G 4G2 Canada
phone: 1-250-782-5251
fax: 1-250-782-5233
internet: http://www.nlc.bc.ca

Northlands College
PO Box 1000
La Ronge, Saskatchewan S0J 3G0 Canada
phone: 1-306-425-4480
fax: 1-306-425-3002
internet: http://www.sasked.gov.sk.ca/reg_col/northlands/norcoll.html

Northwest Community College
5331 McConnell Avenue
Terrace, British Columbia V8G 4C2 Canada
phone: 1-250-635-6511
fax: 1-250-635-3511
internet: http://www.nwcc.bc.ca

Nova Scotia Agriculture College
PO Box 550
Truro, Nova Scotia B2N 5E3 Canada
phone: 1-902-893-6600
fax: 1-902-897-9399
internet: http://www.nsac.ns.ca

Nova Scotia Community Colleges
Department of Education
5685 Leeds Street, PO Box 1153
Halifax, Nova Scotia B3J 3C4 Canada
phone: 1-902-491-6722
fax: 1-902-491-4646
internet: http://www.nscc.ns.ca

Nunavut Arctic College
PO Box 160, Aeroplex Building
Iqaluit, Northwest Territories X0A 0H0 Canada
phone: 1-867-979-4114
fax: 1-867-979-4118
internet: http://www.nunanet.com/~nachq

Okanagan University College
North Kelowna Campus, 3333 College Way
Kelowna, British Columbia V1V 1V7 Canada
phone: 1-250-862-5421
fax: 1-250-860-8806
internet: http://www.okanagan.bc.ca

Olds College
4500 - 50th Street
Olds, Alberta T4H 1R6 Canada
phone: 1-403-556-8281
fax: 1-403-556-4698
internet: http://www.oldscollege.ab.ca

Open Learning Agency
4355 Mathissi Place
Burnaby, British Columbia V5G 4S8 Canada
phone: 1-604-431-3000
fax: 1-604-431-3333
internet: http://www.ola.bc.ca

Parkland Regional College
290 Prince William Drive, Box 790
Melville, Saskatchewan S0A 2P0 Canada
phone: 1-306-728-4471
fax: 1-306-728-2576
internet: http://www.sasked.gov.sk.ca/reg_col/parkland/prc_home.html

Red Deer College
56th Avenue & 32nd Street
Red Deer, Alberta T4N 5H5 Canada
phone: 1-403-342-3300
fax: 1-403-340-8940
internet: http://www.rdc.ab.ca

Red River College of Applied Arts, Science and Technology
2055 Notre Dame Avenue
Winnipeg, Manitoba R3H 0J9 Canada
phone: 1-204-632-3960
fax: 1-204-632-9661
internet: http://www.rrcc.mb.ca

Ridgetown College of Agricultural Technology
Main Street
Ridgetown, Ontario N0P 2C0 Canada
phone: 1-519-674-1610
fax: 1-519-674-1600
internet: http://www.ridgetownc.on.ca

Saskatchewan Indian Institute of Technology
Asinakaniseekan Askiy Reserve
103A Packham Avenue, Suite 100
Saskatoon, Saskatchewan S7N 4K4 Canada
phone: 1-306-244-4444
fax: 1-306-244-1391
internet: http://www.siit.sk.ca

Saskatchewan Institute of Applied Science & Technology
SIAST - S.J. Cohen Centre
401 - 119 4th Avenue South
Saskatoon, Saskatchewan S7K 5X2 Canada
phone: 1-306-933-7328
fax: 1-306-933-7334
internet: http://www.siast.sk.ca

Sault College of Applied Arts & Technology
443 Northern Avenue, PO Box 60
Sault Sainte Marie, Ontario P6A 5L3 Canada
phone: 1-705-759-6774
fax: 1-705-759-1319
internet: http://www.saultc.on.ca

Selkirk College
301 Frank Beinder Way, Box 1200
Castlegar, British Columbia V1N 3J1 Canada
phone: 1-250-365-7292
fax: 1-250-365-6568
internet: http://www.selkirk.bc.ca

Seneca College of Applied Arts & Technology
1750 Finch Avenue East
North York, Ontario M2J 2X5 Canada
phone: 1-416-491-5050
fax: 1-416-491-3081
internet: http://www.senecac.on.ca

Sheridan College of Applied Arts and Technology
Oakville Campus
1430 Trafalgar Road
Oakville, Ontario L6H 2L1 Canada
phone: 1-905-845-9430
fax: 1-905-815-4043
internet: http://www.sheridanc.on.ca

Sir Sandford Fleming College of Applied Arts & Technology
McDonnel Campus, 526 McDonnel Street
Peterborough, Ontario K9J 7B1 Canada
phone: 1-705-743-5610
fax: 1-705-749-5540
internet: http://www.flemingc.on.ca

South Winnipeg Technical Centre
130 Henlow Bay, PO Box 145
Fort Whyte, Manitoba R3Y 1G5 Canada
phone: 1-204-989-6500
fax: 1-204-488-4152
internet: http://www.swtc.mb.ca

Southern Alberta Institute of Technology
1301 - 16th Avenue N. W.
Calgary, Alberta T2M 0L4 Canada
phone: 1-403-284-8110
fax: 1-403-284-8940
internet: http://www.sait.ab.ca

Southeast Regional College
Souris Valley Campus, Box 2003
Weyburn, Saskatchewan S4H 2Z9 Canada
phone: 1-306-848-2511
fax: 1-306-848-2517
internet: -

ACCC Member List

The following list of institutions appears courtesy of the Association of Canadian Community Colleges (ACCC). The information provided is the most recent available; however, in some cases its accuracy cannot be verified. Please contact the institution directly for further information.
An asterisk (*) indicates that the institute offers instruction in French.

St. Clair College of Applied Arts & Technology
2000 Talbot Road West
Windsor, Ontario N9A 6S4 Canada
phone: 1-519-966-1656
fax: 1-519-972-3811
internet: http://www.stclairc.on.ca

St. Lawrence College
2288 Parkedale avenue
Brockville, Ontario K6V 5X3 Canada
phone: 1-613-345-0556
fax: 1-613-345-2231
http://www.stlawrencec.on.ca

University College of Cape Breton
Place Bay Highway, PO Box 5300
Sydney, Nova Scotia B1P 6L2 Canada
phone: 1-902-539-5300
fax: 1-902-562-0119
internet: http://www.uccb.ns.ca

University College of the Cariboo
900 College Drive, Box 3010
Kamloops, British Columbia V2C 5N3 Canada
phone: 1-250-828-5000
fax: 1-250-828-5092
internet: http://www.cariboo.bc.ca

University College of the Fraser Valley
33844 King Road, RR #2
Abbotsford, British Columbia V2S 7M9 Canada
phone: 1-604-853-7441
fax: 1-604-853-9990
internet: http://www.ucfv.bc.ca

Vancouver Community College
1155 East Broadway, Box # 24620, Station F
Vancouver, British Columbia V5N 5T9 Canada
phone: 1-604-871-7000
fax: 1-604-871-7100
internet: http://www.vcc.bc.ca

Vanier College
821, Sainte-Croix avenue
Saint Laurent, Quebec H4L 3X9 Canada
phone: 1-514-744-7500
fax: 1-514-744-7952
internet: http://www.vaniercollege.qc.ca

Yellowquill College
Crescent Road West, PO Box 1599
Portage la Prairie, Manitoba R1N 3P1 Canada
phone: 1-204-239-1570
fax: 1-204-857-4272
internet: http://www2.portage.net

Yukon College
I00 Lewes Boulevard, PO Box 2799
Whitehorse, Yukon Y1A 5K4 Canada
phone: 1-867-668-8710
fax: 1-867-668-8890
internet: http://www.yukoncollege.yk.ca

education international

The 1999 Guide Series
Guiding Students to Success

Secondary School & English Language Programs

International Guide to Public & Private Secondary Schools in Canada

Features *In-Depth Profiles* of private and public secondary school programs across Canada, providing information such as curriculum, facilities, admissions, expenses and support for international students. Includes an overview of Canadian education and detailed descriptions of provincial education systems.

ISBN 1-894122-37-2, 8½ x 11 inches, US$14.95, C$18.95, soft cover

International Guide to English Language Programs

Features *In-Depth Profiles* of over 200 programs in Australia, Canada, the USA and other countries, providing detailed information on each program: courses offered, costs and other expenses, admission requirements, and more. Lists contact information for more than 900 English Language programs, and contains articles on topics such as living and studying in each country, TOEFL preparation and information on education systems.

ISBN 1-894122-33-x, 8 ½ x 11 inches, US$24.95, C$29.95, soft cover
Also available in single-country format for Australia and Canada (US$9.95, C$12.95 each) and the USA (US$11.95, C$14.95 each). ISBN 1-894122-34-8 (Australia), ISBN 1-894122-35-6 (Canada), ISBN 1-894122-36-4 (USA)

Undergraduate Programs

Guide to Undergraduate Business Programs

Features *In-Depth Profiles* of over 150 programs in Australia, Canada, the USA and other countries, and provides contact information for another 600 degree granting programs. Profiles highlight each program's unique features and areas of concentration, admission requirements and expenses. New for 1999: articles on the different business majors, accounting education and careers in business.

ISBN 1-894122-25-9, 8½ x 11 inches, US$24.95, C$29.95, soft cover
Also available in single-country format for Australia and Canada (US$9.95, C$12.95 each) and the USA (US$11.95, C$14.95 each). ISBN 1-894122-26-7 (Australia), ISBN 1-894122-27-5 (Canada), ISBN 1-894122-28-3 (USA)

Guide to Undergraduate Engineering & Technology Programs

Features *In-Depth Profiles* of over 100 programs in Australia, Canada, the USA and other countries, and provides contact information for more than 400 programs. Profiles highlight each program's disciplines and areas of expertise, admission requirements, expenses, and recognition earned. New for 1999: articles on various disciplines, choosing an engineering program and careers in engineering.

ISBN 1-894122-29-1, 8½ x 11 inches, US$24.95, C$29.95, soft cover
Also available in single-country format for Australia and Canada (US$9.95, C$12.95 each) and the USA (US$11.95, C$14.95 each). ISBN 1-894122-30-5 (Australia), ISBN 1-894122-31-3 (Canada), ISBN 1-894122-32-1 (USA)

education international

General College & University

Guide to Universities & Colleges in Canada

In-Depth Profiles of Canadian colleges are presented in this one-of-a-kind resource. Profiles contain all the information one needs to confidently select a college: academic programs offered, university transfer programs, admission requirements, expenses and financial aid, student support services, and more. Also lists contact information and statistics for more than 200 colleges and university colleges. Includes articles on topics such as the Canadian education system, scholarships, study options like co-op/internships and evaluating a school.

ISBN 1-894122-24-0, 8½ x 11 inches, US$19.95, C$21.95, soft cover

International Guide to Universities & 4-Year Colleges in the USA

Geared to the needs of international students, this unique resource provides in-depth information on over 100 universities and colleges throughout the USA, providing information on admissions, the university and programs offered. Also lists contact information and statistics for an additional 150 American four-year universities and colleges with significant international student populations. Includes articles on topics such as living and studying in the USA, scholarships, study options and evaluating a school.

ISBN 1-894122-19-4, 8½ x 11 inches, US$21.95, C$24.95, soft cover

Graduate Programs

Guide to Graduate Management Programs in Australia

Features *In-Depth Profiles* of Australia's MBA, PhD, and DBA programs. Provides information on full-time, part-time and distance education opportunities, and includes articles on program options and trends, application procedures, the GMAT and more.

ISBN 1-894122-21-6, 8 ½ x 11 inches, US$21.95, C$24.95, soft cover

Guide to Graduate & Executive Management Programs in Canada

Features *In-Depth Profiles* of MBA, Executive MBA, MPA, PhD, executive development and specialized programs such as industrial relations, agriculture and aviation. Provides information on full-time, part-time and distance education opportunities. Includes detailed industry and career descriptions contributed by leading Canadian corporations, institutes and professional associations.

ISBN 1-894122-22-4, 8½ x 11 inches, US$21.95, C$24.95, soft cover

Guide to Graduate Management Programs in the USA

Published in conjunction with the AACSB—International Association for Management Education. Features *In-Depth Profiles* and complete listings of all AACSB-accredited and candidacy school programs, highlighting MBA, MSc, MPA and other master's-level management degrees. Provides contact information and program highlights for non-profiled schools, and includes information on program options and trends, key industries, the GMAT and more.

ISBN 1-894122-23-2, 8½ x 11 inches, US$21.95, C$24.95, soft cover

Guide to Graduate Engineering & Computer Science Programs in Canada

Includes detailed information on over 90 graduate engineering and computer science programs, and features select professional development programs from across Canada. *In-Depth Profiles* include information such as current research areas, specializations of faculty members, research funding, and expenses and financial assistance.

ISBN 1-894122-20-8, 8½ x 11 inches, US$21.95, C$24.95, soft cover

Additional Resources

EDUCATION RELATED ORGANIZATIONS

Association of Canadian Community Colleges (ACCC)

200-1223 rue Michael Street Nord/North
Ottawa, Canada K1J 7T2
phone: 1-613-746-2222
fax: 1-613-746-6721
email:-
internet: http://www.accc.ca/

Created in 1972, the Association of Canadian Community Colleges is a national organization of voluntary members that includes Canadian colleges, institutes, cégeps and university colleges. The ACCC represents the interests of its members to government, business and industry, both in Canada and internationally, and provides a wide range of information services to students.

Association of Universities and Colleges in Canada (AUCC)

350 Albert Street, Suite 600
Ottowa, Ontario K1R 1B1 Canada
phone: 1-613-563-1236
fax: 1-613-563-9745
email: dseldent@aucc.ca
internet: http://www.aucc.ca

The Association of Universities and Colleges in Canada is a nonprofit association devoted to promoting the interests of higher education in Canada. AUCC publishes many publications and administers approximately 140 student scholarships on behalf of other organizations.

Canadian Alliance of Student Associations (CASA)

PO Box 3408, Station D
Ottowa, Ontario K1P 6H8 Canada
phone: 1-613-236-3457
fax: 1-613-236-2386
email: director@casa.ca
internet: http://www.casa.ca

The Canadian Alliance of Student Associations represents 17 student associations, which represent over 275,000 students. CASA, among other things, endeavors to fascilitate the discussion of post secondary issues and increase postsecondary education quality.

Canadian Association of Colleges & University Student Services (CACUSS)

c/o Office of Student Affairs
214 College Street, Room 307, University of Toronto
Toronto, Ontario M5T 2Z9 Canada
phone: 1-416-978-4027
fax: 1-416-971-2037
email: cacuss@cacuss.ca
internet: http://www2.cacuss.ca/cacuss

The Canadian Association of College & University Student Services is a professional association representing those working in the tertiary education and student services/affairs fields. CACUSS's main purpose is to promote the effective use of university and college services.

Ontario Universities' Application Centre (OAUC)

650 Woodlawn Road West, PO Box 1328
Guelph, Ontario N1H 7P4 Canada
phone: 1-519-823-1940
fax: 1-519-823-5232
email: request@ouac.on.ca
internet: http://www.ouac.on.ca

The Ontario Universities' Application Centre was founded in 1971 as a non-profit agency. OUAC is a centralized bureau which processes applications of admissions to all 18 universities in Ontario.

INTERNATIONAL STUDENT RESOURCES

Educational Testing Service (ETS) - TOEFL

Corporate Headquarters, Rosedale Road
Princeton, New Jersey USA 08541
phone: 1-609-921-9000
fax: 1-609-734-5410
email: etsinfo@ets.org
internet: http://www.ets.org/body.html

ETS is the administrative body responsible for managing the TOEFL under the guidance of the TOEFL Policy Council, a group of 15 members from independent academic organizations and government agencies. The service's online network (ETS Net) provides information on a range of subjects from financial aid to teacher certification. Sample TOEFL questions and hints about test preparation and registration are also available on ETS Net.

More on Education International

Education International (EI) provides high-quality information to students, education counsellors, academics and governments worldwide on secondary and postsecondary study opportunities in Australia, Canada, New Zealand, the UK and the USA.

EI publishes a variety of study guides geared to both students interested in overseas study opportunities and those wanting comprehensive information on domestic program offerings. EI's guides help readers compare and evaluate programs based on the most important and relevant criteria. The 1999 series consists of 25 titles spanning secondary school programs; English language programs; undergraduate, graduate and executive business and engineering programs; and universities and colleges. Our guides are distributed in over 80 countries worldwide.

EI extends its global reach through its three websites:

EDUCATION INTERNATIONAL WORLDWIDE

http://www.eiworldwide.com

- contains mini-profiles of almost 500 secondary schools, English language, undergraduate business and undergraduate engineering programs in Australia, Canada, New Zealand, the UK and the USA, as well as 200+ universities and colleges in Canada and the USA
- includes a search engine that allows users to identify relevant programs based on the criteria most important to them
- offers multilingual profiles in as many as eight languages
- allows users to browse information on health care, visas, culture shock, safety and more

GradSciEng.com

http://www.gradscieng.com

The only website devoted to graduate engineering and computer science education in Canada

- profiles over 90 graduate engineering, computer science and professional development programs in Canada
- allows users to search and compare programs by discipline
- users can request more information on a program at the click of a mouse
- contains articles on options and trends, financing an education, and more

GraduateBusiness.com

http://www.graduatebusiness.com

The Web's #1 resource on graduate management programs around the world

- profiles hundreds of graduate and executive management programs in Canada, Australia and the USA
- allows comparison of program features at the click of a mouse
- users can request more information on a program electronically
- contains articles on the GMAT, management trends and careers contributed by leading global organizations

Whether you are looking for a high school, undergraduate, graduate or professional development program, we know that choosing the program suited to your unique needs is the key to success. Our primary objective is to help make that process easier.

We invite and encourage questions, comments or feedback from our readers. Contact us at

EI Education International Ltd.
#205 - 5325 Cordova Bay Road
Victoria, British Columbia V8Y 2L3 Canada
Phone: (250) 658-6283 Fax: (250) 658-6285 Email: educate@eiworldwide.com

Editorial Notes

Education International's style standards anticipate the customs and expectations of its audience. Although spelling and usage vary widely, the majority of the readers of the *1999 Guide to Universities & Colleges in Canada* will be more familiar with British conventions; EI has therefore chosen the ninth edition of the *Concise Oxford Dictionary* as its primary reference text, choosing British over American spelling standards, with a few exceptions. One is in the use of "program," for which the traditional -mme ending has been dropped. Proper names—of universities, programs, organizations, etc.—have not been altered to match EI's style standards.

Current trends in writing are to a simplified style: less use of capitalization, punctuation and hyphenation. Where practicable, EI has adopted this approach (e.g., postsecondary, coursework, PhD).

Metric measures are used as the standard within the guide.

For style standards, EI uses both the *Chicago Manual of Style* and *NAFSA Style: A Manual for Writers and Editors.*

Throughout the guide, the words "international," "foreign" and "overseas" are used to refer to students who study in a nation other than their own.

Within the profiles, "n/a" has been used to indicate statistics that are not applicable to the program or university in question; "not available" has been used to indicate instances where the information is not regularly compiled.

Profile Information

The goal of the guide is to provide as much relevant information as possible in as comparable a format as possible. All of the profiles follow a standard format in order to facilitate comparison between universities and colleges. Statistics used in the profiles are based on the most recent figures available from each university or college.

The *Disciplines/Majors Offered* and *Academic Programs* sections list the fields of study offered by the universities, university colleges, colleges and institutes. Minors and graduate program options are not listed.

The information in the Calendar Year field is intended to indicate only those terms, semesters or quarters during which a full course selection is offered. Additional, partial sessions may be available. Students should contact schools directly for further information.

Information provided under *Student & Faculty Profile* typically shows statistics for the most recent school year; however, in certain cases where this information has not been compiled, the statistics reflect the most current information available.

The information provided under *Admissions Criteria & Procedures* and *Admissions at a Glance* is not intended to be comprehensive, but to provide general guidelines. Students should consult school brochures and contact the institution directly before submitting applications to ensure that they are aware of and will meet the most current requirements and deadlines.

Expenses at a Glance is intended to provide a breakdown of some of the costs associated with postsecondary study. The tuition costs indicated refer to a typical year of full-time, undergraduate degree studies. This section does not take into account additional tuition encountered through specialized degree programs, summer sessions, etc. Any nonacademic supplementary fees or expenses that students may encounter have been excluded. For a comprehensive list of expenses, potential students should consult university/college brochures or contact school representatives.

The textbook costs given are approximations; true costs will vary depending on courses taken.

The expenses given for accommodation are approximations. For residence costs where meal plans are available, these costs have been factored in; for self-catering, private rental situations, a guideline of C$200 per month has been used to account for food costs. Costs may vary depending on individual lifestyle.

Expenses refer to the 1999-2000 school year. Where 1999-2000 figures were not available, the most recent costs available have been used; these figures are followed by an asterisk (*). Dollar amounts given reflect the information available at the time of writing; prices are liable to change and EI makes no guarantee about costs listed.

The Cost of Living field is intended to reflect the relative cost of living in one Canadian city as compared to living in another Canadian city; in some cases this information has been self-reported and its accuracy cannot be verified.

Final Notes

The information used to compile these profiles was obtained through promotional literature from each school and in consultation with school representatives. All profiles have been verified by the respective institution. Although all information is believed to be accurate, prospective students should contact schools directly for further information.

This guide offers general guidelines for individuals who are preparing for international study and is not intended as a complete reference to immigration and visa procedures. Potential students should consult the appropriate embassy or consulate to obtain advice and the materials necessary to prepare for overseas study.

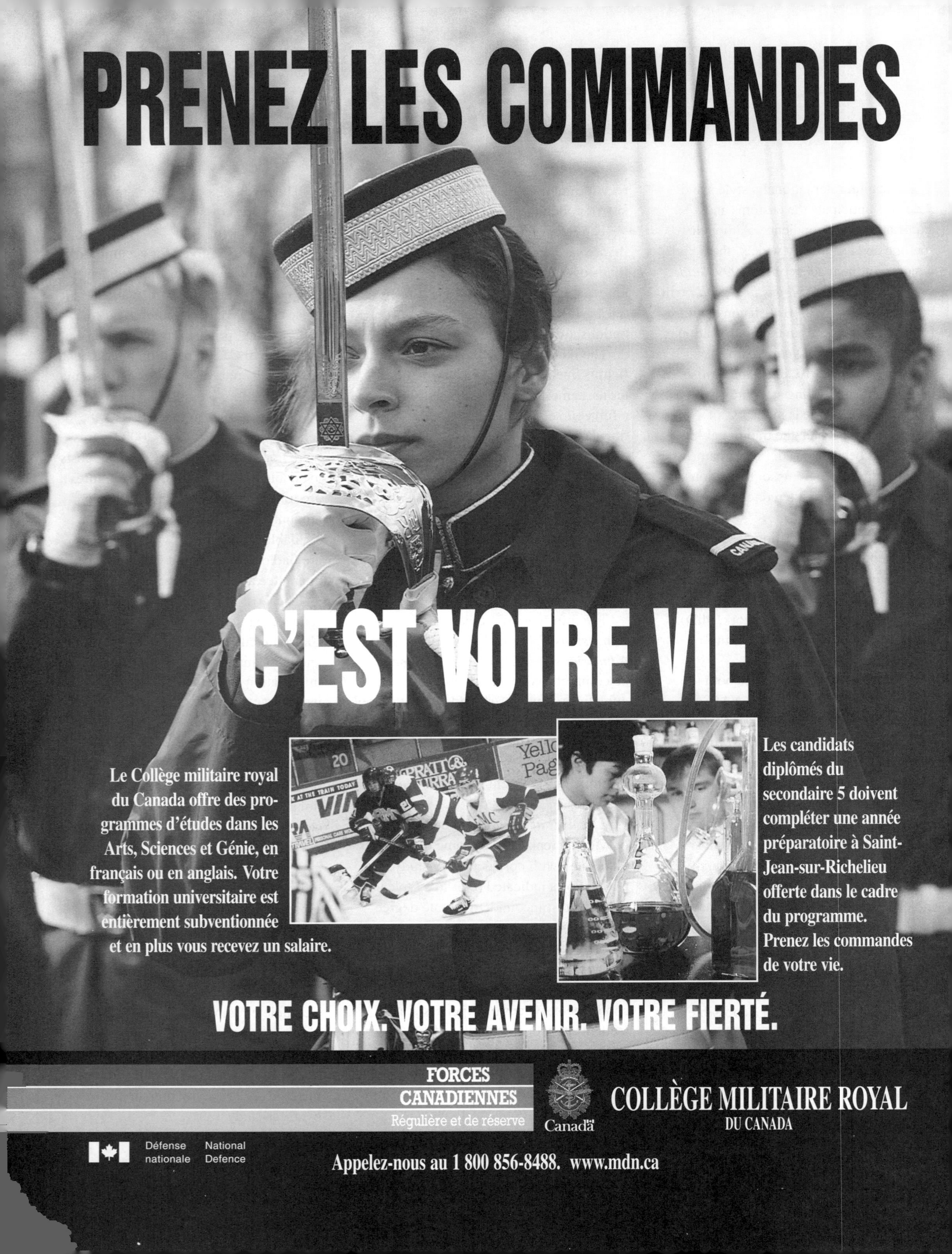
PRENEZ LES COMMANDES
C'EST VOTRE VIE
Le Collège militaire royal du Canada offre des programmes d'études dans les Arts, Sciences et Génie, en français ou en anglais. Votre formation universitaire est entièrement subventionnée et en plus vous recevez un salaire.
Les candidats diplômés du secondaire 5 doivent compléter une année préparatoire à Saint-Jean-sur-Richelieu offerte dans le cadre du programme. Prenez les commandes de votre vie.
VOTRE CHOIX. VOTRE AVENIR. VOTRE FIERTÉ.
FORCES CANADIENNES
Régulière et de réserve
Canada
COLLÈGE MILITAIRE ROYAL DU CANADA
Défense nationale
National Defence
Appelez-nous au 1 800 856-8488. www.mdn.ca

Glossary

Definitions

0-5 Pharmacy Program – a five-year undergraduate Bachelor of Science degree program; this program is slowly being phased out in favour of the 0-6 Pharmacy Program

0-6 Pharmacy Program – a six-year undergraduate Doctor of Pharmacy degree program (leads to a Pharm-D, though it is not a graduate degree); graduates can write (not just fill) prescriptions

3/2 Program – usually refers to a program in which a bachelor's degree and a Master of Business Administration (MBA) degree may be earned in five years; these programs are starting to be available with other master's degrees as well

4-1-4 (terms); 4-4-1 (terms) – refer to the organization of terms by month; in the first, a four-month term is followed by a one-month term and then another four-month term; in the second, two consecutive four-month terms are followed by a one-month term

Academic Adviser – an appointed university representative who provides guidance to students in designing an academic program and selecting courses to meet program requirements

Accredit – to render credible; programs are often accredited by regional and/or general bodies, ensuring that specific curricular standards are met

Advanced Standing (Advanced Placement, Accelerated Study) – direct entry into more advanced levels in the program (bypassing initial components) based on performance on advanced placement tests or academic credit previously earned

Affidavit – a written statement confirmed by oath

Associate Degree – degree granted after completion of a two-year postsecondary program (sometimes used as a transfer degree)

Baccalaureate – a bachelor's degree level of study

Case Study – the application of management principles to simulated or real-life situations in order to give students practice in applying their analytical and presentation skills as well as theoretical knowledge

Class Rank – students' academic standing in relation to their peers' (usually in reference to secondary school grade averages)

College – institution offering associate and bachelor's degrees focusing on education rather than research; also refers to divisions within a university system (e.g., College of Business)

Concentration – a focus undertaken within a major; for example, a student pursuing a degree with a major in business might undertake a concentration in human resources management

Concurrent – simultaneous; occurring at the same time or together

Conditional Acceptance (Admission) – offer of a place in a university/institution degree program to an academically qualified student subject to meeting a specified condition, often completion of English language studies or achievement of a minimum English proficiency test score

Consortium – an association of several bodies

Cooperative or Co-op (Program) – education program that combines theoretical learning with practical experience, generally via alternating periods of classroom study and paid work placements

Core Course – course addressing the main components of a program, generally as a requisite for graduation

Courseload – the number of courses taken or credits earned within a period of study (semester, term, quarter, etc.)

Credit – a measure granted for each course completed; most academic programs require students to complete a certain number of credits for graduation

Credit Hours – a system of measuring credit by the number of hours spent in class a week

Curriculum – subjects included in a course of study; plural: curricula

Deferred Admission – postponing enrolment into an academic program after acceptance for a specified period of time (usually one year)

Distance Education – education program whereby students may complete all or part of an educational program in a geographical location apart from the institution hosting the program; the final award given is equivalent in standard and content to an award program completed on campus

Double Major – the pursuit of two majors during the course of one degree program

Ecumenical – of or representing the whole Christian world

Early Admission – acceptance into a postsecondary institution before completion of secondary school; admission standards are usually higher than for regular admission

Early Decision – a system in which applicants apply earlier than the posted deadline, and, if accepted, withdraw all other applications and agree to enrol at the university

Elective Courses – optional courses that complement the core components of a degree program; credit earned is applied to the final degree

Glossary

Entrepreneurship – the undertaking of a business or enterprise with chance of profit or loss; a common specialization in business programs; program participants study the traits of successful entrepreneurs as well as what is needed to establish a new business

Exchange (Program) – agreement between institutions that permits students to move from one institution to another for short- or long-term periods of study or employment; may offer credit towards a degree earned at the original institution

Faculty – the professors and researchers employed by a university; also refers to divisions within a university system (e.g., Faculty of Engineering)

Foundation (Studies/Year) – preliminary general or specific course of study that forms the basis of subsequent education; frequently offered as a qualifying year for candidates who require skills/knowledge upgrading for entry into a desired degree program

Government Depository – official storehouse for government documents, often situated within a university library or specified building

GPA – grade point average; the average grade achieved by a student during the course of an educational program, calculated on various scales determined by individual institutions

Graduate Study – post-baccalaureate program, usually leading to master's or doctoral degrees

Homestay – housing arrangement in which students are placed with local families; weekly or monthly cost generally includes two to three meals per day

Honours Program – programs of particularly challenging coursework (and often including a major project or thesis) offered to high-achieving students; achievement is recognized on the degree

Interdisciplinary (Curriculum) – study of all aspects of a particular field (e.g., business, engineering) rather than complete specialization in a single area (e.g., marketing, electrical engineering); gives students a broad, well-rounded education

Internship – concentrated period of degree-related, industrial or business placement, for which participant may or may not be remunerated

Joint Degree – pursuit of two degrees (e.g., business and law) at the same time; students achieving joint degrees frequently benefit from special programs enabling a shortened period of study

Liberal Arts – nontechnical work conducted in the humanities and social and natural sciences

Major – the primary academic focus pursued within a degree program; often combined with general education requirements

Matriculation – qualifying by examination or otherwise for admission to a university

Mechatronic – the use of computer hardware and software to control mechanical systems

Minor – a secondary academic focus pursued as a supplement or accent to a major program

Open Admissions – admissions policy under which there are no academic prerequisites with the exception of secondary school completion

Orientation – an organized introduction for new students to the campus, resources and surrounding area; usually occurs just prior to the onset of classes

Parallel-time Co-op – cooperative education system in which students complete classroom instruction and acquire degree-related work experience during the same time period

Placement Test – a test used to determine a student's level in a particular skill area; commonly used for placement in English language programs for non-native speakers; conducted after a student's arrival on campus

Pool (Selection) – determination, with academic advisory assistance, of a schedule of required and elective courses and the appropriate order of completion to fulfil degree requirements

Postgraduate Study – see graduate study

Practicum – concentrated period of degree-related, practical work experience; plural: **practica**

Prerequisite – course required as preparation for entry into a more advanced academic course or program

Private Institution – an institution that relies primarily on non-governmental sources of financial support

Prorated – proportionally; for prorated refunds, the amount of money refunded is proportional to the amount of time passed from a specified date

Public Institution – an institution that receives the majority of funding through the government

Reference (Recommendation) – a commendation from a former teacher or counsellor in the form of a letter attesting to the student's academic and/or personal merits

Registrar – the person responsible for records of enrolment and academic achievement at an institution

Residence Hall (Dormitory) – accommodation located on campus; students usually live in shared or private rooms; cooking facilities are not generally supplied, though many institutions offer cafeteria meal plans

Rolling Admissions – a policy with no set deadline for application submission

Glossary

Sandwich Option – educational program in which a period of paid, supervised industrial work experience is undertaken in the midst of degree studies

Secular – not concerned with religion or religious belief

Self-catering – accommodation type in which housing may or may not be furnished and students are responsible for upkeep as well as food purchase and preparation

Specialization – a focus undertaken within a major; for example, a student pursuing a degree with a major in engineering might specialize in computer science

Standardized Tests – tests administered by an outside body that are used in the admissions process in conjunction with academic transcripts; these include the SAT and ACT

Study Abroad (Program) – agreement between institutions in different geographical locations enabling students to move from one to the other for short- or long-term study periods within a single degree program

Syllabus – program or outline of a course of study

Teaching Assistant – a student (usually graduate) who assists the professor with advising, laboratory supervision, marking and teaching

Terminal Degree – the highest degree that may be obtained in a field (usually, but not always, a doctoral degree)

Tertiary – postsecondary education; education pursued after secondary school (usually in reference to college or university education)

Transcript – official academic records detailing place and time of study, courses completed and grades achieved

Twinning (Program) – arrangement between institutions in different geographical locations in which students complete up to two years of study in a college in their home countries, followed by guaranteed admission to the partner university for completion of a degree program; the degree is granted by the latter institution

Videoconference – a conference conducted through the use of video technology, allowing individuals to participate from separate locations; frequently used by distance education programs

Abbreviations

acc	accounting
adm	admission
admin	administration
adv	advanced
ag	agriculture(al)
app	application
arch	architecture
asst	assistant
assoc	associate/association
avg	average
begin	beginner
bio	biology(ical)
bldg	building
bus	business
chem	chemistry(ical)
comm	communication(s)
comp	computer(ing)
des	design
dev't	development
dom	domestic
dorms	dormitories
econ	economics
educ	education
elect	electrical
elem	elementary
eng	engineering
env	environmental
fin	finance
ha	hectare(s)
Hons	Honours
HR	human resources
info	information
int	intermediate
ind	industrial
IS	information systems
int'l	international
km	kilometre(s)
lang	language(s)
mech	mechanical
med	medical
mgmt	management
mktg	marketing
org	organizations
ops	operations
phil	philosophy
poli	political
priv	private
prod	production
prog	program(s)
psych	psychology
res	resources
qtr	quarter
rehab	rehabilitation
res	residence
sci	science(s)
sem	semester
soc	sociology
stats	statistics
tech'n	technician
tech	technology
uni	university
yr	year

Glossary

Accreditation Bodies, Associations, Councils & Societies

AACSB The International Association for Management Education
AAIEP American Association of Intensive English Programs
ABET Accreditation Board for Engineering & Technology
ACCC Association of Canadian Community Colleges
ACPE American Council on Pharmaceutical Education
ACU Association of Commonwealth Universities
AIESEC Association International des Etudiants en Sciences Eco-nomiques & Commerciales
AUBER Association for University Business & Economic Research
AUCC Association of Universities & Colleges in Canada
CIAU Canadian Intercollegiate Athletics Union
ECE Education Credentials Evaluators
FIYTO Federation of International Youth Travel Organizations
GATE Global Alliance for Transnational Education
OUAC Ontario Universities' Application Centre
OCAS Ontario College Application Service
NAFSA Association of International Educators
NSF National Science Foundation
NRC National Research Council
NSERC National Science & Engineering Research Council of Canada
TESOL Teachers of English to Speakers of Other Languages
UCIEP University & College Intensive English Programs

English Language Tests & Certifications

CAE Cambridge Advanced English Test
CanTEST Canadian Test of English as a Foreign Language
CCSE Cambridge Certificate of Communicative Skills in English
CEIBT Cambridge Certificate in English for International Business & Trade
CEIC Cambridge Certificate in English for International Communication
CPE Cambridge Certificate of Proficiency in English
ECPE Examination for the Certificate of Proficiency in English
ELPT English Language Proficiency Test
FCE Cambridge First Certificate in English
IELTS International English Language Testing System
MELAB Michigan English Language Assessment Battery
MTELP Michigan Test of English Language Proficiency
PET Preliminary English Test
TEEP Test in English for Educational Purposes
TOEFL Test of English as a Foreign Language
TOFFL Test of French as a Foreign Language
TOEIC Test of English for International Communication
TSE Test of Spoken English
TWE Test of Written English

Acronyms

ACT American College Test
CALL Computer-Assisted Language Learning
CD-ROM Compact Disk-Read Only Memory
EMAIL Electronic Mail
ESL English as a Second Language
GCSE General Certificate of Secondary Education
GEC General Education Curriculum
GED General Educational Development (test)
GMAT Graduate Management Admissions Test
GPA Grade Point Average
GRE Graduate Record Examination
HND Higher National Diploma
IB International Baccalaureate
IEE Institution of Electrical Engineers
LAN Local Area Network
MIS Management Information Systems
MMR Measles, Mumps & Rubella vaccination
NAFTA North American Free Trade Agreement
NASA National Aeronautical & Space Administration
NCUR National Conference for Undergraduate Research
OAC Ontario Academic Credit
PC Personal Computer
SAT Scholastic Assessment Test
UFC University Funding Council
UHIP University Health Insurance Plan
UMAP University Mobility in Asia Pacific Scheme
VLSI Very Large Scale Integration
WWW World Wide Web

Fields of Study Index

The following index is a guide to some of the more common undergraduate majors offered by the universities and colleges featured in this guide. It is not intended to be a comprehensive source of information, and prospective students should consult individual schools directly for further information.

A

ALGONQUIN COLLEGE OF APPLIED ARTS & TECHNOLOGY

Please send me information on the following career fields:

- ❐ Business
- ❐ Media
- ❐ Computer Engineering Technology
- ❐ Mechanical Engineering Technology
- ❐ Telecommunications
- ❐ Social/Community Services
- ❐ English Language Training Programs
- ❐ Hospitality & Tourism
- ❐ Health & Life Sciences
- ❐ Electronics Engineering Technology
- ❐ Architectural Technology
- ❐ Transportation/Building
- ❐ Justice/Security

Please send me the following application form(s):

- ❐ International Student Application Form for Language Training at Algonquin College
- ❐ Application for Admission to Algonquin College

Last Name ______________________ First Name ______________________

Address ____

______________________ Postal Code ______________ Country ______________

Telephone (______) ______________ Fax (______) ______________ Email ______________
Area Code Area Code

CUC '99

BOW VALLEY COLLEGE

Please send me information on:

- ❐ English Language Studies for International Students
- ❐ Academic Upgrading
- ❐ English as a Second Language
- ❐ Career Programs: Office Careers; Practical Nurse; Medical Office Assistant; Dental Office Assistant; Hospital Unit Clerk; Hospital Admitting Clerk; Personal Care Attendant; Arborist; Hairstyling

Last Name ______________________ First Name ______________________

Address ____

______________________ Postal Code ______________ Country ______________

Telephone (______) ______________ Fax (______) ______________ Email ______________
Area Code Area Code

CUC '99

COLLEGE OF THE NORTH ATLANTIC
Prince Philip Drive Campus

COLLEGE OF THE NORTH ATLANTIC

Please send me information on:

- ❐ Admission/application Material
- ❐ International Student Materials
- ❐ Other______________________

Last Name ______________ First Name ______________ Age ______ Sex ______

Address ____

______________________ Postal Code ______________ Country ______________

Telephone (______) ______________ Fax (______) ______________ Email ______________
Area Code Area Code

CUC '99

education international

education international

AIR MAIL

You can also fax the other side of this card to us at 1-613-727-7665

ATTACH
AIR MAIL
POSTAGE

ADMISSIONS OFFICE - ROOM C 150
Algonquin College of Applied Arts & Technology
1385 Woodroffe Avenue
Ottawa, Ontario K2G 1V8 CANADA

AIR MAIL

You can also fax the other side of this card to us at 1-403-297-4081

ATTACH
AIR MAIL
POSTAGE

BOW VALLEY COLLEGE
332-6 Avenue SE
Calgary, Alberta T2G 4S6 CANADA

AIR MAIL

You can also fax the other side of this card to us at 1-709-758-7302

ATTACH
AIR MAIL
POSTAGE

REGISTRAR'S OFFICE
College of the North Atlantic
Prince Philip Drive Campus
PO Box 1693
St. John's, Newfoundland A1C 5P7 CANADA

NBCC

NEW BRUNSWICK COMMUNITY COLLEGE

Please send me information on:

- ❐ Admission/Application Material
- ❐ Financial Aid
- ❐ Other (specify)____________________

Last Name ____________________ First Name ____________________

Address ____

____________________ Postal Code ________________ Country ________________

Telephone (______) ________________ Fax (______) ________________ Email ________________
Area Code Area Code

CUC '99

ROYAL MILITARY COLLEGE OF CANADA
COLLEGE MILITAIRE ROYAL DU CANADA

Please send me information on the following programs:/ Veuillez m'envoyer des renseignements sur les programmes suivants:

- ❐ Arts
- ❐ Sciences
- ❐ Engineering / Génie

Last Name / Nom ____________________ First Name / Prénom ____________________

Address / Adresse ____

____________________ Postal Code / Code Postal ________________ Country / Pays ________________

Tel / Tél (______) ________________ Fax (______) ________________ Email ________________
Area Code Area Code

CUC '99

UNIVERSITY OF WINDSOR

UNIVERSITY OF WINDSOR

Please send me information about:

- ❐ Undergraduate ❐ Graduate
- ❐ Academic Programs in ____________________ (specify areas of study)
- ❐ Residence and Food
- ❐ Financial Aid
- ❐ Other (specify)____________________

Last Name ________________ First Name ________________ Age______ Sex ______

Address ____

____________________ Postal Code________________ Country________________

Telephone (______) ________________ Fax (______) ________________ Email ________________
Area Code Area Code

CUC '99

education international
education international

AIR MAIL

You can also fax the other side of this card to us at 1-506-789-2430

ATTACH
AIR MAIL
POSTAGE

NBCC Admissions Services
6 Arran Street
Campbellton, New Brunswick E3N 1K4 CANADA

AIR MAIL

You can also fax the other side of this card to us at 1-613-542-3565

ATTACH
AIR MAIL
POSTAGE

REGISTRAR / SECRÉTAIRE GÉNÉRAL
Royal Military College of Canada / College Militaire Royal du Canada
PO Box 17000, Station Forces
Kingston, Ontario K7K 7B4 CANADA

AIR MAIL

You can also fax the other side of this card to us at 1-519-971-3653

ATTACH
AIR MAIL
POSTAGE

OFFICE OF THE REGISTRAR
University of Windsor
Windsor, Ontario N9B 3P4 CANADA

education international

To find out more about the universities and university-colleges that interest you, circle the name and page number, complete the form and send the card to the address on the back.
You can also fax this card to EI at 1-250-658-6285.

Universities:

Bishop'sU	275	SaintMary'sU	299	UofPrinceEdwardIsland	311
BrandonU	131	SimonFraserU	65	UofRegina	147
CarletonU	189	StFrancisXavierU	303	UofSaskatchewan	151
CMilitaireRoyalduCanada	193	TheUofWesternOntario	237	UofToronto	229
ConcordiaU	279	TheUofWinnipeg	155	UofVictoria	77
DalhousieU	291	TrentU	217	UofWaterloo	233
LakeheadU	197	UofAlberta	135	UofWindsor	241
LaurentianU	201	UofBritishColumbia	69	WilfridLaurierU	245
McGillU	283	UofCalgary	139	YorkU	249
McMasterU	205	UofGuelph	221	**University Colleges:**	
MemorialUofNewfoundland	295	UofLethbridge	143	AugustanaUC	161
Queen'sU	209	UofNewBrunswick	307	MalaspinaUC	83
RoyalMilitaryCofCanada	213	UofNorthernBritishColumbia	73	OkanaganUC	87
RoyalRoadsU	61	UofOttawa	225	TheUCoftheCariboo	91

Last Name ______ First Name ______ Age ______ Sex ______

Address ______

______ Postal Code ______ Country ______

Telephone (______) ______ Fax (______) ______ Email ______
Area Code Area Code

CUC '99

education international

To find out more about the colleges and institutes that interest you, circle the name and page number, complete the form and send the card to the address on the back.
You can also fax this card to EI at 1-250-658-6285.

Institutes:		ColumbiaC	101
BritishColumbiaIofTechnology	119	DouglasC	105
EmilyCarrIofArt&Design	123	GeorgeBrownC	259
SouthernAlbertaIofTechnology	181	LambtonC	263
Colleges:		LangaraC	109
AlgonquinCofAppliedArts&Technology	255	MountRoyalC	171
AuroraC	329	NewBrunswickCommunityC	321
BowValleyC	167	NorthIslandC	113
CamosunC	97	NorthernCofAppliedArts&Technology	267
CoftheNorthAtlantic	317	RedDeerC	175

Last Name ______ First Name ______ Age ______ Sex ______

Address ______

City ______ Postal/Zip Code ______ Country ______

Telephone (______) ______ Fax (______) ______ Email ______
Area Code Area Code

CUC '99

education international

To receive information on all of the schools that are profiled in this guide from a specific region, check the appropriate box below, complete the form and send the card to the address on the back.
You can also fax this card to EI at 1-250-658-6285.

- ❒ British Columbia
- ❒ The Prairie Provinces (Alberta, Saskatchewan, Manitoba)
- ❒ Ontario and Quebec
- ❒ The Atlantic Provinces (New Brunswick, Nova Scotia, Prince Edward Island, Newfoundland)
- ❒ The Northwest Territories

Last Name ______ First Name ______ Age ______ Sex ______

Address ______

City ______ Postal/Zip Code ______ Country ______

Telephone (______) ______ Fax (______) ______ Email ______
Area Code Area Code

Area of Interest ______

CUC '99

education international

education international

education international

AIR MAIL

You can also fax the other side of this card to us at 1-250-658-6285

ATTACH
AIR MAIL
POSTAGE

EI EDUCATION INTERNATIONAL LTD
#205 - 5325 Cordova Bay Road
Victoria, British Columbia V8Y 2L3 CANADA

AIR MAIL

You can also fax the other side of this card to us at 1-250-658-6285

ATTACH
AIR MAIL
POSTAGE

EI EDUCATION INTERNATIONAL LTD
#205 - 5325 Cordova Bay Road
Victoria, British Columbia V8Y 2L3 CANADA

AIR MAIL

You can also fax the other side of this card to us at 1-250-658-6285

ATTACH
AIR MAIL
POSTAGE

EI EDUCATION INTERNATIONAL LTD
#205 - 5325 Cordova Bay Road
Victoria, British Columbia V8Y 2L3 CANADA

N

NATIVE STUDIES/LANGUAGES (+FIRST NATIONS STUDIES, NATIVE AMERICAN STUDIES, INDIAN LANGUAGES)

NATURAL RESOURCES TECHNOLOGY (+NATURAL RESOURCES SCIENCES, NATURAL RESOURCES MANAGEMENT)

NEUROSCIENCE (+BEHAVIOURAL NEUROSCIENCE, NEUROLOGY & NEUROSURGERY)

NURSING (+PRACTICAL NURSING)

NUTRITION & FOOD SCIENCES (+HUMAN NUTRITION, NUTRITIONAL SCIENCES, APPLIED HUMAN NUTRITION, FAMILY & NUTRITIONAL SCIENCES)

O

OBSTETRICS/GYNECOLOGY

OCCUPATIONAL HEALTH (+OCCUPATIONAL HEALTH & SAFETY, OCCUPATIONAL HEALTH & SAFETY TECHNICIAN,)

OCCUPATIONAL THERAPY (+PHYSICAL & OCCUPATIONAL THERAPY)

OFFICE ADMINISTRATION

P

PHARMACY/PHARMACOLOGY (+PHARMACOLOGY & THERAPEUTICS, PHARMACOLOGY & TOXICOLOGY, BIOMEDICAL TOXICOLOGY)

PHILOSOPHY

U

URBAN STUDIES (+URBAN PLANNING, URBAN & REGIONAL STUDIES, REGIONAL & URBAN DEVELOPMENT)

V

VETERINARY TECHNICIAN/VETERINARY

VISUAL ARTS(+ART, FINE ARTS, FINE ARTS & CRAFTS, ART & DESIGN, STUDIO ARTS)

W

WELDING (+WELDING ENGINEER TECHNICIAN, WELDING ENGINEERING, WELDING TECHNIQUES)

WOMEN'S STUDIES

WOOD PRODUCTS MANUFACTURING (+WOOD & RELATED MATERIALS, WOOD PRODUCTS TECHNOLOGY, WOOD PROCESS TECHNOLOGY)

Z

ZOOLOGY (+ANIMAL SCIENCE)

General Index

N

O

P

Q

R

S

T

U

V

W

Y

Notes